D1430275

Graphic Design: A User's Manual

Background Image: 50 Reading Lists - Spin/2 (Reading Lists, page 263)

Foreword

Michael Bierut

In a recent interview with the author of this book, the legendary graphic designer Peter Saville mentioned something valuable he learned ten years into his career: that there is so much more to design than 'just designing'.

Just designing? *Just designing?* As a design student graduating nearly 30 years ago, I would have been stunned to hear this. Designing was everything to me. I had just spent five years in design school. I had entered college as someone who could do a nice pencil drawing of a bowl of fruit. I spent the next 60 months moving shapes around on grids, manipulating squares of coloured paper, resolving compositions, drawing letterforms, learning to tell the difference between Helvetica and Univers and between Herbert Bayer and Herbert Matter, redrawing a logo a hundred times until it was perfect, calculating the column lengths of Garamond set 12/13 on a 35 pica measure, and — for this was the point of it all — learning the difference between good design and bad design. When I graduated, my goal was to work with all my heart to create the former and avoid — nay, obliterate from the face of the earth — the latter. And now I learn that not everything's about designing? What else is there?

But it's true. I spent five years transforming myself into a designer. But what had I been before? That's simple: I had been a regular person, like most other people in the world. And, as it turns out, it's those people who actually make it possible — or difficult, or impossible — for designers to do their work. And most of that work isn't about designing.

This is the secret of success. If you want to be a designer, no matter how compelling your personal vision or how all-consuming your commitment, you need other people to practice your craft. Not all projects need clients, of course. But unless you're independently wealthy, you'll need to finance the production of your work. This means persuading people to hire you, whether it's bosses at first, or, once you're on your own, clients. And people always have a choice. They can hire you or they can hire someone else. How can you get them to hire you? A good question, and although it has nothing to do with actually doing design work, you'll need an answer for it if you ever intend to actually *do* any design work.

Once you're doing design work, you face another challenge: how do you get someone else to approve the work you've created and permit it to get out into the world? But, you might protest, certainly they'll recognize good design work when they see it! After all, you do, and your classmates did, and your teachers did. Ah, but that was in the rarefied world of design school. You are now back in the world of regular people. And regular people require patience, diplomacy, tact, bullshit and, very occasionally, brute force to recognize good design, or, failing that, to trust that you can recognize it on their behalf. Again, this is hard work, and work that, strictly speaking, has nothing to do with designing.

Finally, once your work is approved, your challenge is to get it made. This may mean working with collaborators like writers, illustrators, photographers, type designers, printers, fabricators, manufacturers and distributors. It also means working with people who may not care about design, but who care passionately about budgets and deadlines. Then the whole process starts again. In some ways it gets easier each time. In other ways it's always the same.

I remember a lesson from my first year of design school, a series of exercises that

we did to learn about the relationship
between the figure/ground relationship,
the relationship between the thing that's
the subject of a visual composition and
the area that surrounds it. For me, this
is one of the most magical things about
graphic design. It's the idea that the
spaces between the letterforms are as
important as the letters themselves, that
the empty space in a layout isn't really
empty at all but filled with tension,
potential and excitement. I learned you
ignore the white space at your peril.

In many ways, the lesson of this book is
the same, and it's a lesson that every
great designer has learned one way or
another. Designing is the most important
thing, but it's not the only thing.
All of the other things a designer does
are important too, and you have to do
them with intelligence, enthusiasm,
dedication and love. Together, those
things create the background that makes
the work meaningful, and, when you do
them right, that makes the work good.

Michael Bierut is a partner in the New York office of the
international design consultancy Pentagram. He is a founding
editor of *Design Observer* and a Senior Critic at the Yale
School of Art. His most recent book is *Seventy-nine Short
Essays on Design*.

Introduction

Adrian Shaughnessy

I'm not a design historian. I'm not technically knowledgeable. I didn't even go to design school: I trained in a big studio where I discovered the basic principles of graphic design by endlessly quizzing experienced designers and by doing a lot of looking.

So what qualifications do I have to write a book about graphic design? Good question. Well, I love the subject and never tire of analyzing it and evaluating it. Anything else? I co-ran a design studio (Intro) for 15 years, employing dozens of designers and working with a vast array of clients from record labels to the British National Health Service. I also helped launch a new type of design consultancy (This is Real Art) that functioned with a roster of designers rather than salaried employees. For the past few years I have worked as a self-employed designer and art director, and I have written extensively about visual communication. All these experiences taught me a lot about graphic design, about designers, about clients — and about myself. And they made me want to write a book about what I discovered along the way.

By far the most important thing I learned was that we graphic designers have a self-destructive tendency to become so absorbed in the craft of design that we lose the ability to be objective about ourselves and our work. We rashly suppose that just because we know what we are doing, our clients do too. But if we ever stopped to ask them, we'd discover that although most clients would claim to know what graphic design is, few would claim to know how designers think or what motivates them. Even mundane matters such as knowing how long it takes to complete a project, or how graphic designers charge for their services, are often impenetrable mysteries to bemused clients.

This lack of comprehension is at the core of most of the problems we encounter as working graphic designers. It turns clients into adversaries rather than collaborators; it causes designers to say things like 'clients need to be educated about design', or, 'I'm a professional, clients must respect my opinion.' All nonsense, of course. Clients are usually adversarial because we have made a mess of explaining to them what we've done for them. This inability to explain ourselves is caused by a virus called 'Graphic Designers' Syndrome'.

'Graphic Designers' Syndrome' — you've never heard of it? You're lucky; perhaps you're one of the few who doesn't suffer from it. It's the same virus that causes Plumbers' Syndrome and Lawyers' Syndrome; in fact, it's shared by anyone who knows their job inside out but forgets to explain what it is they do.

Take the case of the expert plumber. Many of us will have been on the receiving end of a lengthy and technical explanation from a plumber about why some vital piece of sanitary ware has suddenly stopped working: yet how many of us understood what we were told? And because we can't do much about faulty shower valves or under-floor piping, we let the plumber get on with it while we wait nervously, hoping for a satisfactory outcome (and dreading a large bill).

Graphic Designers' Syndrome means that we often end up treating our clients in exactly the same way the plumber treated us — except we're not talking about valves and pipes, we're talking about logos and websites. Graphic Designers' Syndrome is caused by becoming so wrapped up in the craft of design that we neglect to properly explain to our clients what we are showing them when we present new work. Like an eager-to-please puppy, we just throw down a chewed stick and say: 'Look how clever I am.'

This wouldn't matter too much if clients didn't question everything we do: there never was a client who accepted a piece of work without asking the designer lots of questions about it. And because graphic design isn't plumbing – we can see graphic design but we can't always see plumbing – clients feel empowered to point and say, 'I don't like that; change it.'

So, if we are going to be accomplished, effective and responsible graphic designers, it makes sense that we learn how to explain to our clients what we do, and how we do it. Simple, really – except it's not. So much of what we do is instinctive and we rarely stop to think about it. We think deeply about our work – we put our hearts and souls into it – but forget about basics like presenting it in a way that non-designers can grasp. In other words, we take a lot of things for granted. This book is about the stuff that gets taken for granted.

Graphic Design: A User's Manual contains entries on subjects that routinely come up when I give talks; it includes some of my pet topics (Ellipses, page 105), and one or two that may raise eyebrows (Rejection, page 265). Apart from some guidance on green issues you will search in vain for instruction on ethical matters. That's not to say I don't believe in designers behaving ethically: I believe passionately in ethical behaviour in all areas of life. But who am I to tell anyone how to behave? The subject is raised (Ethics in design, page 109), yet it seems to me that people convinced of their own rightness, who thus feel compelled to tell other people how they should live their lives, cause most of the world's problems. This is fundamentalism, and it's not a concept to which I subscribe. The only thing I'm certain about is that nothing in this life is certain: the only code of conduct I'd recommend is one we learn for ourselves and which permits us to live peacefully with other human beings.

So if this is not a book that tells people how to behave, what is it then? It's a book for graphic designers who care about the future of graphic design; it's a book for designers who want to make effective and expressive work; it's a book for designers who want to make the world a better place. Now, most graphic designers would sign up to those ambitions. Yet it's getting harder to be that sort of designer. Graphic design is increasingly governed by focus groups and timid marketing departments. It's becoming something that nervous clients demand to be sprayed aerosol-style on to products and services to make them look like other products and services. It's becoming increasingly impersonal and formulaic.

I became a graphic designer because I was drawn to the idea of creating work – marks, images, graphic concoctions – that I could call my own. This is not the same as harbouring a selfish desire to make graphic design to suit myself – what Steven Heller calls 'Me too design'. On the contrary, I've always possessed that essential gene that every graphic designer needs – the wanting-to-please-clients gene. I want happy clients, but I want to have responsibility for what I make for them. In other words, I believe in graphic design being at the service of clients, but I also believe in doing it the way I think best. This seems to be a perfectly logical and sustainable position to take. It doesn't mean I can't be told when I'm wrong, or that I'm incapable of doing substandard work. It means, though, that the best graphic design is always distinguished by a strong element of personal conviction. If you let a committee design a house, you get a house that no one wants to live in.

Despite being attracted to graphic design by the thought of making visual statements

I could call my own, it actually took me a long time to find the courage to do this. For much of my working life I was grimly professional – fixated on pleasing my clients, and stubbornly unaware that designers could have an opinion and a viewpoint. But in the second half of the 1990s, my then studio (Intro) went through a period of growth. For the first time in our existence, we were regularly approached by new clients without any prompting from us. Some even offered us work without the usual palaver of pitches and tendering. Here was a sign that we had acquired a reputation, and that clients were approaching us in the knowledge that we were good at what we did. This radicalized me. It made me see that I needn't live in fear of never getting another assignment. I grew in confidence and went from being a doormat designer, to a designer with a viewpoint and with a creative and professional philosophy.

It also made me re-evaluate everything that I did personally within my working environment, and everything we did collectively as a studio. Did I discover anything? Well, you'll have to read this book to decide for yourself. But it made me realize that – as I've noted already – we designers take a lot of stuff for granted. I also learned that graphic design is mostly a series of paradoxes. If we think something is 'x', it's almost certainly 'y'. What we think to be true is usually false. Here's an example of what I mean: graphic designers love to call themselves problem solvers. Yes, problem solving is part of being a graphic designer (and part of being a human being), but most graphic-design briefs are not 'problems'. In fact, they are the opposite; they are opportunities – springboards even – to create something new and unexpected. If we insist on treating all briefs as problems waiting to be solved, our responses will be constrained by the need to provide rational quantifiable solutions, when

in fact we should be letting rip with the rebel yell of unfettered creativity. For example: the first generation of MP3 players looked as if they had been designed in Frankenstein's lab by engineers more suited to making military equipment. When the iPod came along, the early MP3 players were exposed as crude and inefficient. The iPod wasn't a problem waiting to be solved, it was an opportunity waiting to be taken by anyone willing to think the unthinkable (Problem solving, page 254).

So, this is a book about some of the paradoxes of graphic design. And of course the first paradox is that anyone who sets themselves up as an expert is almost certainly going to be wrong in most things. But as I said earlier, I'm not going to tell anyone what to do. I believe in the heuristic principle* of learning, and by giving my take on some of the less commonly discussed aspects of graphic design, I hope designers will be encouraged to question and interrogate every aspect of what they do as a designer. In its purest sense, this is what graphic design is – a thorough interrogation of a subject resulting in a graphic presentation of the findings.

*adjective 1 Enabling a person to discover or learn something for themselves. 2 Computing: proceeding to a solution by trial and error or by rules that are only loosely defined. www.askoxford.com

Accessibility

Universal access is fast becoming one of the most important aspects of modern graphic design. Legislation means that designers can no longer disregard the needs of people with visual impairment, for example. So does this mean lots of third-rate graphic design?

Opposite
A new typeface called FS Me™, specially crafted by typography firm Fontsmith in consultation with the learning disability charity Mencap. The typeface improves legibility for a wider audience.
www.mencap.org.uk
www.fontsmith.com

Modern architects have successfully incorporated accessibility into their thinking, and no public building, no matter how adventurous in design, is without universal access. In graphic design, however, thinking about accessibility is less prevalent. But it's a growing concern, especially in web design where it's a hot issue.

The United States Congress amended the Rehabilitation Act[1] in order to compel federal agencies to make their electronic communications accessible to people with disabilities. As yet there are no requirements for private-sector websites to adhere to these rules; commercial sites are encouraged to follow the guidelines laid down by the World Wide Web Consortium's rules on web accessibility.

According to the US Department of Commerce, there are over 54 million people in the United States with disabilities.[2] The increasing number of elderly citizens means that a huge swathe of the population has failing eyesight. So you might wonder why anyone would ever want to create design that prevented so many people from gaining access to it – either online, in print or in signage.

If we are designing something that purports to communicate with a mass audience, we should give as much help to the disabled user as possible. There's plenty of practical guidance available. The Internet has many sites that offer assistance, and there are free online utilities that give web designers the chance to evaluate their designs for people with visual impairment.[3]

Most of the advice on accessibility is common sense, and there can't be many graphic designers who don't instinctively know what is required to make something accessible: designers understand factors such as ensuring

Friendly terminal finish, very subtle softness

Subtle foot and cursive round into stem feature & alternate 'b' stem join

Defining flick that gives ownership and stability to the letter

Subtle curving of the thin 'k' stroke

Large dot for clarity

Subtle curving of the thin 'v' stroke

Bottom flick

Top flick

Open single tiered 'g' for clarity

Low stem join to define 'r' in a character combination of 'rn' so it doesn't look like 'm'

Large dot and long comma tail for clarity

1 www.access-board.gov/508.htm
2 www.designlinc.com
3 www.vischeck.com/vischeck

maximum colour contrast, and the way typography can be used to ensure legibility and ease of comprehension. And increasingly, in the era of multi-platform publishing, the need to offer visual material that works on PDAs, 3G phones, etc., means that designers have to think in terms of universal access anyway.

But does this mean sub-standard design? Not necessarily. Architects have managed to produce daring and uncompromised buildings while still catering for users with disabilities. For graphic designers, the same challenge beckons. Advances in technology mean that the web developer, the broadcast designer and the signage designer are often able to offer facilities such as voice activation, Braille conversion programs and the facility to allow users to reconfigure websites to suit themselves.

There can't be many graphic designers who don't instinctively know what is required to make something accessible.

Comparisons with the world of sport are useful here. No one advocates abandoning sport because there are people with physical disabilities. Instead, as a civilized society, we must create a climate where they have opportunities to participate in sport in ways that suit them. The same applies to design. We should not abandon experimental design because some people are visually impaired; rather, modern designers have a duty to search for ways to allow access to everyone without relying on infantile layouts and typography. It's our duty as human beings.

So how does this book approach the question of universal access? An electronic edition of the book (or eBook) is available from the publisher's website. Fully downloadable, it will allow visually impaired users to alter type size, leading and colour contrast to suit their needs.

Further reading: www.designlinc.com

Account handling

Many design groups use account handlers. Some account handlers do a good job, but in most cases account handling leads to clients being divorced from the creative process and imagining that design is an invisible procedure. When this happens, problems ensue.

During the time that I ran a design studio, and despite having some blue-chip clients and, at one giddy moment, 40 members of staff, I never employed account handlers. Why? Because 'account handling' was something done by advertising agencies and big soulless design groups as a way of distancing their clients from the messy business of creativity, and this was the opposite of what my studio stood for. We believed in letting clients see the blood on the floor.

But in truth, account handling was what I mostly did: hand-holding nervous and mistrustful clients;

listening to them; placating them; remonstrating with them; and sometimes admitting to them that we'd screwed up. But although this is what I did, I refused to call it account handling. I called it: looking after clients, and showing them what we do, and letting them know where and how their money was being spent.

My reasoning was that a lot of misery in client-designer relationships is caused by clients not knowing how their work is done, who it is done by, and what is involved in doing it. Designers often think that by sheltering clients from the often untidy business of design, they are streamlining the relationship. In fact, the opposite is true. Clients usually find the workings of design studios – and the creative process itself – a mystery. They haven't a clue what goes on after a project has been briefed. But showing them how we operate, how we brief internally, how our creative processes work, and revealing how we do our research, can reap enormous benefits. By exposing clients to our processes, by being transparent in the way we operate on their behalf, we build a climate of trust and understanding. Operating behind account handlers is not the best way to do this.

There's nothing easier for a client than rejecting work when someone with no personal stake in the project is charged with presenting it.

Yet what we call the role is unimportant; it's who does it that matters. And in my view the people who do the work – in our case designers, project managers and me, as creative director – should handle the accounts. Clients should work in partnership with designers and the people who have a personal stake in the work they produce. In the case of account handlers, this notion of a stake – a sense of authorship – is often absent.

Forcing clients to deal with account handlers downgrades the creative process and turns it into a mess of indecision and rejection. There's nothing easier for a client than rejecting or brainlessly modifying work when someone with no personal stake in the project is charged with presenting it. It's much harder to tell a designer, or someone intimately involved with the creative production of a piece of work, that their efforts are rejected. Of course, this is why many clients prefer to deal with account handlers; they can be bullied.

Furthermore, account handlers in agencies and big design groups often develop a greater loyalty to their clients than to their own creative teams. This is hardly surprising. They are encouraged to bond with their clients – that's their job. But clients sense this, and, like lions finding a lame antelope, they rip creative work to pieces.

The progressive London advertising agency Mother confronted this problem head-on when it opened for business in 1996. It set out to create a 'different kind of agency', and one of the first things it did was dispense with account executives. In an online article one of the agency's partners explains their philosophy: 'People assume we've stripped out a layer. We haven't. We just don't have a group of people that are called account handlers. Whenever a creative person picks up the phone and talks to a client about the size of an end frame or what director they can use, they're being an account manager. The client doesn't just have one relationship with one person called an account man or whatever – they have relationships with everybody.'[1]

Account handlers in agencies and big design groups often develop a greater loyalty to their clients than to their own creative teams. This is hardly surprising. They are encouraged to bond with their clients.

This nails it for me. In the modern design studio everyone does 'account handling', and every phone call, email or meeting is an opportunity to 'look after clients'. For solo designers, the same applies. They spend half their time being a designer and the other half being an account handler – not to mention accountant, debt chaser, production controller, spellchecker, light-bulb changer and a dozen other roles. To put it as bluntly as possible – all designers have to learn to become account handlers all the time.

1 Mother Knows Best
www.ideasfactory.com/art_design/features/
artdes_feature50.htm

Further reading: David Ogilvy, *Ogilvy on Advertising*. Prion, 2007.

Advertising design

Why do the advertisements in magazines and on websites look as if the same person has designed them all? Why do they look as if they've been designed by someone who hasn't looked at any of the developments within graphic design from the past 30 years? Why do we ignore most advertisements?

I was once asked by an advertising agency to create a series of posters. The agency had seen some of my studio's work, and thought we'd be suitable for the task they had in mind. They briefed me and I produced a range of ideas, which were presented to the creative team at the agency. The response was lukewarm; they told me they didn't think their bosses or their client would like the work.

A few days later they asked me to start again. And to 'assist' me, they showed me some advertising posters they considered to be successful examples of poster design. I looked at the posters and felt that little wave of unease we get when we sense that a bottomless ravine has just opened up between our client and us. Each poster had a look of adland blandness and formulaic sameness – effective up to a point, but aesthetically sterile. I told the agency team that I thought individuals who had no interest in graphic design had designed them:

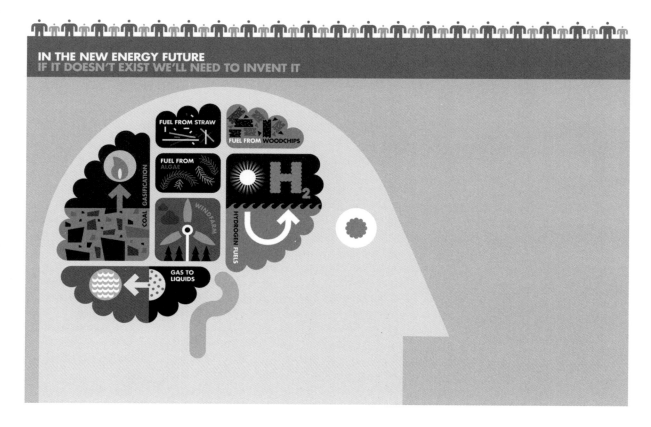

IN THE NEW ENERGY FUTURE
IF IT DOESN'T EXIST WE'LL NEED TO INVENT IT

FUEL FROM STRAW

FUEL FROM WOODCHIPS

FUEL FROM ALGAE

H₂

COAL GASIFICATION

WINDFARM

HYDROGEN FUELS

GAS TO LIQUIDS

Above and opposite
Project: Shell ads
Date: 2008
Client: Shell
Designer: Peter Grundy
Agency: JWT
Creative Director: Jim Chambers @ Antidote
Peter Grundy is represented by Debut Art
Series of colour ads which ran in the
UK national press highlighting Shell's
commitment to finding future energy sources.
A rare example of un-formulaic design in
mainstream press advertising.

'Ah, yes,' they said, 'but the execution is only there to convey "the idea".'

I knew what they meant; in advertising the idea – the message – is everything. But the problem with this approach is that it justifies some of the dreariest design you'll ever see and, furthermore, it sends out a signal that says, 'This is a press ad, it's just like all the others, no need to bother with it.' Paul Rand wrote about the design of advertisements: 'The designer must often steer clear of visual clichés by some unexpected interpretation of the commonplace.' But the graphic design element of most advertisements relies on the commonplace. Too many of them scream, 'Ignore me!'

The reason for design's poor showing in advertising agencies is the widely held view within them that designers are mere technicians tolerated only as opinion-free foot soldiers, ready to do the bidding of others. When you factor in the belief held by the majority of advertising people that unless it's on television it doesn't really count (a view that appears increasingly Luddite in the

> **In advertising, the message is everything. But the problem with this is that it justifies some of the dreariest design you'll ever see.**

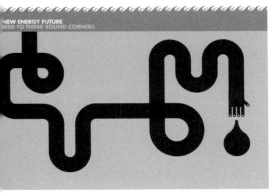

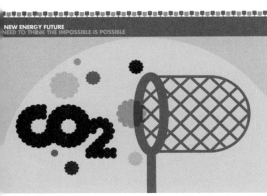

digital era), you realize that design comes pretty low on the adland scale of importance.

Additionally, many creative people in agencies are not much interested in doing stuff themselves; they prefer to have ideas and direct others to make their ideas come to life. Nothing wrong with this – but the system tends to fall down when it's applied to graphic design. I once did a job with a well-known advertising agency which, as with the posters mentioned above, ended in failure. (Not all my work ends in failure – it's just that we tend to learn more from car crashes than car journeys.) When I presented our work to the creative director of the agency, she shook her head and said it wasn't what she wanted. I offered to do more work. 'OK,' she said, 'but I want to send someone round to your studio to sit with you.' The job came to an abrupt end at that point.

Paul Belford, one of Britain's most award-garlanded advertising designers, gives other reasons for adland's inability to create intelligently designed advertisements in *Typographics 65*:[1] 'Nervous clients and their over reliance on consumer research can be a huge problem. Innovative advertising makes focus groups uncomfortable because, by definition, they have not seen anything like it before, so they are not sure about it. The mind-numbing straitjacket of ill-thought-out corporate guidelines handed over by branding consultancies … and yes, advertising agencies sometimes fail to come up with sufficiently interesting solutions or, we fail to sell them to our clients.'

Writing in the same issue of *Typographics 65*, Paul Cohen, another adman with a commitment to good design, asks the question: 'Why is it perceived by so many marketing directors that the more derivative and bland a print or poster is, the better it will work?'

Design for advertising wasn't always poor. In the 1960s, a golden age for advertising design, some of the most accomplished designers of all time, many of them European émigrés, and many of them disciples of Modernism, created a new language of advertising. Designers like Paul Rand, Herbert Matter, Alvin Lustig and Ladislav Sutnar helped to develop the New Advertising, what the designer and writer Richard Hollis came to describe as advertising 'where the spectator was active, not passive, where curiosity was aroused and intelligence needed to complete the sense'.

This hardly seems like a description of what can be seen today. Yet there are some notable exceptions.

Designers need to think more like advertising people, but advertising people need to recognize the value in Rand's 'unexpected interpretation of the commonplace' and not settle for one-size-fits-all graphic design.

Occasionally there are advertisements that don't simply trade in cliché and look as if they might want us to engage with them rather than just skate past them. The designer Paula Scher has noticed a change in advertising design. 'I'm not sure that the graphic design community as a whole is paying any attention to this,' she writes. 'I don't see very many speakers from the advertising community invited to speak at design conferences (except for the very few who lead branding groups at agencies and in some circles they are still considered the enemy). I don't read about it on design blogs, and I'm not seeing books published about it. I'm not seeing advertising, in any form, turn up in any design museum exhibitions, not at the Modern, not at the Cooper-Hewitt. The Cooper-Hewitt National Design Museum has an annual designer award category for Communication Design and I've never seen an advertising person nominated since the award's inception. How can the design community be so insular? Something has definitely changed here, and the design community is missing it. Too bad.'[2]

In my view, designers have much to learn from advertising people. Designers are habitually bound up in detail and aesthetic consideration, and forget about the need for compelling emotive ideas. Advertising people are much better at looking at the bigger picture. Designers need to think more like advertising people, but advertising people need to recognize the value in Rand's 'unexpected interpretation of the commonplace' and not settle for one-size-fits-all graphic design.

Further reading: Clive Challis, Helmut Krone, *The Book*. The Cambridge Enchorial Press, 2003.

1 *Typographics 65*, The Advertising Issue, June 2006.
2 Paula Scher, *Advertising Got Better*, February 2008. http://creativity-online.com/?action=ne ws:article&newsId=124983&sectionId=pov

Aesthetics

Why is it painful when clients tell us to change red to blue and make the type bigger? It's painful because sometimes clients are right. But also because they are usually insisting that we go against our aesthetic judgement. And if we believe in what we do, that's hard to accept.

Aesthetics is a term with a rich and complex history. My dictionary defines it as a 'set of principles concerned with the nature and appreciation of beauty, especially in art'. It goes on to describe aesthetics as a 'branch of philosophy which deals with questions of beauty and artistic taste'. When we use the word 'aesthetics' in design we are referring to the visual appearance of a work rather than its content or message – although any deep reading into the subject of aesthetics reveals that the two are inseparable. Is it possible, for example, for something to be evil and also beautiful? For designers, however, aesthetics is a term that has become interchangeable with 'style' and 'visual appearance', although it is not only used to describe design that is beautiful or representative of good taste. Terms such as 'trash aesthetic' and 'vernacular aesthetic' are commonplace.

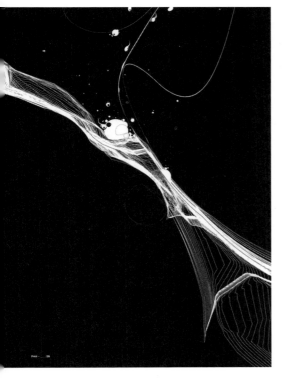

Above
Project: On/Off – Birth
Date: 2006
Client: Maxalot
Designer: Michael C. Place/Commonwealth
Licorice series; 2-D graphics morph into
custom CNC-milled 3-D frames. On/Off
show with Build (UK) and Commonwealth (NYC),
curated by Maxalot.

For designers, the most important aspect of aesthetics is that we develop an aesthetic way of seeing. In other words, we see the appearance of something before we see the content. Typically, we might pick up a magazine and feel disgust – or delight – at the typeface that has been used. This way of seeing is different from the way non-designers see, and is the cause of much disconnectedness between designers and their clients. It's always worth remembering that when we present work to clients, they tend not to see it the way we do. They tend not to view it aesthetically.

The question of aesthetics runs through graphic design like an open wound. On one side of the gash we have the pragmatists, designers who see design as a service industry supplying the 'packaging' for business messages; and on the other side we have the aesthetes, designers who see design as aesthetic expression driven by inner compulsion. The former group underplays the importance of aesthetics; the later group overplays the importance of aesthetics.

The arch pragmatist – but also a designer responsible for a great deal of elegant and refined work – is Massimo Vignelli. In an interview with Steven Heller, Vignelli defines the split with Helvetica-like precision: 'There are two kinds of graphic designers: one is rooted in history and semiotics and problem solving. The other is more rooted in the liberal arts – painting, figurative arts, advertising, trends, and fashions. These are really two different avenues … one side is the structured side, the other is the emotional side.'[1]

But even Vignelli's problem solvers have aesthetic impulses. In a famous essay called 'Why I Write', George Orwell lists the 'four great motives' for writing.[2] He defines them as sheer egotism, historical impulse, political purpose and aesthetic enthusiasm. If we were trying to list the 'four great motives' for becoming a graphic designer, most people would give aesthetics as one of their reasons, although it would vary from designer to designer in the importance given to it. But even the pragmatists tend to care passionately about how their own work looks, and in my experience there aren't many designers who don't have personal aesthetic reasons for their actions.

Is it possible to be a graphic designer without having an interest in aesthetics? Possibly; but it would be a bit like trying to climb Everest in ballet pumps. You might be able to do it, but not without difficulty.

> **Genuine aesthetic conviction is real and deeply felt, and when we are asked to go against these convictions we find it difficult.**

I've known one or two designers without aesthetic instincts, but they weren't very good designers. Aesthetic feelings in design – our innate taste and allegiance to colours, shapes and visual stylings – are powerful drivers. It's why it's often painful when we have them trampled on by insensitive clients. Of course, a lot of 'pain' is down to too much sensitivity (being thin-skinned) on our part, and an inability to take reasonable criticism (due to lack of confidence in our abilities). But genuine aesthetic conviction is real and deeply felt, and when we are asked to go against these convictions we find it difficult.

Now, the tough-minded pragmatists will say: 'Get real. We're here to serve our clients; if they want it blue – if they want the type bigger – do it, and don't be a cringing wimp.' This takes us to the essential conundrum at the heart of graphic design: aesthetics are personal, yet design is not personal; design is about objectivity.

How we deal with this conundrum determines the degree to which we find a life in design fulfilling or frustrating. As designers we can never have complete aesthetic freedom. But most of us find ways of channelling our aesthetic judgement into dealing with a client's demands and needs. It also helps if we develop a thick skin – but not so thick that we lose our sense of touch.

Further reading: David Pye, *The Nature and Aesthetics of Design*. Cambium Press, 1995.

1 Massimo Vignelli on *Rational Design, Design Dialogues* by Steven Heller and Elinor Pettit. Allworth Press, 1998.
2 Essay from 1946, reprinted in *George Orwell Essays*. Penguin, 2000.

Annual reports

They used to be sparkling examples of innovative graphic communication. Now it's rare to find an annual report that gives an indication of a company's personality, and increasingly the reports are being done online. In the future, all annual reports will be electronic.

Corporations with shareholders, and many publicly funded institutions, are obliged to publish an annual statement prepared by independent auditors showing financial performance from the previous year. Many companies have traditionally also used these reports to provide additional information to shareholders and interested observers, and to act as image-enhancing documents.

In the past, corporations were usually reluctant to scrimp on their annual reports: good paper, high-grade printing and immaculate design and art direction were obligatory. These often lavish publications provided graphic designers with well-funded projects that encouraged the deployment of the full range of graphic techniques and skills – typography, art direction, photography, illustration, information design and high-end production.

The annual report reached its apogee in the corporate frenzy of the deregulated 1980s and early 1990s. In the United States and Europe, it became a tool of corporate bravado. Firms vied to outdo each other in ostentation. The corporate feeding frenzy of the Thatcher and Reagan

years provided plenty of scraps for hungry and ambitious designers, and numerous design firms were set up just to produce annual reports.

In recent times, the annual report has come to reflect a more sober business environment, and the look and content of most documents are now governed by three overriding contemporary issues: firstly, new trends in corporate governance; secondly, accessibility concerns; and thirdly, the move to the online domain. In a post-Enron world, corporate hype is frowned on: waste and ostentation are discouraged – bloated and glossy documents that look as if they might have contributed to a decline in a firm's profitability are a thing of the past. Accessibility issues have now moved to centre stage; firms are keen to show a caring face to the world, and no corporate communications department will allow a designer to deploy subtle graphic effects and distracting imagery that might alienate investors – information must be clear and devoid of frills. And the sustainability message has arrived in boardrooms. For many corporations, their ability to change their core activity – or even lessen its environmental impact – is limited: an airline can hardly stop flying, for example. But they can change their corporate message, and it is advantageous to publish online (usually in conjunction with a stripped-down print version).

The notion of an annual report delivering a compelling narrative is increasingly rare.

Graphic designers are allowed to shed a small, salty tear at this pragmatism. There have been some wonderful annual reports. Take Helmut Krone's famous and influential design for the 1970 Cybermatics report, which instead of using photographs of the corporation's president and vice-president, used documentary-style shots of its messengers, cleaners and mailroom people. Krone rendered the images as exquisite duotones, and humanized corporate America at a stroke. And throughout the 1990s in America, the work of Bill Cahan provided a blueprint for radical, thought-provoking and effective annual report design.

So is it possible to produce a report that fulfils all the regulatory requirements, as well as offering accessibility and environmental credentials, and yet one that shows originality and distinctiveness? While the aims of such a document are entirely laudable, responding to all of them tends to result in dullness and uniformity. The notion of an annual report delivering a compelling narrative is increasingly rare.

Further reading: *Graphis Annual Reports Annual 07/08*. Graphis Press, 2008.

Above
Project: Annual Report 1970
Client: Cybermatics
Designer: Helmut Krone
Spreads from the revolutionary Annual Report for Cybermatics, showing the 'service guys' from the company, not the bigwigs.

Art direction

Art direction is generally considered to be the act of giving visual expression to an idea with the help of others, in roughly the same way that a film director 'directs' a film using both technical and creative collaborators. But what makes a good art director?

Some of the most important figures in graphic design and advertising have called themselves art directors – George Lois, Alexey Brodovitch, Lester Beall. Yet it's a term that confuses clients who often think it only relates to the creative direction of photography. Philip Meggs doesn't even list it in the index of his *History of Graphic Design*, first published in 1983. The term came to the fore in the early 1960s with the arrival in advertising of the 'big idea'. Here was a new form of advertising where a carefully formulated message was articulated through a central idea, often requiring the merging of text and image in a compelling mix that gripped the viewer. It's easy to see how the term 'art direction' fits into this context. Someone like George Lois had an idea and then enlisted the services of a photographer, a typographer and any number of other skilled practitioners to make it come alive on the page.

> **A good art director will always have a clear idea where the final destination is, but they will also allow the people working with them to contribute to this journey.**

As a job description, art direction still flourishes in advertising, but also in fashion and in magazine publishing. It is also used in movie-making to describe a slightly different activity.[1] In advertising it means directing the appearance of communications of all kinds – press advertisements, television commercials, websites and digital messages. In graphic design, a good art director moulds a palette of visual and verbal elements into a coherent whole. Typically, these elements might include photography, retouching, typography and specialist skills such as 3-D modelling, animation, audio: creating the design might also entail casting, prop hire, model-making and location-finding. But the one defining characteristic is that art direction always involves directing other people.

To be a good art director, three attributes are essential:

A clear vision of the final outcome
The art director takes his or her collaborators on a journey. A good art director will always have a clear idea where the final destination is, but they will also allow the people working with them to contribute to this journey. If we suffocate our collaborators they will feel reluctant to bring all their resources to the project.

A working knowledge of the various technical disciplines involved in creating a successful result

Opposite
Project: Manic Street Preachers
Lifeblood album
Date: 2004
Client: Sony
Designer: Farrow Design
Photographer: John Ross
Dramatic collaboration between art director and designer Mark Farrow and photographer John Ross, for what many describe as Manic Street Preachers' best album.

There are two views on this. Many art directors believe that it's best to know next to nothing about technical matters. They argue that if they ask their collaborators to do the impossible, they might just do it. I take the opposite view: the more we know, the better we can cajole and encourage. This doesn't mean that art directors have to be able to take photographs as competently as the photographers they employ, or operate complex 3-D software as skilfully as the operators they work with. But they have to be conversant with the functionality, limitations and potential of the crafts they are directing. An art director who hasn't a clue about the technicalities of photography, and makes unreasonable and ill-informed demands on a photographer, cannot expect an outstanding result, while one with a sympathetic understanding of lighting, film stock, digital processes and composition can 'negotiate' a more successful outcome. I also think it is important to 'own up' to a lack of knowledge when we encounter technical matters we don't understand. Technical people usually relish explaining their craft.

An ability to inspire a sense of joint authorship
The best art directors make their collaborators want to do great work; they are able to 'persuade' them to go further than they imagine themselves capable of going. This is done by thoughtful and respectful communication. There never was a good art director who was a bully; you can be demanding and hard to please, but if you want to get great results you have to allow your collaborators a sense of joint authorship.[2]

Further reading: Steven Heller and Veronique Vienne, *The Education of an Art Director.* **Allworth Press, 2006.**

1 The IMDB defines the movie art director as 'the person who oversees the artists and craftspeople who build the sets'.
2 Shared authorship can sometimes lead to disputes and unhappiness over who has the right to show work once it is completed. We've all seen creative work touted around by someone who only played a minor role in its creation, therefore it is always advisable to agree credits and insist on proper 'billing' from the outset.

Art v design

**Design and art are often seen
as polar opposites. Yet most
contemporary art and most big-
money designs are entirely
conceptual; as a result, neither
is primarily concerned with the
purely aesthetic. So perhaps
they're not so far apart
after all?**

In 1961, the Italian artist Piero Manzoni placed his
own excrement in 90 small cans which he then sealed. He
calculated the value of the cans in accordance with the
market value of gold at the time. Today, his creation is
described as Conceptual art, and the cans are in museums,
galleries and private collections around the world. If
a can of human shit can be called art, we shouldn't have
too much trouble defining graphic design as art. If only
it was that easy.

In our post-Modern world, as Manzoni demonstrates,
anything can be art – even graphic design. I get as much
aesthetic pleasure from a poster by one of the great
Swiss masters as I do from a painting by one of the great
masters of the Renaissance. But even if we accept that
as human beings we are free to find art in Swiss posters
or celebrity photographs, we must also
accept that the intentions behind
the posters and the photographs are
different from the intentions behind
classical paintings. There is a design
sensibility and there is an artistic
sensibility, and they're not the same
thing. Occasionally, both sensibilities
are found within the same person, but
genuine graphic designer/artists are
rare. Traditionally, the main difference between a graphic
designer and an artist is that a graphic designer requires
a brief and needs to be given content to work with.
Artists, on the other hand, write their own briefs
and create their own content.

> **There is
> a design
> sensibility
> and there is
> an artistic
> sensibility,
> and they're not
> the same thing.**

But let's go back to Piero Manzoni. He didn't produce
a can of shit for it to be enjoyed in the way art is
normally enjoyed. He wanted people to 'think about the
relationship between the body and art'.[1] In other words,
he had a conceptual message that was more important
than the visual qualities of the can. Strangely, this
means that much contemporary art is remarkably like
much commercial graphic design: both are conceptual
and both have a message that is more important than
the artwork itself. On the surface there appears to be
a vast difference between a big super-efficient design
group working on projects for the mass market, and a
contemporary artist producing strong personal visions
in tiny quantities intended for display in galleries,
to be sold to private or institutional collectors.
Yet when we look closely at these two seemingly opposing
forms of expression, both are concerned with what their
work is telling us and not with its aesthetic merit.

The notion of anyone enjoying either the works
of big, global design agencies or the offerings of
contemporary artists for purely aesthetic reasons is

anathema to both groups. They want us to engage with what they have created on a motivational or conceptual level. Our deriving aesthetic pleasure from them comes as a secondary consideration, if at all.

Yet – paradoxically – aesthetic pleasure is the motive behind the work of many designers. Let's call them the 'auteurs'. These are designers who follow their own instincts. They set their own creative agendas. They are not shy of offering clients self-expression and radical gestures that come from the same impulse as the need to produce art. Not all auteurs are interested in aesthetics – some are politically or ethically motivated. And being aesthetically inclined doesn't mean that individuals or studios are not interested in communicating messages, and using the tools and conventions of commercial graphic design. But their primary aim is to create work that delights the retina. And this seems to me to be a fundamental – if rather old-fashioned – characteristic of art.

The main difference between a graphic designer and an artist is that a graphic designer requires a brief and needs to be given content to work with.

One of the few books to address this question is a modest yet inspirational volume entitled *Art Without Boundaries*.[2] It was published in 1972, and was written by three British graphic designers and teachers. In it the authors make a compelling case for the demolition of the fence that separates design and art. They write: 'At one time it was easy to distinguish between the "fine" artist and the commercial artist. It is now less easy. The qualities which differentiated the one from the other are now common to both. The painter who once saw the commercial designer as a toady to the financial pressures of industry, may now find that the dealer can impose a tyranny worse than any client. During the last 20 years or so, barriers have broken down; and they are still being broken down.'

The authors of *Art Without Boundaries* may be guilty of some post-1960s utopianism, and the dream they expounded was to be blown apart by the stupendous rise in the value of the art market and the commercial design boom of the 1980s and 1990s. But they are correct in assuming that the old division has gone. Both art and design are consumed by commercial intentions and, as always, it's the personal vision of the creative individual that counts, regardless of whether that individual is working in landscape gardening, Conceptual art or graphic design.

Further reading: Julian Stallabrass, *Art Incorporated. The Story of Contemporary Art*. Oxford University Press, 2004.

Opposite
Project: VOID
Date: 2007
Client: Self-initiated
Designer: Lesley Moore
The design is inspired by Droste-effect images. 'Droste-effect' is the term used to describe images that repeat themselves ad infinitum within an overall plan.

1 www.pieromanzoni.org/EN/works_shit.htm
2 Gerald Woods, Philip Thompson and John Williams, *Art Without Boundaries: 1950–70*. Thames & Hudson, 1972.

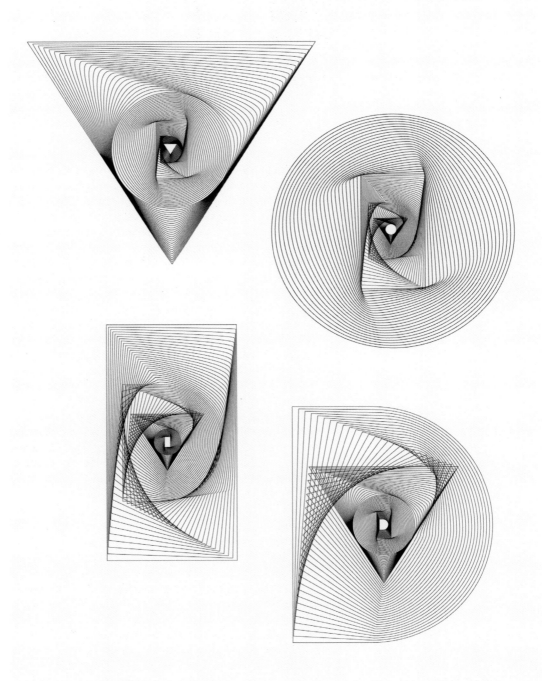

VOID

VOID N° 2
by Lesley Moore & Annouck

Asymmetric design

Centred layouts are like wearing socks with sandals – no one gets hurt, but it's not a good look. When designers want an easy life, they centre everything. But asymmetry is how we give typographic layouts dynamism and zip. For many designers, only wedding invitations are centred.

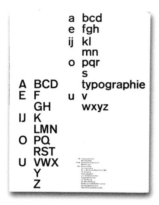

Above
Project: Covers for *Typografische Monatsblätter*
Date: 1960
Client: *Typografische Monatsblätter*
Designer: Uncredited
Two covers showing asymmetric typography created for *Typografische Monatsblätter*, the Swiss journal of typography, writing and visual communication. The publication first appeared in 1933.

As a self-taught designer, all my early efforts to create typographic layouts were timid and cautious. I was terrified of doing anything bad so I centred everything. I did this because it was safe and required minimal judgement. I also did it because – back then – I never bothered to read the type I was asked to lay out, and as a consequence I didn't care a hoot about the reader. As long as it looked 'balanced' I was happy. I was producing work that, if I looked at it now, would make me blush until the blood vessels in my face burst.

When I began to study typographic layouts more closely (and this is what I mean by saying I was self-taught – I did a lot of looking) I saw that the really gripping stuff was the great Modernist asymmetric designs for books and posters. I was also drawn to non-formal design – psychedelic, punk and other forms of outsider expression – and this was neither symmetric nor asymmetric; it was unsymmetric. Suddenly, centred type looked crude and unsophisticated.

And as I looked more deeply, I also noticed that the design element that excited me most – and also the one that antagonized clients the most – was white space.

As Jan Tschichold put it: 'In asymmetric design, the white background plays an active part in the design. The typical main display of the old typography, the title page, showed its black type on a white background that played no part in the design. In asymmetric typography on the other hand, the paper background contributes to a greater or lesser degree to the effect of the whole. The strength of its effect depends on whether it is deliberately emphasized or not; but in asymmetrical design it is always a component.'[1]

Tschichold's advocacy of asymmetric type was not a style affectation. It was part of his ferocious commitment to clarity in typography. In his view, 'old typography' was arranged around a central axis, and was therefore hard to read since it didn't follow the sense of the text. He wrote: '… it is wrong to arrange a text as if there were some focal point in the centre of a line which would justify such an arrangement. Such points of course do not exist, because we read by starting at one side (Europeans for example read from left to right, the Chinese from top to bottom and right to left). Axial arrangements are illogical because the distance of the stressed, central parts from the beginning and end of the word

Asymmetry has come to dominate most typographical forms of communication. So much so, in fact, that centred type in any sort of serious design setting is almost a subversive gesture.

sequences is not usually equal but constantly varies from line to line.'[2]

Today, the asymmetric Modernist approach to typography has come to dominate most typographical forms of communication. So much so, in fact, that centred type in any sort of serious design setting is almost a subversive gesture. I was recently acting in a consultancy role to the publishers of a magazine. It was a magazine with radical intentions and an intelligent readership. The designer proposed introducing some centred text. The effect was startling and subversive. I liked it.

Further reading: Jan Tschichold, *Asymmetric Typography*. Faber & Faber, 1967.

1 'The Principles of the New Typography', PM, June/July 1938. Reprinted in Steven Heller and Philip B. Meggs (eds), *Texts on Type*. Allworth Press, 2001.
2 Ibid.

Avant Garde design

Historically, various avant-garde movements in design have driven the discipline to new heights. Avant-garde activities are usually oppositional and contrarian. They shock. In the twenty-first century, today's shocking visual gesture is tomorrow's haircare packaging.

The avant-garde movement of the first two decades of the twentieth century was a loose coalition of 'isms': Futurism, Constructivism, Dadaism, Expressionism and Vorticism. It included such resonant names as Filippo Tommaso Marinetti (Italy), Guillaume Apollinaire (France), Hannah Höch (Germany) and Wyndham Lewis (United Kingdom). It was a period of furious artistic energy that saw art and design melded into a force that was to jump-start the look of the modern machine age and the era of mass communications. Do we have avant-garde design today? Or is the radical spirit in designers most likely to be channelled into a Nike promotion, or a website for a street fashion label? Avant-garde movements in the early twentieth century were oppositional. They were about rebellion and the shock of the new. Today, we don't have rebellion and opposition. And even radical campaigning groups and individuals realize that if they want to communicate their message regarding green matters, social and political injustice or local issues, they have to do so with the slickness and impeccable manners of big-bucks advertising. In addition, the commercial world is now so dominant that as soon as new styles and graphic modes of expression emerge they are absorbed into advertising, marketing and branding.

Do we have avant-garde design today? Or is the radical spirit in designers most likely to be channelled into a Nike promotion, or a website for a street fashion label?

Further reading: Roxane Joubert, *Typography and Graphic Design*. Flammarion, 2006.

Avant Garde typeface

A typeface of lasting genius or a soulless conflation of Art Deco and sans serif Modernism? It was famously designed by Herb Lubalin – but does he deserve sole credit for its creation? Or is it, like so much graphic design, of uncertain parentage?

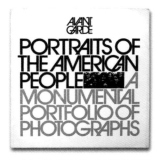

Above
Front covers of *Avant Garde* magazine, a publication founded by editor Ralph Ginzburg. Designer Herb Lubalin created the magazine's masthead – or logogram. He later developed the lettering into the highly successful Avant Garde family of typefaces. *Avant Garde* the magazine ran for 16 issues, from January 1968 to July 1971.

Avant Garde the typeface was created by advertising art director and typographer Herb Lubalin. Lubalin was one of the leading American designers/art directors of the twentieth century and founded the typographic journal *U&LC*, and established the International Typographic Corporation (ITC).

Avant Garde began life as a 'logogram' for the magazine *Avant Garde*, and it was only when Lubalin's geometric interlocking letterforms generated waves of interest that he created the full ITC Avant Garde family of weights. The font was ubiquitous in the 1970s, and is enjoying a period of voguishness today among young designers who like its sharp modernity, but are not tainted by its initial massive overuse on everything from packaging to album covers.

The typeface contains echoes of Art Deco and Futura, and is distinguished by its radical ligatures (although, as Steven Heller noted in a brilliantly researched article,[1] Lubalin was heard to 'curse the day that Avant Garde was released due to the abominable use of these ligatures'). It is an example of a font that was only made possible by computerized typesetting.

Yet Avant Garde is a font with a story. Like most elements of graphic design, its provenance is of mixed parentage. It was commissioned by Ralph Ginzburg, who launched *Avant Garde* magazine as a publication 'for intellectuals with a sense of humour'. He asked the normally reliable and fast-responding Lubalin to produce the masthead. After a few, uncharacteristic failed attempts by Lubalin, Ginzburg's wife and collaborator, Shoshana Ginzburg, went to his studio to reiterate the concept of the magazine. Heller reports her briefing technique: 'I asked him to picture a very modern clean European airport (or the TWA terminal), with signs in stark black and white. Then I told him to imagine a jet taking off the runway into the future. I used my hand to describe an upward diagonal of the plane climbing skyward. He had me do that several times.' Ginzburg's hand gestures are clearly visible in the sloping characters of Avant Garde.

Lubalin was to make a lot of money out of his font. But, as Heller points out, it was drawn up by Lubalin's then partner Tom Carnase 'from Lubalin's scribbles'. Yet when the money started rolling in, neither the Ginzburgs

Avant Garde is a font with a story. Like most elements of graphic design, its provenance is of mixed parentage. It was commissioned by Ralph Ginzburg, who launched *Avant Garde* magazine as a publication 'for intellectuals with a sense of humour'.

1 Steven Heller, 'Crimes Against Typography: The Case of Avant Garde', *Grafik*, no. 20, August 2004. Reprinted in Michael Bierut, William Drenttel and Steven Heller (eds), *Looking Closer 5*. Allworth Press, 2006.

nor Carnase earned any money out of Avant Garde's success. No one disputes that Lubalin, a type designer of real genius, was its creator but, as Heller shows, he wasn't the only author. Few stories better illustrate the complexity of claiming sole authorship in graphic design; somewhere along the line you have to get other people to help carry the load. Graphic design is only rarely a solo activity.

Further reading: John D. Berry, *U&LC: Influencing Design & Typography*. Mark Batty Publisher, 2005.

Awards

Worthless beauty parades or useful thermometer readings of design's health? We love them when we win and scoff at them when we lose. For many, the granting of awards is a sinister process overseen by elites. For others, awards offer a sort of natural justice enabling the good to rise?

Designers love to win awards, but we also love to moan about them. We've all looked at winners and thought: why? And we've all looked at work that hasn't received any recognition (usually our own) and wondered: why not? I have just Googled 'design awards' and got 19,400,000 links. That tells us something.

The arguments against design awards are persuasive. There is an undeniable element of randomness in the allocation of prizes that renders most award schemes mildly farcical. For many, the notion of design as a competitive race with winners and losers is ideologically unpalatable. And, in truth, the idea that one piece of design can be adjudged to be 'better' than another is hard to rationalize. For a start, you have to enter your work; if you're not in the line-up, you can't hope to win the race. Not only that, you usually have to pay to enter. This precludes many worthy designs being considered since much good work is done by individuals and small groups who are unable to afford the entry fees or allocate the vast amount of time required to prepare and dispatch entries (organizers appear to have no cognizance of the amount of work they require from entrants).

And it gets worse. Most design awards are judged by other designers, so how can we be sure of a fair trial? How can we be sure of impartiality or avoid being victims of cronyism? We can't. We have to rely on the honesty of the juries, and the good intentions of the various awards bodies. Perhaps, as in criminal trials, entrants should be given the right to vet juries: any juror with a history of overusing Helvetica, for example, could be objected to and sent home as being unlikely to look fondly on work that incorporated decorative typefaces and floral flourishes.

In defence of awards organizers, they invariably advise jury members about the need for impartiality and the obligation to declare personal involvement. But designers are human beings, and total impartiality is impossible. I was once sitting on a design jury and found myself agonizing over a piece of work. I genuinely

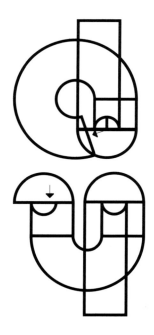

liked the item, but I wasn't sure if I liked it enough to hold it up to my fellow jurors and say it was worthy of consideration. Until, that is, I found the designer's name in a remote corner of the work. His identity was officially supposed to be concealed but there it was, plain for all to see. As it happens, he was one of my favourite designers, and my hesitation evaporated.

Would design awards be any better if the entries were judged by members of the public? Or what about allowing clients to judge them? One or two awards schemes use clients to adjudicate – in Britain the Design Business Association (DBA)[1] uses them as judges. Naturally, clients will bring different criteria to bear. They will automatically be more interested in results than in intangibles like aesthetics and craft-based considerations. There's not much evidence to show that using the balance sheet to assess the entries, and allowing non-designers (clients or civilians) to sit in judgement on them, leads to anything other than rewarding the safe and the predictable.

The arguments against design awards are persuasive. There is an undeniable element of randomness in the allocation of prizes that renders most award schemes mildly farcical.

Yet, despite their flaws, awards are one of the few outlets that enable designers to stake a claim for design. Design award schemes, with all their warts and snaggle-toothed imperfections, are all we've got.

One last thought. I've sat on awards juries on many occasions, and almost without exception doing so has been an unqualified joy. The debate is elevated; the discourse lively; the wit flows. I've learnt a great deal from listening to the ways in which other designers look at work, and I've made more friends by sitting on design juries than through just about any other activity I've ever indulged in. And what's more, I'm disappointed to report that I've never encountered any skulduggery or malpractice. Quite the opposite: most designers take jury service seriously – even if they often have to look at vast amounts of work in a short space of time – and stick up for fairness and even-handedness.

It's a view corroborated by Pentagram partner Michael Bierut: 'People who enter design competitions, particularly people who enter and lose design competitions, comfort themselves by imagining that something sinister goes on in the tomb-like confines of the judges' chambers. When you judge a competition yourself, you learn that nothing could be farther from the truth. Behind the closed doors are table after table covered with pieces of graphic design. Like most things

Above
Project: *There Is A Light*
Date: 2008
Client: Tokyo Type Directors Club
Designers: Non-Format
Spreads from book, commissioned by the Tokyo Type Directors Club, as part of its 20th anniversary celebrations. TDC runs one of the world's most prestigious awards schemes.

in life, only a few of these are really good. Each judge moves along the tables, looking at each piece just long enough to ascertain whether he or she likes it. It takes a long time and a lot of people to produce even a modest piece of graphic design. The judging process takes less than a second.'[2]

Before you make your mind up about the value of design awards, inveigle your way on to a design jury (it's easily done; just ask the organizers – they're always keen to have new blood) and then make a final assessment about the messy business of design competitions.

Further reading: http://designawards.wordpress.com

1 www.dba.org.uk
2 Michael Bierut, *You May Already Be a Winner*. www.designobserver.com

B

Bad projects

For designers, there are good jobs and there are bad jobs. Bad ones tend to be more prevalent than good ones. And why is it that other people always seem to get the good jobs, while we end up with the bad ones? But what makes a bad project? Clients? Poor budgets? Not enough time? Or are designers to blame?

Bad projects are projects that end up as disappointments. They can be disappointing on many levels. They can be creatively disappointing; they can be financially ruinous; they can fail to communicate with their intended audiences.

So who is to blame when jobs go bad? As designers, we are quick to take credit – individually and collectively – for successes. We love to see our names in the pages of the awards annuals, and we have no problem accepting the kudos that comes with triumph. But when it comes to failure, we are never quite so keen to claim acceptance. Yet it's only by owning up to culpability that we can ever hope to avoid disaster in the future.

It's easy to say that the brief was too restrictive, or that the client was unreasonable or set the budget too low. Yet even when clients are to blame for projects going wrong, there's nothing to be gained from blaming them. What we need to do is look at ourselves. There might well be a troublesome client, but clients are difficult for a reason, and I usually find on closer inspection that I hadn't identified what this was; if you know why a client is unhappy you can usually do something about it.

Even when clients are to blame for projects going wrong, there's nothing to be gained from blaming them. What we need to do is look at ourselves.

It's one of design's great myths that other people get the good jobs and we get the duff ones. There are very few great clients and even fewer great jobs. Instead, there are jobs that have to be turned into great jobs. All the good work we see in books and magazines has been achieved by hard graft and the utilization of more skills than purely those of graphic design. Read *Sagmeister: Made You Look* if you think superstar designers glide from one triumph to the next. No one does. But the people who do good work take responsibility for their actions and don't blame clients, budgets or the size of the moon.

Further reading: Peter Hall, *Sagmeister: Made You Look*. Thames & Hudson, 2001.

Banks

Dealing with banks is as much fun as chewing your arm off. Until that is, we remember that we are the clients and the banks are our suppliers. Just try not to get a loan from them. One of the best things about design is you don't need a lot of money to get started.

What are banks doing in a book about graphic design? Good question. Let's get rid of them. No, wait. If you run a studio, or work as a freelancer, or even draw a salary, you will have to rub up against the world of banking. So it's advisable to have some understanding of how banks work. Banks used to be intimidating places, but in the new service culture we all inhabit we've learnt not to be cowed by them. We've also learnt not to sign up with the first bank we walk into. We ask around first. We ask designer friends for recommendations, but we also visit the banks they recommend and decide for ourselves.[1]

For designers starting up in business the big rule is: don't borrow money from a bank. Try not to borrow money from anyone, but never from a bank. Why? Because you don't need to. One of the great things about being a designer is that the entry cost is invitingly low. You can set up in your bedroom, or a garden shed, or in the corner of a friend's studio, and all you need is a computer, some software, a phone and an Internet account; you might want to think about a desk and a chair, and maybe a good coffee machine, but you don't need much more than this. You will have some scary months while you wait for people to pay you, and you will have to survive on air and rainwater. But no matter what the pressure, avoid getting a loan from a bank.

Beyond that, the only other rule is to talk to your bank often and regularly. If there's a problem on the horizon, let your bank manager know before the problem becomes unmanageable. The later you leave it, the harder it is to clean up the mess afterwards. Bank managers are our best friends when we've got money in our account, but the minute we step out of line they start behaving like someone with a nest of wasps in their mouth. We can avoid most problems by being upfront with them. We often hope financial problems will go away; but by hiding from them, we usually make them worse. If you've got a client who is unwilling or unable to pay, for example, tell your bank manager. He or she won't always be willing to help, but they are more likely to accommodate you if you've warned them.

Bank managers are our best friends when we've got money in our account, but the minute we step out of line they start behaving like someone with a nest of wasps in their mouth.

Treat banks like any other supplier: be tough and fair with them. If they make mistakes, remonstrate and ask for compensation. If they don't measure up, move your account. If they are helpful and accommodating, stick with them.

Further reading: Marcello Minale, *How to Run and Run a Successful Multi-Disciplinary Design Company*. Booth-Clibborn Editions, 1996.

1 These words were written before the global financial meltdown that took place from September 2008 onwards. Since then nearly every banking institution in the West has turned into a basket case, many requiring to be bailed out by national governments. We were encouraged to think of bankers as heroes. They turned out not to be. Another reason to avoid borrowing money from them.

Binding

A badly bound document is like a badly designed document. Not much good. Glued, stapled, riveted, stitched, perfect bound, hot glued or cold glued: the way we bind our documents says as much about our abilities as designers as the way we kern our type.

A graphic designer friend of mine said to me recently: 'I stare at a screen all day and move pixels around with a mouse. I want to find something that lets me work with my hands, with organic materials, and with stuff that smells.' He took up bookbinding at an evening class.

Everything the print designer comes into contact with, other than posters and single sheets of paper, has to be bound in some way. And yet bad binding is a frequent source of unhappiness. It causes more frustration than just about anything else in graphic design; there's nothing more hopeless than a document that won't lie flat, or one that splits when you open it too far, or one that is bound so poorly that pages fall out.

The English designer Paul Jenkins runs a studio called Ranch. He and his designers work mainly for charities and arts-based organizations, which means they rarely have the luxury of big production budgets. And yet Ranch's printed brochures always look beguiling and distinctive, with much of their attraction coming from the varied and inventive binding techniques used. 'We love all types of binding,' says Jenkins. 'Rivets, thread sewing, industrial staples (done individually with

Above
Project: Binding techniques
Clients: Pathe (top); The Sales Company
(middle); The Sales Company (bottom)
Designer: Paul Jenkins at Ranch Associates
Range of binding techniques; cover stab-
stitched and creased at spine and then
bookbinders tape applied (top); stab-
stitched with industrial carton staples
(middle); hole-punched and tied together
with torn red cloth (bottom).

a foot-pedal machine), coloured wires, even good old comb binding; there's a whole world of different bindings out there.'

How does a designer decide which type of binding to use? Any decision surrounding sophisticated binding has to begin with a discussion with a printer. But there's a problem here: most print reps are not binding experts, and since most print firms farm out binding to specialists it is hardly surprising that the printer who has sound advice to give on paper stock, dot gain and the use of special colours might be less reliable on the difference between hot glue and cold glue.

Jenkins bases his binding decisions on a mixture of aesthetics and functionality. As he explains: 'Let's take the easy one first, functionality. Basically, if you do not want to be limited to four-page sets, then a type of binding other than the industry-standard saddle stitch (or stapling) is called for. A lot of our work is based on using unusual materials, and quite often we want to insert different stocks in different places within a brochure. If the pagination can be single sheets instead of four-page sets we can achieve this without a different piece of material "coming out at the other end of the brochure". Aesthetically, it's amazing how an unusual binding method can "flavour" a brochure. Something as simple as stab-stitching a brochure (staples going through the face of the brochure to the back rather than through the spine) creates a cruder more honest feel.'

And now that digital printing has made small print runs feasible it is increasingly important that designers are able to utilize simple 'home-made' types of binding: an elastic band holding together a dozen sheets of folded stock, for example. 'A rubber band can be beautifully simple,' notes Jenkins. 'They come in colours, and they seem to magically keep everything in place, as well.' But as he observes, these 'domestic' methods are not necessarily the cheapest. 'A different binding will usually call for slightly more budget than a saddle stitch,' he says, 'so even though some of these crude bindings look cheap they are in fact not. Aesthetics plays a big part as mentioned above. I think it's really about suitability; you don't want to be pressing crude metal eyelets into a bank's annual report, but these would look great for a gritty Ken Loach film brochure.'

> There's nothing more hopeless than a document that won't lie flat, or one that splits when you open it too far, or one that is bound so poorly that pages fall out.

Further reading: Daniel Mason, *Materials, Process, Print*. Laurence King Publishing, 2007.

Blogs

Design blogs have had a pronounced – and growing – impact on design. A weblog means that anyone can publish anything, any time they like, for a global audience. For some, blogs are the sketchpads for the new design seriousness, for others they are a platform for the new design egotism.

In recent decades we've been urged by critics, historians, educators and high-minded designers to take design more seriously: to debate it, analyze it and theorize it. There have always been designers with strong philosophical and theoretical interests willing to subject their craft to analysis, but it wasn't until the 1990s and the arrival of radical designers like Rudy VanderLans at *Émigré*, and the publication of *Eye*, that the notion of a critical debate surrounding graphic design gained a serious foothold within professional practice. A decade or so later, the process has been accelerated by the arrival of design blogs.

It has become both fashionable and necessary to monitor daily – sometimes hourly – the design discourse online. Designers who might shy away from a 4,000-word *Eye* article are happy to dip into online discussions.

The design blogosphere is dominated by a few big United States-based sites that offer contributors a platform to write freely and spontaneously on any design-related subject. *Design Observer* (to which I am a guest contributor) and *Speak Up* dominate the terrain. *Design Observer* is 'older' and retains a journal-like seriousness. *Speak Up* is 'younger', with a greater professional focus. Other blogs deal with online design, typography, branding and illustration. Most of the design magazines have blogs, a tacit acknowledgement that most of the action has moved online, and that print media are unable to move with a fraction of the speed that is possible on the Internet.

The blogs enjoy vast readerships – far more than any design journal. They attract huge numbers of comments from vociferous posters. Comments range from the precise and detailed (often eclipsing the original posting for sharpness and insight), to boorish abuse no better than playground insults. Commentators often exhibit a pugnacity they wouldn't show if they were talking face to face with the person they are berating: everyone is brave in cyberspace.

At their best, personal design blogs offer a new ecosystem of shared thoughts, images and news and a brain-fry of web feeds and links to compelling material.

There's another sort of blog, far more prevalent than the kind mentioned above – the personal blog. There are countless personal design blogs. Blogging software allows designers to publish texts, images, animation and audio without the restrictions of cost and space normally encountered in traditional publishing. At their best, personal design blogs offer a new ecosystem of shared thoughts, images and news and a brain-fry of web feeds and links to compelling material. At their

AisleOne

An inspirational reso
graphic design, typo
minimalism and mod

Home Shop Wallpapers About Contact

Wallpapers

ABC 123

1920x1200

ROME WAS NOT BUILT IN A SUIT

1920x1200

1920x1200

1920x1200

GRIDS ARE GOOD FOR THE SOUL

Helvetica - 1920x1200

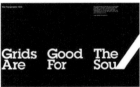

Lubalin Graph - 1920x1200

I LOVE TYPOGRAPHY

worst they are embarrassing pile-ups of egotism, dreary self-advertisement and pointless twittering. Many are the equivalent of sitting on a long train journey and listening to someone on a mobile phone discussing the contents of their fridge; when design studios attach blogs to their websites there is an unmistakable whiff of self-aggrandizement about them, and judging by the prevalence of 'Comments (0)' tags at the end of articles there isn't much 'commentary' going on either.

By trawling the blogosphere we discover vast amounts of interesting and unexpected material – both text and images. And while there are too many sites to offer any sort of authoritative appraisal, there are three important effects of design blogging.

The first is the welcome promotion of discussion and comment, not to mention more practical benefits such as software tips and shared information that make the life of a designer less solitary. Anyone who became a designer in the era before blogging – and before the great design-publishing boom of the 1990s – will know that designing was often an isolated occupation; there simply wasn't enough information around. Now, thanks to the plethora of design books – and design blogs – there's no shortage of shared knowledge, practical help and inspiration. And that's a good thing, even if we occasionally feel overwhelmed by the sheer amount of material.

The second effect is also beneficial: blogging is turning designers into editors. The posting of self-generated text and self-sourced images is forcing them to present content in a way that rarely happened before. A few designers write (and design) their own books, but now hundreds – perhaps thousands – produce blogs brimful of their own writings, photographs and graphics. Occasionally these sites are chaotic and far too self-absorbed to be of interest to anyone other than the blogger's circle of friends; but a huge number are smart, engaging and sharply presented. Some of this is down to the sophistication of the blogging software, but mostly it's down to designers unleashing instinctive editorial and presentation skills they barely knew they had.

The third effect is less obviously beneficial. Blogging is threatening to supplant books and magazines as the primary source of information on design. Even as far back as 2004, Rudy VanderLans was able to say: 'I think blogs are making a lot of design magazines

Occasionally these sites are chaotic and far too self-absorbed to be of interest to anyone other than the blogger's circle of friends; but a huge number are smart, engaging and sharply presented.

obsolete.'[1] At first glance this appears to be a bad thing; it's increasingly likely that books and magazines will lose out to the Internet – who wants to pay to see stuff that you can view free on the computer screen? But I mentioned a less obvious benefit. What I think will happen (in fact, it's already happening) is that publishers, writers, editors and designers of books and magazines will have to start producing better books and magazines. And, furthermore, they will have to find ways to integrate books with the online world. It seems increasingly likely that books and magazines will coexist in physical and electronic versions. And that seems like a benefit to me.

Further reading: www.designobserver.com

Opposite
Project: Wallpapers on the AisleOne blog
Date: 2008
Designer: Antonio Carusone
Typographic wallpaper designs created on strict grid systems, downloadable at www.aisleone.net

1 'An Interview with Rudy VanderLans: Still Subversive After All These Years', Steven Heller, 2004. www.aiga.org/content.cfm/an-interview-with-rudy-vanderlans

Book design

When designers tell you, with pained expressions, that they are 'designing a book', the pain is usually mixed with pride. Designing a book is a badge of honour, and although it is usually poorly paid it is one of the most satisfying things a designer can do.

There is no better advertisement for the value and grace of good graphic design than a well-designed book. When everything is in harmony – typography, images, grids, margins, print quality, paper stock, format, binding and finishing – the effect is a kind of perfection. A well-designed book not only looks good, it also delivers information in a uniquely satisfying manner; we may live in a screen-based culture, with all the advantages this brings, but for the elegant delivery of ideas and most forms of information, a well-crafted book is unsurpassed in ergonomic terms. It even smells good.

For the elegant delivery of ideas and most forms of information, a well-crafted book is unsurpassed in ergonomic terms.

William Morris, the Victorian designer, artist, writer and utopian socialist, believed in the inherent dignity of craft, and in well-designed artefacts as a perquisite of civilization. In 'The Ideal Book',[1] a paper written in 1893, he stated: 'The picture-book is not, perhaps, absolutely necessary to man's life, but it gives us such endless pleasure, and it is so intimately connected with the other absolutely necessary art of imaginative literature that it must remain one of the very worthiest things towards the production of which reasonable men should strive.'

But it's also true that book publishing is an intensely competitive and cost-sensitive industry with punishing deadlines and strained editorial and production resources – not to mention increasingly demanding marketing constraints. Designers who want to dwell on the minutiae of book design are rarely given enough time. Yet, somehow, wonderful books continue to emerge, and few designers can turn down the opportunity to design one. It is a staple of graphic design – a rite of passage even – and despite the financial hardship, and despite

Above and opposite
Project: *Making of the Universe/Book*
Date: 2009
Client: Paul A. Taylor @ Mute records
Designer: Adrian Shaughnessy
Artwork: Tea Design
Photographers: Daniel Miller and
Ferg Peterkin
96pp book with photographs of Depeche
Mode recording their album Sounds of the
Universe. Available as part of the Sounds
of the Universe Deluxe Box Set.
www.depechemode.com/sotu_box_set.html

the fact that few books were ever designed in less time than had been estimated, designers still queue up to design them.

One of the masters of modern book design is Derek Birdsall; his *Notes on Book Design*[2] is the one of the best works on the subject. Reviewing the volume in a national newspaper, the critic John Manning noted: 'Most readers take the appearance, layout, shape, size and feel of a book for granted. As Birdsall ruefully admits: "In book work, the best layouts appear to have designed themselves." We instinctively know when the design is right, and when it is horribly wrong. If the design thrusts itself on our attention, it is probably wrong. There should be a natural harmony and rhythm in such matters, as the form matches content, images marry text, and text flows from one opening to the next with pleasing aesthetic logic. Appearances to the contrary, these things do not happen by themselves. They are the result of care, thought and meticulous attention to detail.'[3]

Phrases like 'natural harmony' and 'aesthetic logic' are inspiring. But how do we achieve this with a publisher throwing marketing instructions at us, and editors and production people giving us energy-sapping deadlines?

Before designing a book, designers have to make a fundamental decision. Even before we decide on formats, grids, fonts, colour palettes, paper stock, materials and binding, there is a basic philosophical question to be asked: do we create a design that reflects the spirit, tone or flavour of the book, or do we create a neutral design that 'most readers will take for granted' and which allows the subject matter – pictorial and textual – to occupy all their attention?

Take the example of a book about fast cars. We have a choice: we can incorporate 'go faster stripes' and other 'auto-graphic' detailing, or we can allow the pictorial content to carry the visual message, and use typography, layout and graphic elements to underscore the content in an 'invisible' way. Here's another example. Imagine you are asked to design a book on Indian cuisine. What is it to be: faux Sanskrit fonts and pointed arches, or a cool, understated, typographically neutral system that makes the recipes easy to follow?

Both approaches have their merits. How do we decide? Of course, publishers, marketing departments and even book retailers will have a view, and it is up to the

It is a staple of graphic design – a rite of passage even – and despite the financial hardship, and despite the fact that few books were ever designed in less time than had been estimated, designers still queue up to design them.

designer to negotiate these sometimes competing demands. But ultimately the designer has to ask the question: does the content demand an interventionist approach, or does it simply need an unobtrusive design that presents the content with clarity? As the great Dutch book designer Irma Boom noted in an interview: 'I always read the text of the books I design. If I don't know the content I can't design. Because I know the content I can go further than other people.'[4]

Once we've decided on our 'philosophical' approach, what practical steps can we take to ensure a good design? The trick is to envision the book in its totality. Designers tend to think in terms of spreads. Two pages fit snuggly on to our computer screens – they are manageable. But readers view books with a wider perspective, and readers do annoying things like start at the back, or flick randomly. For me, the most important part of a book's design is its rhythm. As we move from page to page, is there a sense of consistency but also of variation? I'm not talking about the hyper-variation we find in most commercial magazines, where every spread is an explosion of change as publishers strive to keep readers in a state of constant alertness. Rather, I'm talking about the sense of controlled change that occurs throughout all well-designed books.

For 'controlled change' we need a grid. I've devoted an entire entry to grids (see Grids, page 132), but here

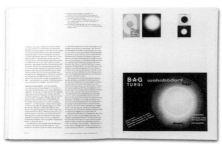

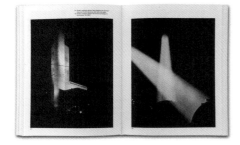

Above
Project: *Hans Finsler und die Schweizer
Fotokultur Werk, Fotoklasse, moderne
Gestaltung 1932-1960*
Date: 2006
Designers: Prill & Vieceli
Clients: Museum für Gestaltung Zürich
Thilo König, Martin Gasser (eds.)
*Hans Finsler und die Schweizer Fotokultur.
Werk, Fotokolasse, moderne Gestaltung 1932-
1960*. gta Verlag Zürich, Zürich 2006
© for this edition: Zürcher Hochschule der
Künste (ZHdK), 8005 Zürich and gta Verlag,
ETH Hönggerberg, 8093 Zürich
© photographs by Hans Finsler © Stiftung
Moritzburg, Halle/Saale, DE
Designed by the Swiss duo Tania Prill
and Alberto Vieceli, the black-and-white
photographs of Hans Finsler are placed in
balanced arrangements surrounded by refined
and restrained typography. A clear sense of
hierarchy emerges, with nothing to distract
the eye.

it's enough to say that the grid is absolutely fundamental to the structure and flow of a book's content. A grid is like the framework of a house: it gives inner strength to external appearance. A grid gives a book its sense of architecture and, as with buildings, you can have a clumsy construction with no sense of design, or you can have one that functions properly and also looks good.

The process of envisioning the overall design of a book has become more difficult now that it is common to receive the contents digitally. This means the designer is required to design the book without being able to hold its contents in his or her hands. Digital files make the technical execution of the design relatively easy, but by relying on thumbnails and text files we bypass the opportunity to physically assess the nature of the content. Nothing beats holding images and text in our hands, so wherever possible a good way to start designing a book is to lay out all the contents on a table – printouts of photographs, text, graphs, headlines, etc. This allows the designer to create an overview – to have a sense of the book's totality. In small studios this is not always possible. But spreads can be pinned on the wall to get a sense of pace and rhythm. I often use the floor – anything that helps to give a view of the book as something more than a succession of isolated spreads.

The process of envisioning the overall design of a book has become more difficult now that it is common to receive the contents digitally. This means the designer is required to design the book without being able to hold its contents in his or her hands.

Next in importance is the relationship between text and images. Once column widths and typographic details have been decided, the size and positioning of the images is crucial. Too many different sizes and the book looks overcooked; too few and the pages can look bland. Personally, I like some bleed pages mixed in with non-bleed images. This gives books a dynamic quality. I also have a personal dislike of colour backgrounds. I like white pages. I like black text on white paper. Not very adventurous perhaps, but I tire of colour pages and find text on – or out of – tint backgrounds tedious in anything other than short bursts. Other designers use colour pages to good effect. There are no rules that can't be broken in book design.

Finally, the furniture of a book: the folios, running heads, captions, endmatter, etc. All these details are vital and if they are not well judged the end result will be dowdy and look thrown together. Good designers put plenty of thought into these minor notes in the symphony of a book. They have an impact out of all proportion to the space they take up.

What else can we do? Besides sweating blood, we can attend to one of my main book-design irritations: a cover or jacket that bears no relation to the design of the inside of the book. Nothing makes a book look as though it is suffering from a lack of overall vision more than one that seems to belong to another title. It's true that a cover/jacket is often subjected to greater scrutiny than the book's contents. Marketing departments get involved; foreign sales departments get involved; even bookshop buyers get involved. And the result is that a cover or jacket can drift off like a hot air balloon that's slipped its moorings. I've had this happen many times. (As I write these words I make a mental note not to let it happen to this book.)

Finally, the best skill a book designer can develop is editorial skill. As designers we should approach the task of designing a book in the same way that an editor approaches editing one. Most designers are capable of editorial thinking. They have an instinct for the hierarchical arrangement of information and for points of emphasis. As Irma Boom said: '… I do book design – which is not only design, but also editing – so it's time-consuming. And I'm always involved right from the beginning of a project as part of the editorial board, which makes my design process even more time-consuming, but that's what I like. Because then you can make something special.'[5]

Further reading: Jost Hochuli and Robin Kinross, *Designing books: practice and theory*. Hyphen Press, 1997.

1 www.marxists.org/archive/morris/works/tmp/ideal.htm
2 Derek Birdsall, *Notes on Book Design*. Yale University Press, 2004.
3 'Cover to cover', *Guardian*, Saturday 16 October 2004.
4 Erich Nagler, 'Boom's Visual Testing Ground: the internationally acclaimed book designer Irma Boom talks about her craft', February 2008. www.metropolismag.com/cda/story.php?artid=3175
5 Ibid.

Book cover design

Designing a book cover tests the designer's ability to create precise and immediate visual communication. To simultaneously encapsulate the content of a book and grab the attention of the casual bookshop browser is one of graphic design's great conjuring tricks.

There's no sharper test for the designer, or illustrator, than distilling the contents of an entire book into an incisive, graphic statement. But a designer who doesn't love words and ideas or reading is unlikely to be capable of creating a great book cover: the best ones are designed by designers who like words in the same way that the best record-sleeve designers like music.[1]

OK, so I'm not talking about the covers of airport blockbusters, movie tie-ins, romantic fiction, celebrity biographies or car repair manuals. These are all done to a formula, and deviation would result in lost sales and the spilling of blood in the air-conditioned marketing departments of the big publishers. So let's look away from the displays in our local supermarket, and turn instead to intelligent books for intelligent readers: modern fiction, classic fiction, biography, travel, cooking, the arts and humanities.

Top
Project: *Jilted* by Jill Hoffman
Date: 1994
Client: Simon and Schuster
Designer: Carin Goldberg
Photomontage: Man Ray
Jilted is a novel about a contemporary,
urban, middle-aged artist experiencing
a sexual rebirth. The typography reflects
the dysfunctional and quirky characters
that appear throughout the book.

Above
Project: *Sight Readings* by Elizabeth Hardwick
Date: 1998
Client: Random House
Designer: Carin Goldberg
A collection of Elizabeth Hardwick's essays
on American writers written between 1982
and 1997. This cover was submitted but
never printed.

Book covers must attract the attention of browsers in bookshops. They must be eye-catching because the browser is assailed by hundreds of books all clamouring for attention. And, of course, today it is not enough to create covers that work on the display tables in Borders; the designer has to create designs that also work as thumbnails on the Internet.

Can we design a book cover without reading the book? Yes, but it will be a better-designed cover if we have, in fact, read it. Can we design a cover for a book we have read but didn't like or understand? Yes, but it will show. Book-cover designers – like record-sleeve designers – do their best work when they are working with material that inspires them. The novelist and artist Harland Miller has produced a series of paintings based on Penguin book covers.[2] Writing about cover design in a newspaper article,[3] he quoted the American writer Allan Gurganus, who said the cover of 'one's book is in a sense one of the first acts of literary criticism'. The idea of the cover design being a sort of visual critique of the book is compelling: the designer as visual critic! It means that readers can use the cover as a sort of review.

> **Today it is not enough to create covers that work on the display tables in Borders; the designer has to create designs that also work as thumbnails on the Internet.**

So, what makes a good cover design? The secret is not to attempt to retell the story. Even if we wanted to, this is a near impossible task. The author might have hundreds of pages to indulge in endless detail; the designer has only a small space to visually replicate the book's content. Good cover design uses a visual shorthand, and bypasses the heavy-handed spelling out of the story.

But it's worth pointing out that publishers don't usually see covers in the way designers see them. The first 'critic' is not, as Allan Gurganus suggests, the designer; it is usually the publisher's marketing department. More often than not, book covers are the products of marketing and sales departments. This is not to say that marketing people don't know what imagery will sell a book – but, as with film posters and record covers, the more control they exercise, the more standardized and formulaic the outcome becomes.

The American designer Michael Ian Kaye, one of the best of the modern crop of cover designers, has some interesting things to say about 'marketing requests'. Designers in all spheres can learn from his perceptive comments. In an interview with Steven Heller,[4] Kaye noted: 'When someone asks for large type, for example, is that what he or she really wants? Nine times out of ten, no.

Above
Project: *American Theatre Book of
Monologues for Men/American Theatre Book
of Monologues for Women*
Date: 2001
Client: Theater Communications Group
Designer: Carin Goldberg
These books present the best audition pieces
for actors selected from over 80 plays first
published in *American Theatre* magazine since
1985. The magazine has published many of the
most important contemporary American plays
over the last 15 years, including Angels
in America, Three Tall Women, M. Butterfly,
Talk Radio, The Baltimore Waltz and Buried
Child, to name a few.

Readability, yes. A sense of importance, yes. Clarity,
yes.' He went on to say: 'I do get asked for visual
clichés; big type, foil stamping, embossing, etcetera.
In these cases, I know the concern is readability and
that the book feels important and special. These are
things that can be achieved without succumbing to the
hackneyed tricks of the trade.'

As these comments demonstrate, Kaye isn't defeated
when he's given a marketing instruction. Instead he
'negotiates'. Like a hostage negotiator he looks at
the situation and finds a way out where no one gets
hurt. Sometimes we have to admit defeat in conflicts
with marketing departments but, as Kaye shows, there are
times when we can give our clients what they want, and
at the same time, preserve the integrity of our designs
(see Clients, page 64).

Kaye has earned his right to challenge marketing
diktats. In an online article about him, it was pointed
out that Kaye enjoys a unique position: 'At most
[publishing] houses, design and advertising are separate
departments,' writes Alexandra Lange. 'But as creative
director at Little, Brown, Kaye has control over a book's
design and its advertising – the total look of the product
from galleys to display table.'[5] Most
designers would donate a limb to be
in Kaye's position.

Another leading book-jacket
designer is New York-based Carin
Goldberg. For her, designers have
an obligation to 'stimulate, evoke,
cajole, lure and tease the customer
by graphically interpreting the
tone and the intent of the author's
words and ideas similar to the way
a dancer might respond to music.'
But she thinks that an excess
of timidity among commissioners
prevents book covers from being better. 'A jacket has
to compete with hundreds of other jackets on the shelves,'
she notes, 'so the challenge is to graphically compete
among a visually over-stimulating and competitive
environment. I don't believe that a book jacket is
fully responsible for selling a book. A good review and
celebrity endorsements are much more effective. But, a
cover can certainly tip the scales. Therefore there is no
excuse for bad design or even just OK design for a book
jacket. I believe most designers understand this but
unfortunately, editors, publishers and marketers too often
undervalue the power of brave, evocative design. Given the
huge number of books published each year there should be,
but are not, many more excellent covers on the shelves.'[6]

**More often than
not, book covers
are the products of
marketing and sales
departments, and as
with film posters
and record covers,
the more control
they exercise, the
more standardized
and formulaic the
outcome becomes.**

Yet no matter how wonderful a cover design may be, it is unlikely that this alone will be the reason someone buys a book. Design might play a crucial role in alerting a potential customer to a book's presence; it might encourage someone to pick up a book and it might also play a role in helping someone decide to buy the book they have in their hand. But design alone is unlikely to be the sole reason for purchase. Even Chip Kidd who, like Michael Ian Kaye and Carin Goldberg is acclaimed as a book designer of genius, doesn't think a book can be sold solely on its cover: 'I cannot make you buy a book, but I can try to help make you pick it up,' he says. 'There are so many factors that go into whether somebody buys a book – the cover's just one of them.'[7]

For wannabe book designers – as well as hardened book-trade pros – a study of the design history of Penguin books is enlightening. The venerable publisher began producing cheap paperbacks for a mass market in 1935. Since then, it has consistently pioneered good design at a sustained level that no other publishing house has equalled. Two excellent books have recently been published showing its commitment to design.[8] What is striking when you read the Penguin story is the way the company has nearly always combined a high-minded commitment to excellent graphic design and, simultaneously, a sound commercial outlook.

No one ever got rich designing book covers, but smart designers will always want to design them, if only because this allows them to perform in an arena that combines culture, ideas and commercial activity.

Further reading: Chip Kidd, *Chip Kidd: Book One: Work: 1986–2006*. Rizzoli, 2005.

1 As with most sweeping observations, there are exceptions: the great Reid Miles, designer and photographer of so many immortal *Blue Note* album covers, famously disliked jazz. OK, no more generalizations.
2 www.whitecube.com/artists/miller/
3 'Judge the book trade by its covers', Harland Miller, *Guardian*, 7 July 2007.
4 Michael Ian Kaye on book covers; interview with Steven Heller, in *Steven Heller and Elinor Pettit, Design Dialogues*. Allworth Press, 1998.
5 Alexandra Lange, 'The Bookmaker', December 1998. www.metropolismag.com/html/content_1298/de98boo.htm
6 Conversation with author.
7 Anya Yurchyshyn, 'How to Make People Buy Books. Chip Kidd, art director at Alfred A. Knopf, reveals the tricks of the trade', June 2007. www.esquire.com/the-side/qa/chipkidd061807
8 Phil Baines, *Penguin by Design, A Cover Story 1935–2005*. Allen Lane, an imprint of Penguin Books, 2005; Phil Baines and Steve Hare (eds), *Penguin by Designers*. Published by Penguin Collectors Society, 2007, in an edition of 1,250 copies.

Branding

In the post-industrial West the only things we 'make' are brands. This means lots of work for designers, but is it also the death knell for radical expression and innovative graphic design? By turning design into branding, designers have handed over the keys to the castle.

During the 1990s, I noticed the word 'branding' turning up in design meetings. At first, I stubbornly refused to use it. I clung to old-fashioned words like 'identity' and 'logos' and 'marks'. I also urged colleagues – and clients – not to use the 'B' word. I had three reasons for this.

Firstly, I felt that branding didn't have much to do with design. Brand status was almost entirely dependent on qualities earned over a period of time, and could not be acquired – or granted – instantaneously by a metaphorical squirt from the graphic design aerosol. Yet many of the clients who walked through my door requested a 'brand identity' that would express concepts like trust and reliability, and they wanted this to be facilitated by a new logo and some branded communication materials. I felt that trust and reliability should be earned.

Secondly, branding strategies frequently seemed to be camouflage for third-rate ideas. Branding appeared to be saying: 'You can have a lousy business – or product – but if you "brand" it properly you'll get away with it.' Branding linked design to hype and spin, and other contemporary black arts. Let's face it – Enron was well branded. As Jeffrey Keedy said in a 2001 *Adbusters* article: 'Brands should be memorable because they are good, not because they are omnipresent.'[1]

The third reason was that I never heard ordinary people talk about brands or branding. When media-world professionals referred to a jeans manufacturer as a brand rather than a fashion label, or shops as retail brands, they seemed to be breeding an arrogant them-and-us culture; they appeared to be saying: 'We will tell you what to think about a company or product.'

Then I saw in my local paper a photograph of a recently deceased teenager's grave. Her friends had commissioned a floral tribute. The flowers spelt out the word 'Gap'. If it had been the name of a boy band I wouldn't have batted an eyelid, but teenagers building a floral tribute to a dead friend in the shape of a shop logo was a sign that branding had triumphed. Today, everyone talks about brands. Branding is accepted wisdom. Clients love it. It's easier to understand than 'design', a term that most of them fear. Clients regard branding as a science. They like this because it means they can apply a formula to the creative process. They can even show 'brand equity' on a balance sheet.

But by allowing graphic design to become branding, designers have inflicted a self-induced wound. Give a marketing department a set of brand guidelines (see Brand guidelines, page 45) and they imagine they can conquer the world – not to mention the guidelines allowing them to sidestep huffy graphic designers with their funny ideas and endless chin stroking. Yet when clients are in charge of creative expression the result is always mediocrity. By turning design into branding we've allowed creativity to pass into their control. By abandoning its mystique for the dull science of branding, we've lost the one incalculable gift we can give our clients – the rebel yell of genuine creative vision. We've swapped this for a branded world of sameness.

Paradoxically, I was confirmed in this line of thinking by a visit to one of the world's leading branding companies. In early 2008, Patrick Burgoyne of *Creative*

When clients are in charge of creative expression the result is always mediocrity. By turning design into branding we've allowed creativity to pass into their control.

Above and overleaf
Project: Macmillan Cancer Support branding
Date: 2009
Client: Macmillan Cancer Support
Design: Wolff Olins
Macmillan Cancer Support used to provide nurses to look after people with cancer. But the nurses were often misperceived as 'angels of death'. With 1.2 million people in the UK living with cancer, Macmillan needed a much broader role. Wolff Olins helped the charity by imagining the organization's future, clarifying its ambition, changing its name ('cancer relief' to 'cancer support'), developing a brand idea and personality, and creating a radical new brand expression. The striking typography creates a distinctive and effective brand identity.

Review asked me to write a profile of Wolff Olins, which had just emerged from the media firestorm of the logo for the London Olympic Games in 2012.[2] I had been a vocal critic of the logo, but I also sensed that it was an attempt to do something different in that most difficult of arenas – the public arena.

I interviewed chairman Brian Boylan and senior creative director Patrick Cox. I asked Boylan to give his view of branding: 'The brand is no longer a single neat and tidy logo that you stick in the same place every time,' he said. 'Our thinking on brand has moved on. The brand is the platform, the brand is flexible, the brand is a place of exchange, and it is not fixed, so there is not one logo. There is recognizable form and recognizable communication and behaviour, but it's not one type of constrained and fixed thing.'

As is customary with big branding agencies, Wolff Olins offer their clients strategy and business thinking. But crucially they combine these with a magic ingredient: intuition. It's a word Boylan used often. He was keen to emphasize that strategy is no good if it results in what he calls branding by numbers. 'Our process is about getting a deep understanding of our clients,' he said, 'which is why we have people who come from a more strategic and business background. But then we start exploring, and that's where the intuition comes in. All in all, from beginning to end, it's a creative process, as opposed to a step-by-step logical process. Because if you only followed a logical process you'd inevitably arrive at a dry answer. Some of the answers we arrive at are beyond logical processes.'

Boylan's competitors have spent the last few decades removing intuition from the design process in a desperate attempt to make themselves attractive to businesses who, they imagine, don't understand such airy concepts as intuition and creativity. But Wolff Olins have proved that the smart companies of today want intuitive thinking and the vibrant creativity that comes with it. It's why Wolff Olins are booming, with clients clamouring to hire them.

But there's another reason why it is a bad idea to allow design to become a subset of branding: by aligning itself so thoroughly with branding, graphic design risks being sucked down with it, when as with most business credos, branding falls out of fashion or becomes discredited – and don't think it can't happen. Look at what happened to Wall Street's Masters of the Universe

By aligning itself with branding, graphic design risks being sucked down with it, when as with most business credos, branding falls out of fashion or becomes discredited – don't think it can't happen.

1 Jeffrey Keedy, 'Hysteria, Intelligent Design not Clever Advertising', reproduced in Steven Heller and Veronique Vienne (eds), *Citizen Designer, Perspectives on Design Responsibility*. Allworth Press, 2003.
2 www.creativereview.co.uk/crblog/wolff-olins-expectations-confounded

in the fall of 2008. Who would have guessed that these financial wizards would be exposed as not much better than bandits and they'd have to go begging to the government for a bailout?

I think we are already in the post-brand era. Branding – as practised by designers – has a role to play in the identity and identification of products and services, but the impoverishment of most brand-related thinking, and its cumbersome and occasionally sinister efforts to invade every aspect of our lives and turn us all into brand junkies, have been exposed as shallow and out of tune with the new era of participatory media. In the age of the Internet, when consumers can band together in cyberspace and challenge, refute and reject a company's brand values, branding will have to be more collaborative and less dictatorial. If this leads to more honesty, openness and plain speaking we'll all benefit.

Further reading: *Brand Madness* Special Issue. *Eye* 53, 2004.

Brand guidelines

What are they for? Are they essential rule books for the professional maintenance of design standards and consistent brand identity, or are they creative straitjackets that impede effective communication, and turn clients into control freaks and designers into mere implementers?

Brand guidelines ('brand books' as they are often called) are rules devised to govern the correct and consistent usage of typefaces, colours, logos, photography and graphic elements. They exist to ensure that companies and organizations maintain a consistent 'look and tone of voice' across all their communication materials. These brand books used to be called 'corporate identity manuals', and for the implementation of consistent and well-managed identities they have long been considered indispensable. They used to be printed documents – an airline might have 20 individual books of rules; MTV famously used one sheet of paper – but today they are likely to be online.

There are two conflicting views on brand guidelines. The first is the traditional view that strict guidelines are a prerequisite for the efficient control and management of an organization's identity across all media. With the arrival of cross-media communications (web, broadcast, mobile, print, outdoor, etc.) they have assumed a new level of importance. The task of maintaining a coherent visual identity across so many diverse platforms (a global corporation might have hundreds of different design groups around the world working on branded communications) means that precise instructions relating to the correct usage of all graphic elements is essential. This pragmatic view of brand guidelines regards them as a framework that designers should respond to with imagination and ingenuity, but also fidelity. Their advocates point out that design is, after all, about problem solving, and that navigating the restraints of the guidelines should bring out the best in designers.

The alternative view of brand identity manuals is more cynical and questioning. Most of the graphic design we encounter today is governed by brand guidelines. What this means is that nearly all the graphic design we see is done not by the people who designed it, but by others who are following instructions. There aren't many graphic designers who would advocate anarchy – graphic designers are rarely anarchists – but the controlling omnipresence of brand guidelines in modern visual communications means that design is often sterile, unimaginative and impersonal. In the eyes of many people who are asked to work with them, guidelines function like a boa constrictor, and squeeze the life out of graphic expression, resulting in 'blanding' (a neologism that neatly summarizes the effect of most branding strategies).

There aren't many graphic designers who would advocate anarchy – graphic designers are rarely anarchists – but the controlling omnipresence of brand guidelines in modern visual communications means that design is often sterile, unimaginative and impersonal.

Is there anything in this argument? Why should brand guidelines act as inhibitors? The reason is not the guidelines; it's the people who police them. Brand books are used by non-designers to control the visual presentation of an organization. Some marketing departments do this well, but when an organization becomes a slave to its brand guidelines the result is sterility. No set of guidelines – no matter how comprehensive and intelligent – can cater for every situation. It is therefore unavoidable that, from time to time, digressions from the rules are both necessary and desirable. The problem here is that the non-designers who police brand identities are rarely capable of the sort of flexible judgement that allows for imaginative deviations.

Typically, this problem is highlighted when branding-based design groups create guidelines that have to be adhered to by advertising agencies. The ability to create vibrant and effective advertising is frequently compromised by lumbering and rigid rules produced by graphic designers pandering to clients who imagine that inflexibility is the hallmark of a good set of brand guidelines, and who have never had to design an end frame for a television commercial, a billboard or press ad.

Of course, there is a breed of designer – highly disciplined and meticulous – who is attracted to devising brand guidelines. Often the manuals themselves are striking and handsome pieces of visual communication.

Opposite
Project: Brand guidelines
Date: 2004
Client: Moving Brands
Designers: Bibliotheque
Double-sided poster giving instructions for the implementation of independent brand agency Moving Brands' brand identity. Guidelines and identity designed by Bibliotheque.

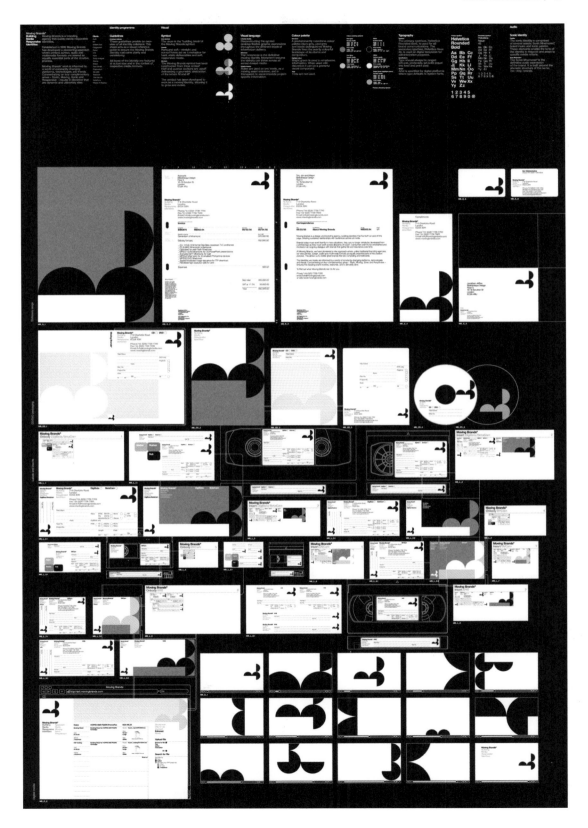

The almost academic approach to visual expression that they require is deeply impressive. There are brand books that are profoundly beautiful documents, yet ultimately they are doomed to be ignored, resented and endlessly flaunted. No good designer likes to be told what to do by another designer. And here is the reality of brand guidelines. Clients should look away, and hard-line professional designers who advocate 'professionalism' and obedience to the wishes of the client should also avert their gazes – the only successful brand guidelines are those that are implemented by the designer who made them in the first place.

Further reading: www.designerstalk.com

Briefs

How a designer responds to a brief is the most important factor in determining the outcome of a project. Briefing documents need to be studied closely, yet following them slavishly is not always advisable. We should challenge bad briefs and dig deeper into good ones.

Although designers like to kick out at the restrictions in design briefs, the simple truth is that they need briefs like cars need fuel. Yet a frequent complaint among clients is that designers ignore briefs. This is an astonishing allegation, but one I hear often. There are two reasons why clients say this. The first is that some designers do indeed ignore briefs and do what they want to do. The other – probably the more common – reason is that most designers give clients better work than they want, and clients mistakenly see this as a failure to follow the brief.

Once the practical issues are defined, we need to see if the brief is comprehensible. Is what is expected of us obvious?

Briefs are rarely what they appear to be. No matter how thorough and detailed they are, they always leave something unsaid. This is just as well, because if clients could write perfect briefs there would be no need for creative thought. Clients know what they want when they commission a designer, but they rarely know how to achieve their aim. Sometimes they will try and impose the 'how' bit, and we should recognize these briefs for what they are – they are not creative. But good clients know they can't do the 'how' bit and leave it up to designers.

Although a brief normally arrives as a document, its most important aspect is the person, or persons, who issued it. In other words, a brief isn't just a brief, it's a piece of communication from a human being with thoughts, prejudices, fears and concerns, and it's only by dealing with the human being – the brief's creator – that we can squeeze out its real essence. A good written brief is a prompt for a discussion more than a set of definitive instructions.

The AIGA defines a design brief as follows:

INCISIVE INFORMATION:
TECH. SPEC. DEADLINE, FEE,
TARGET-GROUP, etc. etc.

'A written explanation given by the client to the designer at the outset of a project. As the client, you are spelling out your objectives and expectations and defining a scope of work when you issue one. You're also committing to a concrete expression that can be revisited as a project moves forward. It's an honest way to keep everyone honest. If the brief raises questions, all the better. Questions early are better than questions late.'[1]

In most cases, by the time a brief arrives we have already met its creator – our client – and discussed the project. Yet just because we've done this, we mustn't assume that the briefing process is over. It isn't. It is nearly always necessary to go back and ask more questions – and in any case, asking questions shows commitment to the project, and clients always like to see commitment.

Before we go back to the client, though, we need to look at the practical requirements. Does the brief state the deliverables? Does it give full technical specifications? Does it supply the various delivery dates that we are required to work to? And, of course, does it provide budget details? We need to get these matters nailed down and agreed before anything else.

Once the practical issues are defined, we need to see if the brief is comprehensible. Is what is expected of us obvious? Are we required to work within existing brand guidelines or are we working on a blank canvas? Who is our intended audience? Have we been given all the 'parts' (logos, images, text, etc.) that we need? How do the practical arrangements (budgets, timings, etc.) impinge on our response? If we can't see the answers to these (and other relevant queries) the brief is in need of clarification and we must start questioning the client.

Not all briefs are written. With well-established clients, people we've worked with for a number of years, we will often be given a verbal brief. This is fine up to a point. But it's also dangerous, and can lead to misunderstandings. After receiving a verbal brief it's a good idea to fire back a confirmation email or letter that spells everything out. In other words, we need to write our own brief and send it to the client. This may seem unnecessary and pedantic, but it's a good discipline, and it shows the client that we don't take them for granted. It also avoids the 'Oh, I thought you meant …' argument.

A brief isn't just a brief, it's a piece of communication from a human being with thoughts, prejudices, fears and concerns, and it's only by dealing with the human being that we can squeeze out its real essence.

Above
Drawing by Paul Davis, 2009

If we are writing our own brief, never be frightened to state the obvious; it helps everyone focus. This is also the reason why I invariably begin presentations of creative work with a restatement of the brief (see Presentation skills, page 250). It ensures client and designer are on the same wavelength, and highlights any divergence of purpose. Clients also find it reassuring.

We also need to decide whether a brief is worth responding to. Honest evaluation of a brief requires – honesty. We usually need the work, and we've often fought hard to get it, but now that it is in our hands we have to be tough and ask some tough questions. Is this a good brief? Is it possible to produce high-quality work from this brief? Is it possible to make a profit?

Briefs are rarely what they appear to be. No matter how thorough and detailed they are, they always leave something unsaid. This is just as well, because if clients could write perfect briefs there would be no need for creative thought.

If we can answer all these questions to our satisfaction, we should proceed. If not, we need to challenge the brief. But how do we do this? By discussion, and by standing up for what we believe in. If a client is open-minded, it is sometimes possible to rewrite, or at least remould, the brief. Of course, some clients will be unhappy about this, but if we believe in our point of view we must be prepared to take a stand.

Finally, we reach a point where we can immerse ourselves in responding to the brief. In every brief there are a number of instructions and demands. Follow these and we will probably end up with an acceptable result. But in most briefs there is also a hidden or unspoken element – a key that unlocks the creative solution to the task. How do we find this key? Well, by doing research. I'm a passionate believer in talking directly to the audience that a brief is targeting. If you are aiming to reach fifteen-year old skate kids, go and talk to them. You'll almost certainly be surprised by what you hear. I was recently involved in a project to design a journal aimed at doctors; I spoke to a few doctors and they turned out to be one of the most adventurous and open-minded groups of people I've ever worked with – far more adventurous than my client, an over-cautious publisher. But I only found this out by talking to them. The way to find the creative key that unlocks a brief is through ruthless interrogation – of the client and the audience; and, most importantly, of ourselves.

The final part of the briefing process is delivery of the creative response. Here is the moment of truth. In my experience, it's rare for a designer to serve up a dud response. It is far more common to over-deliver. Now, this is not to say that designers can't get it wrong. Rather, it is saying that our natural inclination is to give clients better work than they want which ironically is often seen as a failure to understand the brief. So it's often necessary to develop strategies to convince clients that the narrow outlines of their expectations can be exceeded. From the outset I challenge clients to expect an unexpected response. Sometimes this backfires and I'm sent packing, but usually it opens up minds and raises awareness of solutions and responses that are not the normal formulaic ones.

Further reading: Peter L. Phillips, *Creating the Perfect Design Brief*. Allworth Press, 2004.

1 http://www.aiga.org/resources/
  content/3/5/9/6/documents/
  aiga_1clients_07.pdf

Briefing suppliers

Design is increasingly a collaborative activity and, more and more, designers are required to work with other creative people. This means they have to develop sophisticated commissioning skills. A hurried email or garbled phone call isn't usually good enough.

We are always quick to blame suppliers when our work isn't as good as we'd like it to be. Why has the printer trimmed these pages so badly? Don't these coders know all the type has to line up? Bad printing, bad colour reproduction and bad programming of websites are regularly cited when projects don't live up to expectations. Blaming suppliers is easy. Taking responsibility for suppliers delivering perfection is a bit tougher.

There are bad suppliers – no question. But the fact is that most poor work by suppliers is usually down to poor preparation, poor project control and poor briefing by designers. We know we are at fault when we tell suppliers: 'Oh, I assumed you knew …' Mere utterance of the words 'I assumed' is enough to condemn us as guilty without trial, and responsible for any shortcomings in the work delivered to us. 'Never assume' is the first rule of good designer-supplier relationships. Actually, 'never assume' is the only rule of good relationships with suppliers.

> **Most poor work by suppliers is usually down to poor preparation, poor project control and poor briefing by designers.**

Designers are usually good at being suppliers. We are good at looking after our clients; if they treat us well we give them our deathless devotion. But we are often lousy at being clients. We give our suppliers sketchy briefs, unreasonable delivery deadlines and miserly fees, then wonder why we don't get the results we want.

We should brief suppliers in the way we like to be briefed ourselves. All the smart designers I know treat their suppliers as valued equals. They treat them as collaborators; they treat them as people who can make them look good. Briefing should always be done personally, face

to face. This is increasingly difficult in the digital era. Many Internet projects – where the final outcome is a digital file – are bounced around a network of global suppliers. With razor-edged project management, this can be made to work. But nothing beats a meeting around a table. A good supplier will not let us get away with a bad brief – but nevertheless, all suppliers need careful briefing and careful monitoring.

A written brief is essential. Not only should we itemize financial and scheduling details but, if necessary, we must also restate everything discussed in a verbal brief. Failure to do so will result in retribution from the vengeful gods of graphic design. A bad bit of print buying, or commissioning expensive programming, can result in disaster. All good studios will have a system for this; if you don't, get one. Fast.

After writing this entry I was hit by a case of bad supplier briefing. A printer I was working with delivered a job with the wrong paper stock. And this was despite the print rep being told, at a face-to-face meeting, which stock was required. A bright attentive person, she was given its name and weight. I saw her write them down in her notebook. Job done. Except it wasn't. She left the company shortly afterwards and the wrong stock got used. Why? Because I hadn't bothered to put what I wanted in writing.

We should brief suppliers in the way we like to be briefed ourselves. All the smart designers I know treat their suppliers as valued equals. They treat them as collaborators; they treat them as people who can make them look good.

Further reading: Catharine Fishel, *Inside the Business of Graphic Design: 60 Leaders Share Their Secrets of Success.* Allworth Press, 2002.

Above
Drawing by Paul Davis, 2009

British design

Why do non-Brits think current British design is so good? There is lots of world-class design in the United Kingdom, but it's not all good. And besides, in the era of globalization, isn't identifying national design signatures almost impossible?

Above
Project: *Design Magazine*, covers
Date: 1955 (top); 1961 (above)
Client: The Council of Industrial Design
Art Director: Ken Garland
British designer Ken Garland served as art editor for *Design Magazine* for six years. The journal was published by the UK Council of Industrial Design. The cover of the 1955 issue features a logo for The Design Centre for British Industries, designed by Hans Schleger. Ken Garland's work can be viewed at www.kengarland.co.uk

When I go abroad I'm often told how good British design is, and how much healthier the design scene is in Britain. There is a widespread belief, even in countries that also have a claim to be considered the best in the world, that British graphic design is a world leader. I can see why people might think this. Contemporary British graphic design is often dazzling; there's a real appetite for experimentation among United Kingdom designers; and there's a healthy design culture centred around studios, magazines, shops, lectures, exhibitions and websites. As American designer and writer Jessica Helfand states: 'As an incorrigible Anglophile, it is difficult for me to find fault with anything British, let alone its graphic design. Mind you, I grew up with a father who collected *Punch* and bound volumes of old Giles cartoons. I remain addicted to anything packaged by Boots or Waitrose, and long, long ago – though this will date me – my sister and mother and I were besotted with all things Biba. And don't even get me started on the Wellcome Institute. Besides, how can you criticize a country whose national font is Gill Sans?'

But there is also a vast ocean of dismal design – vacuous commercial statements that threaten to engulf the good stuff, and the history of modern graphic design shows that for most of the twentieth century British design couldn't compete with the best work from Europe, the United States, Russia and Japan.

In the catalogue that accompanied 'Communicate', the exhibition of British graphic design that he curated in 2004, Rick Poynor wrote: 'In 1954, two tutors at the Royal College of Art's School of Graphic Design published *Graphic Design*, a textbook aimed at young designers. Revisited today, this sedate, unhurried volume contains little that a contemporary viewer and consumer would recognize as energetic modern graphic design. The authors, John Lewis and John Brinkley, present page after page of book plates, wood engravings and genteel illustrations by graphic artists such as Barnett Freedman, Edward Bawden, and Lynton Lamb …'[1] The key word here is 'genteel', and up until the 1980s British design was pallid and lacking in fire – although it was characterized by flashes of brilliance by British-based (although not always British-born) mavericks such as Eric Gill, Abram Games, Edward McKnight Kauffer,[2] Robin Fior, Dom Silvester Houédard, Keith Cunningham, Anthony Froshaug, Romek Marber and Ken Garland.

The history of modern graphic design shows that for most of the twentieth century British design couldn't compete with the best work from Europe, the United States, Russia and Japan.

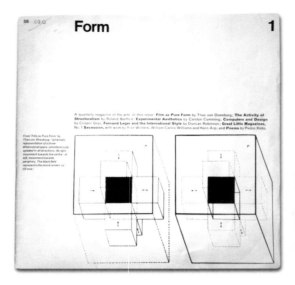

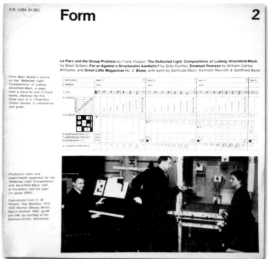

Above and opposite
Project: *Form*, issues 1-4
Date: 1966 (1-3); 1967 (4)
Form 1 shows diagram from 'Film as Pure
Form' by Theo van Doesburg; *Form 2* shows
projection cabin and experimental apparatus
for the 'Reflected Light Compositions', with
Hirschfeld-Mack (left, at the piano) and his
team in about 1924. *Form 4* shows Sanctuary
by Josef Albers, lithograph, 1942.
Designer: Philip Steadman
Editors: Philip Steadman, Mike Weaver (USA)
and Stephen Bann
Published by Philip Steadman
Described as a quarterly magazine of the
arts, *Form* ran to 10 issues in the 1960s.
At a time when most British publications
were locked into more traditional forms
of graphic presentation – or dabbling with
anarchic psychedelic styles – *Form* is a model
of quiet understatement and the adoption of
European Modernist design thinking. Designer,
editor and publisher Philip Steadman is
the author of a number of important books
including *Vermeer's Camera*. He is currently
Professor of Urban and Built Form Studies
at UCL in London. Original copies loaned
by Mason Wells.

But something happened in the 1980s. Graphic design
ceased to be a purely professional activity driven by
formalism and characterized by British reserve and a
fixation with tradition. Instead, it became part of pop
culture. The reason for this was that it was an integral
part of pop music. Album covers were, for many people,
their first and most meaningful encounter with graphic
invention. It was pop music graphics that first attracted
the British design superstars of the 1980s – Malcolm
Garrett, Peter Saville and Neville Brody – and it was
these designers who were to inspire hundreds of young
Brits to go to art school and study graphic design.
Prior to this, people studied design only if they had
shown an aptitude for technical drawing at school, or
if they had a facility for drawing and painting, or,
as was most likely, they had ended up at art school
purely by chance. Graphic design rarely featured on
any list of career options.

During the 1980s graphic design became hip. If you
couldn't play in a band, you did the next best thing and
became a graphic designer. This process has accelerated
to the point that today thousands of school-leavers study
design – of all kinds – and its popularity as a career
option is growing rapidly, and university courses are
full the world over.

But what about contemporary British design? Is it
any good? There are two strands and both are different.
Commercial design in the UK is like commercial design in
any other industrialized Western nation: highly polished
and suave with impeccable manners, but with nothing to
distinguish it as being British. It speaks in the lingua
franca of international communications – bland, anonymous
and tasteful. It has also yoked itself to branding and

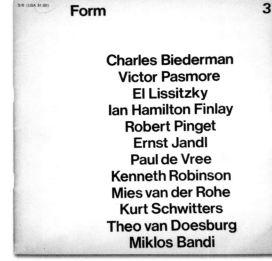

business strategies, with the result that all notions of contrarian thought or maverick statements are expunged. Yet, as someone like the retailer Paul Smith has proved, it is possible to thrive in the global economy by not adopting the dull overcoat of globalized greyness. Smith makes a virtue out of a post-Modern dicing up of British styles. This is uniquely attractive to a global audience, yet other UK manufacturers don't follow Smith's lead.

Elsewhere, away from corporate and mass-market sameness, individualism rules. The independent British graphic design scene couldn't be stronger or more confident. It contains a multiplicity of voices; it contains stylistic and political diversity; it contains visual flair with conceptual quirkiness. There are designers with links to fashion, music and style, and there are designers with strong campaigning and ethical instincts. But overriding all this is a strong design culture; in other words, an interest in design for design's sake. This can be interpreted as either an unhealthy narcissism or an inspiring love of the craft of design and visual communication.

I think it's the latter. The British obsession with graphic design has created its own vigorous subculture. It's a subculture with its own following and its own terrain. Most of the work is done for tiny record labels, small fashion houses and under-the-radar arts and music events. But it's this world that provides British design with its claim to a place at the top table of graphic design.

Further reading: Rick Poynor, *Communicate: Independent British Graphic Design Since the Sixties*. Yale University Press, 2005.

1 Rick Poynor, Communicate: Independent British Graphic Design Since the Sixties. Yale University Press, 2005.
2 Edward McKnight Kauffer, for example, was American, but he lived and worked in Britain from 1914 until 1940.

Broadcast design

People who normally pay no attention to graphic design notice broadcast graphics. Design for broadcast used to be a minor strand of graphic design. Today it's a prestigious activity that marries technical and design skills in a way previous generations of designers wouldn't recognize.

Above and opposite
Project: N Channel intro
Date: 2007
Client: N Channel
Design, shoot and animation: Stiletto NYC
Music/Sound Design: Marcus Schmickler
The design team at Stiletto NYC designed
the intro for N Channel's movie programming.
Due to the short time span allowed for the
spots, the designers used a filmstrip to
spell out the name of the show and have
the projector pull it in.

We think of broadcast graphics as a recent invention, but in 1954 the BBC recruited the British designer and filmmaker John Sewell as the corporation's first graphic designer.[1] In Sewell's era, television graphics were shakily displayed on boards held up in front of a camera. In this black-and-white period of poor screen resolution and snowy reception, there wasn't much the broadcast designer could do; design was rudimentary.

The first broadcast designer of any significance in the United Kingdom was Bernard Lodge in the early 1960s. Lodge alerted designers – and TV people – to the potential of television as a medium for graphic inventiveness with his title sequence for the cult show *Doctor Who*. This spooky, effects-laden sequence has passed into broadcast and pop culture legend. Part of its success was due to its remarkable, other-worldly music (by the BBC Radiophonic Workshop), but Lodge's work 'effortlessly epitomized the most unusual, imaginative and economically-innovative drama series ever to hit British (and eventually worldwide) TV screens.'[2]

In the 1970s, television channels began to incorporate moving graphics as part of their brand identity and, again, the United Kingdom led the way. In 1982, the designer Martin Lambie-Nairn used the new computerized equipment that was becoming available to television designers (mainly Quantal Paintbox) to create the animated 3-D logo for the new Channel 4. He went on to create striking station identities for other British broadcasters, including the BBC. His witty and inventive idents for BBC2 helped to define the modern era of broadcast graphics.[3]

With its launch in 1981, MTV became a playground for visual experimentation in television graphics. The channel heralded the break from conventional television design standards: it used flash frames, distressed imagery and predetermined interference, and pushed the boundaries of what was acceptable within broadcast conventions. Here the work of designers and animators enjoyed equal billing with the wall-to-wall music videos that the channel played. Post-MTV anything was possible, and if television was the most powerful communication medium known to human beings, then graphic designers suddenly had a seat at the top table. Designers, many without prior television experience, were able to create work that had an impact that was impossible in any other arena. In McLuhan's

The networks fight back by using broadcast graphics as a battering ram. The multi-channel environment is a battleground for competing broadcasters that use every marketing trick they can find to compel viewers to tune in.

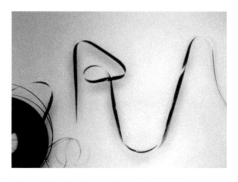

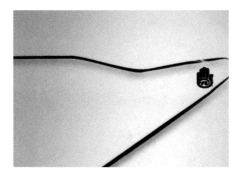

global village, the broadcast graphic designer was a skilled artisan, not a horny-handed toiler in the fields.

By the 1990s, broadcast design had become established. Graphic designers created the stings, idents, interstitials, title sequences and programme graphics that colonized television. These packages were often of superior quality to the programmes they book-ended. Budgets for television graphics soared. Design studios were established purely to service the insatiable desire of TV stations for a manicured graphic environment – no station could broadcast without a 'bug' reminding us which channel we were tuned to. Broadcast design became less about signposting and more about branding.

According to Mark Webster, a seasoned watcher of the motion graphics scene, and the creator of an informative website on the subject[4] 'Broadcast design is the most important domain for motion graphic design work and the wealth of creative output has increased largely with the increase in digital channels over the past ten years. For me, some of the least exciting broadcast design is done by news channels such as BBC World, ITN, CNN and all the others – where they have found themselves recreating the early Internet layout and have disappointingly got tied up in the all too prominent rectangular form. If it isn't another split screen then you soon find yourself watching and reading information boxes within boxes, alongside distracting and poor moving typography.' But Webster singles out one European broadcaster for praise: 'Arte which is a Franco-German public TV channel, has some of the most thoughtful broadcast designs I've ever seen, even for the news!'[5]

Today, in the multi-channel electronic souk of global television, the viewing public hardly notices – or cares – which channel they are watching. Now that we have endless choice, we exercise it. We channel hop, we time shift, we screen out the advertisements and the bits we don't care about; we even watch television on the Internet and on mobile phones. The networks fight back by using broadcast graphics as a battering ram. The multi-channel environment is a battleground for competing broadcasters that use every marketing trick they can find to compel viewers to tune in. In London, as in other cities around the world, it is commonplace to see billboards that once would have promoted pet food, automobiles and confectionery, advertising television shows. In New York, Jakob Trollbäck runs the design house

In London, as in other cities around the world, it is commonplace to see billboards that once would have promoted pet food, automobiles and confectionery, advertising television shows.

Trollbäck + Company. Roughly half its turnover comes from broadcast work. The studio's clients include leading United States broadcasters such as HBO, Discovery Channel and TCM. For Trollbäck, the biggest challenge in all broadcast design is that 'there usually are two separate teams for on-air and off-air promotion at the network. Every commercial client that we work with has a well thought-out and cohesive identity and message across platforms. For us, since we are very into figuring out a clear message for the network, it can be frustrating to see a completely different identity off-air. In some good scenarios we have created both, but those are rare exceptions.'[6]

The battle rages on. Channels utilize every pixel of on-screen real estate to persuade, cajole and browbeat the viewer into becoming a statistic in their ratings war. And yet, compelling and inventive work still appears. In Britain, the crown for broadcast graphics is held by Channel 4. The station – known for its radical and progressive approach to broadcasting – has produced a series of elegant idents that define the territory.

Broadcast design is both simultaneously more important than ever before, and more ephemeral than ever before. In a world where there is only dwindling channel loyalty design is often seen as the last best hope to retain viewers. As a result, TV stations change their on-air look almost as fast as their viewers change channels. Today's designers need to understand complex broadcasting systems that enable real-time information to be delivered to an audience that demand instant information. Being a broadcast designer has never been more demanding.

Further reading: *Broadcast Design*. Daab Books, 2007.

1 http://motiondesign.wordpress.com/
category/1960/
2 'Doctor Who: Evolution of a Title Sequence'.
http://www.bbc.co.uk/dna/h2g2/A907544
3 http://idents.tv/blog/
4 http://motiondesign.wordpress.com
5 www.arte.tv/fr/
6 www.trollback.com

Brochure design

Multi-page documents are a staple of graphic design. But in the digital online age, and with green issues rising in importance, brochures and printed documents are in danger of becoming things of the past; so does the Internet and sustainability mean the death of brochures?

A few years ago I was commissioned to produce a book of recent brochure design.[1] I contacted lots of designers whose work I liked and asked them for contributions. Nearly everyone I spoke to told me the same story: 'Sorry, haven't designed a brochure in ages.' And when I stopped to think about it, I hadn't either. Finding suitable specimens – and by this I mean engaging and unformulaic examples – became hard work. To fill my book, I had to stretch the definition of a brochure almost to breaking point, and ended up including any sort of bound, multi-page document.

Brochures still exist. But they tend to be either heavily laminated productions for luxury goods – if I'd wanted to fill my book with yacht brochures I could have done so many times over – or dull, low-grade leaflets

Above
Project: Holzmedia Look book_2.0
Date: 2008
Client: Holzmedia GmbH
Design: Projekttriangle Design Studio
Image brochure for premium media furniture
manufacturer Holzmedia. Projekttriangle is
responsible for the brochure's conception
as well as design, editing, photography
and writing.

1 Adrian Shaughnessy, *Look at This:
Contemporary Brochures, Catalogues and
Documents*. Laurence King Publishing, 2006.
2 www.annikuan.com

selling mass-market products such as consumer electronics, insurance and DIY products. With one or two glorious exceptions, the days when designers were routinely asked to design beautiful multi-page documents with high production values and exquisite design are gone.

Why? The Internet, of course. Clients have moved their budgets to the online world. It's understandable, really: websites are updatable, cheap to produce and offer unlimited distribution – all attributes lacking in printed documents.

Designers are allowed to shed a tear over the demise of the brochure. To create a striking multi-page document requires a designer to use all his or her core skills: layout, typography, art direction of photography and illustration, not to mention a keen grasp of colour reproduction, paper, printing and finishing technology.

Today, anyone who wants to design multi-page documents will have to use imagination and resourcefulness. With most clients reluctant to fund expensive printed documents, the modern designer has to box clever. Here's a good example of what I mean. In my book of brochure designs I featured some examples by Stefan Sagmeister. Sagmeister invariably uses cunning to create traffic-stopping work. For his girlfriend, the fashion designer Anni Kuan,[2] he designed a printed document to promote her label. She made only one stipulation: it mustn't cost more than the promotional postcards she was currently mailing out. Displaying the ingenuity that has made him one of graphic design's few household names, Sagmeister created a 'newspaper' for the cost of a postcard. As he explains: 'The idea of doing all these newspaper items came completely out of her tiny budget. Before we took over her graphics, she sent out a 4-cent postcard to all her buyers. Someone mentioned this Korean newsprint place in New York. They print a 32-page paper for the price of a postcard.'

> **To create a striking multi-page document requires a designer to use all his or her core skills: layout, typography, art direction of photography and illustration, not to mention a keen grasp of colour reproduction, paper, printing and finishing technology.**

Further reading: Adrian Shaughnessy, *Look at This: Contemporary Brochures, Catalogues and Documents*. Laurence King Publishing, 2006.

C

Charities, working for

Graphic designers have prospered in recent decades because they've catered for the rich minority of the world's population. We can only charge high prices if we have rich clients. But what about the world's poor and disadvantaged – surely they deserve good design too?

Graphic designers are often guilty of imagining that the world revolves around graphic design. Yet designers are social animals, and many have a strong impulse to do work that has a social or charitable benefit. But if we try offering our services to one of the big charities, we find that unless we have a track record in mass-market branding, direct mail and the techniques of customer relations marketing, our offer won't be taken seriously.

The designer Lucienne Roberts, a signatory of the 1999 First Things First manifesto,[1] and someone with a strong commitment to responsible and ethical design, noted in an article: 'Now I have meetings with communications directors who worked for McDonald's in a previous life, call people who donate money "clients" and model their strategic thinking on the mass market and mainstream. Yuck. This wasn't what I signed up for.'[2]

Charities argue that to compete in the consumerist economy of the West, they have to become marketing savvy and business-focused. But it seems odd that so many of them have chosen soulless corporatism as their model.

The American designer Jason Tselentis notes: 'The question I like to ask charities and not-for-profits is, why do you want to be like the enemy? It's true, they often liken their perceived approach to McDonalds-Nike-Gap branding methods. Oftentimes, they respond by saying, we want to make money. The biggest challenge is how do you

If we try offering our services to one of the big charities, we find that unless we have a track record in mass-market branding, direct mail and the techniques of customer relations marketing, our offer won't be taken seriously.

get them to innovate and carve their own niche in today's culture. It's as much a problem for not-for-profits as it is for any other client. They all love clichés.'

So, what can we do if we have an altruistic instinct and want to use our skills to do some good? In fact, there are lots of small charitable organizations that will welcome offers of help from graphic designers. All charitable bodies need to raise funds, and all fund-raising initiatives need communication materials to help them do it. If we approach organizations with offers of help, many will welcome us.

But we have more to offer than just our professional skills. Corporate social responsibility (CSR) has been widely adopted by large corporations as an essential part of their corporate ethos. Yet it's not only large corporations that have CSR programmes. Small design studios can have them too. In an article in *Design Week* Gill Parker, joint managing director of BDG Workfutures, an international design consultancy focusing on strategy and design for working environments, listed some options: 'payroll giving; loaning out meeting space; volunteer days; advertising a charity on your website; a charity leaflet/appeal in your regular business or customer mailings; putting a message in your franking machine; and using email footers.'[3]

It seems odd that so many charities have chosen soulless corporatism as their business model.

Further reading: Lucienne Roberts, *Good: An Introduction to Ethics in Graphic Design*. AVA Publishing, 2006.

Above
Project: Breakthrough Breast Cancer Annual Review
Date: 1997
Client: Breakthrough Breast Cancer
Photographers: Clare Park (left), Fleur Olby (right)
Designer: Lucienne Roberts
Breakthrough Breast Cancer is the UK's leading charity committed to fighting breast cancer through research and education. Designer Lucienne Roberts' Annual Report marked a change in Breakthrough's approach to publicity. At the time, 1-in-12 women in the UK were diagnosed with breast cancer. The report included the story of a woman who froze meals for her family before she died. www.breakthrough.org.uk

1 http://www.eyemagazine.com/feature.php?id=18&fid=99
2 Lucienne Roberts quote.
3 Gill Parker, 'It pays to be the good guys', *Design Week*, 17 January 2008.

Clichés

Clichés in design are often unavoidable since design deals with universal symbols and universal messages. But if the purpose of graphic design is to deliver messages, clichéd communications should be avoided, since clichés are invisible due to their familiarity.

Above and opposite
Project: *Pocket Canons* series
Date: 1997
Client: Canongate Books Ltd.
Designer: Angus Hyland, Pentagram
The *Pocket Canons* is a series of small paperbacks featuring the texts of individual Books of the Bible, with introductions by famous secular authors. The *Pocket Canons* series was designed by Angus Hyland for the progressive publisher Canongate Books. Hyland avoids the obviously clichéd response: no Biblical lettering, no bearded prophets and wan religiosity. Instead he produces covers that exude modernity and distinctiveness, and proves that the clichéd response isn't always necessary.

Design clichés are like clichés in any other area – dull, tiresome and best avoided. Think of Hollywood blockbusters; with a few rare exceptions, these steroid-injected cinematic eruptions are usually unbearable thanks to the grinding familiarity of recycled plots and seen-it-before sequences. The effect is numbing. When we make clichéd graphic design, we create exactly the same effect.

The best that can be said about clichéd design is that it is a sort of background radiation rendered almost invisible by its parrot-like repetition of the familiar. Its sameness means that we just don't see it. Yet, despite this, many designers – and clients – fall back on cliché-ridden communications (insurance brochures featuring pictures of Photoshop-fresh nuclear families walking in the countryside, for example) with the outcome that, like pictures we've had on our walls for ages, we simply don't see them.

Yet clichéd graphic design is not confined to corporate or mainstream design. Clichés thrive in fashionable circles too. To stay hip and trendy we have to use the language of hip and trendy, and many designers do this with the same slavishness that the marketing manager of a finance company employs when putting a picture of a stock-library family on the front of a pensions brochure. Hip clichés are as bad as unhip clichés.

Developments in technology and software can also lead to clichés. Look at the current obsession with objects mirrored in reflective surfaces – a device featured extensively by Apple and now almost impossible to use without looking derivative and lazy. In recent years we've had a superabundance of vector graphics (see Vector illustrations, page 295) – and just think how quickly these became tired and groanworthy.

There are no surprises to be found in clichés. If we want our work to resonate with its audience, if we want it to be noticed, we have to avoid hackneyed visual effects and overused graphic tropes.

The result of all this, as the writer Dan Nadel has noted, is that, 'One artist is nearly indistinguishable from another because they are all using the same tools and all operating from the same set of visual clichés, learned in, most likely, the same places. Rather than heightening the mystery, the effect is to deaden the work, sealing it off from the curious onlooker.'[1]

Designers have often spoken about the need to introduce an element of 'surprise' into their work. Not a good idea, perhaps, if we are asked to create the instructions on a medicine bottle, but most items of communication are improved by an element of controlled surprise. And since most communication is there for a

purpose – for either commercial or purely informational reasons – it's self-evident that the communication will fail if it doesn't get noticed. An element of surprise is the best way to get people to notice.

The book jackets by the British designer and Pentagram partner Angus Hyland for the series of biblical paperbacks published by Canongate are a stellar example of avoiding the obvious. In 1999, Canongate published the Bible in the form of single books. Had Hyland and the publisher followed the conventional marketing diktats of the genre they would have used classical art depicting Biblical scenes, and accompanied it with ornate 'biblical' typography. Instead Hyland used starkly modern photography and sans serif type. The effect was startling and invigorating; it was startling and invigorating because it was unclichéd.

There are no surprises to be found in clichés. If we want our work to resonate with its audience, if we want it to be noticed, we have to avoid hackneyed visual effects and overused graphic tropes.

However, it's not practical to reinvent the language of graphic design every time we create a piece of work. We've all encountered the witty designer who has decided to 'play with' the male and female symbols found on public toilet doors. It's usually in ritzy nightclubs or swanky restaurants that we come **Clients will always veer towards safeness, and safeness usually means taking refuge in clichés.** across this designerly playfulness, yet almost without exception it leads to confusion. We've all hesitated in front of an ambiguous rendering of the symbols, and wished the designer hadn't bothered. Here, and in other quotidian situations, reliance on universal symbols is usually the best – and safest – idea.

Clients will always veer towards safeness – and safeness usually means taking refuge in clichés. Yet if we alert them to the dangers of clichéd thinking, if we alert them to the dangers of sameness, we can often wean them off their obsession with the visual clichés of modern life. Of course, it will help if we can give them viable and compelling alternatives. Not easy, and we won't always succeed, but if we stop trying we mustn't be surprised if our work lacks vigour and effectiveness.

Further reading:
http://designarchives.aiga.org/entry.cfm/eid_367

1 Dan Nadel, 'Design Out of Bounds', reproduced in Michael Bierut, William Drenttel, Steven Heller (eds), *Looking Closer* 5. Allworth Press, 2006.

Clients

When projects go wrong, designers tend to blame their clients. But it's usually designers who are to blame. Yes, there are bad clients, but they are often turned into bad clients by designers treating them badly. Designers get the clients they deserve – the good, the bad and the indifferent.

Whenever I hear a designer announce that we must 'educate our clients' I reach for the sick bag. Instead of educating our clients, we must educate ourselves in the ways of our clients. Then – and only then – will clients listen to us and take us seriously.

And here's another paradox: the best way to understand clients is to become one. On the few occasions that I've been a client this has taught me more about being a designer than just about anything else I've ever done. It's only by commissioning – and paying for – graphic design ourselves that we discover that most of us are not very good at articulating to our clients what we think and how we work. For many clients, designers seem to operate on the principle expressed by the architect hero of Ayn Rand's *The Fountainhead*: 'I don't intend to build in order to have clients. I intend to have clients in order to build.'

This sense that we are pleasing ourselves at the expense of our clients is the source of countless conflicts and relationship meltdowns. Of course, there is an element of 'pleasing ourselves' in what we design. This needn't be a bad thing – even the most pragmatic designer does things because he or she 'likes them'. But design's unspoken secret is that we have to find ways to combine satisfying our own desires with serving our clients. It's a conundrum that designers have to wrestle with throughout their entire careers; it never goes away.

But let's spare a thought for our poor clients. How should we deal with them? Is there a right and a wrong way? All clients are different but broadly speaking there are three distinct ways of dealing with them:

Just when we think we've learnt how to deal with clients, we find one who doesn't fit our game plan. In truth, all we ever learn to do is handle a particular client. When another comes along, we have to start all over again.

We can be 'yes sayers'.
We can be hectoring bullies.
We can be equal partners.

Guess which option is best? Well, it's not being a 'yes sayer'. Mind you, if we only ever say yes we are destined to have an easy life. Assignments will come our way, and we will be patronized by clients who also want an easy life. But will great work emerge from this arrangement? Sometimes. But not often.

What about the 'bullying' route? Lots of designers talk about 'not taking crap' from their clients. They talk about 'laying down ground rules' and 'not compromising'.

SOON WE WILL OBLITERATE ANY TALENT YOU THOUGHT YOU POSSESSED.

Above
Drawing by Paul Davis, 2009

Well, this sometimes works too. But is it a good way to produce consistently great work? Not really.

What about the third route? How does becoming an equal partner with a client help? Surely we need the upper hand? And surely they want the upper hand? True and true; yet it's only through mutual respect and the honest and frank exchange of views (on both sides) that we can hope to create worthwhile work. Designers often say that if only they had an indulgent client like so-and-so (here they name the client of a famous designer who has commissioned a dazzling body of work), they too would create brilliant designs. But there are no dream clients. When we see great work it is because there is a mutually respectful and well-balanced designer-client relationship.

And the only way to build these great designer-client relationships is to create them ourselves. We can't rely on our clients to do it. The onus is on us to make these equal partnerships happen. But how do we do this? In a word: empathy. I discovered early in my career that I had a gift for client empathy. By this I mean I was quick to see the client's point of view, and quick to intuit what they really wanted.

We must listen to our clients for the simple reason that clients will only listen to those who listen to them. If we fail in this, the work will almost certainly fail too.

Empathy is a great attribute for a designer: it provides understanding and objectivity. And yet, although empathy is a useful 'skill' to have, it also means that those of us who possess it are fated to always see the world in a grey tint (Pantone 427, I'd guess), while others less burdened with it see the world in stark black and white. I am often envious of people with the ability to view every situation with monovision, but as an 'empathizer' I see the world in stereo; I am cursed to always see the other person's point of view.

I say cursed because, although empathy is undoubtedly useful in graphic design, it also has a downside. What happens when a client wants something that is wrong or runs against our aesthetic grain? Ah well, that's the problem with empathy. Too much of it is like too much certainty – not healthy.

So, to return to the question posed earlier: what is the best way to guarantee an equal partnership with clients? We need empathy mixed with a bit of inner certainty. If we are all empathy and no conviction we will not achieve the balance that is necessary for a good designer-client relationship. We must listen to our clients for the simple reason that clients will only listen to those who listen to them. If we fail in this, the work will almost certainly fail too.

And just when we think we've learnt how to deal with clients, we find one who doesn't fit our game plan. In truth, all we ever learn to do is handle a particular client. When another comes along, we have to start all over again. Clients can be capricious. They can be fickle and indecisive. This is a hard thing to contend with. But no one ever escapes it. Personally, I've always found being ruthlessly professional helps establish good relationships with clients. Doing all the dull stuff like written quotes, establishing payment terms and agreeing schedules is essential. Even when clients are casual and relaxed it is vital to maintain professional standards. When we complain that clients don't treat us like 'professionals' it is usually because we haven't behaved professionally.

I've always found it beneficial to admit my mistakes and errors of judgement. Too many designers work on the principle that they are never wrong, or imagine that they can never admit to having got things wrong. I've always tried to own up when I've made a mistake, and usually the outcome is that the relationship moves on to a stronger footing.

Think of it like this. Imagine going to your dentist. When you get there his or her white clothes are dirty. The surgery is messy. The dentist doesn't remember seeing you a month ago. Your files are missing. How much trust would you give this person? None, I'd guess. Well, it's the same with being a designer. It's no good saying, 'Trust me, I'm a professional' if you behave like a non-professional. The great American illustrator Brad Holland nailed this when he said: 'A lot of artists seem to think they'll be better artists if they're bad businessmen.'[1] Holland was talking about illustrators, but his view extends to graphic designers: I know a lot of designers who think its cool to behave like Jackson Pollock. It's not — unless you are as talented as Jackson Pollock.

Yet we mustn't ignore the human touch in all this. Clients are people, and if we treat them impersonally they will behave impersonally. For example, I've always found it beneficial to admit my mistakes and errors of judgement. Too many designers work on the principle that they are never wrong, or imagine that they can never admit to having got things wrong. I've always tried to own up when I've made a mistake, and usually the outcome is that the client/designer relationship moves on to a stronger footing. Clients respond to honesty and frankness. What they rarely like is bullish certainty.

Before I got to know the English designer Daniel Eatock,[2] I'd been told that he was 'uncompromising'.

ARE YOU AVAILABLE FOR A LOW-PAID, LENGTHY POINTLESS and SOUL-DESTROYING JOB THAT'LL MAKE NO DIFFERENCE TO ANY ONE OR ANYTHING, ANYWHERE?

When I got to know him I asked him if this was true. He said: 'If a client has a better idea than mine, I'm happy to incorporate it.' This is my view too. I've never believed in the notion that the designer is always right; I think it's a dangerous premise on which to do business. Of course, it is also true that we have to be uncompromising when a client gives dumb instructions. It's about being mentally and temperamentally flexible: knowing when we are wrong and knowing when we are right. Also, we must realize that every situation is unique, and that we can't adopt a blanket approach.

Our clients commission us to do something, and they agree to pay us some money, but the fact of the matter is they have no idea what they will get until they've got it.

The only other universal rule with clients is that most of them are in a state of constant terror. Why? For many clients (I'm tempted to say all clients but that wouldn't be quite true) commissioning design is like entering a lottery. They commission us to do something, and they agree to pay us some money, but the fact of the matter is they have no idea what they will get until they've got it. Yes, they can look at our past work; yes, they can brief us meticulously. But none of this guarantees that we will give them what they want. Hence the terror. And the fear and loathing.

But there are many things we can do to assuage this terror. We can show them work in progress, talk to them while the project is under way, and present our work with care (see Presentation skills, page 250). Instead, most of us rush off and work in a little bubble of self-absorption; we exclude the client from the process they are paying for, and then wonder why they reject, or interfere with, the end result.

One last thought. At a recent design conference, where various speakers railed and moaned about clients' venality and crassness, the moderator of the discussion, the veteran designer Ken Garland,[3] concluded the evening by saying he wanted to counter these negative comments. He said he'd enjoyed some of the most rewarding relationships of his life with his clients. Looking at Garland's rich back-history, you can see the wisdom in his remark. We have to love our clients – even when they don't deserve it.

Above
Drawing by Paul Davis, 2009

1 Jo Davies, 'Pictures for Articles Not Yet Written', interview with Brad Holland, *Varoom*, June 2008.
2 www.danieleatock.com
3 www.kengarland.co.uk

Further reading: Anne Odling-Smee, 'Ken Garland is known for First Things First, but his work is playful and personal as well as political', interview with Ken Garland, *Eye* 66, Spring 2008. www.eyemagazine.com/feature. php?id=152&fid=653

Commissioning creatives

Design is increasingly a collaborative undertaking. This means that designers often have to commission other creative professionals. This is not easy and means that designers have to become a bit more like clients. We are rarely at our best when playing the role of client.

Designers tend to be overly sympathetic to fellow creative practitioners. Perhaps because of a fear of appearing to be overbearing and unsympathetic – in other words we don't want to behave like an ogreish client – we are frequently too indulgent with creative suppliers and collaborators and then wonder why we end up with results that are disappointing. Sometimes, of course, we do the opposite. We treat them with too much severity and impose on them the sort of restrictions and prohibitions that we would resent if they were inflicted upon us.

As you might guess, a middle way is best. We must allow creative suppliers to retain a sense of authorship in what they do for us, but we must also use a degree of firmness to ensure that we get the results we want. Diplomacy and tact, matched by a clear vision of the final outcome, are essential. Let your creative suppliers know what you expect – but make sure you leave them space to do what they do. To use a cliché: treat them as you'd like to be treated yourself.

It is also essential to follow some basic housekeeping rules. It is the nature of creative projects that they always over-run and always involve more work than was estimated at the outset. So we must plan accordingly. The easiest way for a studio – or a freelance designer – to lose money is to enter into an open-ended agreement with a creative supplier and find, when a project over-runs, huge bills arriving that cannot be passed on to the client who, having a smart business brain, has tied us down to a fixed price. It is imperative, therefore, to establish financial parameters with creative suppliers. We must assume that all projects will over-run, and so we need to insist on suppliers working to fixed prices wherever possible. However, this arrangement must be fair, and if the client makes changes to the brief that necessitate us giving new instructions to suppliers, we have to allow them to charge – wherever possible – for this extra work (having first secured an additional fee from the client).

In addition, we must agree the technical specifications of the project and how the final work is to be delivered. It's also worth nailing the rules on copyright, usage rights, credits and press exposure. This often seems counter to the warm spirit of creative enthusiasm with which most projects begin, but when we see our work on a supplier's website without our credit (see Credits, page 79) we might wish we'd agreed beforehand what rights he or she was entitled to.

> **Let your creative suppliers know what you expect – but make sure you leave them space to do what they do. To use a cliché: treat them as you'd like to be treated yourself.**

Above and opposite
Illustrations by Andy Martin depicting the notion of commissioning illustrators. Produced specially for this book.
www.andy-martin.com

Commissioning illustrators

The commissioning of illustrators is creatively riskier than commissioning photographers, who tend to produce dozens – sometimes hundreds – of images, greatly increasing the likelihood of finding one that is suitable. With illustration, on the other hand, there is usually only one final output, which means it has to be right. Illustration is the least malleable of the graphic arts. Despite it being mostly digital today, it is more resistant to tinkering and alteration than typography or photography. Besides, making changes to a fellow professional's work is something all good designers avoid instinctively.

So how do we become good at commissioning illustrators? Well, we get to know them. I once spoke to an illustrator who told me he had never met any of his commissioners. He only ever received briefs via email, which he responded to by emailing back rough sketches. These were commented on (via email) and then he sent a PDF of the finished illustration to his client. Both parties are at fault here. The illustrator should have insisted on a face-to-face meeting, and the commissioner should consider a career change; anyone who thinks it is acceptable to commission illustration without any personal contact – ever – is in the wrong job.

The English illustrator Paul Davis (who has contributed illustrations to this book) receives many of his commissions from designers. He is a favourite with them. What does he think of the way they commission illustration? 'Sometimes it can be the most painful undertaking known to humankind,' he notes. 'You wake up sweating and full of that heady mix of dread and reluctance to get out of bed; and then other times you leap out smiling knowing it's a great project because you're being asked to do what you want to do and screw the focus groups. Yes, it depends on the person commissioning and whether that person has an open mind. I like it best when you're given text and a size and then trusted to come up with something good. Your arse is on the line so you do a better job.' Davis touches on the key to good commissioning here, when he says freedom means he is more – not less – responsible.

Giving illustrators freedom is essential. But sometimes we have a precise requirement that we want an

The worst thing we can do to a creative person is brief them and then, when they show us what they've done, point out that we needed something else. No creative person objects to a clear and precise brief. What every creative person resents is being given a precise brief *after* they have delivered the finished project.

Above
Project: Liam, Steel Fixer.
Date: 2008
Client: London and Continental Railways
Photographer: Brian Griffin
Art Director: Greg Horton, IC Art and Design
Striking image by photographer Brian
Griffin for the book *Team*, a portrayal of
the workers and management who constructed
High Speed 1, together with the modernization
of St Pancras Station into St Pancras
International.

illustrator to adhere to. How do we deal with this? The worst thing we can do to a creative person is brief them and then, when they show us what they've done, point out that we needed something else. No creative person objects to a clear and precise brief. What every creative person resents is being given a precise brief *after* they have delivered the finished project.

Commissioning photographers

Designers tend to be reverential about photography and photographers. We see photographers as enviable and glamorous figures. Most are extroverts. They are often entertaining and good to have around; they are often highly sociable individuals.

Photographers make themselves easy to brief; they are quick to grasp what is required of them and usually bring buckets of hepped-up enthusiasm to any project. The good ones often contribute ideas that add both technical and creative heft to the job. I always think it's a good sign when a photographer brings along a pile of books showing the work of other photographers – it indicates commitment and passion and, on a personal note, has been my introduction to the work of photographers who were previously unknown to me. Photographers are generally pretty clued-up about copyright and usage rights,[1] and because of this it's worth the designer establishing what rights he or she, and the client, are entitled to, and putting any conclusions in writing.

Beyond the vitally important questions of scheduling and money (there may be production matters concerning the hiring of models and props, as well as stylists and location fees) there are two main issues to resolve. The first is art direction and the second is the post-production question.

In most commercial photography, good art direction (see Art direction, page 18) can add hugely to the success of a shoot. Photographers are usually

If we turn up at a shoot and hope to make it up as we go along, we might find tempers fraying and a one-day shoot turning into a two-day one. Planning and agreeing the extent of the art direction is essential.

happy to be art directed. They like the shared creative experience of it. Occasionally, art direction can be resented and seen as interfering, but this is rare and it's usually the fault of ill-prepared art directors – and meddlesome clients. But the biggest problem with art direction is lack of pre-planning. If we turn up at a shoot and hope to make it up as we go along, we might find tempers fraying and a one-day shoot turning into a two-day one. Planning and agreeing the extent of the art direction is essential, and in most cases it is achieved easily. Occasionally, though, the art direction brief needs to be firmed up prior to shooting.

Post-production planning is as important as preparing for the shoot. In the pre-digital era, photographers took responsibility for delivering colour-balanced transparencies or prints. In the digital era, while most of them still see it as part of their job to deliver correctly adjusted files – usually in Photoshop – others see it as an extra commission that needs to be paid for or as being the responsibility of the designer. Either way, who does what has to be agreed.

When the photographer Brian Griffin started out in the 1970s, he was described as the 'new Robert Frank'. Having worked with many leading designers and photographers in Europe and the United States, he has simple but radical advice for designers attempting to get the best out of photographers. 'Throw away being preoccupied with design when commissioning a photographer,' he says. 'Instead, generate a photographic concept which in itself triggers off the eventual design. Be too focused on the design of the page and it could destroy the photographic magic. Design your pages after viewing all the shoot material. Let the photography drive the graphic concept. Photographs are so powerful when executed by a top photographer, let them breathe.'

Further reading: www.theaoi.com/client/commission.html www.copyright4clients.com/faqs

1 Photographers are usually better than designers and illustrators at protecting their copyrights – and maddeningly, clients are quicker and keener to recognize the copyright in photographs than graphic design and illustration (see Copyright, below)

Copyright

Few topics have greater potential for disaster than copyright. Designers and clients knowingly and unknowingly infringe someone's rights every day. Copyright is a minefield but few of us know where the mines are buried. How do we avoid being blown up?

My studio was once asked to do a movie poster for a film company. We hadn't worked for the company before, nor had we done much movie-related work. The only reason we'd been commissioned was because the director of the film had insisted on us doing the poster – apparently she didn't want a 'typical movie poster'. We were happy to oblige.

The film company approved our fee, and the project was completed using a heavily treated still from the film (supplied by the client for use on the poster). On acceptance of the design, an invoice for the agreed amount was submitted. End of story. Or so I thought.

A few weeks later, a United States film company with the American rights to the movie called me to ask how much we'd charge to let them use the artwork. I named a figure, but said I'd need to check with our United Kingdom client that this was acceptable since the image was theirs. I spoke to our client and within minutes I was contacted by the company's in-house lawyer. She said we were not entitled to any additional income if the poster was used

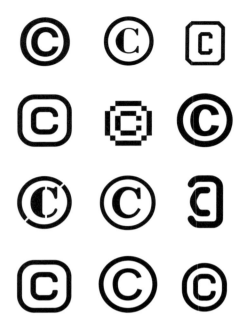

by a third party. I agreed not to give the artwork to anyone else, but I also pointed out that she couldn't allow anyone else to use our artwork. I reminded her that our Terms and Conditions (which had been sent to her) stated that 'no additional usage rights other than those stated on the invoice' were granted 'without prior agreement'. She said none of the other companies she worked with insisted on this. I asked her if this meant she didn't recognize copyright in creative work. She replied that her company always acknowledged copyright in photographs and illustration. In my huffiest voice I asked if this meant she didn't think there was any copyright in design. We got our additional fee.

In practice, most designers live happily without the need to assert their rights, and copyright becomes a concern only when it is infringed, either by a client or a third party.

What became clear in talking to the lawyer was that her company wanted to sell poster usage rights to the US company, thus recouping their initial outlay, but had no intention of sharing any of the income with me. By insisting on my rights I had disrupted this arrangement.

I retell this story not to gloat over a small victory (well, OK, there's a little bit of gloating) but because it illustrates the fundamental complexity of copyright as it relates to graphic design. The movie company that had commissioned us operated on the principle that because it gave regular work to a small group of studios, this allowed them to exploit the work in any way that suited them; the designers on their roster never asserted any of their rights because they wanted regular work from the company. Another aspect of copyright complexity was revealed by the difficulty I had in assigning usage rights to the poster to a third party since the central image (albeit radically altered) was the property of the commissioning film company.

The United States Copyright Office defines copyright as a 'form of protection provided by the laws of the United States to the authors of "original works of authorship", including literary, dramatic, musical, artistic, and certain other intellectual works'. Significantly, this definition doesn't mention design. Copyright in relation to design is described by the AIGA in its excellent online *Guide to Copyright*[1] as defining 'the ownership of work created by a designer'.

But the first thing to note is that copyright law is not universal. There is no 'international copyright', and laws vary from country to country. Simon Stern is a British illustrator and book designer who has made a study of copyright. I asked him if United States

Above
Range of copyright symbols taken from various typographic alphabets.

and European copyright laws are the same. 'No, but all copyright laws are somewhat similar, as the countries concerned subscribe to the Berne Convention, a set of minimum standards. So the broad principles are the same.'

Copyright, as it relates to illustration and photography seems straightforward. The end result – an illustration or a photograph – is usually the work of an individual who owns the copyright unless they enter into an agreement with the commissioner to assert otherwise. But the situation becomes muddier when we talk about graphic design. 'It's never clear cut because there's so much that's never been tested in court,' notes Stern. 'This is a result of the sheer expense of intellectual-property lawyers and the fact that many cases end up turning on a point of contract law. Also graphic designers tend not to worry about it, though they should. Fees for graphic design are very rarely user-dependent. Instead they are based on a day rate or an estimate of the time a job will take. If an illustrator grants a licence for limited use for a set fee, it follows he/she must retain the copyright. Designers come across copyright as an issue when buying in creative supplies, when clients and suppliers can sometimes have different expectations.'

The AIGA guide notes that 'most graphic design should be copyrightable'. It states that, 'Basic geometric shapes, such as squares and circles, are not copyrightable, but artistic combinations of these shapes can be copyrighted. Typeface designs are also excluded from being copyrightable.'

The AIGA guide notes that 'most graphic design should be copyrightable'. It states that, 'Basic geometric shapes, such as squares and circles, are not copyrightable, but artistic combinations of these shapes can be copyrighted. Typeface designs are also excluded from being copyrightable.' The omission of protection for typefaces is significant since they are an essential building block for nearly all graphic design, and many designers create their own fonts for logos and specialist uses. However, this failure to grant protection to typeface design is a feature of US copyright law, and is unique in the Western world.

But how realistic is it for designers to retain copyright in their work? When a designer creates a logo for a client it would be unrealistic to retain the copyright in that logo. No client would want to have to come back to a designer to negotiate each new usage. Stern points out that 'any agreement could be made about a logo, as long as the client would put up with it. As a matter of fact, in the UK, a client could manage fine with a wide-ranging exclusive licence since the 1989 Copyright Act, but it is usual to transfer the copyright of the logo.'

For designers, though, the situation is further complicated by the fact that if we create a piece of work while being employed in a studio, it is generally understood that the work is owned by our employer. In America this is called 'Work for Hire' – a feature of US law not recognized in the UK.

Yet another complication in attempting to copyright graphic design is the fact that graphic work is often made up of many copyrights (typefaces, images, other people's logos, etc.); 'These so-called "embedded copyrights",' notes Stern, 'preserve their individual protection, even if the graphic design as a whole is also copyrighted. Embedded copyrights can make it hard to bring an action for copyright infringement.'

There is also the widely held belief among clients that all graphic design is purchased on the 'buyout' principle. In other words, most commissioners imagine that once they have paid for a design, ownership passes to them.

As if navigating through the copyright minefield isn't difficult enough, there is also the widely held belief among clients that all graphic design is purchased on the 'buyout' principle. In other words, most commissioners imagine that once they have paid for a design, ownership passes to them. For example, if we design a brochure for a client they generally regard it as acceptable to pass on any design components to a web designer for use in the creation of a companion website. How can designers prevent this without threatening legal action every five minutes of the working day? 'Only by making their terms clear at the outset of the commission,' advises Stern. 'Really the question boils down to what economic or aesthetic interest does the designer wish to protect?'

Stern gets to the nub of the matter here. In reality, financial and aesthetic reasons govern designers' thinking in relation to copyright. Few designers are interested in exploiting the copyright inherent in their work. They are reluctant to go to the cost and effort of registration via national copyright offices, and instead they only want a realistic fee for a project; once they have been paid, designers are generally happy to allow clients to benefit from the design. However, designers are generally unhappy when their work is used badly by third parties. I've had instances where my work has been legitimately passed on to other people and been badly implemented with my design credit included.

But by far the biggest worry for designers is the risk of infringing someone else's copyright. In the digital sphere, where images can be captured in an instant, this is an ever-increasing risk. How many of us can say we haven't used copyrighted elements when working on design proposals? Even photocopying material out of a book or magazine is an infringement of someone's copyright. Even using a snippet of recorded music as a soundtrack to accompany a piece of test motion graphics constitutes infringement. The utmost caution is required when dealing with material that is published. As my film poster story shows, it is essential to ensure that all the work that leaves our studios – even those slick proposals that use our favourite photographic images – is original.

In practice, most designers live happily without the need to assert their rights, and copyright becomes a concern only when it is infringed, either by a client or a third party. But designers need to have protection built into the Terms and Conditions they give to their clients, and they need to agree all usage rights before parting with work. And they need to question every element that goes into a work of design. Missing something could be a costly oversight.

Further reading: Simon Stern, *The Illustrator's Guide to Law and Business Practice*. AOI, 2008.

1 www.aiga.org/resources/content/3/5/9/6/ documents/aiga_copyright.pdf

Creative block

Is there such a thing as creative block or is it a convenient excuse for a lack of ideas? Designers are not robots and everyone has spells when ideas dry up. If this happens, what do we do? Is there a plumbing service we can call to unblock the blockage?

I always have creative block. It's not that I don't have ideas – I have lots. Its just that I'm never happy with them. They rarely seem good enough, and I always want them to be better. It's as if I know that behind every idea there's a better one waiting to burst out; or, if not a better idea, then a way of making the first idea better. Even when I have an idea that others tell me is good, I'm not convinced and always look to dig down to another layer.

This state of semi-permanent creative turmoil is familiar to many designers. We are biologically conditioned to agonize over our work. It is natural – desirable even – to fret over it. I'm not talking about torturing ourselves. I'm talking about relishing and accepting the process of pushing, extending and sculpting ideas. When we stop doing this we inhabit a state of mind that is far more debilitating than mere fretfulness; it's called self-satisfaction, and it's the mortal enemy of creativity.

But ideas can sometimes be hard to find, and just as great sports people have off days, designers can experience spells of creative inertia. Are there any practical steps we can take to dislodge creative

blockages? First, we have to look at why blockages occur. One reason is that we become over-reliant on our tools. Designers the world over use the same tools, and over time we come to accept the limitations they place on us and start working in ways that are familiar and repetitive. Often the first step towards avoiding creative stagnation is to change our tools: ditch the computer and pick up a pencil; change the book we sketch in; change the place we work in; change the surroundings we function in.

We have to look at why creative block occurs. One reason is that we become over-reliant on our tools. Designers the world over use the same tools, and over time we come to accept the limitations they place on us.

Another reason is that it takes time to develop ideas. If we only rely on instant thinking we will miss the opportunity to develop an idea fully. If we can give ideas time to gestate we stand a better chance of producing new and fresh expressions. But time is a scarce commodity in design. Ask most designers what they'd most like more of and many will say – time. Yet, despite never seeming to have enough of it, by juggling deadlines we can often give our psychic engines time to generate new thoughts.

When we have a creative block we should move on to something else and go back to the task that's causing the problem at a later date. This usually results in a new perspective. However, it's worth emphasizing that it's important not to suspend work on a project when a blockage is at its worst; we should only put a job to one side when we have reached a psychological point where we are not experiencing extreme despondency. We should keep going until we feel some inkling of confidence that there will be a suitable outcome, otherwise we will be reluctant to go back to the project.

If all else fails, try reading a chapter of *Alice's Adventures in Wonderland*. Any book will do as long as it provides a glimpse of genius, but Lewis Carroll's Victorian surrealist masterpiece is hard to beat for unfettering the imagination.

Further reading: Lewis Carroll, *Alice's Adventures in Wonderland*, illustrated by Sir John Tenniel. Macmillan & Co., 1865. Available in various reprinted editions.

Above
Drawing by Paul Davis, 2009

Creative directors

Creative directors need two sets of eyes: one set to see things from the viewpoint of the designers they are directing, and the other to see things from the viewpoint of their clients. Perfect knowledge about the project also helps, as does lots of generosity – meanness doesn't work.

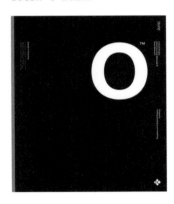

Above
Project: *Soon: Brands of Tomorrow*, book cover
Date: 2001
Client: Getty Images
Creative Directors: Lewis Blackwell, Chris Ashworth
Collaborators: Design – Chris Kelly, Robert Kester, Cameron Leadbetter, Carl Glover, Chris Ashworth; Copy – Lewis Blackwell, Jonathan Mackness; Photography – Ian Davies; Project Management – Nicola Rose; Research – Fay Dowling, Rebecca Swift; Production – James Moore, Gary McCall, Daniel Mason, Lloyd Bromhead
Book, exhibitions, website. 25 leading creative studios each imagine and create a brand of the future.

How many of us would recognize Wikipedia's description of a creative director? 'A person who has to interpret a client's communications strategy and then develop proposed creative approaches and treatments that align with that strategy. Another is to initiate and stimulate creative ideas for and from everyone involved in the creative process. Creative directors normally oversee creative service agencies or departments within a corporation. In advertising agencies, this consists of copywriters and art directors. In media design firms, the team can include graphic designers and computer programmers.'

I prefer Steven Heller's more succinct definition. Heller describes a creative director as someone who 'usually did not directly do the design but probably oversaw, consulted or at least signed off on it'. When I had my studio I had the words creative director on my business card. Occasionally, clients would be unsure about what my title meant; one or two even asked me what I did as creative director. I said I dictated the creative direction of the studio, but that I also protected the interests of our clients – I was their eyes in absentia. But I also stressed that, unlike many other creative directors, I didn't dictate every aspect of the studio's output. And I might also have pointed out that it was also part of the job to ensure that there were toilet rolls in the toilets, and to placate the enraged window cleaner who turned up at 8.00 a.m. and demanded money when I couldn't find the key to the petty-cash box.

A good creative director cajoles, enthuses and inspires; a good creative director is not afraid to say when something is wrong. I once worked for a creative director who was incapable of telling anyone they had produced bad work, or that a client had rejected their work. Instead he'd wait until the miscreant designer had gone home and then he'd change the work himself. The good creative director knows how to tell designers how to rectify errors, without destroying confidence or enthusiasm. It's easy to crush someone by telling him or her they've produced rubbish, but it's much harder to tell them they have produced sub-standard work and then give them the confidence to go on to produce good work. But above all else, a good creative director needs generosity. A creative director who can't praise and inspire isn't going to get far: there's no room for meanness in the role. None whatsoever.

> **It's easy to crush someone by telling him or her they've produced rubbish, but it's much harder to tell them they have produced sub-standard work and then give them the confidence to go on to produce good work.**

Above
Project: *The Big Idea*, DVD cover
Date: 2002
Client: Getty Images
Creative Directors: Lewis Blackwell,
Chris Ashworth
Collaborators: Art Direction – Tobin Lush;
Design – Tobin Lush, Adrian Britteon; Project
Management – Nathan Gainford; Copywriting
– Dave Masters, John O'Reilly; Interviews
– John O'Reilly; Research – Fay Dowling;
Production – James Moore, Gary McCall.
DVD, seminars, website. Six leading film
practitioners each create a one-minute film
about a 'big idea'.

Creative directors have to defend the work of the team they lead, but they also have to act as their client's custodian. These roles often cancel each other out: creative directors can either take the studio's 'side' and defend its work to the death; or they can take the client's side and crush initiatives that are likely to challenge and antagonize them. In fact, good creative directors do both. To be a good creative director you have to strike a balance between both interests, and to do this a mixture of humility and arrogance is needed.

Chris Ashworth was creative director of the Getty Images studio in Seattle. He was in charge of over 30 designers and likened the role to being a trapeze artist. 'It's a delicate balancing act, being inspiring to your team when needs must, and most importantly being able to draw out the best from others, week in, week out. Your team are there to learn and grow, they want to be creative and they want to be seen to be contributing, even driving the bus sometimes – making the difference.'

Prior to Getty, Ashworth had worked on his own and spent eight years 'doing everything myself'. But he quickly realized that his new role as creative director gave him 'a special opportunity'. He says: 'A lot of the designers were way smarter and way more creative than me. I saw my role as steering them when needed and being someone who could draw ideas out of them. Fantastically rewarding all round. And incredibly healthy, if you can pull it off.' Ashworth is clear about what characterizes the bad creative director: 'Dictatorial. Controlling. Loud-mouthed. Arrogant,' he observes.

If you are a designer obsessed with doing, you are unlikely to make a comfortable transition to having the words 'creative' and 'director' on your business card.

The world wouldn't end if creative directors were abolished, but they are not a great evil either. For designers ready to take on the ermine of creative directorship (remember the toilet rolls) elevation usually entails becoming less of a do-er and more of a facilitator. If you are a designer obsessed with doing, you are unlikely to make a comfortable transition to having the words 'creative' and 'director' on your business card. But many designers grow tired of the mechanical side of design and prefer to think rather than make. Good creative directors derive pleasure and fulfilment from seeing talent develop, and this doesn't happen if we insist on doing every job ourselves.

Further reading: *Portrait of a Successful Creative Director*. www.thecreativeforum.com/forum/archive/index. php/t-137.html

Credits

Design credits can be a source of pride, but they can also be the cause of disgruntlement. For many designers, credits are the lifeblood of design; others believe they are incompatible with being a professional designer and claim that design should always be anonymous.

Above
Project: *Reasons to be Cheerful: The Life and Work of Barney Bubbles* by Paul Gorman
Date: 2008
Publisher: Adelita
The English graphic designer Barney Bubbles famously declined to put a design credit on his many groundbreaking record covers from the 1970s, preferring to work anonymously or sometimes pseudonymously. Bubbles (real name Colin Fulcher) was a hugely influential figure, acting as a source of inspiration for many of the leading names in British graphic design. He committed suicide in 1983.

I was thumbing through the stock in a vintage poster shop. Most of it was high-quality travel posters from the 1930s – expensive stuff aimed at the collectors' market. But I came across a modest black-and-white poster from the 1970s that exuded an understated graphic panache. It was marked by the dealers as 'anonymous', and as a consequence it was cheaper than most of the other named specimens. But tucked away in a corner of the poster I found, in 6-point type, the name of the Dutch designer Jan van Toorn. I bought the poster.

While it has always been commonplace for illustrators and photographers to receive published credits, it is much less common for designers to have them. Traditionally, design credits – for either a studio or an individual – were considered antithetical to the spirit of professional problem-solving design. It was accepted wisdom that the designer remained anonymous. To be credited with a design was to draw attention to it in a way that was widely regarded as unprofessional.

There have always been exceptions. Record companies and book publishers have allowed designers to be credited for the design of album covers, and books and their covers. It's no accident, therefore, that many of the best-known designers of recent decades have been either record-cover designers or book designers. As book-cover designer Chip Kidd observed: 'I think that I get recognition for my work only because it's standard that your name gets put on the back flap of the book if you're a book designer. It's not standard for most graphic designers.'[1]

Most graphic design goes uncredited. Take the packaging for consumer goods, for example. Who knows who designed the pack for the biscuits we bought at the supermarket? Who ever saw a design credit for a television station ident? Who knows who designed our newspapers? Or railway timetables?

The arguments in favour of design credits are persuasive. Credits are an important mechanism for designers to promote themselves. They help to prevent plagiarism and mindless copying. They help to promote an understanding of design among non-designers. And they are personally satisfying to designers, since recognition is fundamental to the act of creativity. We also want potential clients to notice our credit and contact us (hence the fashion for publishing urls as design credits).

It is natural, therefore, for creative people to want to see themselves credited for the work they do.

Most graphic design goes uncredited. Take the packaging for consumer goods, for example. Who knows who designed the pack for the biscuits we bought at the supermarket?

Normally, this is reassuring to clients, who are happy to see that we endorse what we have done for them, and most of them are generous enough to agree to the inclusion of a 'design by …' line. (It's also worth remembering that they can take offence when we request not to be credited for our work.) Others, however, are not so accommodating. If a client doesn't want a designer to have a credit there isn't much the designer can do about it. And it gets worse: increasingly, clients are vetoing credits for reasons of commercial confidentiality. They are even denying designers the right to publicize work in trade journals or on websites, or to enter it in competitions. This is a growing trend and one that designers should resist.

> If a client doesn't want a designer to have a credit there isn't much the designer can do about it. And increasingly, clients are vetoing credits for reasons of commercial confidentiality.

But credits are fraught with paranoia. Studio credits sometimes disguise the fact that a project is the work of an individual. Conversely, individuals sometimes take credit for work that was dependent on the input of many people.

I'm in favour of simple and discreet design credits, although, as Jonathan Barnbrook has noted, designers can sometimes be too self-effacing: writing about his famous book for the artist Damien Hirst,[2] Barnbrook noted: 'I put my design credit very small in the book, I thought "those who knew, would know". Instead all that happened was that most people thought Damien Hirst did the whole thing. It taught me that being subtle is not always a good idea.'[3]

There's one last thing to say about credits. When I ran my studio I allowed individual designers to have credits: the designer's name appeared alongside the studio name. This was done only when a designer had produced a piece of work that could be rightfully called his or her own. Of course, it was understood (and I didn't let anyone forget) that even heroic acts of solo graphic creation benefited from the organizational structure of a studio, and that work was never done in complete isolation. But the personal design credit gave satisfaction to the designers and contributed to making them feel happier and more appreciated than if their work had been lumped under a generic studio credit. Occasionally it led to small problems when clients approached designers directly, but this was rare and was easily dealt with. For studios looking for ways to make designers happy, the personal design credit is a good place to start. Try it.

Further reading: Paul Gorman, *Reasons to be Cheerful: The Life and Work of Barney Bubbles*. Adelita, 2008.

1 *At Home With the Closest Thing to a Rock Star In Graphic Design*. www.mediabistro.com/unbeige/graphic_design/default.asp
2 Damien Hirst, *I Want to Spend the Rest of My Life Everywhere, with Everyone, One to One, Always, Forever, Now*. Booth-Clibborn Editions, 1997.
3 Jonathan Barnbrook, *Barnbrook Bible. The Graphic Design of Jonathan Barnbrook*. Booth-Clibborn Editions, 2007.

Criticism in design

CDs by boy bands are reviewed critically in the national press, but not graphic design. Why? What would happen if design was subjected to systematic critical scrutiny in the way novels, movies, plays and even computer games are? Could design take it, or is it a step too far?

There are two sorts of criticism in graphic design. The first is the criticism we receive from clients and colleagues – and sometimes even the audience for which our work is intended. The second comes from a small coterie of design writers – design critics – who write about design from a critical standpoint. It is the latter group we are concerned with here: with writers capable of discussing graphic design in an objective manner, and able to place it in both its historical and contemporary contexts. Unfortunately, despite a surge of interest in design among non-designers, the kind of genuine criticism described above is still a rarity.

This is odd. Graphic design is omnipresent, constantly demanding our attention and colonizing our environment. More people are exposed to it than listen to boy bands, see movies or read fiction, yet it is pretty much ignored.

The design press reviews books and exhibitions that deal with design, yet only occasionally offers formal criticism of the vast amount of work these feature. There are a handful of journals where graphic design is critiqued with thoroughness, although this higher criticism tends to attract only academics and a handful of people interested in theory and critical thinking. However, salvation of sorts has come through the countless blogs (see Blogs, page 33), where graphic design is discussed in an intelligent and questioning, if sometimes chaotic and partisan, manner.

The opponents of a critical presence in design point out that graphic design is a service industry paid for by clients and not by the public, and that it is therefore pointless to critique it.

Why is there not much appetite for developing a real critical discourse around graphic design? When I mention this to designer friends, I'm usually told that 'criticism' exists to support consumer choice; its purpose is to answer such questions as which movies to see, which books to buy, which galleries to visit. The opponents of a critical presence in design point out that graphic design is a service industry paid for by clients and not by the public, and that it is therefore pointless to critique it. End of story.

But it's a narrow view of criticism that says it is only worth critiquing something if it can be purchased by members of the public. Take architecture: upmarket national newspapers employ architecture critics, and the subject is frequently discussed intelligently on television and radio, despite the fact that its practice is a purely 'professional' activity.

The consequences of a popular critical framework developing around architecture have been dramatic. The subject has been simultaneously demystified and elevated. In Britain, for example, our famous traditionalism and bulldog-like insularity in architecture has been replaced by experimentation and innovation. Today clients are much less likely than they were to commission lousy buildings, and are more aware of the benefits of good design.

Perhaps the real reason why graphic design is not critiqued with the same rigour as pop music, architecture – even restaurants – is that graphic design is simply not ready to submit itself to the searchlights of critical investigation. Take the furore over the logo for the 2012 Olympic Games in London. It was widely condemned: criticism by design pundits, journalists and members of the public caused a tidal wave of revulsion to crash through newspapers, television and the Internet. And while the level of debate wasn't especially elevated (criticism rarely rose above the level of observing that the logo looked like Lisa Simpson engaging in a lewd sex act), at least it was refreshing to see design talked about in the mass media.

One of the best ways to 'educate' clients would be to have graphic design assessed by astute critical voices capable of dissecting its social, business and aesthetic effects.

But in a letter in *Design Week* from a prominent British 'executive creative director' we find a passionate plea asking fellow designers to desist from publicly criticizing the logo: 'This was a moment where our industry should have stood together to value the contribution, or kept a dignified silence, even if it was not to everyone's taste. The small-minded backstabbing has done us all no service at all.'[1]

The writer has a point, yet an unwillingness to be subjected to criticism is also damaging. We designers are a bit too sensitive. We're not used to the lash of external critical scrutiny, and this communicates itself to public and clients. We appear petty and immature.

The benefits that would ensue from putting graphic design under the critical microscope seem obvious. Designers constantly bemoan – arrogantly it seems to me – the lack of 'design education' among clients. But one of the best ways to 'educate' clients would be to have graphic design assessed by astute critical voices capable of dissecting its social, business and aesthetic effects. Public criticism would make designers fight harder for better design, and make clients shy about commissioning the sort of work that might earn them a good kicking from a beady-eyed critic. Of course, poor-quality graphic design would not be eradicated – just as schlocky movies continue to get made despite routine critical maulings – but there would be less of it.

Yet the emergence of genuine design criticism seems unlikely in the foreseeable future. Where would the critics come from? We can't rely on fellow designers for critical impartiality – friendships as much as professional enmity preclude this. And because of design's current obsession with dull, obvious branding, it is unlikely to attract the sort of lively minded independent brains needed to do the criticizing.

A cause for optimism has arrived with the establishment in the United States, and in the United Kingdom,[2] of degree courses teaching design criticism. Writer and critic Alice Twemlow is chair of the Design Criticism MFA Program at the School of Visual Arts in New York. The two-year, 64-credit curriculum provides the 'skills and knowledge relevant to those who wish to write about design on a full-time, professional basis; or pursue alternative critical practices, such as curating, publishing or teaching.'

It will take time, but if Twemlow and those others who are offering courses in critical thinking can create a new climate of critical discovery, perhaps design can join other contemporary modes of expression and receive healthy scrutiny. If design fails to attract critical interrogation it risks remaining on a par with knitting – a craft practised with great love and dedication by many, but ignored by everyone else.

Further reading: www.schoolofvisualarts.edu

1 'Should designers stand by each other's work …'; letter from Peter Knapp, executive creative director, Europe and Middle East, Landor Associates Branding and Design Consultants. *Design Week*, 28 June 2007.
2 A one-year full-time (or two-year part-time) course run by writer and academic Teal Triggs. Course details can be found here – www.designwritingcriticism.co.uk

Cultural design

Working for institutions like museums, galleries and theatres has been widely seen as having greater value than purely commercial activities such as designing confectionery wrappers. But is this still the case when many public institutions behave like confectionery-makers?

In *C/ID, Visual Identity and Branding for the Arts*, the Pentagram designer Angus Hyland looks at the ways in which various arts institutions around the world present themselves. He quotes Brian Eno's definition of culture as 'everything we don't need to do'. You can see how Eno's definition might appeal to those graphic designers who can commonly be heard to say: 'We only do cultural work.' By embracing cultural design they are aligning themselves in opposition to the hard-faced commercial work most designers need to do in order to stay solvent.

Cultural design is widely seen as having a greater value than purely commercial work. And, crucially, it is also mainly regarded as having more creative freedom than commercial forms of design. But there's a catch; the arts and commercialism are merging. Arts and cultural bodies have become immersed in branding and marketing strategies and, like converts to any new cause, they are fanatical in the way they have embraced the new commercial creeds.

PROA-Regular

In *C/ID* the design writer Emily King describes how in the arts it has become 'commonplace for institutions to create well-designed, coherent identities for themselves with the aim of attracting both audiences and funding. Alongside these design innovations, they are employing savvy CEO-style directors, marketing experts and micro-managing administrators.'

She continues: 'There is a pragmatic assumption that culture must compete with other forms of entertainment (even by those who don't believe that culture is entertainment). It is generally accepted that an institution with a smart identity and some snappy advertising is in the best position to hold its place in the ever-expanding line-up of contemporary entertainment.'

So, far from escaping from commercial demands when we enter the world of cultural design, we are often back in the realm of focus groups, market forces and branding strategies. Yet, as *C/ID* goes on to show, arts institutions still produce some remarkable visual identity work. Three examples that demonstrate the richness of cultural design are: Experimental Jetset's Stedelijk Museum CS in Amsterdam (the temporary home of the famous Stedelijk Museum while it is being refurbished); Graphic Thought Facility's Shakespeare's Globe Theatre in London; and the CDDB Theatre de Lorient, in France by m/m paris. There are a dozen others that are equally good, and leafing through the book it's hard to see where the crisis is. But designers who work for arts organizations will tell you that all design decisions are tethered to strict commercial imperatives. As Emily King points out, many people don't regard culture as entertainment. Equally, there are lots of people who fail to see why culture should be promoted by marketing techniques more suited to mass entertainment.

Further reading: Angus Hyland and Emily King, *C/ID*, *Visual Identity and Branding for the Arts*. Laurence King Publishing, 2006.

Left
Project: Typeface for PROA identity
Date: 2009
Client: Fundacion Proa
Design: Spin
Creative Credits: Tony Brook, Creative Director; Patrick Eley, Senior Designer; Josh Young, Designer
Buenos Aires art gallery Fundacion Proa briefed London design group Spin to create an identity for the institution's revamped gallery. Shown here is the custom typeface that Spin designed, based on the architecture of a bridge situated close to the gallery.

D

Debt chasing

The need to chase debts is a problem faced by freelance designers, small studios and big design agencies owned by stock market-listed conglomerates. Getting paid quickly is the key to financial stability and security. But what is the best way to ensure prompt payment?

It's a problem faced equally by designers who are anti-capitalist idealists and by those who align themselves with the design-is-business ethos. It's a problem that afflicts all designers – whether they are ultra-talented or mediocre. But you won't read about this subject in design history books; you're unlikely to be taught anything about it in design school; and you'll only rarely hear designers talking about it in interviews. Debt chasing is a grubby business.

Designers who receive monthly pay cheques don't have to worry about this problem (although their employers do), but for designers who depend on invoicing for their services it's a battle that has to be waged incessantly. When we prepare an invoice we often feel that warm glow of satisfaction that comes with billing a decent amount of money; but we also feel a twinge of anxiety over the length of time we know it will take to get paid. Until the money hits our bank account, it's just so much ink on paper or pixels on a computer screen.

The need to chase our debts is like a dark secret that mustn't be spoken about.

But the need to chase our debts is like a dark secret that mustn't be spoken about. So it is refreshing when someone does discuss the subject. Take the designer Michael C. Place. Michael and his wife Nicky run a studio called Build. Among students and design fans, Build couldn't be more highly regarded. It is seen as a hypercreative studio overwhelmed with perfect projects and the adulation of adoring clients. Yet here's what Nicky said in *Creative Review*: 'Generally invoices take a long time to get paid. Ours state that payment "is due in 30 days", which is quite normal. So when chasing one after a

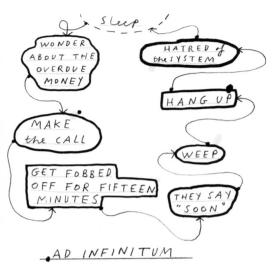

Sleep

WONDER ABOUT THE OVERDUE MONEY

HATRED of the SYSTEM

HANG UP

MAKE the CALL

WEEP

GET FOBBED OFF FOR FIFTEEN MINUTES

THEY SAY "SOON"

AD INFINITUM

Above
Drawing by Paul Davis, 2009

month has lapsed, you'll probably find that it is "still waiting for approval" before it even gets to the accounts department … who might pay up in a week or two … but who generally have a backlog of other invoices which have been waiting for two months. Why should yours go to the front? Because it's overdue.'[1]

Cash coming in faster than it goes out is a prerequisite of running a design business. In fact, it is a prerequisite of all businesses. We can negotiate overdrafts and lines of credit, but there will always be a biblical-style day of reckoning; at some point we have to be cash positive, and to do this we have to chase our debts.

But there are few things designers are less well suited to than chasing outstanding debt. Usually we are too emotionally involved in our craft to make good debt chasers. We lose our tempers, we become discourteous and we are unsystematic in the way we go about getting paid. Of course, there are many designers who are financially literate and who have good systems for ensuring that they get paid promptly. So what can we do to make this process less painful and more effective?

Not much, is the depressing answer. It is the nature of the imperfect capitalist system in which we operate that since everyone in business is playing the same shuffling game to maintain their own liquidity, we are destined to endlessly chase the money we are owed and delay making the payments we owe. We can adopt a high moral stance and say no one should commission design if they can't pay for it, but the world's financial systems are based on credit – and very few of us, in either our business lives or our private lives, don't use it in some form or other.

Since everyone in business is playing the same shuffling game to maintain their own liquidity, we are destined to endlessly chase the money we are owed and delay making the payments we owe.

But let's not get too gloomy. There are one or two things we can do to help get cash in the door. The first thing we should do is ensure that our invoices are 100 per cent accurate – no unexpected extras added at the last minute, or irregularities that give a client an opportunity to send an invoice back unpaid. We can try invoice factoring. This is a system that enables businesses to turn invoices into cash. Factoring agencies purchase outstanding invoices and the business receives immediate funds. The agency will take a percentage of the invoice as their fee, and they will also impose restrictions that may be as much trouble as they are worth. So it's necessary to take good advice before signing up to a factoring service.

Above
Project: Type Shop Invoice
Date: 2006
Client: Type Shop (Hong Kong)
Designer: Michael C. Place
Part of the Type Shop stationery
set. Designer Michael Place calls
it a 'Typographic history lesson'.

1 Partner Nicky Place, from 'A Month in the
Life of ... A Graphic Designer', *Creative
Review*, August 2007.

Left to our own devices we can try levying penalties for late payment. It is common to see on invoices that a charge will be made for this. This can encourage certain clients to pay up on time. But it won't make anyone who is determined to delay payment pay any quicker; plus, sending out late payment charges can introduce a level of bad feeling that ends up in the termination of a working relationship (not necessarily a bad thing, but best avoided if possible).

One of the few procedures that really makes a difference is advance billing; this is where designers charge – and receive – a percentage of the fee before commencing work. It is common practice in many creative sectors, but is less common in graphic design. Yet securing an upfront payment will help cash flow, and reduce the strain of working on projects for long spells without income.

I've noticed that people who are good at debt chasing are unemotional about it. When they call accounts departments they don't sound cross or chippy – they sound relaxed and professional. Getting testy is nearly always useless (until, that is, you've tried every other avenue, when a bit of teeth-grinding rage can sometimes help). The reason it is mostly counterproductive to get angry with people in accounts departments is that they are rarely the problem. The problem is more likely to be the people who haven't yet approved the invoice, as Nicky Place describes above. Most accounts departments like to pay people: part of their job is to pay people; it makes their books tidy. So, make friends with them. Treat them with respect and dignity. It pays.

Of course, there are such things as bad debts – debts that are unrecoverable, for example, when an invoice is in dispute or a client becomes insolvent. When this happens we need to take expert financial and legal advice. But we must do everything in our power to ensure we don't get to this position. One of the first things designers do when their studios grow is employ a good bookkeeper/accountant, one of whose main duties is to chase debts and manage the credit allowed to clients. But until they can employ someone to do this, debt management is a feature of being a designer as much as being proficient in Photoshop or knowing how to kern a line of type.

When we prepare an invoice we often feel that warm glow of satisfaction that comes with billing a decent amount of money; but we also feel a twinge of anxiety over the length of time we know it will take to get paid.

Further reading: www.direct.gov.uk/en/MoneyTaxAndBenefits/ ManagingDebt/CourtClaimsAndBankruptcy/DG_10023133

Default design

Not all graphic design is fixated with stylish seductiveness. There's even a school of design that uses computer presets and default settings. It might just be the descendant of Modernist purity and rationality, but like every anti-style, it automatically becomes a style itself.

In the early years of the new millennium, a handful of influential designers pioneered a new, raw, template-driven approach to graphic design that rejected seductive refinement and typographic nuance. Sometimes called 'default design', it has its roots in late 1990s British and Dutch graphic design, and was a self-conscious rejection of over-wrought and over-refined graphics.

One of the pioneers of the default style was Foundation 33, the studio founded in 2000 by Daniel Eatock and Sam Solhaug. It only lasted four years, but during its short life it developed a blunt, non-aestheticized approach to graphic design that relied on default typefaces and computer presets. An 'essay' by Daniel Eatock, 'Call For Entries… Feature article without content', was published in the second issue of *Dot Dot Dot* magazine in 2000. It contained the legend: 'Say YES to fun & function & NO to seductive imagery & colour!' This slogan was to become the unwitting war cry for this new trend in design.

I first became aware of the existence of default design (it can't be called a movement as it never acquired enough adherents, or enough influence) with the publication of a remarkable and under-recognized book called *Specials*, in 2001.[1] This was the first cataloguing of a new post-millennial sensibility in design. The rejection of decoration was just one of the stylistic strands it featured. In an essay in the book, after pointing out the huge changes in design wrought by technology, Claire Catterall noted that 'some designers have been retracing their steps in an attempt to cut down to size, the over-arching influence of digitalization. They've done this in a number of ways; mainly by "mucking about with" and undermining the digital aesthetic itself …'

In the case of the default designers it was more a case of embracing an unrecognized aspect of the digital aesthetic. Computers enabled designers to create ever richer and more elaborate graphic design – the sort that gave consumerism its gene pool of imagery. In a discussion on the subject between Rob Giampietro and Rudy VanderLans, Giampietro defined default design as making use of the 'preordained settings found in common design programs such as Quark, Photoshop, and Illustrator that a user (or designer) must manually override. Thus, in Quark, all text boxes have a 1-point text insert unless one enters the default setting and changes this. Put simply, defaults automate certain aspects of the design process.'[2]

With default designers it was a case of embracing an unrecognized aspect of the digital aesthetic.

Late Card

Write an excuse or apology in no more than
fifty words to explain why this card is late.

Sign and date

Greeting Card

Using a red pen delete all descriptions that
are not relevant to card's recipient.

Mum	Cousin	Enemy
Dad	Nephew	Stranger
Daughter	Niece	Teacher
Son	Twin	Boss
Sister	Girlfriend	Neighbour
Brother	Boyfriend	Other*
Grandma	Wife	
Grandad	Husband	
Aunt	Friend	
Uncle	Lover	

*Please specify

Above and previous page
Project: Utilitarian Greeting Cards
Date: 2003
Client: Self-initiated
Designer: Daniel Eatock
Daniel Eatock is a pioneer of the new neutral
graphics. His utilitarian multi-purpose
greeting cards are light years away from the
customary over-purposed greeting cards we
see in chain stores and high streets. The
cards are produced in editions of 500 sets
and printed on recycled Dutch greyboard. The
reverse is printed fluorescent yellow.

He went on to say: 'Default colors are black and
white, the additive primaries (RGB) and the subtractive
primaries (CMY). Default elements include all preexisting
borders, blends, icons, filters, etc. Default sizes are
8, 10, 12, 18, 24 pt. in type, standard sheet sizes for
American designers, ISO sizes for Europeans, etc. With
standardization, it's argued, comes compatibility. Objects
(particularly printed objects) are reproduced 1:1, and
images and documents are shown with minimal manipulation.'

The default school which, paradoxically, I found
deeply seductive, had its antecedents in 1990s
architecture where natural materials and industrial
products were being used in a completely non-ingratiating
way. It also had echoes in Dogme 95, the radical mid-1990s
filmmaking movement started by the Danish directors Lars
von Trier and Thomas Vinterberg with the signing of the
Dogme 95 Manifesto and the Vow of Chastity. The aim of
the manifesto was to purify filmmaking by refusing to use
special effects and post-production trickery. Von Trier
and Vinterberg believed that by concentrating on filmic
purity a renewed focus could be brought to bear on the
story and the actors' performances.

Dogme had its most obvious graphic design counterpart
in a manifesto written by the designer John Morgan for
students at St Martin's School of Art and Design in London
in 2001.[3] Morgan writes: 'Produced with tongue in cheek
and in direct reference to the Dogme 95 "Vow of Chastity"
for filmmaking by Lars von Trier and Thomas Vinterberg.
These design rules had the expressed goal of countering
"certain tendencies" in graphic design at St Martins. Each
first-year student had to sign up and swear to submit to
the rules for the duration of the project...'

The Vow of Chastity
I swear to submit (for the period of this project)
to the following set of rules drawn up and confirmed
by DOGME 2004:
1. Content matters: design nothing that is not
worth reading. The job should speak for itself (if
it doesn't, the designer hasn't learned to listen).
Books showing pictures of other designer's work
must not be referred to (unless as part of
a critical study).
2. Images must not be used unless they refer directly
to the text. (Illustrations must be positioned where
they are referred to in the text; foot/sidenotes
must be positioned on same page as the text they
refer to.)
3. The book must be hand-held (and designed from the
inside out). 'Coffee-table books' are not acceptable.
4. The first text colour shall be black; the second

colour red. Special colours, varnish and lamination are not acceptable.
5. Photoshop/Illustrator filters are forbidden.
6. The design must not contain superficial elements (maximize the data-ink ratio, no chart junk).
7. Temporal and geographical alienation are forbidden. (That is to say that the design takes place here and now. No pastiche.)
8. Genre design is not acceptable. (No 'smile in the mind'. Leave graphic wit to comedians. No thoughtless application of style.)
9. Formats must not be 'A' sizes. Paper must be chlorine free. It must be off-white.
10. The designer must not be credited (unless all other workers are also credited). Designing and making is collective work.

Furthermore, I swear as a designer to refrain from personal taste! I am no longer an artist. I swear to refrain from creating a 'work', as I regard the instant as more important than the whole. My supreme goal is to force the truth out of my characters and settings. I swear to do so by all the means available and at the cost of any good taste and any aesthetic considerations. Thus I make my VOW OF CHASTITY.

The default style lingers on — mainly among the small group of designers who pioneered it. You can see it in Daniel Eatock's ultra-functionalist website,[4] but it has failed to jump the species barrier into the mainstream. Nevertheless, it remains an approach to design that in its quest for purity of expression resembles that of the early Modernists. No frills.

Further reading: www.studio-gs.com/writing/default.html

1 Booth-Clibborn Editions, *Scarlet Projects and Bump, Specials*. Booth-Clibborn Editions, 2001.
2 'Default System design, a discussion with Rob Ciampietro about guilt and loss in graphic cesign', *Émigré 65*, 2003. Also www.studio-gs.com/writing/default.html
3 *Dot Dot Dot 6*, 2003; Michael Bierut, William Drenttel and Steven Heller (eds), *Looking Closer 4: Critical Writings on Graphic Design*. Allworth Press, 2002.
4 www.eatock.com/

Design books

There are books covering most design topics. But what is the point of design books in the age of the Internet when so much material can be viewed online? Is the design book destined for the dustbin of history or does it still have a useful role to play in the lives of working designers?

In an article I wrote about design books a few years ago I fantasized about someone producing a book of lost-pet posters; I imagined it filled with handmade posters stuck on trees by distraught pet owners looking for missing animals. The editor who commissioned me pointed out a book on this subject already existed.[1]

Today, there are books on most design subjects. Sometimes there are three or four covering the same topic, and there is no sign of a slowdown in the rip tide of new books hitting the bookshop shelves. But I wonder whether this orgy of design publishing has made us better designers. Has it helped to make clients and non-designers more knowledgeable about, and appreciative of, graphic design? Has it increased the number of people willing to

Above and opposite
A tiny selection of the dozens of books used by the author in the preparation of this book.

study the subject? Has it raised the quality of graphic design around the world?

The answer to all these questions is a qualified 'Yes'. Anyone who started work before the great design publishing boom of the 1990s will know that good books were depressingly scarce. Today, it's the opposite; design books (as well as magazines and, increasingly, the Internet) are helping to drive a huge surge of interest in, and activity around, graphic design – most of it positive.

The modern design publishing boom might be said to have begun with Neville Brody's two monographs – the first published in 1988[2] and the second in 1994.[3] In the 1990s, designer monographs sold in big numbers. *The End of Print: Graphic Design of David Carson* (2000) was a worldwide smash hit. The market was driven by influential books – you can tell which ones these are; every studio has a copy.

Today, design books divide into three main categories: 'how to' books; compilations of both past and present work; and collections of essays on theory, criticism and design history. Since design is a competitive industry where employment opportunities are hotly pursued and jobs go to the most skilled and competent, 'how to' books are perennial best-sellers. Their success is further driven by the huge increase in the number of students studying graphic design. This is a global phenomenon; from Seattle to Beijing, design courses are oversubscribed. It's a hugely popular subject, and like any subject that needs to be studied, it requires a body of practical literature to feed it.

Why would we spend a hefty sum of money on a book when we can view the contents free online? The speed of the Internet further conspires against books that strive to appear fresh and up-to-date; what purports to be new and fresh in their pages might have been available online for some time.

Publishers thrive by catering for the global demand for design books. But how long can this demand last? Increasingly, the market is beset by overproduction (I should know, I contribute to it); time and again I pick up a thick compendium of recent work only to find material I've just seen in another book, and material I've already seen on the Internet.

The Internet has changed the nature of design-book publishing. Publishers will tell you that monographs, even of famous designers, no longer sell. This is understandable, since there aren't many designers who don't have a website containing images of most of, if not all, their work. Why would we spend a hefty sum of

1 www.papress.com/bookpage.tpl?isbn=1568983379
2 Neville Brody and Jon Wozencroft, *The Graphic Language of Neville Brody*: v.1. Thames & Hudson, 1988.
3 Neville Brody and Jon Wozencroft, *The Graphic Language of Neville Brody*: v.2. Thames & Hudson, 1994.

money on a book when we can view the contents free online? The speed of the Internet further conspires against books that strive to appear fresh and up-to-date; what purports to be new and fresh in their pages might have been available online for some time. Books are slow technology; the Internet is fast technology.

The consequence of all this is a recalibrating of the design-publishing industry. Monographs may have faded in popularity, but the book remains a designer staple. Even small studios boast shelves of books. Most studios have a book budget. Designers buy books insatiably. And as the Norwegian designer Kjell Ekhorn noted when I asked him why designers still bought books when they could see everything on the Internet: 'The problem with the Internet is that you stumble across interesting stuff, but you often can't find it again when you need it, and also, nothing beats having a book by your side, open and flat on the desk, as you are working.'

What do we want from design books? Since the Internet provides us with instant fixes of imagery, we naturally crave commentary, analysis and information. We also want production values. How well a book is designed is essential to the desire to acquire it. I recently contributed an essay to a book; it wasn't about design, but it was on a subject that many designers are interested in. The publisher commissioned a shoddy design. Lots of friends told me they'd like to have bought the book but were discouraged by the bad design. For most designers, good design is a good reason for buying a book.

But mostly we want the permanence and integrity of well-designed, well-written and well-edited books. While publishers continue to produce them, designers will willingly hand over their cash.

Further reading: http://www.designersreviewofbooks.com/

Design conferences

The problem with design conferences is too much design and not enough real life. They may be expensive and time-consuming, yet who can resist the allure of an exotic location and the opportunity to indulge in unrestrained socializing with fellow designers?

A rather smug person once told me he'd been to a three-day IT management conference. On the first day, the event's moderator had announced that if anyone got up and stood on their seat the rest of the audience would automatically give them a round of applause. My guy got up immediately and did in fact win himself a rapturous ovation. Like I said, smug.

I often think about him when I attend design conferences. I feel a compulsion to stand up on my seat – not to receive a round of applause, but to let rip with a scream of frustration. The insularity, the navel-gazing, the self-absorption encountered at design conferences can be maddening. They often remind me of going to church as an atheistic child: boring and repetitive.

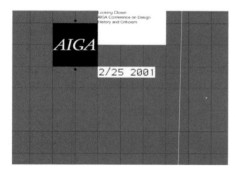

Above
Project: Looking Closer: AIGA Conference on
Design History and Criticism
Date: 2001
Client: Alice Twemlow, American Institute of
Graphic Arts
Designers: Paul Elliman and David Reinfurt
Paul Elliman and David Reinfurt were
responsible for the design of a promotional
poster, the speaker title slides, signage,
and a website for a conference on graphic
design history and criticism chaired by
Steven Heller and Alice Twemlow. The graphic
programme for the conference was based on
test patterns, beginning with the poster
that reproduced a Xerox copying test card.
The website re-purposed existing computer
monitor tests. The conference title slides
used modified LCD projector test sequences
to announce each speaker and event over the
course of the conference.

Why is this? Alice Twemlow has organized numerous design conferences. In an article in *Eye*,[1] she made the point that 'the first frequently cited problem with graphic design conferences is that their featured speakers tend to be graphic designers. Designers, whose very vocation means that they have chosen to express themselves visually, are summoned on stage in front of thousands of people to expound, to narrate, to inspire – orally.' In truth, it's rare to find designers who can deliver a convincing lecture. The work invariably looks good when projected on a giant screen, but with only a few exceptions the insights tend towards the banal or the overfamiliar.

Until recently I've thought of design conferences purely as social functions with the added bonus of an opportunity to travel. Nothing wrong with this. The presentations and panel discussions act as a sort of glue that holds everything together, while the real action takes place in the bars and cafés where designers meet and swap war stories from the front line. Designers are usually good company, and the chance to engage in some intensive socializing away from the demands of studio life is usually a good enough reason to attend a design conference.

But how often do we get real debate and real insight? Not often enough. And the reason for this is that design conference organizers invite too few outsiders. By restricting speakers and panellists to other designers, the conferences show up design's insularity – its unexpected disconnectedness from the ocean currents of life. Designers talk to designers, and not much happens.

It is only by bringing in outside elements that conferences can hope to rise above the level of self-congratulatory trade shows. Bring in the critics; bring in the clients who think designers are selfish onanists; bring in the outside world in all its messy profusion.

Today, design conferences are held all over the world: the United States, South Africa, India and China. More are planned every year. Which forces us to ask the question, should I spend my money attending a gathering of designers in an exotic location, which almost certainly involves expensive and environmentally damaging travel not to mention registration and accommodation fees?

In reality, attendance is usually dependent on design studios and employers funding employees. It would be a wealthy designer who could afford to attend out of his or her own pocket. So the question needs to be reframed for employers and the principals of design studios: is

Design conference organizers invite too few outsiders. By restricting speakers and panellists to other designers, the conferences show up design's insularity.

it worth sending your employees (and yourself) to design conferences at the company's expense?

If the conference expands the attendees' horizons, if it makes designers readdress their priorities and assumptions, if it reinspires and reinvigorates them, the answer is 'Yes'. But how do we know if a particular event will do these things? We don't. It's a bit like the way clients feel when they commission design: they don't know what they are getting till they get it. Sobering thought, isn't it?

Further reading: Alice Twemlow, 'Conference madness', *Eye* 49, Autumn 2003.

1 Alice Twemlow, 'Conference madness', *Eye* 49, Autumn 2003.

Design press

It's rare to hear designers talk enthusiastically about the design press. We are much more likely to hear someone say that magazine 'x' has 'gone off' or 'I've stopped buying magazine "y" because it's always full of the same old people'. So what do we want from our design press?

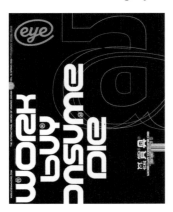

When the design press writes about big-shot designers, readers complain that ordinary designers are being ignored. When journalists write about issues such as ethics and green matters, designers moan about a lack of professional focus. When editors commission long pensive articles, designers demand shorter texts and more pictures. When magazines feature designers who show work in galleries, other designers say that most design is done in the furnace room of commerce. When print design is written about, it is pointed out that the reality of modern design is screen-based. It's impossible to please everyone.

So what do we want from our design press? Well, most designers would agree that it's better than it used to be. The standard of design journalism has risen over the past few years, and what was previously an indiscriminate cataloguing of the new – all show and not much tell – has now been augmented by more critical and issue-based articles. We still go to the design press for professional news and the presentation of new and groundbreaking work, but increasingly we also go for engaging writing and critical thinking. Yet the suspicion remains that the design press is merely a giant shop window that enables designers, illustrators and photographers to display their wares in the hope of being picked up by advertising agencies and corporate clients. Those magazines that can't shake off this accusation are destined not to rise above the level of glorified portfolios.

The design press was forced to raise its game by the arrival in 1994 of *Eye*, the International Review of Graphic Design.

The design press was forced to raise its game by the arrival in 1994 of *Eye*, the International Review of Graphic Design. Under the editorship of Rick Poynor, it made most design magazines look parochial, badly designed

Above and previous page
Project: *Eye 71* and *Eye 70*
Date: 2008/2009
Client: *Eye*
Designers: Simon Esterson, art director;
Jay Prynne, design
Simon Esterson is only the magazine's
third art director since its launch in
1990. Under Esterson (who is also a co-
proprietor of the publication) *Eye*'s layout
is sophisticated and sure-footed; layouts
have become busier and more conversational.
The magazine remains the house journal for
design's intellectual wing.

and narrow in outlook. Up until the arrival of *Eye*, the design press had seen itself simply as a promoter of design; its enthusiastic boosterism had helped graphic designers to come out of their craft-based nook and become players in international commerce.

Coinciding with the arrival of *Eye*, the design press also received a wake-up call with the emergence of theoretical thinking in influential United States design schools, which, along with magazines like *Émigré*, helped to usher in the design world's first period of mass introspection and self-doubt. Suddenly designers – although by no means all designers – started to question their role in consumer society, and their participation in a culture of persuasion and manipulation.

The design press responded – at least partially – to these undercurrents and upped its performance: magazines realized that it was no longer possible to rely on show and tell, and the good ones developed a recognizable editorial ethos, occasionally offering readers vibrant writing, heated debate and controversy.

The standard of design journalism has risen over the past few years, and what was previously an indiscriminate cataloguing of the new – all show and not much tell – has now been augmented by more critical and issue-based articles.

More recently, an even bigger seismic shift has been caused by the arrival of blogging and designers' colonization of the web – a shift that carries hefty commercial implications for the future of all print-based media, but which seems to have particular implications for the design press. The blogs (see Blogs, page 33) are making the design press look slow, they are attracting vast audiences, and they are forcing magazine editors and publishers to reappraise the role of printed magazines.

Most magazines are responding to the threat of blogging – and the Internet in general – by belatedly migrating to the web. The web offers real-time speed. It offers audio and video. It provides embedded links. It offers searchable archives. And, most alluringly of all, it allows reader interaction. Suddenly, a monthly publishing schedule and a past-its-sell-by-date letters page are as dull as stale bread. It's hard to see how the design press will be able to survive in its printed forms when we reach a point where publishers can attract advertising online more easily than they can in print.

And yet, I don't see printed magazines dying out. As the editor of one myself,[1] I sincerely hope not. There's still a kudos to print and paper that the Internet, despite its many advantages, can't compete with. And, of course, there is the question of money. It is a widely held view that if something is online it has to be free, and because of this all magazines (and not just design magazines) have abandoned attempts to get readers to pay for what they see online. For the time being a fluid interchange of content, where electronic and print media live side by side, looks like the model for the future. But the debate about editorial standards and the remuneration of writers will rumble on. Free is good if you are the receiver; not always so good if you are the provider.

The only way to compete against the online free show is for magazines to improve their offerings: better writing, better coverage, better discourse. Designers will pay for professional content and they will pay for genuine insight into their profession. And as a relative newcomer to the scene – *Dot Dot Dot* – has proved there's always space on a designer's bookshelves for anyone who wants to approach an old formula in a new way.

Further reading: David Crowley, 'Design magazines and design culture', in Rick Poynor (ed.), *Communicate, Independent British Graphic Design since the Sixties.* Laurence King Publishing, 2004.

1 *Varoom* – the journal of illustration and the made-image. Published three times a year by the Association of Illustrators. www.varoom-mag.com

Dutch design

Holland is a tiny country – cultured and progressive. In graphic design terms it punches above its weight. To outsiders, Dutch design appears central to commercial, cultural and public life. Could it be that graphic design from the Netherlands is the best in the world? This author thinks so.

Dutch design makes non-Dutch designers sigh with envy and admiration. Why is there so much graphic energy in this small sea-threatened nation? It's hard to think of a great Dutch novelist, but surely there must be a Dutch gene that produces all this visual dynamism? The Netherlands is the country that gave us Hieronymus Bosch, Vermeer, Rembrandt, van Gogh and Mondrian, so perhaps we shouldn't be surprised that it has produced a regular supply of graphic giants who in the modern era have had a hand in nearly all the major developments in progressive graphic design around the world.

What are the reasons for the country's graphic design pre-eminence? Dutch culture undoubtedly bequeaths its artistic legacy to each generation of art and design students, but graphic design can only thrive where there are enlightened and tolerant clients. Post-Second World War prosperity, and a tradition of enlightened patronage among clients with artistic and social ideologies, have encouraged design to prosper in the Netherlands. Unprecedented levels of state support back this up; sponsorship is readily obtainable for publishing projects, and generous start-up funds are available to fledgling creative enterprises. But the state is also Dutch design's best client. Government bodies have a tradition of commissioning radical design for stamps, bank notes,

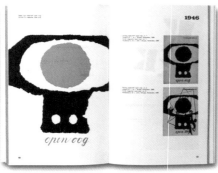

Above
Project: Sandberg
Date: published 1986
Book Design: Adri Colpaart
Cover and spreads from 80-page book showing
the work of pioneer Dutch designer Willem
Sandberg (1897–1984). His work had a rough-
edged illustrative quality, which he combined
with sophisticated Modernist typography.

passports and public institutions. And in the PTT – the Dutch postal, telegraph and telephone authority – Dutch designers can boast of a visionary client who has passed into design history as an exemplar of what can be achieved in the realm of public communication.

Radicalism has been a feature of Dutch graphic design since its earliest days. Even when done for firms that made such quotidian products as bacon-slicing equipment, Dutch graphics exude avant-garde virility and courageousness. Dutch design looks revolutionary, and this revolutionary fervour began with the De Stijl movement named after the journal founded by Theo van Doesburg in 1917. Mondrian was closely associated with De Stijl, as were the influential designers Piet Zwart and Paul Schuitema, who were to pioneer a fertile period of Dutch Modernism characterized by a more experimental flavour than the drier varieties found in Germany and Switzerland. Early Dutch design was stylistically and temperamentally closer to the Russian Constructivists.

Zwart had a profound influence on Willem Sandberg, who designed posters and catalogues for the Stedelijk Museum in Amsterdam and, in a typically Dutch twist, was the museum's director from 1945 to 1962. Sandberg was actively involved in the Dutch resistance movement during the Second World War and forged identity cards. Other designers and typographers lost their lives at the hands of the Nazis because of their illegal printing activities. When we read about the activities of designers during the war, we can see why graphic design has acquired a centrality in Dutch national life.

The modern era began with Wim Crouwel, one of the great innovators of Dutch design. He was among the first designers to recognize the importance of the computer and computerized design. As early as 1970 he was designing typefaces for the computer screen, but 'on the eve of the explosion in personal computing, Crouwel abandoned his own discoveries and returned to graphic design that remained faithful to the modernist tradition'.[1] In 1963, with Benno Wissing, Friso Kramer and the Schwarz Brothers, he founded design studio Total Design, a revolutionary design group with a continuing legacy. One of their clients was PTT.

In 1988, PTT was privatized – a recurring theme in European countries at the time – and Studio Dumbar was commissioned to update its identity. Under the leadership

In the PTT – the Dutch postal, telegraph and telephone authority – Dutch designers can boast of a visionary client who has passed into design history as an exemplar of what can be achieved in the realm of public communication.

Above

Project: KONG
Date: 2006
Client: Kong Design Store, Mexico City
Designer: Richard Niessen (Niessen & de Vries)
This poster is a splendid example of current Dutch graphic design. It was made for the opening of Kong Design Store and Gallery in Mexico City. Designer Richard Niessen was 'inspired' by the movie *King Kong*, and by the computer games Pong and Donkey Kong. He has created a cityscape built out of the letters K, O, N and G.

1 Emmanuel Bérard, 'The Computerless Electronic Designer', in *Wim Crouwel: Typographic Architectures*. Galerie Anatome, F7, 2007.

of Gert Dumbar, the studio revolutionized corporate identity by creating a fluid and expressive design – governed by a four-volume style manual that is a classic of modern graphic design.

Dumbar is a significant figure in Dutch design – and the period when he taught at the Royal College of Art in London had a galvanizing effect on a group of young British graphic designers in the late 1980s. His greatest contribution to the vocabulary of graphic design was the way in which he replaced the conventional flatness of much graphic communication with naturalistic depth. His posters for numerous cultural events show this to vivid effect.

While most Dutch graphic design gives the impression of a profound love of the craft for the craft's sake – the sense that it is closer to art than to design is commonplace – the designer Jan van Toorn was interested in its social and educational role. His work was the opposite of the manicured style of Crouwel and Dumbar, and exhibited a raw, almost punk-like directness. Rather than achieving purely professional objectives, it has an emotional heft that stems from his exploration of visual meaning and the role of design in society. Van Toorn was an influential teacher.

Other designers such as Hard Werken (a design studio founded by Rick Vermeulen, which grew out of the influential magazine of the same name), Karel Martens and Anton Beeke extended the range of Dutch graphic design as it moved into the digital era. It was a comfortable transition for most Dutch designers. The layering and densely overlapping effects that could be effortlessly achieved with a computer had long been a feature of their work. The adjustable set square had been replaced by software and computer processing power. Minimalism was rarely a feature of Dutch design.

In the new millennium, Dutch design has not abandoned its idiosyncratic voice. *Super Holland Design*, published in 2008, features work by young designers. At first glance it looks as if this new generation has lost something of the austerity of the best Dutch design. The book features a rich stew of images – many of which seem closer to illustration than graphic design. Yet the old rigour remains. Even at its most frenetic and anarchic, there's a controlled sense of structure and purposefulness about most new Dutch design. And in Experimental Jetset – perhaps the most famous of the new generation – Dutch design has a voice that offers a distinctive mixture of visual playfulness, editorial wit and graphic precision, and which also remains unmistakably Dutch.

Further Reading: Tomoko Sakamoto and Ramon Prat (eds), *Super Holland Design*. Actar, 2008.

E

Education of a designer

How much can students learn about graphic design in a few years of study? Not much. But a design education isn't about becoming an oven-ready graphic designer. It's about learning how to learn, because there never was a designer who didn't have more to learn.

I didn't go to design school. Instead I trained to be a graphic designer by working in a studio, and was taught by the designers I worked alongside. As a result I developed a highly pragmatic approach to design. I was a 'pro' from the outset, and couldn't imagine why anyone needed to go to design school. Learning on the job was the smart thing to do; or so I thought. But over time I realized that my view of design was far too narrow and that my work was unremarkable. I was a designer, but not an educated one. It took me a long time, but eventually I discovered that the true purpose of education is to learn how to learn.

Graphic design has rules and conventions. There are software skills and vast amounts of technical knowledge to acquire. But we learn these through training (usually on the job), and we shouldn't confuse training with education. Both are essential, but they are different: training gives us technical and mechanical skills; education gives us something more valuable – the ability to approach professional life with a mental aptitude for learning. And if we are lucky, a good education also gives us the wherewithal to understand ourselves and the world we live in.

You'd have thought that it would be enough for design schools to produce inquisitive graduates with the mental apparatus to learn the vast array of new skills that modern designers need. But employers – many of them the beneficiaries of a design education themselves – demand more. Most expect a supply of fully trained graduates ready for a productive life in the design business. You can see this in the recruitment advertisements that specify extensive software skills and experience. It's a depressing thought, but I've yet to see a recruitment ad, placed by a design firm, that offered training

Above
Project: Women on Top
Date: 2008
Design School: School of Visual Arts,
New York
Designer: Kimiyo Nakatsui
Women on Top addresses the lack of female
representation in U.S. and international
politics. An artefact of traditional female
roles, each apron represents a 'campaign'
ir support of female leadership – leading
families, cities and nations. By maintaining
a distinctly feminine sensibility, the pieces
invite women to both embrace tradition and
defy stereotype.

and development. The fact that very few employers see
it as part of their role to continue the education of
graduates is the cause of a great deal of unhappiness.
And as long as the vast majority of studios remain small
operations – with only a handful of employees – this is
unlikely to change.[1]

When I first started employing designers (in the
late 1980s) I had a typical employer's view of design
graduates. I selfishly wanted them to be ready for
immediate combat, and I was critical of schools that
seemed to do nothing to prepare them for the battles
of professional life. But over time I came to change
my mind. I found that I wanted free-thinkers with a
degree of personal confidence and – most importantly –
a willingness to learn.

I realized that if I took on young designers there
was a responsibility on me to train them, and so I evolved
a studio policy that recognized that it took a graduate
between six and 18 months to become an effective member
of the team – in other words, someone who could be given
projects without heavy-duty supervision. This meant I had
to devote time to graduate recruits; I had to see it as
part of the studio's function to train them. All I asked
the schools to do was produce bright candidates with a
sense of personal worth and a willingness to learn. Some
of the better schools did this; others failed miserably.

When I first started visiting British design schools
in the late 1980s, I was struck by the pragmatism of the
teaching. It seemed that students weren't encouraged to
think beyond becoming fodder for the
'design business'; there was no sense
that they were entering an arena where
it might be possible to have a voice
or an opinion. Later, in the 1990s, I
noticed a shift in emphasis: students
were being encouraged to think more
freely; to look at the designer as
being more than a value-free service
provider. They were being encouraged
to have a voice and an opinion.

This radicalism, taught by tutors
who themselves had been radicalized by
the explosion in design thinking in the
1980s and 1990s, was refreshing. Yet today the pedagogical
pendulum has perhaps swung too far towards high-minded
notions of personal expression and the designer-as-author,
at the expense of more mundane skills. The simple truth is
that the modern designer needs both approaches because it
is possible to use both of them in contemporary design.

So what is the correct formula for a design
education? In a perfect world, students would emerge

In the 1990s, I noticed a shift in emphasis: students were being encouraged to think more freely; to look at the designer as being more than a value-free service provider.

from their schools with a grasp of basic technical skills; they would have a flair for research and creative thinking; they would acquire knowledge of design history and contemporary theory; they would be equipped with an understanding of professional practice; and, most important of all, they would have broad cultural awareness. This is a tall order. The only students I have met who come close to ticking all these boxes are students who have done postgraduate degrees and who have spent time – possibly as much as a year or more – in professional practice.

This last point seems to me to be critical. Design courses that specify a mandatory period of working professionally seem closest to establishing the correct and most effective formula for a rounded education.

Sarah Temple is course director of the Diploma in Professional Studies, and head of Personal and Professional Development, at the London College of Communication (previously the London College of Printing, and the alma mater of many of Britain's leading designers, Neville Brody among them).[2] Temple is pioneering courses that combine study with work experience. 'It's a healthy ratio,' she notes. '3:1 education and professionalism, which is a good balance and comes at the right time for the students in year three of a four-year course.'

Design courses that specify a mandatory period of working professionally seem closest to establishing the correct and most effective formula for a rounded education.

Students are prepared over two terms with live projects, meeting clients, making studio visits, developing presentation skills and attending portfolio tutorials. Next, they develop an individual proposal. 'This can be anything they wish to try,' explains Temple. 'Working in Tokyo for a designer they admire, for example. Or researching first-hand their dissertation subject, setting up an exhibition, taking on a freelance project, putting a book idea together and taking it to a publisher, volunteering for a charity abroad in a design or photographic capacity, crossing a discipline, working with a product designer in Iceland or an architect in Holland, exploring a specialism such as letterpress, moving image, interactive design, with mentors across the world. I make them research extensively and I encourage them to be ambitious.'

What do the students get from this? Temple views it as a creative and productive 'gap' year. 'It's a period of standing on their own two feet,' she says. 'It's a time to work out what they're good at, and where their weaknesses lie. It gives confidence, amazing networking benefits, and

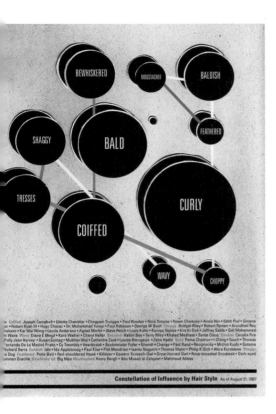

Constellation of Influence by Hair Style As of August 31, 2007

Above
Project: Constellation of Influence by
Hair Style poster
Date: 2008
Design school: The School of Visual Arts,
Designer as Author
Designer: Devon Kinch
Milton Glaser invited a group of students to
design a poster that summarized their life
to date. Devon Kinch listed his personal
influences and organized them 'by hairstyle'.

a CV to graduate with that is often more impressive
than that of a graduate who has been working for three
or four years. They are likely to perform very much
better at degree and are very much more focused on when
they graduate – hence much quicker to set up on their own
or be offered a good position.'

Not all educationalists think this is a good idea.
They see the role of education as encouraging the
acquisition of knowledge through learning and tuition.
Yet Temple seems to be offering the
best of both worlds; 'The danger is,'
she states, 'that as the industry
becomes more competitive, students
simply find it impossible to "position"
themselves correctly without help,
and wonderful talent gets squandered.
Critics just need to look at the
figures to see that with professional
knowledge, the very best experimental
students can not only obtain degrees
of the highest level but are also able
to propel themselves into the most
important and key positions in the
design industry, and most crucially,
not just domestically but in India and
China, and other emerging economies.'

Temple's course takes four years
instead of the usual three, and she
notes ruefully that new government
strategies in the United Kingdom are
threatening to make four-year courses
impossible. This is regrettable since her model offers a
near-perfect blend of the practical and the theoretical,
and just as learning a language is done best by living in
the country where that language is spoken, the practical
aspects of design are best learnt in a studio.

Temple is advocating a heuristic approach to
education. My dictionary defines the word as teaching that
encourages learners to discover solutions for themselves.
Heuristic teaching is a method that allows conclusions to
be reached through trial and error rather than by learning
rules. In my view this is the only way design can be
taught. As John Thackara notes: 'Learning is a complex,
social, and multi-dimensional process that does not lend
itself to being sent down a pipe – for example, from a
website. Knowledge, understanding, wisdom – or "content"
if you must – are qualities one develops through time.
They are not a thing one is sent.'[3]

**'Learning is
a complex,
social, and
multi-dimensional
process that does
not lend itself
to being sent
down a pipe –
for example,
from a website.
Knowledge,
understanding,
wisdom – or
"content" if
you must – are
qualities one
develops through
time. They are
not a thing one
is sent.'**

**Further reading: Steven Heller, *The Education of a Graphic
Designer*. Allworth Press, 1998.**

1 A recent survey in the UK discovered
  that large design consultancies are
  relatively rare and the design industry
  is overwhelmingly characterized by very
  small businesses: 59 per cent of design
  consultancies employ fewer than five people
  and a further 23 per cent employ five to ten
  people. www.designcouncil.org.uk
2 www.lcc.arts.ac.uk
3 John Thackara, *In the Bubble. Designing in a
  Complex World.* MIT Press, 2005.

Editing text

Designers have to work with the written content that is supplied by clients. Sometimes content is good; sometimes it's bad. There are certain things we can't change, but there isn't much written content that can't be made better by editing. If it's bad – consider changing it.

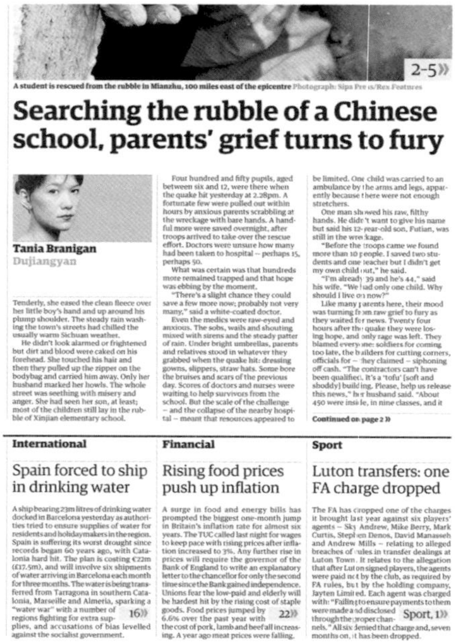

2-5»

A student is rescued from the rubble in Mianzhu, 100 miles east of the epicentre Photograph: Sipa Press/Rex Features

Searching the rubble of a Chinese school, parents' grief turns to fury

Tania Branigan
Dujiangyan

Tenderly, she eased the clean fleece over her little boy's hand and up around his plump shoulder. The steady rain washing the town's streets had chilled the usually warm Sichuan weather.

He didn't look alarmed or frightened but dirt and blood were caked on his forehead. She touched his hair and then they pulled up the zipper on the bodybag and carried him away. Only her husband marked her howls. The whole street was seething with misery and anger. She had seen her son, at least; most of the children still lay in the rubble of Xinjian elementary school.

Four hundred and fifty pupils, aged between six and 12, were there when the quake hit yesterday at 2.28pm. A fortunate few were pulled out within hours by anxious parents scrabbling at the wreckage with bare hands. A handful more were saved overnight, after troops arrived to take over the rescue effort. Doctors were unsure how many had been taken to hospital – perhaps 15, perhaps 50.

What was certain was that hundreds more remained trapped and that hope was ebbing by the moment.

"There's a slight chance they could save a few more now; probably not very many," said a white-coated doctor.

Even the medics were raw-eyed and anxious. The sobs, wails and shouting mixed with sirens and the steady patter of rain. Under bright umbrellas, parents and relatives stood in whatever they grabbed when the quake hit: dressing gowns, slippers, straw hats. Some bore the bruises and scars of the previous day. Scores of doctors and nurses were waiting to help survivors from the school. But the scale of the challenge – and the collapse of the nearby hospital – meant that resources appeared to be limited. One child was carried to an ambulance by the arms and legs, apparently because there were not enough stretchers.

One man showed his raw, filthy hands. He didn't want to give his name but said his 12-year-old son, Futian, was still in the wreckage.

"Before the troops came we found more than 10 people. I saved two students and one teacher but I didn't get my own child out," he said.

"I'm already 39 and he's 44," said his wife. "We had only one child. Why should I live on now?"

Like many parents here, their mood was turning from raw grief to fury as they waited for news. Twenty four hours after the quake they were losing hope, and only rage was left. They blamed everyone: soldiers for coming too late, the builders for cutting corners, officials for – they claimed – siphoning off cash. "The contractors can't have been qualified. It's a 'tofu' [soft and shoddy] building. Please, help us release this news," her husband said. "About 450 were inside, in nine classes, and it

Continued on page 2 »

International

Spain forced to ship in drinking water

A ship bearing 23m litres of drinking water docked in Barcelona yesterday as authorities tried to ensure supplies of water for residents and holidaymakers in the region. Spain is suffering its worst drought since records began 60 years ago, with Catalonia hard hit. The plan is costing €22m (£17.5m), and will involve six shipments of water arriving in Barcelona each month for three months. The water is being transferred from Tarragona in southern Catalonia, Marseille and Almeria, sparking a "water war" with a number of regions fighting for extra supplies, and accusations of bias levelled against the socialist government.

16»

Financial

Rising food prices push up inflation

A surge in food and energy bills has prompted the biggest one-month jump in Britain's inflation rate for almost six years. The TUC called last night for wages to keep pace with rising prices after inflation increased to 3%. Any further rise in prices will require the governor of the Bank of England to write an explanatory letter to the chancellor for only the second time since the Bank gained independence. Unions fear the low-paid and elderly will be hardest hit by the rising cost of staple goods. Food prices jumped by 6.6% over the past year with the cost of pork, lamb and beef all increasing. A year ago meat prices were falling.

22»

Sport

Luton transfers: one FA charge dropped

The FA has dropped one of the charges it brought last year against six players' agents – Sky Andrew, Mike Berry, Mark Curtis, Stephen Denos, David Manasseh and Andrew Mills – relating to alleged breaches of rules in transfer dealings at Luton Town. It relates to the allegation that after Luton signed players, the agents were paid not by the club, as required by FA rules, but by the holding company, Jayten Limited. Each agent was charged with: "Failing to ensure payments to them were made and disclosed through the proper channels." All six denied that charge and, seven months on, it has been dropped.

Sport, 1»

Above
On a daily basis, the *Guardian* demonstrates the value of good sub-editing. The paper's editorial and design team adopt a disciplined and consistent policy towards word counts. The result is a highly structured and ordered publication that never descends into muddle or confusion.

It's unlikely that a client will allow a designer to change the company's strapline, and no designer would dream of interfering with properly edited text or important factual data. But designers who acquire the confidence to suggest alterations and alternatives to text find that the appearance of their work is improved, and its effectiveness is enhanced. If we adopt a passive approach to content, we mustn't be surprised if we are treated like a passive partner in the communication process.

Just as there is always more than one way to render a piece of text typographically, so there is usually a variety of ways to reformulate written meaning. Designers are confident about the former, but less so about the latter, yet it's unusual to find text that can't be improved by good copy-editing. The ability to do this – to change, mould and shape written content supplied by clients – is one of the most useful skills the graphic designer can acquire. I worked for a long time as a designer before I realized I could – where appropriate – change a client's copy. When I think about the hours I spent as a novice designer copy-fitting poor-quality text into spaces it wouldn't fit into, I could weep.

Designers often make good editors. Their ability to order and structure text and images is a valuable skill.

At first I was hesitant about suggesting alterations to copy, but gradually I learnt that the way to do it was to show alternatives; I'd rewrite headlines, edit body copy and even provide new text where I thought the original version could be improved. To do this, you need a certain amount of linguistic confidence. But there aren't many designers who lack the ability to suggest alterations to a headline which result in a more comprehensible – and better looking – message.

There is a step beyond this, which takes us into the area of the designer as editor. Designers often make good editors. Their ability to order and structure text and images is a valuable skill. I worked with the designers Non Format[1] on a book project, and was stuck for a title. Instead of waiting for me to come up with one, Non Format came to me with a combined text and visual idea which I adopted.[2] It was a good example of how designers can seize the initiative and take control of their projects. Try it.

Further reading: Luke Sullivan, *Hey, Whipple, Squeeze This: A Guide to Creating Great Ads*. John Wiley & Sons, 1998.

1 www.non-format.com
2 Adrian Shaughnessy, *Look At This: Brochures, Catalogues and Documents*. Laurence King Publishing, 2005.

Ellipsis …

In the pursuit of radical graphic expression it is necessary – and often desirable – to break typographic rules. When typographic rules are contravened, it suggests insurrection and anarchy. Except when it is the one typographic rule that cannot be broken. Ever.

Above
Project: *Trainspotting* poster
Date: 1995
Client: Polygram Filmed Entertainment
Designer: Mark Blamire/Rob O'Connor, Stylorouge
Detail of quad poster to promote the seminal film made from the novel by Irvine Welsh. The film poster by London studio Stylorouge became a benchmark for radical film poster design. The use of the ellipsis is both eye-catching and textually engaging – we want to know more.

1 One of my favourite films is the 1960s British movie *If . . . . .* My affection for this wonderful film is severely tested by the fact that it has a four-dot ellipsis in its title.

Radical, avant-garde and oppositional graphic design has always attacked typographic convention as symbolic of established values relating to order and power structures. Or, to put it more plainly, when we want to demonstrate our rebelliousness as designers we chuck out typographical law. The Dadaists of the 1920s did it and the psychedelic poster artists of the 1960s did it, as did the punk designers of the 1970s. No gesture advertises our radicalism more effectively than thumbing our nose at typographic convention.

But there's one rule that can't be broken. It was the first typographic rule I learnt, so perhaps I give it undue importance, but it has always seemed to me that if you don't use the proper ellipsis you are committing an unpardonable crime against nature.

An ellipsis is a run of baseline dots used to imply gaps, elisions and unfinished statements in text. Certain writers use this device frequently, others rarely. But what is the correct way to set an ellipsis in text? When in doubt about typographic conventions, go to Robert Bringhurst's *The Elements of Typographic Style*. He writes: 'Most digital fonts now include, among other things, a prefabricated ellipsis (a row of three baseline dots). Many typographers nevertheless prefer to make their own. Some prefer to set the three dots flush … with a normal word space before and after. Others prefer . . . to add thin spaces between the dots.'

> **When designers want to demonstrate rebelliousness they chuck out typographical law.**

This short statement contains all that anyone needs to know about the ellipsis. But the most important bit of information is that there should only ever be *three dots*. I'm astonished by how often I see four dots, even five or six.[1] Only a lunatic would use more than three, and I'll go to my grave insisting on the moral rightness of the three-dot rule. But Bringhurst adds a comment that makes my eyes pop: 'When the ellipsis occurs at the end of a sentence, a fourth dot, the period, is added and the space at the beginning of the ellipses disappears….'

Well, I'm sorry, but that's one typographical convention I'm not going to adopt. Four dots are like a wig on a bald man. Not a good idea.

Further reading: Robert Bringhurst, *The Elements of Typographic Style*. Hartley & Marks, 1992.

Empathy

If you asked designers to name the most important attribute of the modern designer, few would say 'empathy'. Yet it might just be the most valuable skill a designer can acquire – although, as those who have an empathetic nature will attest, it comes at a price.

My dictionary defines empathy as the ability to identify with and understand another person's feelings or difficulties. When you think about it, empathy is a valuable psychological asset for working graphic designers to possess. The objectivity that they derive from having an empathetic nature is invaluable.

I discovered early in my working life that by using a sort of automatic psychological profiling I could intuit what clients were expecting. In other words, I had empathy with them. Over the years this sixth sense grew. It sometimes became difficult when I was dealing with groups of people rather than individuals, but even here I found I could usually grope towards identifying a collective desire. I knew what clients wanted and I gave it to them.

But as I developed my own philosophy of design, the ability to know what a client wanted started to become a burden. Sometimes what they wanted was wrong: wrong for the intended audience, wrong for them, and wrong for me. I realized I would be a better designer if I didn't have so much empathy.

> **Designers are either empathizers or egotists. Most of us are empathizers; we want to please both our clients and the users of the things we design.**

Designers are either empathizers or egotists. Most of us are empathizers; we want to please both our clients and the users of the things we design. And we are happy to forgo some personal gratification in favour of giving our clients what they want. But egotists are interested only in getting their own way; they have a fundamentalist certainty about themselves and their work.

I once saw a brilliant illustration of the difference between empathizers and egotists while sitting on a jury judging magazine design. The jurors were a mix of designers and non-designers, mainly editors and publishers. A magazine appeared on the table. It had been spectacularly successful on news-stands and had also caused a stir in design and publishing circles. Around the judging table the non-designers cooed over it. They thought it was terrific. It must be good, they said, it sells gazillions of copies every week.

When it was my turn to speak I did a bit of fence sitting, and said that although I didn't like the magazine's design I thought it was worth noting that it didn't follow the current magazine-design template – I couldn't bring myself to dismiss it without pointing out that it had some redeeming features. One of my co-jurors had no such scruples; the British designer David King took one look at the magazine and threw it across the table. 'Rubbish,' he grunted.

IRRITATING
OFF-MESSAGE
INDULGENT
SUBJECTIVE
LISTLESS
IRKSOME
BOLLOCKS
STUPID
SHALLOW
MUNDANE
UGLY
RUBBISH

Above
Drawing by Paul Davis, 2009

Employment

As if learning to be a designer wasn't hard enough, we then have to find employment. Business gurus tell us the job is dead. Finding employment has become harder than ever. Yet designers are better equipped to deal with the new world of work than most.

Much as I admired King's frank and blunt response, I wasn't capable of doing the same. My empathetic nature wouldn't allow me. And just as empathy forces me to see merit in others' efforts, it also forces me to see that even difficult clients have a viewpoint and a reason for being the way they are. But I also accept that too much empathy can lead to designers becoming overcompliant – and the consequence of too much compliance is mediocrity.

To be successful, a designer needs empathy and egotism. If we have empathy we will always find clients willing to employ us. But if we can combine empathy with a bit of stubborn inner conviction, our work will be richer and more effective. It will be richer and more effective because it will have the stamp of confidence and personal commitment. You can tell the work that doesn't have these ingredients. It is bland and formulaic – or, to put it another way, it is work that is drowning in empathy.

Further reading:
www.designobserver.com/archives/029038.html

Funky Business is a book by two Swedish business academics: 'The job is dead,' they write. 'No longer can we believe in having a piece of paper saying job description at the top. The new realities call for far greater flexibility. Throughout most of the twentieth century, managers averaged one job and one career. Now, we are talking two careers and seven jobs. These days the long-serving corporate man, safe and sound in the dusty recesses of the corporation, are long gone. Soon, the emphasis will be on getting a life instead of a career, and work will be viewed as a series of gigs or projects.'[1]

This was first published in 2000. It was mildly prophetic then; it is reality today. Interestingly, for many designers, this has always been the way. Stability of employment is rare in design; studios expand and contract, and designers rarely stay with the same employer. But this process has accelerated. It is now standard practice for designers to move jobs frequently: it is common for designers to be employed on short-term contracts; it is common for designers to be in full-time employment during the day and run their own studio at night. It is also common for designers to be self-employed, hiring themselves out to whoever offers them work, and moving on to someone else when that dries up.

Designers are well suited to the job-is-dead future envisaged by the authors of *Funky Business*. They have enjoyed a precarious relationship with stable employment for decades. Even in times of boom, contraction and redundancy were always lurking ahead. Now, it's a case of the rest of the world adapting to a situation that designers have lived with since the 1960s.

So how should the modern designer approach employment? We need to understand a number of fundamentals about the world we live in. Jobs for life don't exist. Short-term and freelance contracts are common. In fact, working in the same place for a long time is, in the eyes of many employers, a sign of lack of ambition. We also need to accept that in our early years we will change jobs regularly. It is common for recent graduates to do this every year or so, and rely on short-term contracts, internships and work experience. None of this need be a bad thing. We may regret not building up long relationships with inspirational employers, but by changing jobs frequently we gain valuable insight into the working methodologies of studios, and we rub up against all sorts of people who shape and mould us in ways we hardly realize.

Designers are well suited to the job-is-dead future envisaged by the authors of *Funky Business*. They have enjoyed a precarious relationship with stable employment for decades.

Employment in the future will be an increasingly survivalist activity. We must be prepared to be flexible, entrepreneurial and bold. Employers are spoilt for choice – there are plenty of good designers to go round. So we need to offer something extra: an aptitude for new design platforms, a gift for organization, an additional creative skill such as programming or illustration. It's simply no longer good enough to be a good designer. We have to be good designers plus …

1 Jonas Ridderstråle and Kjelle Nordström, *Funky Business*. F.T. Prentice Hall, 2002.

Further reading: Jonas Ridderstråle and Kjelle Nordström, *Funky Business*. F.T. Prentice Hall, 2002.

Envy

What's envy doing in a book about graphic design? Well, envy runs through design like a forest fire. But what's so bad about a bit of envy? Nothing, just so long as it doesn't turn into the poison of jealousy. Perhaps it's actually a useful spur encouraging us to do better work?

Consider this. In an interview, Stephen Doyle of Doyle Partners in New York, makes the following observation: 'Down deep, designers really loathe each other's work. We'll never admit it, but we only feel safe truly admiring the work of the dead. Everybody else, at some level, is the competition.'[1] Doyle has a point. When he uses the word 'loathe' – a pretty strong word – I think he is talking about jealousy, and I'd say that most of us feel a jealous dislike of the work of others at some time in our careers. But I'd argue that rather than the corrosive emotion of jealousy, we are more likely to feel the milder emotion of envy when we view the work of other designers. Envy in design can be expressed in the frequently heard phrase, 'I wish I'd done that'.

Envy is a healthy, even necessary, emotion for the designer. My guess is that when we stop looking at work and saying 'I wish I'd done that' we've stopped noticing anything new. Envy seems unavoidable if we are to care about our personal development as designers. Dazzling work surrounds us. New designers arrive on the scene every day. Nations with a previously unremarkable track record in graphic design suddenly produce talent whose work makes us sit up and gaze admiringly. If by envying this work we improve our own, envy serves a useful purpose. If we allow it to become jealousy, we need to recognize that envy is a symptom of our own doubts and inadequacies; when we are jealous of others, we are really hating ourselves.

Morrissey once sang 'We hate it when our friends become successful'. This may be true in the febrile world of music, but I've noticed that the opposite tends to be true in design. All the good designers I've ever known are quick to congratulate and praise the work of others. They may cast envious glances at the work of others, but this doesn't stop them from acknowledging that they are good. It also helps keep at bay the toxins of jealousy.

Further reading: Peter Salovey, *The Psychology of Jealousy and Envy*. The Guilford Press, 1991.

Above
Drawing by Paul Davis, 2009

1 'Stephen Doyle on Humor in Design', in Steven Heller and Elinor Pettit, *Design Dialogues*. Allworth Press, 1989.

Ethics in design

For some designers – and for many clients – ethics are about as important as the boiling instructions on a packet of rice. But that's changing. Today, more and more designers are thinking about the ethics of what they do. It's no longer something we can choose to ignore.

We are all obliged to take personal responsibility for what we do in our working lives, and to think constantly about the implications of how our actions impact upon society. In fact, this applies to all occupations and not just designers. Bankers and road sweepers have to consider the ethical implications of what they do. Bankers have to make judgements that might result in people being evicted from their homes; road sweepers have to decide whether to pick up the blood-caked syringe they find in the gutter or leave it for someone else to stumble upon. There isn't much in life that doesn't involve ethical decision-making.

There seems, however, to be something about design that makes designers especially sensitive to ethical questions. Why is this? Perhaps it is to do with design's proximity to many of the key issues that confront us today: consumerism, overconsumption, green issues, economic growth, commercial propaganda and media proliferation. It might even be because designers have a natural inclination towards ethical conduct.

But let's take a step back and look at graphic design from a distance. Put simplistically, design is done by people who (in the industrialized West, at least) offer their services for hire in a democratically governed, free-market society – just like estate agents, plumbers,

A manifesto

We, the undersigned, are graphic designers, photographers and students who have been brought up in a world in which the techniques and apparatus of advertising have persistently been presented to us as the most lucrative, effective and desirable means of using our talents. We have been bombarded with publications devoted to this belief, applauding the work of those who have flogged their skill and imagination to sell such things as:

cat food, stomach powders, detergent, hair restorer, striped toothpaste, aftershave lotion, beforeshave lotion, slimming diets, fattening diets, deodorants, fizzy water, cigarettes, roll-ons, pull-ons and slip-ons.

By far the greatest time and effort of those working in the advertising industry are wasted on these trivial purposes, which contribute little or nothing to our national prosperity.

In common with an increasing number of the general public, we have reached a saturation point at which the high pitched scream of consumer selling is no more than sheer noise. We think that there are other things more worth using our skill and experience on. There are signs for streets and buildings, books and periodicals, catalogues, instructional manuals, industrial photography, educational aids, films, television features, scientific and industrial publications and all the other media through which we promote our trade, our education, our culture and our greater awareness of the world.

We do not advocate the abolition of high pressure consumer advertising: this is not feasible. Nor do we want to take any of the fun out of life. But we are proposing a reversal of priorities in favour of the more useful and more lasting forms of communication. We hope that our

society will tire of gimmick merchants, status salesmen and hidden persuaders, and that the prior call on our skills will be for worthwhile purposes. With this in mind, we propose to share our experience and opinions, and to make them available to colleagues, students and others who may be interested.

Edward Wright
Geoffrey White
William Slack
Caroline Rawlence
Ian McLaren
Sam Lambert
Ivor Kamlish
Gerald Jones
Bernard Higton
Brian Grimbly
John Garner
Ken Garland
Anthony Froshaug
Robin Fior
Germano Facetti
Ivan Dodd
Harriet Crowder
Anthony Clift
Gerry Cinamon
Robert Chapman
Ray Carpenter
Ken Briggs

Published by Ken Garland, 13 Oakley Sq NW1
Printed by Goodwin Press Ltd, London N4

lawyers and accountants. And as long as we don't break any laws we are able to do pretty much what we like.

The design profession is free from regulatory codes. Various professional bodies around the world offer gentle guidance on ethical issues, but membership to these organizations is not compulsory and their main focus tends to be professional not ethical – their main interest seems to be making design attractive to clients. This puts huge pressure on individual designers to make up their own minds on ethical matters, which may partly explain why they become preoccupied with ethical questions – if there are no rules we go looking for them (it's a designer foible!).

In my opinion there are two strands to this: the personal and the professional. Or to put it another way: the moral and the ethical. The personal strand is clearly stated. Each of us has our own moral code and every day we must decide whether to abide by that code or not. In our professional lives, however, we have ethics. These are the mainly public codes that we adopt to govern our professional behaviour. Of course, the two strands overlap, and for some designers morality and ethics may be the same thing. But for most of us they are separable. Like a lawyer defending a rapist, we might choose to work for a client we don't approve of on the grounds that we are being professional; on the other hand, we may personally find this same client morally repugnant and refuse to work for them. The choice is ours.

It is going to be increasingly hard not to take an ethical stance on design. More and more client companies have corporate social responsibility programmes.

Here are three examples of instances that require an ethical as well as a purely professional response: 1. We are asked to design a website for a landmine manufacturer. 2. We are asked to design the packaging for a new fizzy drink that is full of sugar and dubious chemicals, but which promotes itself as 'fun'. 3. We are invited to design a hang tag for a jeans company with exploitative labour practices in developing countries.

The landmine example offers a simple choice. Most designers wouldn't want to assist in a barbaric exercise like promoting sales of landmines and would therefore decline the project – although there must be some who would be willing to do this work. (I'm guessing here, but I suppose landmine companies have websites. I'm too squeamish to look.) In this case, both our ethical and our moral codes are alerted.

But what about the fizzy drink? Here there is still a moral dimension, but it is not on the same scale as landmines. If we thought the drinks company was

Above and opposite
Project: First Things First manifestos
Date: 1964 (opposite) and 2000 (above)
Designer: Ken Garland (opposite),
Nick Bell (above)
The First Things First manifesto was
published in 1964 by Ken Garland. It argued
against the unthinking absorption of design
into the consumerism engulfing Britain in the
affluent post-war years. It postulated the
belief that graphic designers had an ethical
responsibility to contribute meaningfully
to society and not to be mere pawns in
commercial life. In 2000, a new group of 33
designers produced their own version. It
appeared in various publications and aroused
criticism from design's conventional wing.
The version shown appeared in *Eye* 33.

contributing to poor health among the young and vulnerable
we might decline to work for them. But if they were
producing a product that did not claim to promote health,
and if they made the contents clear on the packaging,
most of us would find it professionally expedient to take
on the project. If, however, the company claimed their
product gave the people who drank it strength and vigour
this would become a moral issue, because they are asking
us to lie.

On the surface, the hang tag appears to be
straightforward; most designers would relish the
opportunity to make it look beautiful. Yet the fact that
the jeans are made in sweatshops in developing countries
would cause many of us to think about our actions. We
might abhor the thought of fashionable denim being made
by exploited labour, but what would be
gained by not doing the work? Firstly,
few of us can say how the workers might
feel if their admittedly paltry incomes
were withdrawn. Secondly, the jeans
company pays taxes (we hope) which
help to run hospitals and fund welfare
programmes (as well as funding wars, of
course). Thirdly, by taking on the work
we are in a position to state our views
on exploitation in developing countries
to the people doing the exploiting.
This might make us unpopular with our
client. It might even cause us to be sacked — but in my
experience most clients are happy to have this sort of
discussion as long as it is conducted rationally and
without hypocrisy.

Have we reached a point where we need an ethical code to govern our activities? Designers have had codes regulating the way they work in the past — why not now?

Hypocrisy is an important issue here. How many of
us can criticize the activities of clients with a clear
conscience? Do we know where every item in our homes is
made? Do we know where our insurance policies or pension
funds are invested? Do we run our own businesses with
ethical rectitude? Have we ever loaded a print bill to
a client? Ever added a few hours to a time sheet to
inflate our hourly charges? Ever employed an intern
without paying them? How many of us can answer these
questions without blushing?

For me, it boils down to notions of personal
conviction. By this I mean that I believe in the freedom
of the individual. I don't want to be told what to do and,
just as importantly, I don't want to tell anyone else what
to do. I believe in exercising free choice in questions of
personal morality, but I also believe in democratically
arrived at laws that prevent the oppression of others.
I also believe that the price of my soul is a personal
matter. If I sell it cheaply, that's my decision. I must

live with the consequences. But my being a designer does not set the price — it is set by my membership of the human race.

As designers, when we are faced with ethical questions we can deal with them in two ways. We can say, 'This is business and I can't afford ethical quibbles.' Or we can adopt the lawyerly route and say, 'I may think that this project is dubious, but as a professional person I'm obliged to do it to the best of my ability.' Yet, perhaps there's a third way. Have we reached a point where we need an ethical code to govern our activities? Designers have had codes regulating the way they work in the past — why not now?

I've always enjoyed the freedom of working in an unregulated business, and I've always resented any attempts to introduce codes of practice or professional accreditation. But the world is changing. The green issue alone means we can no longer be safely left to decide what is right and what is wrong. All mature businesses and professions accept the need for ethical guidelines. And, surely, signing up to a sensible, fair-minded and voluntary ethical code would also help to resolve professional issues like free pitching, copyright and plagiarism?

But what if this code had rules on rates of pay for interns? What if it had strict guidelines on marking up print and other third-party services? What if it curbed our ability to make money in a business that is already tough and competitive? Would we be so keen to sign up? Or is it the case that any initiative that doesn't further the self-interests of designers is doomed to failure?

In fact, the opposite is happening. It is going to be increasingly hard not to take an ethical stance on design. More and more client companies have corporate social responsibility programmes. Many of these are adopted in name only, with corporations and public bodies paying lip service to the notion of social responsibility. But many organizations are accepting responsibility for their actions and they are insisting that their suppliers do too. As has been already noted (see Accessibility, page 8) the United States federal agencies are obliged by law to make their electronic communications accessible to people with disabilities. We can expect more of this. Increasingly, clients are going to insist on working with designers who, like them, have ethical policies. It's a shame we have to leave it to others to put our own house in order.

Further reading: Lucienne Roberts, *GOOD: an Introduction to Ethics in Graphic Design*. AVA Publishing, 2006.

F

Fashions in design

**Slavishly following fashion
is lazy and unimaginative,
yet when we stop being excited
and informed by new trends
it's usually a sign that we've
stopped caring about our
personal development, and that
we've stopped caring about the
evolution of design in general.**

Fashions in graphic design are like fashions to be found in any other area. Some survive for a few months, others are absorbed and have a longer-lasting contribution to the enlargement of graphic design's vocabulary. All the same, it's fashionable to dismiss all fashions in graphic design as ephemeral and diminishing. Purists talk about the merits of tradition. And undeniably there is merit in design traditions and those styles and idioms that have survived over time. But design without fashions? Design without the fizz of the new? Sounds like a very dull world to me.

Of course, when we encounter new fashions we need to distinguish between the worthwhile and the vacuous. And most of us manage to do this without too much bother. But I'm often wary of the automatic dismissal of fashion. As designers get older, it is natural that they think less about fashionable gestures and more about permanent things. But accepting that the ebb and flow of fashion is part of design's evolutionary instinct, and accepting that everything new isn't automatically bad, is an essential part of being an alert and open-minded designer. The rip tide of fashion – even when we hate it – causes us to examine and re-examine what we do. When we stop being interested in fashion, it's usually a sign that we have become sealed off in some sense.

Without the conflict and skirmishing caused by fashion, design is likely to stagnate.

Take the case of *Super Super*, which first launched in Britain in 2006. It carried a blast of steroid-pumped magazine design that made designers sit up like meerkats at the approach of a leopard. Unsurprisingly, it excited outrage and approval in equal measure. But most of all,

Above
Project: *Super Super* magazine cover
Date: 2009
Creative Director: Steve Slocombe
Super Super caused a furore in UK design
circles when it crash-landed in 2007.
Dismissed by some as fashionable opportunism,
it became the house journal for the Nu-rave
generation. The magazine's confidence, its
garish use of colour, its raw typographic
stylings, and it's unashamedly fashionable
pose, sent a day-glo bullet through the
heart of tasteful magazine design.

1 www.creativereview.co.uk/crblog/super-super-
like-nothing-and-everything/
2 www.crystalreference.com/DC_articles/
English74.pdf

Finding a first job

**Emerging into the job market
is the most daunting moment in
a young designer's life. But
although landing a first job is
tough, there are many simple
rules to make it easier, and
it's amazing to see how many
designers don't bother with
these basic strategies.**

it excited curiosity, and it was widely debated on
the *Creative Review* blog.[1] As *Creative Review*'s editor
Patrick Burgoyne wrote: '*Super Super*'s wilfully distorted
typography, day-glo colours and total rejection of the
holy tenets of magazine design are enough to give more
mature art directors a fit of the vapours. It's MySpace
made flesh, with all the clashing cacophony that concept
brings to mind.'

Bloggers critiqued and commented with their usual
fervour (and their usual aversion to capital letters):
'Isn't it made by cheap students who can't use Photoshop
properly? Looks like national enquirer but with bad
taste, and z list celebrities.' And the counterview
would also be expressed: 'The thing that I find
fascinating and exciting about this magazine is the way
that it naturally and internally relates to other media
in the same way its audience does. If you read a music
review, you go online to listen to the track. Hear about
an interesting designer, you google them and look at
their stuff. A lot of *Super Super*'s content is in the way
that the magazine prompts the reader to go to MySpace etc.
to find out more, either by actually supplying the link or
by just assuming that the reader will google
it themselves.'[2]

Without fashions flaring up, design would be
far less likely to evolve. Without the conflict and
skirmishing caused by fashion, design is likely to
stagnate. If design doesn't admit rude intruders from
time to time, it will atrophy. We don't have to embrace
every fashion, but we have to admit that it is fashion
that reinvigorates design.

**Further reading: Angela McRobbie, *In the Culture Society.
Art, Fashion and Popular Music*. Routledge, 1999.**

Students ask how they can get jobs when every advertised
vacancy seems to demand at least two years' experience.
Well, when studios say they want two years' experience
they don't really mean it. What they mean is they want
someone good. If you are good enough, two years doesn't
mean two years; it's code for no second-rate designers.
So the first rule of job hunting is don't make yourself
appear second-rate.

The second rule of job hunting is: spare a thought
for the employers and give them a helping hand. At the
point in the year when graduates start hitting the
employment trail, letters start appearing in the design
press from disgruntled job seekers complaining about
the callous way studios and employers treat potential
recruits. These letters are followed by letters from

disgruntled employers complaining about the poor level of preparation they find among graduates. Employers have a point here: I've interviewed countless young designers and it's bewildering to see how poor most of them are at communicating their merits. Many of them make it difficult for the interviewer to see their potential. If an employer has to struggle to see the potential in a recruit, the recruit is falling at the first hurdle.

For most of the graduates who flood the market each year, finding a job is a daunting task. But the good news is that it needn't be. Doing it properly is easy. So easy, in fact, that it's remarkable it is ever done badly. Let's look at the three key elements in landing a job. Conveniently, they all begin with the letter P – they are preparation, presentation and psychology.

Preparation

Job hunting begins with research. Waiting for the perfect job usually entails a long and ultimately disappointing wait. Designers have to prepare. There are many ways to find out about jobs. Often opportunities come through personal recommendations, which means it is essential to maintain a network of contacts. It also helps to ask around to see whether anyone knows about vacancies. Jobs are advertised in design magazines, on design groups' websites and on online recruitment sites. Signing up with a professional recruitment firm is also an option.

> **For most of the graduates who flood the market each year, finding a job is a daunting task. But the good news is that it needn't be. Doing it properly is easy.**

Designers should begin by finding the names of studios and firms they'd like to work for – but what they mustn't do is approach only the cool studios. These are inundated with applications. Be smart and choose places that are likely to hire people. How do you know whether studios hire? Well, you can try the direct approach and call them up and ask them. But you can also look for clues. Do they advertise jobs or internships on their website? Do you know anyone who has worked for them? The more research you do, the more likely your chance of being granted an interview.

Once targets have been identified you need to find out everything you can about them. Turning up for an interview knowing zilch about a prospective employer is like turning up with a sticker on your forehead saying, 'Don't hire me'. It is also imperative to find the names of the people responsible for hiring. If this information isn't on a studio's website, call them up and ask who you should send your CV to. Most studios will happily provide

this information. If a studio deals with an enquiry rudely or snootily it's probably a sign that you won't want to work for them. All well-run studios have a policy of dealing with job applications. It's a good first test of an employer's suitability.

Now that you have a list of people to contact, what's the best way to send them your details? Letter, email, or personal visit? Personally, I prefer to receive a letter, although an email is a close second. But, either way, never begin with 'Dear Sir or Madam'. This shows you haven't taken the five minutes required to find out the person's name and, furthermore, it's easy for a potential employer to ignore a letter/email that begins in this way and much harder for them to ignore one that is personally addressed. One more thing: make sure you spell the person's name correctly. Failure to get this small matter right signals a lack of attention to detail, and that's a firing-squad-at-dawn offence in graphic design. As for turning up in person – don't do it unless you are a design genius.[1] How do you know whether you are a design genius? You won't be worrying about interviews; studios will be chasing you.

Don't assume you will walk into the first job you apply for (but don't assume you won't). Be positive, but expect setbacks – everyone has knock-backs at the outset of their careers, and how we deal with them determines how we develop as creative individuals and as human beings.

So what should the letter or email say? Not much. Three paragraphs will do. Give your name, list any relevant experience and state clearly that you only want an interview. This last instruction is crucial. Always ask for an interview, not a job. Very few studios will refuse a request for an interview, even if they are not hiring. By making an interview their primary target, a job hunter gains three vital advantages. The first is interview experience and valuable portfolio feedback. The second is that every interviewer becomes a contact – a contact you can keep in touch with, a contact who might remember you when future vacancies occur, and a contact who might recommend you to someone else. The third is that by setting an interview as the target, you avoid the discouragement of failing to land a job.

If you choose to write a letter, it should be laid out with care and devotion. It should be on good stock, and it should be on letterheaded paper. Any designer who can't be bothered to design his or her own letterhead is like a plumber who turns up to fix a leak without a wrench. The same rules apply to emails. There is less scope for sophisticated presentation (avoid html emails,

Opposite and above
Project: *Never Sleep* book
Date: 2008
Publisher: de.MO
Editors: Wayne Kasserman, Gibson Knott,
Caitlin McCann
Designer: Melissa Scott
Never Sleep is written by Andre Andreev
and G. Dan Covert who run Dress Code,
a New York design group. Their book is
a frank and revealing attempt to demystify
the transition from student life to working
life. They include work from their first
design class alongside recent client work.
The book contains interviews with mentors,
teachers and peers. In the words of the
authors, 'this book serves as the ultimate
companion for design students, educators,
and anyone breaking into a creative field'.
www.neversleepbook.com

they often fall foul of firewalls) but make sure the text is correctly laid out with a distinctive and easy-to-read email signature.

Should you send samples of work with your letter? Definitely. Not too many – five or six items only – but a few pieces of work attached to a letter are essential. In the case of emails I'd avoid large attachments. Instead, provide a link to a personal website (see Online portfolio, page 218).

There is one other job-hunting avenue: the novelty mail-out. I've received some pretty strange mailings from designers looking for work. They tend to fail. The fact is, in most cases what seems innovative and fresh to a young designer will often be grimly familiar to potential employers. Designers have to be clever to come up with something that hasn't been done before. And anything that can't be filed or stored properly, anything that looks wasteful, and anything that is time consuming, is likely to connect only with the inside of a recycling bin.

Even getting a letter or email in front of a prospective employer is hard work. But it doesn't end there. In most cases you will need to make a follow-up phone call; this is pretty well obligatory. You will probably have to make a few calls to get hold of your target. If you make three and fail to reach the person you want to speak to, you can take it that they are probably not interested in you or – more likely – they simply aren't hiring. I always **As a recent graduate you have an attribute that a designer with two years' experience doesn't have: you cost less.** made a point of replying to every job application I received, but this was an onerous task and occasionally some slipped through the net. Preparation is everything. Without good pre-planning, the next two steps aren't worth taking. Don't skimp on the prep.

Presentation:
The way you present your work – and yourself – is more important than the work you show. No matter how good it is, if you present it sloppily, or present yourself sloppily, you will struggle to find employment. But if you do it well, the seemingly insurmountable mountain of landing a first job becomes a stroll on the beach.

The decision to award an interview is almost always based on the impression your approach as a prospective employee has made on your potential employer. This means your presentation has to be as immaculate as you can make it – pitch-perfect in every respect. No one expects lavish, high-concept presentations from graduates, or great displays of confidence and bravado – but every employer expects a level of basic competency and clarity of communication.

So, what is the most effective way to present work? Elsewhere in this book I describe techniques for showing work to clients (see Presentations skills, page 250). Many of these are also relevant to the interview situation. When preparing for a job interview, there are two primary considerations: paper or electronic? Usually, this will be determined by the nature of your work. For web designers and moving image designers, there isn't much point in showing it on paper. When showing screen-based work, show it on a laptop. This means taking your own. Don't assume that you can use the studio's kit. Studios are busy places – I've interviewed people in broom cupboards because at the time of the interview every square inch of space was in use.

Do you take printed samples of your designs? Yes, if this adds to the understanding of the work: no, if it complicates the presentation.

If work is being shown on paper, you will need a case to carry it in. The black ring-binder portfolio is pretty much a dinosaur these days. It's much better to go for a simple black box with a hinged or lift-off lid, and fill it with sheets of A3 run outs in protective acetate sleeves. Do this so that the sheets can be handed round. Avoid cluttering up each page with lengthy descriptions of the work.

Do you take printed samples of your designs? Yes, if this adds to the understanding of the work: no, if it complicates the presentation. I've often been shown a few attractive pages of a book, and then been handed a huge bulky tome to look through; in most instances, the two or three sample pages were enough. I'm often asked whether drawings showing preliminary work are required. Only if they show genuine developmental thinking. Personally, I like to see at least one set of working drawings, but no more.

A final word of caution: when you are presenting work make sure it is facing the interviewer. You'd be staggered to know how many designers – even quite senior ones – treat interviews as opportunities to show their work to themselves. I've lost count of the number of times I've had to strain my neck to see a portfolio because the designer was more concerned about seeing his or her work than he was about showing it to me.

To sum up: make your presentation as good as you can. Be prepared to change it after two or three interviews if it's not getting a good response. And adopt a confident but unprejudiced view about any opportunities that present themselves.

Psychology:

Adopting the correct frame of mind is vital. By frame of mind, I mean having the right attitude and managing your expectations. Don't assume you will walk into the first job you apply for (but don't assume you won't). Be positive, but expect setbacks – everyone has knock-backs at the outset of their careers, and how we deal with them determines how we develop as creative individuals and as human beings.

Don't be too lofty about where you should work. By all means be ambitious and aim high, but don't turn your nose up at opportunities that don't conform to your vision of the ideal job. In my view, there is no such thing as a bad job in your first two or three jobs. Nor is there anything wrong with having three or four jobs in your first few years of working life. If a first, second or third job doesn't work out, move on. And remember: we learn more from the bad jobs than we do from the good ones.

When you are presenting work make sure it is facing the interviewer. You'd be staggered to know how many designers – even quite senior ones – treat interviews as opportunities to show their work to themselves.

Make it your mission to attend as many interviews as you can. Learn from each one. Find out what you are doing well and what you are doing badly. Ask the interviewers to tell you. Most of them will do this happily.

Finally, as a recent graduate you have an attribute that a designer with two years' experience doesn't have: you cost less. Also, you will be willing to do many of the mundane things that someone with two years' experience is less willing to do. So don't see yourself as disadvantaged. See yourself as possessing the precious quality most employers want: unrestrained enthusiasm and willingness.

Today, there are more graduates than there are vacancies. What does this mean? It means that the current generation of young designers has to be more entrepreneurial than previous generations. In order to do the sort of work you want to do, you may have to consider setting up on your own sooner rather than later in your career. I think it's best to spend a few years working in studios (even mediocre ones) before doing this. But the reality is that for ambitious graduates, starting a studio – or working as a freelancer – is sometimes the only option.

Further reading: Andre Andreev and Dan Covert, *Never Sleep: Graduating to Graphic Design.* **de.MO, 2008.**

1 I say never turn up in person, yet I employed two people who did just this. Both appeared unannounced and requested an interview (not at the same time, I should add). Both were hired on the spot. But this is rare. Very rare.

Focus groups

Focus groups are anathema to most designers. Brave and original ideas have a way of getting killed by 'research'. But surely if design is good enough, if it is conceptually solid, it has nothing to fear from scrutiny? You'd have thought so, but this is rarely the case.

Above and opposite
Project: Braniff ads by George Lois
Date: 1969
Client: Braniff Airways
Art Director: George Lois
A selection of ads by George Lois for
Braniff Airways showing his famous pairings
of unlikely celebrities. Thanks to George
Lois for kind permission to reproduce.
See more of George Lois's groundbreaking
work here: www.goodkarmacreative.com

Why are designers terrified of focus groups? Most of them will give you the standard anti-research rant, but few have done it more eloquently than George Lois. In an interview with Steven Heller, Lois recounts his experiences working for Braniff airlines.

'I came up with the "When you've got it, flaunt it" idea. I said to Harding Lawrence (the CEO), "If you're going to research this, forget it; it's going to be a dog." He said, "Well, we've got to research it." So they researched it, and I think 84 per cent of the people who saw the ads and flew Braniff said they would never fly it again. That's how much the test groups hated the campaign. But Lawrence had balls, and he gave me his okay. I did spots with Salvador Dalí telling Whitey Ford how to throw a curveball, and Sonny Liston eyeballing Andy Warhol as he explained the significance of soup cups, and Mickey Spillane, of all people, explaining the power of words to the great poet Marianne Moore. Braniff's business went up 80 per cent. You can't research an idea like that. The only ideas that truly research well are mediocre, "acceptable" ideas. Great ideas are always suspect in research.'[1]

Focus groups become more prevalent as businesses become less and less willing to take risks or trust the judgement of their management – not to mention, the judgement of creative advisers. So we had better get used to them. They are not going to go away. And surely the opinion of an intelligent bunch of people will tend to improve rather than diminish a piece of work? Not so. If you ask someone for their opinion, and especially if you pay them for their opinion, they will feel compelled to give you one, and that opinion is likely to be critical because if it's not, the opinion-giver will feel they aren't doing their job.

The problem with focus groups – and the reason why designers get so miffed by them – is that they usually take place after all the hard work has been done. It would be much more constructive to have them pronounce on a project in its early stages. But this rarely happens because marketing departments think focus groups need to see the finished product before they can make meaningful comments.

My personal experience of focus groups has been, generally speaking, a series of happy encounters. The ones I have been exposed to have, in the main, been end-users. For a couple of years I worked on redesigning a group of business magazines. After each redesign was approved by

Focus groups become more prevalent as businesses become less and less willing to take risks or trust the judgement of their management – not to mention, the judgement of creative advisers.

1 'George Lois on Advertising'; interview in Steven Heller and Elinor Pettit, *Design Dialogues*. Allworth Press, 1998.

the client, it was sent to a focus group of subscribers. In nearly every case, the feedback was approving and sometimes enthusiastic. Although it's probably worth noting that in only one instance was a proposal that could be called radical put forward.

But there's one trick I learnt during this experience: try to attend the focus group sessions personally. It's not always possible to do this. In many instances it's forbidden, and the more important the project (in other words, the more money being spent) the more unlikely it is that you will be allowed to attend. But always ask, and if the answer is yes, grab the opportunity. It can be painful to hear your work discussed, but it can also be enlightening to see what people think about its effectiveness (even in the artificial surroundings of a focus group session). However, the real purpose of attending sessions is to do some 'jury fixing'. You won't be allowed to influence the group unduly, but it is sometimes possible to 'explain' things. If it isn't possible to attend the sessions, at least attempt to speak to the person running them. This is a useful way of prepping the organizers with a few useful responses to the inevitable questions.

Of course, we can't attend all the focus groups our work is given to, so we must learn to live with their opinions, and hope that when a supine verdict is recorded there's someone, like the Braniff CEO, who is brave enough to ignore it.

Further reading: Malcolm Gladwell, *Blink, The Power of Thinking Without Thinking*. Allen Lane, 2005.

French graphic design

When we think of France we think of it as one of the global centres of visual art, but we tend not to think of it as a centre of graphic design. Yet much French design is unsurpassed, and a new generation of practitioners is continuing a noble tradition of radical expression.

Art movements with deep French roots, such as Art Nouveau, Art Deco and Cubism, and artists like Toulouse-Lautrec and Henri Matisse, have profoundly influenced and shaped today's graphic design. In Pierre Bonnard and Jules Chéret, France had two of the pioneers of the modern graphic poster. Yet compared to designers in neighbouring Germany, Holland and Switzerland, French designers have made a relatively small contribution to the history of graphic design. But what French design lacks in quantity, it makes up for in quality.

The international view of French graphic design can be compared to the way French pop music of the 1960s and 1970s was, for so long, dismissed and vilified by both critics and audiences. Yet today, we look back on it as idiosyncratic and self-assured. The same is also true of much of French graphic design; at its best it offers sophisticated visual expression that rivals anything produced by France's European neighbours, and which –

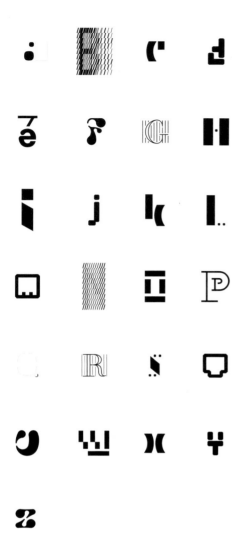

even today – maintains a uniquely Gallic flavour. Yet it's easy to see why French graphic design – with its quirkily indigenous typefaces[1] – didn't become the International Style in the way Swiss and German design did. It's just too – well, French.

In an essay on the celebrated French poster artist Cassandre, the graphic designer Pierre Bernard, founder of the radical design collective Grapus, wrote: 'Cassandre was the first modern French designer … even in his early posters, geometry and light are mingled, the images are clear, often literally radiant. Instantly captivating. Long before being read, they meet our eyes with generous obviousness, strong and reserved at the same instant.'[2] Cassandre's exquisite posters were done mostly between the First and Second World Wars. He even designed a collection of typefaces – Bifur, Peignot and Acier Noir – all radically different from each other, yet unmistakably French. In his posters, with their potent mix of Art Deco styling and geometric Modernism, Cassandre showed how image and typography could be melded to create a humane and rational iconography for advertising and public graphics.

Yet Cassandre's brilliance failed to become the guiding light for either mainstream French design or advertising. In the same essay Bernard writes: 'Nowadays, in our country, visuals and signs of public life, deformed by this advertising idiom, contaminate our social space day in, day out.' Among young French designers commercial design is regarded with revulsion, but away from the stuff that 'contaminates', we find plentiful examples of isolated graphic brilliance. If we look beyond the shiny billboards and dreary advertising, we find French graphic designers working in styles and idioms that engage and delight.

In the early 1960s, designer Robert Massin produced experimental typography for the French publisher Editions Gallimard that anticipated the fluid typography of the computer era by four decades.

The origins of stylistically radical French graphic design can be traced back to the 1960s and 1970s. In the early 1960s, designer Robert Massin produced experimental typography for the French publisher Editions Gallimard that anticipated the fluid typography of the computer era by four decades. The student riots in Paris in May 1968 were the catalyst for Bernard and two colleagues to start Grapus. Philip Meggs writes: 'The shocking verve of [Grapus's] statements, especially the dynamic informality of its spatial organization and casual, graffiti-like lettering, was copied by fashionable advertising.'[3]

Above
A variety of letterforms by designer Philippe Apeloig. Apeloig worked as a trainee at Total Design in Amsterdam. In 1985 he was taken on as graphic designer by the Musée d'Orsay in Paris, and in 1988 he obtained a scholarship and moved to Los Angeles where he worked with April Greiman. He returned to Paris and opened his own studio. His typographic work is cosmopolitan, yet retains an unmistakable Gallic accent.

Above
Project: Edit! Norms, Formats, Media,
Date: 2009
Client: Fine Arts School/Town Hall —
Bordeaux, France
Designer: Christophe Jacquet dit Toffe
The work of Parisian designer Toffe. He
describes it as a 'kind of illustration about
graphic design and names'. It was created
for an International Symposium in Bordeaux.
The work references wine and includes a
vectorized title to represent 'edit!' It also
contains decorative elements in the 'style of
Fernand Leger'.

1 The leading French typeface designer of the
  modern era was Roger Excoffon. He created a
  suite of typefaces as quintessentially Gallic
  as Beaujolais, berets and Edith Piaf. They
  include Banco, Mistral, Nord and Antique
  Olive. He died in 1983.
2 Pierre Bernard, 'Cassandre – All cap –
  Ante-ad or the future of Graphic Design
  in France'; essay in the catalogue for the
  Chaumont poster festival, 2005.
3 Philip Meggs, *Meggs' History of Graphic
  Design*. John Wiley and Sons, 2006.
4 www.ville-chaumont.fr/festival-affiches/
  index.html

The contemporary scene is invigorated by a new breed of maverick designers who are comfortably able to resist the blandishments of advertising and find opportunities in the cultural sectors, as well as in fashion, publishing and music. No star glows brighter in the French graphic cosmos than that of m/m paris. Formed in 1992, the duo, Michael Amzalag and Mathias Augustyniak, are well known for their work for Björk, fashion houses, galleries and their art direction of French *Vogue*.

In Philippe Apeloig, France has a designer whose typographic rigour and cool restraint make him as effective as any typo-based designer at work today. A few others, such as H5, Vier 5, Ultralab and the solo designer Toffe, offer vivid and idiosyncratic work.

France was to have a sharp if unexpected influence on graphic design in the 1990s, when the thinking of various French post-Modern philosophers influenced a generation of young American designers. These giants of the post-Modern scene rarely, if ever, mentioned graphic design in their writings, but their views on semiotics and deconstruction, and notions such as the death of the author, shaped graphic thinking for a decade. The theories of Derrida, Barthes and others entered the bloodstream of American design through the design department at Cranbrook Academy of Art, where graphic design became viewed as a component of popular culture and the subject of critical analysis, rather than a purely commercial practice.

In 2005 I attended the Chaumont poster festival in France.[4] This famous event is centred around an international poster competition, and for one week each year the small town of Chaumont, two hours from Paris and deep in Champagne country, becomes a graphic design town. Armies of students, venerable French designers and famous names from the international scene gather to talk about graphic design, and view exhibitions of work. Churches are turned into galleries, and municipal buildings are filled with earnest designers scrutinizing the displays with unhurried reverence. Only in France.

Cassandre showed how image and typography could be melded to create a humane and rational iconography for advertising and public graphics.

Further reading: Michel Wlassikoff, *The Story of Graphic Design in France*. Gingko Press, 2006.

G

Gill sans

It was designed by perhaps the most controversial designer who ever lived. Eric Gill makes today's designers-cum-rock stars look like extras in a junior school nativity play. His sexual morality was askew, but his skill as a designer/artist and typeface designer is unassailable.

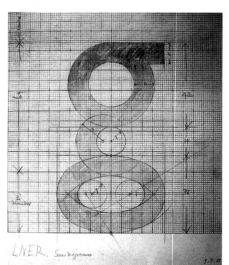

LNER. Sans serifs

Eric Gill's reputation as a human being is in tatters. He had sex with his daughters, experimented with bestiality and, despite espousing a fundamentalist brand of Catholicism, indulged in sexual promiscuity on a grand scale. Modern Western society forgives most transgressions, but not incest and not sex with minors.

I'm not an apologist for Gill's sexual activities. Anyone interested in the man as well as his work can come to their own conclusions. But Gill was undoubtedly a creative genius. He was a sculptor, a stonemason, an engraver, a lettering artist, a typographer and, in everything but name, a graphic designer. No British figure has the same genius for graphic precision and emotive use of line as Gill. Anyone who knows him only for his three immortal typefaces – Gill Sans, Perpetua and Joanna – should hunt down his drawings. He offers a master class in reductive expression.

Gill was born in 1882 and died, aged forty-eight, in 1940. He was a student of Edward Johnston, the calligrapher who in 1916 created the alphabet for the signage of the new London Underground: Johnston Sans. According to Johnston, it was designed to be legible from a speeding train. When Gill came to design Gill Sans, he based it on Johnston's typeface, but where Johnston had retained links with calligraphy (the dot of the 'i' is a square such as would be drawn by a flat-nibbed pen) Gill pushed into more geometric territory. Yet there is something not quite modern about Gill Sans

Anyone who knows Gill only for his three immortal typefaces – Gill Sans, Perpetua and Joanna – should hunt down his drawings. He offers a master class in reductive expression.

that distinguishes it from the mechanistic purity of the great Modernist sans typefaces like Futura and Helvetica, and it is widely used today by designers seeking a sans serif typeface with a humanistic (and British) flavour. Today its use suggests simplicity and an almost monastic lack of showiness. Gill's legacy as a graphic designer lives on in numerous places, but perhaps it exists most intriguingly in the work of Jonathan Barnbrook. Gill's austere, ecclesiastical Modernism permeates Barnbrook's work at all levels.

Gill Sans was the first typeface to make an impression on me. I discovered it in childhood, although at the time I didn't know there were such things as typefaces. It was only when I discovered that there was a typeface called Gill Sans that I realized it was the one that had been used in the book with which I learnt to read.

Further reading: Fiona MacCarthy, *Eric Gill*. Faber & Faber, 1989.

Opposite and above
Drawing by Eric Gill of the typeface for the London & North Eastern Railway. This typeface evolved into Gill Sans.
The 'Eye and the Hand' symbol was often used by Gill as his personal signature.

Gothic type

In the Middle Ages, Gothic letterforms were used in legal documents and to transcribe the word of God. Today, we associate Gothic type with horror films, exotic underwear catalogues and heavy metal album covers. Do we have the Nazis to thank for this?

Above and overleaf
Use of Gothic letterforms by designer Corey Holms. Above: ambigram logo for Fighting Records (ambigram is a mark that can be read from different orientations – this one works both rightside up and upside down). Over: Brea typeface. Holms says: 'I would consider this typeface a remix, since it is constructed from black letter typography – I really liked the idea of treating a typeface completely anachronistically.'
www.coreyholms.com

The Gothic style appeared in the twelfth century. It began as an architectural style and its ornate severity can be seen today in European cathedrals from that period. As a type of lettering (also known as black letter and Fraktur), Gothic scripts were dominant in Europe for two centuries until they were challenged by the Renaissance (1300 onwards), when the Gothic style was considered too barbaric for the new humanist era. The Renaissance saw a return to the classical culture of ancient Greece and Rome, and for this a more humanistic style of letterform was needed, as well as letters that could be used in mechanical printing.

When Gutenburg created his Bible in 1455 it was set in a script called Textura, which closely resembled the calligraphy in monkish hand-lettered manuscripts, and which we recognize today as Gothic. Soon afterwards, black letter began to disappear in France and Italy where they were replaced by lettering created by visionary type designers such as Nicolas Jenson, Claude Garamond and Aldus Manutius, the creator of Bembo. However, Gothic scripts remained in use in Germany, and when Martin Luther published his translation of the New Testament – as a rebuke to the power of Rome, and thus instigating the Protestant reformation – Schwabacher and Fraktur, new variants of the traditional black letter, were used.

Today the word 'Gothic', its abbreviation Goth, and the use of Gothic typefaces in general is associated with anything to do with the macabre, or anything relating to mid-1980s bands who used lots of black leather and

1 As Stephen J. Eskilson has pointed out, Hitler is said to have favoured the classical style: roman typefaces, centred in the classical style and accompanying heraldic imagery. Eskilson writes: 'In 1949 the Nazis abruptly instituted a total elimination of fraktur in favour of roman type. The reason for this shift was not immediately clear, as the official communiqué made use of the Nazi's catchall theme of the "Jewishness" of Fraktur. While no scholar would attempt to explain Nazi policy in entirely rational, human terms, the notion that black letter script represents a tradition or Judenletter (literally "Jewish letters") is an especially bizarre fabrication even for a regime led by anti-Semitic monsters.' Stephen J. Eskilson, 'Typography under the Nazis', in *Graphic Design: A New History*. Laurence King Publishing, 2007.

black mascara, and wrote doleful lyrics about death and suicide. When we use Gothic letterforms in contemporary graphic design, it is usually to signal oppositional or transgressional activities. Norwegian death metal bands are not inviting us to think of them as twinkly-eyed charmers when they use Gothic type on their album covers.

It is tempting to see the use of Gothic letterforms in contemporary settings as having its origins in Nazi propaganda. In the 1970s, when UK punks wanted to shock their bourgeois detractors, they used the swastika. No designer would dare to use the swastika today, but perhaps using Gothic script is a way of borrowing the forbidden allure of Nazi style without resorting to actual Nazi iconography.

The Nazis were bitterly opposed to Modernism and the New Typography. They closed the Bauhaus in 1933 and compelled illustrators and designers to reject Modernism which they associated with Communism, in favour of wholesome German nationalistic styles. This resulted in Nazi propaganda being swathed in menacing Gothic scripts and over-romanticized illustrations of square-jawed Aryan types.[1]

It's doubtful that many contemporary designers actually have Nazis in mind when they use Gothic scripts in steamy underwear catalogues, or on flyers for bondage clubs. And we can be sure that when celebs are tattooed with them they don't want their admirers to start thinking of the Third Reich. But the Gothic style has filtered down from the Nazis and is now an international lingua franca for rebellion and transgressive behaviour.

Further reading: Judith Schalansky, *Fraktur Mon Amour*. Princeton Architectural Press, 2008.

Graphic authorship

Can graphic designers ever be authors? Can the designer of the graphics for a packet of frozen burgers be said to be indulging in an act of authorship? Or does the designer who wants to claim the title 'author' have to originate work from a self-written brief?

When the French post-Modern theorist Roland Barthes pronounced that 'the author is dead' he was observing that the meaning of a text was determined as much by the reader of the text as by its writer. It doesn't sound so dramatic, but his notorious dictum might just as easily have been phrased as 'everyone is an author' since everyone – or nearly everyone – is engaged in finding meaning in texts of all kinds.

Among design historians and critics the term 'graphic authorship' has been coined to describe the activities of designers who generate their own content and create work without the sponsorship of a client. It is also known as self-initiated work. And there are many examples of this. The American designer Elliot Earls is often cited as a graphic author. So too are the British designers Fuel. Many other designers produce books, magazines, websites,

VOLUME 1. NUMBER 4. Remember 1999? The close of the last millenium? This was the year Lance Armstrong won his first *Tour de France*, the Dow Jones Industrial Average closed at over 10,000 for the first time and the Denver Broncos won the Super Bowl for their second consecutive year. It was the year Putin replaced Yeltsin as president of Russia and William Jefferson Clinton went on trial for impeachment charges in the US; the year Apple brought out its first iBook; the year Nickelodeon introduced SpongeBob and global sales of Pokémon cards went through the roof. But 1999 was also a year of tragedy, claiming the lives of thirteen innocent people outside Denver in the Columbine High School massacre. It was the year an earthquake devastated Turkey, NATO launched airstrikes in Kosovo and EgyptAir 990, a twin-engine Boeing 767 on its way from New York to Cairo, crashed in the Atlantic Ocean killing all 217 people aboard. True, it was also a year of accomplishment: *Medecins Sans Frontières* won the Nobel Peace Prize, Norman Foster won the Pritzker Prize and Michael Cunningham won the Pulitzer Prize for fiction. Yet the American Center for Design's coveted prizes never materialized, as the organization closed its doors before it could publish that year's winners. This issue of *Below the Fold:* brings ACD's long-overlooked exhibition to light, casting a lens on a world we may no longer clearly recall. Though less than a decade old, this body of work was produced in a different century — before iPods, before blogs, before the ravages of 9/11. Long lost, now rediscovered: this is a snapshot of design at the end of the millenium. SUMMER 2007.

Above
Project: *Below the Fold: Volume 1*
Date: 2006
Client: Winterhouse
Design: Winterhouse
A self-initiated project by Jessica Helfand and William Drenttel at Winterhouse. *Below the Fold* is an occasional journal from the Winterhouse Institute, each issue exploring a single topic through visual narrative and critical inquiry.

1 Author (noun) 1. a writer of a book or article. 2. a person who originates a plan or idea. www.askoxford.com
2 Ellen Lupton, 'The Producers', 2003. www.elupton.com/index.php?id=48

films, T-shirts and music without a client and without a client brief.

But how is this fundamentally different from the designer who designs the packaging for a packet of frozen burgers? For me, a graphic designer who creates a new visual entity where one didn't previously exist is indulging in an act of authorship. Not only that, but working for a client doesn't preclude the ability to have authorial intent.

The word author has its roots in the word authority, yet authorship carries no implication of quality or measurement: Jeffrey Archer is an author, as is Don DeLillo;[1] we may prefer DeLillo to Archer (or vice versa) but both are engaged in authorship. We may also decide that designing the packaging for frozen burgers does not require the same degree of authorial skill as DeLillo used to write *Underworld*, but designing the pack still requires the designer to make something that wasn't there before, and requires them to do it with authority. And it's this act of originating something that makes creating original design into an act of authorship — in spite of the word's etymological origins in authority. After all, the package for the frozen burgers might have been designed by a designer with a track record in successful and innovative food packaging — an 'authority' figure in his or her chosen field.

Of course, there are many designers who have no desire to claim authorship of their work. As Ellen Lupton notes: 'Typically, graphic designers provide the spit and polish but not the shoe.'[2] Designers are often happy to be hired hands, ready to do the bidding of clients. And yet, show me a designer who doesn't feel the warm glow of authorship when he or she produces work created by a combination of imagination, skill and professional judgement; it's a glow that contemporary human beings crave as keenly as our prehistoric ancestors craved a fire and full belly.

> **Designing the packaging for frozen burgers does not require the same degree of authorial skill as DeLillo used to write *Underworld*, but designing the pack still requires the designer to make something that wasn't there before, and requires them to do it with authority.**

**Further reading: Michael Rock, 'The Designer as Author',
Eye 20, 2001.**

Green design

**As designers we have to accept
our share of the blame for the
causes of environmental damage.
And yet, as designers we are
often not fully in control of
the work we do. It is our clients
who call the shots. So is it even
possible to be a green designer?
Yes, but it's not easy.**

Above and opposite
Project: Evo brand launch
Date: 2006
Client: Evo
Designer: Patrick Walker with Erika Rand —
host and collaborator
Brand launch for the San Francisco Green
Festival 2006, by the Sheffield-based
designer Patrick Walker. Included marketing
material, stand design and screen. A good
example of design for a green cause which
doesn't wear a hair shirt.

I have never met a graphic designer who didn't fight for
his or her ideas. Let me rephrase that: I have never met
a good designer who didn't fight for his or her ideas.
No one is surprised when designers battle for the survival
of their creative ideas. It is hard-wired into their
psychology. It's natural.

Today, there can't be many designers who don't
recognize the importance of adopting a green approach to
professional design — as well as to life in general. I'm
sure there are designers who don't feel any sympathy for
the green cause; and there are plenty of designers who
are acutely sensitive to environmental questions yet take
the view that 'there's not much I can do'. But imagine if
designers adopted the same attitude towards creativity and
said, 'There's no point in pushing for creativity, clients
are not interested in it'. It's an unthinkable scenario.
Countless great design innovations have come through the
tenacity of designers pushing for ideas to be accepted
by sceptical clients.

It is becoming increasingly clear that if designers
want to be green, they are going to have to integrate
green practices into their work in the same fundamental
way that creativity — not to mention the other skills
that designers possess — is integrated. It is no longer
an excuse to say, 'My clients won't buy green design'.
Clients have to be convinced to adopt green policies in
the same way that they have to be convinced to buy smart
and challenging ideas.

Graphic designers may not rank alongside oil
companies, mining conglomerates and car manufacturers
as the planet's leading despoilers — but we are up to
our black polo necks in culpability, and we have to
accept responsibility and not hide behind design's
apparent junior status. The situation is made more
difficult by the fact that the economics of professional
graphic design (in other words, earning good fees or
having a good salary as a designer) are overwhelmingly
dependent on clients constantly driving up consumption
by offering new products and services — which, of course,
demands the brainpower and energy of designers. And here's
where the crux of the problem lies: as designers it is in
our economic interest to persuade clients to do lavish new
brochures with huge print runs, or to commission elaborate
electronic displays that require a 24/7 energy source to
keep them running. In the past I've often urged clients
to produce additional items that weren't in their original
request. It's what running a financially successful design
business is all about — the more our clients spend on
materials the better it is for designers.

So, does achieving a green planet mean we have to
stop the wheels of commerce, don a hair shirt and work in

a cave in the Himalayas? No. Society can't step back from its technologically sophisticated position, but it has to use all its talent and ingenuity to devise ways of not turning our greeny-blue planet into a yellow desert unfit for human habitation. And the green battle has to be fought on the front line of commerce, and for designers this means tackling clients head-on and demonstrating that green doesn't mean plunging profits; and that it doesn't mean grubby and second-rate. Green is the colour of the shining future.

It is no longer an excuse to say, 'My clients won't buy green design'. Clients have to be convinced to adopt green policies in the same way that they have to be convinced to buy smart and challenging ideas.

Most professions are ahead of graphic design in the adoption of sustainability practices. Product designers and architects are at the forefront of radical green strategies, and a rising number of large corporations – the 'enemy' in the eyes of many environmental activists – are actively engaged in green activities even if some of them are open to accusations of 'greenwashing' (see Greenwashing, page 131). In fact, the uptake of green strategies is so rapid that graphic design runs the risk of being left behind. We've reached a stage where anyone starting a design practice today would be well advised, for business reasons alone, to establish one that is genuinely green. There are many clients (although still too few) who have green purchasing policies and who have a remit to work with green suppliers. Increasingly, it is a feature of public sector tendering that suppliers must meet sustainability criteria in the way they already have to meet types of criteria for professional indemnity, for example, and health and safety.

But let's take this back to a more ground-level discussion. What does it mean to be a green designer? There are key areas where designers can play a positive role, yet most of the steps we can take are commonsensical ones and are equally applicable to other walks of life and not just design.

Sophie Thomas is a partner with Kristine Matthews in the London-based design group thomas.matthews. Formed in 1997, the studio has an unapologetic approach to green issues. On their website they state: 'thomas.matthews believes in two things: good design and sustainability.'[1] This clear statement of their intentions may dissuade some potential clients, but for others it will establish green matters as a factor to be contended with from the outset of a project rather than something to be brought up later in the process.

On their website, thomas.matthews list the ten ways in which they design to fight climate change. The list is simple and realistic. It doesn't ask for miracles. It reads: 1. Re-thinking. 2. Re-using. 2. Using friendly materials. 4. Saving energy. 5. Sharing new ideas. 6. Designing to last. 7. Staying local, buying ethical. 8. Supporting what we believe. 9. Inspiring, having fun. 10. Saving money.

Sophie Thomas advises designers to clean up their own backyards first. 'You cannot preach if you do not practise,' she says. 'Cycle to work, switch to green energy suppliers, sort your rubbish and get it recycled, turn off your computers and displays when you go home. Do an audit on your office to get a grip on your impact.' Simple stuff – but how many of us can say we take even these elementary steps? Thomas urges designers to become 'agents for change'. She urges us to: 'Re-design the way you design. This comes under two categories; logical and lateral. Logical changes the way you practise – scrutinize the paper stock you specify, the printers you use and everything that you spec to create your design. Lateral changes the way you think. Don't see environmental impact as an add-on, place it at the beginning of your brief. Closing off some doors will open up a whole new set that you hadn't thought of before.'

The writer John Thackara also points out that designers have to start early. In his *In the Bubble* he writes: 'If the so-called green design approach (better known in the United States as "design for the environment") has a limitation, it is that it intervenes at the "end of the pipe". It modifies individual products or services but does not transform the industrial process as a whole.'[2] Thackara is thinking of design in the holistic sense, but his view applies as much to graphic design as it does to architecture and product design.

Small studios and independent designers can easily adopt many of the strategies described above and, as we've seen, there are clear advantages in doing so. However, introducing good practice is more difficult for designers who work for firms, studios or clients that don't have an environmental policy. Many employers and clients are blind to ecological issues; some are even ideologically opposed

Most professions are ahead of graphic design in the adoption of sustainability practices. Product designers and architects are at the forefront of radical green strategies, and a rising number of large corporations – the 'enemy' in the eyes of many environmental activists – are actively engaged in green activities even if some of them are open to accusations of 'greenwashing'.

Above
Project: Airplot campaign logo
Date: 2009
Client: Greenpeace
Design: Airside
Greenpeace's Airplot campaign questions the need for a third runway at Heathrow. London-based design group Airside created an identity based on a plane's-eye view of patchwork fields – the fields that would be destroyed by the controversial third runway.

Opposite
Project: Ecofont (www.ecofont.eu)
Date: 2008
Client: Self-initiated
Font created: SPRANQ
For designers, printing out work is an unavoidable part of the design process. But when we print our work we use paper and ink. What if we could use less ink? Inspired by Dutch 'holey cheese', the Utrecht-based creative communications agency SPRANQ has developed a new font. The Ecofont uses up to 20 per cent less ink, is free to download and free to use. There is now a professional version for use in large organizations.

ABCDEFGHIJ
KLMNOPQRS
TUVWXYZ01
23456789,.:;
""!?*/&%£$()
[]{}@

1 www.thomasmatthews.com
2 John Thackara, *In the Bubble: Designing in a Complex World*. MIT Press, 2005.

Greenwashing

There are companies who wave the green flag and pretend to be green, when in reality they do nothing. Graphic designers are the first people companies turn to, to help create the illusion of greenness. When businesses do this it's called 'greenwashing', and it leaves a bitter taste when we encounter it.

to environmentalism. Of course, the easy response here is to say change jobs (or clients), and for some this is feasible. But for others it isn't. However, despite such difficulties we shouldn't feel helpless. There is a sea change the world over, and to raise environmental issues in the business place is no longer heretical. It's normal.

But to raise green matters with short-sighted employers and clients we need to do research, and accumulate evidence to demonstrate that there is another way; that it is possible to be environmentally aware and run a successful business. We will only be able to do this if we are properly informed and if we build sustainability into our thinking. It has to be a fundamental part of the design process and not something we might think about only if and when our clients express an interest. Clients who don't want to know about green issues are worse than clients who don't want good design. And we all know how bad they are.

Further reading: www.threetreesdontmakeaforest.com

In our professional lives we are free to ignore most, if not all, green issues. There are laws surrounding waste disposal, but if we want to specify foil blocking and use toxic inks we are free to do so. If we want to leave our computers on overnight, and drive to our studios in our 4x4s, we are not prohibited from doing so.

But there's an area where designers have a special responsibility. This is the activity that has become known as 'greenwashing' – the process whereby corporations and other bodies pretend to have a green ethos in order to make themselves appear environmentally responsible, when in reality they do little or nothing to make themselves genuinely green. As green credentials become increasingly important in corporate and brand-image building, designers are frequently asked to apply 'greenwashing' strategies to make their paymasters look responsible. In other words, they are asked to lie. And when faced with a request for 'greenwashing', the individual designer needs to decide on his or her response. We can accept or decline. The choice is ours.

For designers who decide that greenwashing is unacceptable, there is an alternative option. It is the opposite of greenwashing. I'm talking about the pressing need to explain green issues to a bewildered public. This is an area where designers have an important role to play by helping to make clear the complex arguments put forward by scientists in relation to global warming and dangerous emissions. Difficult scientific arguments can often be explained more effectively by graphic means – diagrams, illustrations, charts – than by scientific language. If designers can produce the seductive imagery and beguiling commercial messages that are leading us to catastrophe, then surely they can use these tools to help 'package' the moral, scientific and practical information that might lead us to salvation.

Further reading: George Monbiot, *Heat: How We Can Stop the Planet Burning*. Penguin, 2007.

Grids

When detractors attack graphic design – Swiss design in particular – they point out that visual expression based on mathematical grids must be dull and inexpressive. In fact, the opposite is true. Grids mean freedom. And what's more, artists have always known this.

A designer friend, a keen student of Swiss design, asked me recently whether I knew who invented the grid in graphic design. Surely, I said, grids were like the weather, they'd always been there – how else would you organize text and images on a page? The Celtic monks who created the Book of Kells didn't use a grid, but if you looked hard enough I'm sure you would find one – or at least find enough recurring patterns to suggest an underlying master plan to deal with the placing of elements on successive pages. And let's face it, that's all a grid is.

The design historian Roxane Joubert sees the grid system within design as having its antecedents 'inscribed in the act of writing itself, already evident in the ruled lines of medieval manuscripts and the earliest systems of writing'.[1] In fact, mathematical grids had been in existence since 1692, when the French type designer Philippe Grandjean constructed letterforms using grids.[2]

In *Swiss Graphic Design*, Richard Hollis notes that grids grew out of hot-metal typesetting, '… type metal, cast in a rectangular base, was composed in horizontal lines arranged in vertical columns, and locked in a rectangular framework. Unlike the infinite scale possible in digital systems fifty years later, type and spacing material were produced in fixed sizes: typography was a modular system.'[3]

Josef Müller-Brockmann, the patron saint of grids, and the designer who did the most to develop a science of modular, grid-based design, wrote: 'The reduction of the number of visual elements used and their incorporation in a grid system creates a sense of compact planning, intelligibility and clarity and suggests orderliness

The Celtic monks who created the Book of Kells didn't use a grid, but if you looked hard enough I'm sure you would find one – or at least find enough recurring patterns to suggest an underlying master plan to deal with the placing of elements on successive pages.

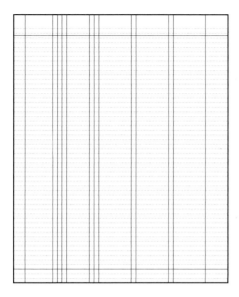

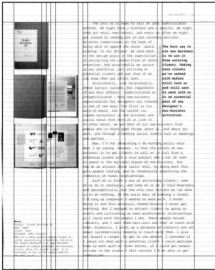

Above
The five-column grid for this book.

of design. This orderliness adds credibility to the information and induces confidence. The grid determines the constant dimensions of space. There is virtually no limit to the number of grid divisions. It may be said in general that every piece of work must be studied very carefully so as to arrive at the specific grid network corresponding to its requirements.'

Most designers will instinctively understand Müller-Brockmann's reasoning. And most designers will instinctively create a grid as a first step to the physical realization of a design. Yet grids are infinite in their variety, so how do we decide what system works best for any given situation? Grids are determined by what we put into them (content) and what we require them to deliver (functionality), and only when we have defined the content and functionality, can we hope to arrive at an appropriate grid.

The excellent Mark Boulton, who writes with clarity and authority on many technical aspects of design, notes the importance of mathematics in grid-based design: 'Ratios and equations are everywhere in grid system design. Relational measurements are what define most systems, from simple leaflet design to complex newspaper grids. To design a successful grid system you have to become familiar with these ratios and proportions, from rational, whole-number ratios such as 1:2, 2:3, 3:4, and those irrational proportions based on the construction of circles, such as the Golden Section 1:1.618 or the standard DIN sizes 1:1.414. These ratios are ubiquitous in modern society, from the buildings around us to patterns in nature. Using these ratios successfully in a grid system can be the deciding factor in whether or not a design not only functions, but has aesthetic appeal too.'[4]

This degree of rationality and mathematical precision is beyond me. My grey matter isn't up to it, and I'm assaulted by images of myself in maths classrooms struggling with numeracy while others filled pages with complex equations and answered questions without hesitation. But I know how to use a pencil, and so my attempts at formulating a grid always begin with sketching. I try to arrive at a grid that is determined by content (headlines, sub headings, pull quotes, pictures, etc.), and by functionality (what the content is meant to do), but also by aesthetics (the need for visual interest). For me, a grid comes out of a juggling act

> **Grids are determined by what we put into them (content) and what we require them to deliver (functionality), and only when we have defined the content and functionality, can we hope to arrive at an appropriate grid.**

between these three factors. Neglect one of them, and we end up with a grid that fails.

I instinctively gravitate towards the Rule of Thirds: by intuition I divide space into blocks of one-third ratio to two-thirds. But I don't measure this; I sketch it. In my hand-drawn, mini layouts I try to approximate the accuracy that can be achieved with software, but I don't go to the computer until the design is fully (or nearly fully) realized on paper. It's a bit like assembling flat-pack furniture. We lay out all the components on the floor and start assembling the larger bits, taking care not to screw anything together too tightly in case we have to undo it. Only at the end do we tighten everything up to make the piece of furniture rigid and self-supporting.

A grid is fundamentally about spatial relationships. Every spatial relationship needs to be considered.

For me, a grid is fundamentally about spatial relationships. Every spatial relationship needs to be considered. Putting together the internal bracing of a layout is one of the great joys of design, and once all the relationships are in place – arrived at through the examination of all the factors involved – we are free to take as many liberties with the grid as possible.

Grid-based design is being re-evaluated in the context of web design. There is now a vital area of visual communication where the graphic designer is no longer fully in control of his or her grids. Web users can change fonts, sizes and column widths, not to mention varying screen ratios, browsers and resolutions – and the problems that come with attempts to align horizontal elements in web pages. Most web grids are vertical and the horizontal is discounted; and in the era of multi-platform publishing – when websites have to be viewable on mobile phones, for example – the notion of a grid being anything other than entirely vertical is almost unthinkable.

For many clients, grids have become templates. They are highly usable, idiot-proof systems that allow anyone (often non-designers) to lay out text and images. The result is the death of the notion of the grid as a living breathing structure, and the establishment of the idea of the grid as a rigid structure that anything can be poured into.

Further reading: Josef Müller-Brockmann, Grid Systems in Graphic Design. Arthur Niggli (bilingual edition), 1996.

1 Roxane Joubert, *Typography and Graphic Design*. Flammarion, 2006.
2 French type engraver known for roman and italic types called Romain du Roi.
3 Richard Hollis, *Swiss Graphic Design*. Laurence King Publishing, 2007.
4 Mark Boulton, *Five simple steps to designing grid systems*. www.markboulton.co.uk/journal/comments/simple_steps_to_designing_grids

H

Handwriting/calligraphy

The handwritten message is the most elemental form of graphic communication. Calligraphy, on the other hand, is a noble art with its own culture and traditions. Yet it's rare to see either used convincingly in modern graphic design. They tend to signal ersatz authenticity.

Since the arrival of Modernism in the early half of the twentieth century, design has been joined at the hip to technology. The Modernist movement in design and art was partly a response to the arrival of industrialization, and modern graphic design developed in strict parallel with industrial production techniques. Today, it walks shoulder to shoulder with digital technology.

One of the many consequences of design's marriage to mechanical reproduction techniques is that hand lettering is viewed sniffily by most designers. Its grown-up sibling, calligraphy (literally, beautiful writing), is regarded as only slightly more acceptable, but it is widely seen as an amateurish craft closer to knitting than the sophisticated practice of typography: after all, everyone can write a few words or make a symbolic scribble, but not everyone – even in the age of the personal computer – can make properly formulated typographic statements.

Professional calligraphers will bristle at this. They will say that within calligraphy there is a rich historical tradition (much older than typography) with a set of stylistic codes, and a range of demanding techniques that have to be learnt formally. Calligraphy even has its own technology: brushes, pens, inks and papers. In the Far East, it is a fine art. Jan Tschichold understood this, and towards the end of his life he made a study of oriental calligraphy.

Calligraphy was once common on signage, and on shop fronts and window displays, but today it rarely intersects with the professional world of graphic design. When it is used, it tends to be used in rarefied, oddball contexts such as New Age literature, or the personalized gift market. The calligrapher Bernard Maisner is often asked

to re-create lettering styles in Hollywood films (he's worked for Tim Burton and Martin Scorsese). In an interview, he noted: 'On the subject of signs, one of the saddest things to me about the demise of hand lettering and the rise of computer-generated font/signage is the absolute ugliness of current signage in society. Sign painters were so talented and creative, and their genius truly beautified shops and public streets. Look at photographs of old New York and Paris and small-town America – the signs were gorgeous. Walk up and down the street now, and with all our developed technology, modern signage is profoundly ugly.'[1]

I've often been asked by clients to render certain messages in handwriting. They suggest this because they imagine it will signal intimacy. But it's rarely a good idea.

Calligraphy may be a diminishing art form, but handwriting is alive and well. Statements rendered as handwriting can be seen widely in advertising where the smack of the authentic is often required. What we see in advertisements and other commercial settings tends not to be 'real handwriting': it is usually heavily doctored to give it a fluid elegance, which often works against the need to be authentic. Many clients are instinctively drawn to handwriting because they understand it in a way they don't understand typefaces. I've often been asked by clients to render certain messages in handwriting. They suggest this because they imagine it will signal intimacy. But it's rarely a good idea; for most designers, hyper-attuned to the nuances of typographic semiotics, there is always the danger that informality and intimacy are replaced by amateurishness and sentimentality.

Handwriting and calligraphy may be relegated to the marginalia of graphic design, but hand-drawn letterforms are suddenly everywhere. I'm talking about hand-rendered versions of well-known typefaces, or freely drawn letterforms that sidestep the mechanical precision of type. They are especially prevalent in book-jacket design where the tone of a book – humour, for example – can be easily expressed by zany hand-rendered lettering. The covers for 'chick lit' books are especially prone to hand-drawn letterforms. Yet these renderings tend not to be done by graphic designers: they are mostly the work of illustrators, and are an example of illustrators capitalizing on modern graphic designers' unwillingness to use hand-rendered elements in their work.

For many illustrators, hand-rendered text is now an established part of their repertoire. The British illustrator Paul Davis pioneered an elegant style of hand lettering (semi-formal but also full of the quirks and

Above
Project: *Constance* book
Date: 2008
Client: Jonathan Ellery
Designer: Jonathan Ellery/Browns
Slipcase and spread from catalogue produced to accompany *Constance*. Both poster and book demonstrate Ellery's elegant and distinctive use of his own handwriting.

Previous page
Project: *Constance* poster
Date: 2008
Client: Jonathan Ellery
Designer: Jonathan Ellery/Browns
One of two A0-size posters designed to promote *Constance*, a live performance by Jonathan Ellery, first exhibited at the Wapping Project in London.

irregularities that can be achieved only through hand-rendered reproduction). This is not new in illustration, but it's one of the ways illustrators are asserting themselves in visual communications at a time when graphic design is dominant (see Illustration, page 149). Designers will continue to be cautious in their use of calligraphy and handwriting, but when hand lettering is used by someone as adept as Davis it seems odd that his example is not more widely followed.

Further reading: www.ejf.org.uk (The Edward Johnston Foundation).

1 'The Hand Is Mightier Than the Font: An Interview with Bernard Maisner', Steven Heller. www.aiga.org/content.cfm/the-hand-is-mightier-than-the-font-bernard-maisner

Helvetica

For some designers, Helvetica is the democratic and rational solution to all typographic tasks. For others it is a problematical typeface that smacks of authoritarianism and sterility. Yet for most designers, it is a handy fall-back option that gets us out of typographic jams.

Overleaf
Project: Weight series (Helvetica) T-shirts
Date: 2007
Client: www.blanka.co.uk
Designer: Mark Blamire — Neue
Range of T-shirts designed for the 50th anniversary of Helvetica. The weight of the typeface determines the size of the garment or the weight of the user. The shirts were available at the Blanka website, which is run by designer Mark Blamire. The shirts sold out soon after their launch.

First, a history lesson. Helvetica (originally called Neue Haas Grotesk) was created in 1957 by the Swiss designer and typeface salesman Max Miedinger, with assistance from Eduard Hoffmann, his boss at the Haas type foundry in Switzerland. Haas spotted a need for a modern alternative to Akzidenz Grotesk, and Helvetica's parentage can be clearly seen in this venerable typeface.

Neue Haas Grotesk was considered an unsuitable name for the international market, and in 1960 Haas' German parent company, Stempel, changed it to Helvetica — derived from Confederatio Helvetica, the Latin name for Switzerland. With its smart new name, and the whiff of clean Swiss mountain air, not to mention the mechanical precision of its seemingly perfect letterforms, Helvetica conquered the world. Today it is one of the most widely used typefaces, and 50-plus years after its inception it is the alpha-font; the big beast that stands for order, discipline and the elimination of chaos.[1] There's even been a film made about it.[2]

But it's not without its share of controversy. For some, Helvetica is the only typeface – the *ne plus ultra* of typefaces. A symbol of order in a world of chaos. Yet for others Helvetica is soulless and mechanistic, and is part of the discredited Modernist doctrine of authoritarianism and inflexibility. In the 1970s, Helvetica along with the International Style became the default style of corporate America, and as a consequence it was also seen by many as a typeface associated with capitalistic power and authoritarianism.

Helvetica is undoubtedly a great modern typeface, and its ubiquity is testament to its rugged durability and its imperviousness to fashion and stylistic fads. But here's

Helvetica looks best in single-word applications or short phrases. When it is used in a mix of sizes and weights its fabled robustness tends to evaporate.

1 In a 1972 essay for the *Village Voice*
entitled 'This Typeface is Changing Your
Life', the writer Leslie Savan wrote about
the impact of Vignelli's work for New York's
Metropolitan Transportation Authority: 'In
contrast to the subway's filth and potential
for violence, the cleanly and crisply
lettered signs lend a sense of authority.
They assure us that the train will come and
diminish the chaos created by the graffiti-
scrawled walls.' Reprinted in Michael
Bierut, Jessica Helfand, Steven Heller and
Rick Poynor (eds), *Looking Closer 3: Classic
Writings on Graphic Design*. Allworth Press,
1999.
2 *Helvetica*. A documentary film directed by
Gary Hustwit. DVD released on Plexi Film.

the thing: it's a surprisingly difficult typeface to use.
Helvetica is unforgiving. It looks best in single-word
applications or short phrases. As soon as it is used in
a mix of sizes and weights its fabled robustness tends
to evaporate. It is also a typeface that requires
immaculate kerning: poor kerning drains it of its
mechanistic perfection.

Personally, I prefer its ageing parent Akzidenz,
which has all the clarity of Helvetica but retains a
warmth and intimacy that the newer typeface lacks.

Further reading: www.helveticafilm.com

History of design

**What's the value of design
history? Can we learn from the
past, or is its value in the
opportunity it gives us to
plunder design's back catalogue?
Is it possible to be a good
designer and know nothing about
history? Or does knowledge of the
past better equip us to deal with
the future?**

When I started working as a designer I didn't know any
design history. I was interested in art and knew that
artists had manifestos, and that they belonged to schools
of thought and had personal philosophies. I didn't realize
there were designers who had philosophical approaches
to design. As a result I had no design ethos myself, no
personal philosophy, and it was only when I dipped my toe
into the pool of design history that I began to develop a
personal design philosophy.

There is nothing wrong with not having a personal
philosophy; but without one we are unlikely to produce
work that has any value beyond the purely pragmatic. To
go beyond the pragmatic we need to develop a philosophy
of design. And we acquire this by firstly identifying the
things that matter to us, and secondly by studying the
drift and flux of history.

According to the writer and academic Francis
Fukuyama, we have now reached the 'end of history'.[1]
Fukuyama states that thanks to the ending of the Cold
War and the supremacy of liberal democracy, there are
no more lessons to be learnt from it. This view has its
supporters, not least in the business sector. At the
height of the dotcom boom it was said that employers in
the new digital industries had no interest in employing

Above and overleaf
Project: Saks Fifth Avenue 2009 Spring Want
It! Campaign
Date: Spring 2009
Client: Saks Fifth Ave
Designer: Studio Number One
Creative Direction: Shepard Fairey and
Florencio Zavala
Art Direction, Design and Illustration:
Cleon Peterson
Example of how historical motifs –
in this instance taken from Russian
Constructivism – are used in modern
commercial settings without any sense
of disjuncture. The plundering of design
history is routinely done throughout
contemporary graphic design.

anyone over twenty-five. This was not because the over-twenty-fives didn't know anything about digital technology; it was because the under-twenty-fives didn't know anything about anything, and were therefore predisposed to thinking and functioning in a completely new and unrestricted way. Well, we all know what happened to the dotcom boom.

And yet there is something in the dotcom-ers argument. So many aspects of modern life have no precedent in history. Everywhere we look we see instances of the world transformed by advances in genetics, medicine and digital culture. This morning I heard on the radio that mobile phone masts will soon cover Africa. When mobile phones appeared as a consumer product in the 1980s they were a luxury item used by affluent Westerners. Yet a few decades later, Africa is the fastest-growing market for mobile phones. Nothing in history has happened on this scale and with this speed. What possible lessons can we learn from a study of history?

I resisted the history of design for a long time. I felt comfortable with the contemporary: I liked the cool and the new; old was dull. I imagined that the only people who were interested in design history were people who had nothing left to say, or who were frightened of the new and sought sanctuary in the past. I also equated history with conservatism and reactionary thinking. But the route that had taken me to the history of pop music eventually encouraged me to study design history. I had noticed that all the musicians I liked had musical heroes they were always willing to talk about. I was impressed with the way they spoke about these men and women with candour and a lack of subterfuge. Gradually I reached a point where I only respected and liked the music of musicians who had assimilated identifiable influences into their work. There was something shallow about anyone who had no reference points. Designers, with their traditional reluctance to name people who have influenced them in case they are labelled copyists, were slower to cite reference points. Yet over time it became fashionable to talk about influences, and for me this opened the cellar door of history.

For many designers, an encounter with the greatest hits of the past can provide the key to our own aesthetic and philosophical visions of the world. It's not about copying; it is more about being signposted to what is already inside us.

For most creative practitioners the benefits of history are purely visual. We look at great work from the past, and with our eye for graphic booty we see things we can use in our own work. This is the post-Modern 'plunder'

theory of history. As it becomes harder and harder to do something new, designers are forced to synthesize the past. Some do it with panache and inventiveness; others do it like masked raiders in a jewellery store.

Yet for many designers (I include myself in this group) an encounter with the greatest hits of the past – or even some of design's dark neglected crevices – can provide the key to our own aesthetic and philosophical visions of the world. It's not about copying (although it may start as that); it is more about being signposted to what is already inside us. In an essay about the benefits of teaching the history of design, Steve Heller writes that students should know how to 'research and analyze design's history, how to apply their historical knowledge in critical analyses about contemporary design, how to collect artifacts, and how to write history. They should understand the intertwining, ongoing influences of design, art, politics, culture, and technology. Schools should encourage design students to create not only a portfolio, but also a body of scholarship and critical writing.'[2]

But what practical help can we derive from knowledge of design history? Will it help us to get a better job? Will it help us to do better work? Will it help us to stop clients treating design like an aerosol spray that can be squirted on to any surface to provide instant sheen and gloss? Surprisingly the answer is: yes. Knowledge of design history can help us in many ways. By studying the way designers have grappled with creative, social, philosophical and practical issues in the past we will become better thinkers, and our own understanding of our craft will be enhanced. Although the world may be going through its most accelerated period of change, many fundamental aspects of life are unchanged. Problems that designers wrestled with four decades ago are still fundamental problems for designers today.

The most important benefit to be gained from studying design history (or for that matter any sort of history) is the discovery that far from being dead and carved in inert stone, it is in fact a living thing.

Perhaps, though, the most important benefit to be gained from studying design history (or for that matter any sort of history) is the discovery that far from being dead and carved in inert stone, it is in fact a living thing, and is only slightly less volatile than the future. As history is reassessed so it changes and is revivified. What we think to be one thing turns out to be something else.

1 www.sais-jhu.edu/faculty/fukuyama/
  Biography.html
2 www.typotheque.com/articles/design_history

Further reading: www.designhistory.org

Humour in design

As designers, are we too absorbed in our craft to notice anything beyond the world of design? Humour in graphic communication can be a powerful ingredient, yet it's rare to find it. Most graphic design is straight-faced. Odd really, because designers tend to be witty people in 'real life'.

For laughs and witty ideas within visual communication, we tend to look to advertising and not graphic design. When we talk about humour in graphic design we usually mean visual puns. But visual puns are like linguistic puns – briefly funny and quickly tedious.

In 2007, when a quirky, animated film clip called *Original Design Gangsta* appeared on the Internet,[1] it stirred up a mild furore in the design blogosphere. It caused designers to examine the notion of humour in design, and predictably this was done in a rather dour, stubble-stroking kind of way.

The clip is funny. Designer/illustrator Kyle T. Webster depicts himself as a rapper. But the geeky-looking Webster, a Moby lookalike with black-rimmed glasses and a shaved head, is no hardcore South Central rapper. He raps over cutesy, low-octane 'Garageband' beats: 'PMS 187 runs deep in my veins/Metallic 8643 in my gold chains/Got the RAM for the ladies in my G5 tower/when it comes to logos, homies call me Jack Bauer.'[2]

Is it funny? Yes. Does it bear repeated playing? Not really. Would non-designers find it amusing? Doubtful. A lengthy post about the clip by Armin Vit, the founder of hot design blog *Speak Up*, generated mounds of comments from earnest graphic designers. Vit declared his dislike of the clip, while design writer Steven Heller called it 'a pretty funny riff on rap'. Some commentators detected racist overtones, while others found it wildly funny. The most interesting thing about the *ODG* clip is Webster's willingness to use humour not just to raise a dry, designerish, ironic grin, but also to get a belly laugh.

Visual gags amuse us the first time round, yet their appeal rarely extends to a second viewing.

There's no question that designers know how to do 'dry and ironic', but what about other forms of humour? On the surface, there's not much humour in design, either in the big serious brand-based stuff or in the more style-conscious fashionable stuff. Of course, there are designers who employ humour. The late Alan Fletcher's work was full of the sort of wit many designers find amusing – but which often makes non-designers groan. Stefan Sagmeister and Michael Johnson both use humour in their work; Sagmeister's wit comes in a slightly darker hue than Johnson's, but both are capable of producing work that makes us laugh. Humour in design even has its own bible: *Smile in the Mind* is a perennial best-seller, and has become a sort of textbook for 'ideas-based' design. For many designers, witty puns and visual gags are graphic design at its best.

Visual gags amuse us the first time round, yet their appeal rarely extends to a second viewing. It's a feature

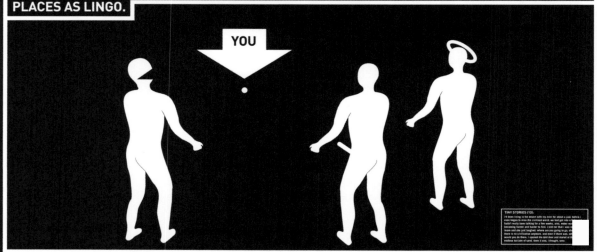

THIS IS NEW! THE UNBEATABLE CUSTOMER SERVICE:

WHAT WE NEED IS LANGUAGE

(LET'S CALL IT LINGO FOR NOW) LINGO IS YOUR FRIEND, MAYBE YOUR BEST FRIEND. IT IS A RESIDENT OF YOUR COUNTRY AND YOU BETTER RESPECT IT. EVERYDAY IT IS WITH YOU, NO MATTER IF IT SNOWS OR RAINS. AND BECAUSE IT IS ALWAYS AROUND YOU, IT IS GOOD FRIENDS WITH GOD HIMSELF AND SEX; OH YES, THESE TWO GUYS HANG AROUND THE SAME PLACES AS LINGO.

YOU

Above
Project: The Unbeatable Customer
Service stories
Date: ongoing
Client: Self-initiated
Designers: Jan Wilker, Hjalti Karlsson
Initially designed for their book *tellmewhy*,
humour has always played a part in New York-
based Karlssonwilker's approach to design
and communication. For a while their website
offered the consultancy for sale, using the
graphic language of cheap discount signage.

1 www.youtube.com/watch?v=QbF-SiCktCg
2 http://kyletwebster.com/

of humour that only the best and most witty stuff bears repeat exposure: even The Simpsons, a show with dazzling wit, needs a lengthy period of time to elapse before an episode stands up to repeat viewing.

Visual humour, too, can only rarely withstand repeat viewing, with the consequence that it is best avoided. Yet there's an irony in all this: designers in private tend to be witty; some of the funniest people I know are designers, but you wouldn't necessarily discover this from their work. Furthermore, designers share an important characteristic with comedians. The best comedy is based on acute observation of the everyday; the sharpest comedians are the ones who are able to look at the mundane and unlock an inner truth about what they see. And when you think about it, that's exactly what you have to do to be a sharp, relevant and effective graphic designer.

**Further reading: Beryl McAlhone and David Stuart,
A Smile in the Mind: Witty Thinking in Graphic Design.
Phaidon, 1998.**

Hyphens

The poor old hyphen – it's only a tiny horizontal bar, yet it causes more problems than just about any other typographical mark. It is common today to see a complete lack of understanding between hyphens and other types of dashes. But does it matter?

A friend of mine designed a brochure for his father-in-law, a silversmith. It was a bold and informative document, with a lot of text. My friend pointed out that his father-in-law had given him a firm instruction: no hyphenation. The result was hours of work massaging the text to ensure no hyphens. The result was impressive. The designer had used a long column measure, so the absence of hyphenation was barely noticeable. But the effect was rather like cosmetic surgery: you couldn't say what was wrong, but you knew something was fake.[1]

Hyphens may be tiny fragments of typographic detail, but they are a hot topic. When to hyphenate and when not to hyphenate vexes writers, editors, readers and the producers of style manuals. *The Economist Style Guide* devotes five pages to the subject. It is worth consulting, as are many of the other good style guides. *The Economist* lists some basic rules: always hyphenate fractions: two-thirds, four-fifths, etc. It advises hyphenating words with prefixes like 'ex' and 'anti': ex-husband, anti-freeze. It urges writers to use hyphens to avoid ambiguities like 'a little-used car' and 'a little used-car'.

For designers, the first lesson is to learn the difference between hyphens and en and em dashes. With desktop publishing, emails and web pages the distinction is becoming harder to maintain. Television captioning seems to have abandoned any attempt to distinguish between the various marks. Does it matter? Only when meaning and sense are distorted. If correct usage means we understand texts better it is important to maintain the differences.

So let's look at the differences between these three marks. An em dash (or long dash) is a unit of measurement defined as the point size of the font. So a 48-pt typeface has a 48-pt em dash. The en dash is half the size of the em dash. The em dash and en dash are both used for parentheses: I got into the car –/– it smelled new –/– and we drove off to the meeting. In the United States the em dash is preferred for this purpose, while in the UK the en dash is more commonly used with a space on either side. The en dash also stands in for the word 'to': 'from 2006 to 2009' appears as 2006–2007. The hyphen is normally a third of an em. It is short and stubby, and is used with no space on either side. It is used to link two words: round-up.

The first lesson is to learn the difference between hyphens, en and em dashes. With desktop publishing, emails and web pages the distinction is becoming harder to maintain.

Further reading: *The Chicago Manual of Style*, 15th edition. The University of Chicago Press, 2003.

1 I wrote these words before I had decided on the layout and typeface for this book. Due to the choice of Fedra Mono as the typeface I have ended up avoiding hyphenation of words. I did this because Fedra Mono is a monospace typeface, and works best – to my eyes anyway – when it is not hyphenated. The mechanical nature of the typeface seems best served by turning off hyphenation. I have allowed words that are already hyphenated to be broken at the hyphen.

I

Ideas

Ideas are widely regarded as the mental building blocks of design. But where do good ideas come from, and is there anything we can do to improve the quality of our ideas by training our minds like an athlete trains his or her body? Or are we stuck with what we've got?

I went to a lecture given by Storm Thorgerson, the album-cover artist. Thorgerson was the founder of Hipgnosis,[1] but since the 1980s he has worked under his own name, mainly for Pink Floyd but also for numerous other bands attracted to his surrealist art direction and heroic implementation of dramatic ideas. No digital fakery for him – when 700 hospital beds were needed for the cover of a Pink Floyd album,[2] he took 700 hospital beds to a beach in Devon, England, and photographed them. The Thorgerson *oeuvre* is full of such madcap and ambitious schemes.

Thorgerson began his lecture by asking for cabbages to be distributed to an audience of about 300 people. He then asked each person to hold a cabbage in front of his or her face. On the stage next to Thorgerson was a photographer who snapped 300 human torsos with cabbages obscuring their heads.

This struck me as a brilliant idea. But where did it come from? Was it a flash of inspiration, or did Thorgerson sit round a table with a group of people and thrash the idea out over a few hours? It seems unlikely that he devised it in a group session. It has the whiff of pure inspiration about it. But if great ideas are the product of a blinding flash of insight, how do the rest of us go about generating them? Is it easy to have great ideas when – as was the case with Thorgerson's lecture – we are 'writing our own briefs'. Is it more difficult to have ideas when we have a client with a brief and all the inherent restrictions that come with that?

I've always been drawn to the theory of an unconscious mind. I've always 'known' there was a part of me that works even when I'm asleep or when I'm thinking about other things. My unconscious mind feels as real to me as does my heart, lungs and liver – I can't see any of

these vital organs, but I know they're there. And I
also know the unconscious mind is where ideas come from,
and over time I've learnt to trust it and to treat it
with respect.

I've also learnt that you can't force ideas, and
that when anxiety builds up because of a looming deadline
or pressure from a client, the effect is to stem their
flow. We have to allow ideas to surface naturally – we
can't make them appear as if by magic. I always try and
allow problems – creative or practical – to percolate
down into my unconscious mind, confident that I'll get
a solution of sorts.

Sometimes I get a lot of ideas quickly. I find
these very seductive and often want to implement them
immediately. But when I look at them closely I'm usually
disappointed. It turns out that
I've failed to see a flaw, or that
an idea is not original, or it is
simply not good enough. Occasionally
the perfect idea arrives oven-
ready – but usually ideas come in
different states of completeness:
sometimes they emerge perfectly
formed, other times they emerge in
scraps and fragments. Sometimes the
response is too slow and we have to
find ways to accelerate the process.

The best ideas are usually made better by other people. Allowing someone, in an informal conversation or in a more formalized group session, to jump on an idea, to add to it, to remix it, even to trash it, usually means that an idea develops and grows.

The work of the English
designer Daniel Eatock[3] is driven by
mental concepts and not by style.
The quality of his thinking is
what draws us to his work. He is a Conceptualist, and
his approach to generating ideas is unusual. Rather than
relying on flashes of inspiration he has accumulated an
'archive' of ideas that he applies to projects he is asked
to undertake. 'If you only look for ideas when you need
them,' he says, 'you will soon get stuck. However, if
you constantly try to generate them and connect things
by making juxtapositions of thoughts, alignments, and by
embracing coincidences, they will be there in abundance.
With a little practice most people can have good ideas.
That's the easy bit; choosing which one to make is the
difficult task.'

I've worked with Eatock, and his 'system' functions
surprisingly well. Given a design brief he scans his
archive and finds ideas that answer it. But anyone who
uses this approach needs a good and extensive archive,
and this means generating ideas constantly. To build up
an archive of ideas means never switching off.

For me, and I suspect most other designers, ideas
come mainly when we are faced with a brief. For ideas to

emerge, we need the stimulus of a brief. And what's more, ideas usually need to be dragged out. The best way to 'drag ideas out' is in a group 'brainstorming' session. Alex Osborn formulated this concept in the late 1930s. An advertising man, Osborn proposed that groups could increase their creative output by using a few simple techniques and rules. He maintained there should be an emphasis on 'quantity of ideas' rather than quality, that there should be no criticism of ideas, that unusual ideas were welcome, and that combining ideas produced better ideas.

But group sessions don't always produce results. Not every designer is suited to the group situation. Sometimes individual designers tighten up when asked to exchange ideas, and it becomes clear that they don't like sharing the authorship of ideas. I've also encountered designers who come to sessions with an idea already formed in their heads and can't be budged from it, or can't open up enough to let some additional thinking expand it. This problem is best dealt with by establishing a studio culture where authorship of ideas is shared. However, a sharing ethos can't be arbitrarily introduced; it has to be worked on and its benefits have to be demonstrated. Of course, there are certain creative people who simply don't function in group sessions and they shouldn't be forced to do so.

Most designers look at books when they want ideas. Others pound through the Internet. This is fine. But we should force ourselves to go to unlikely books and unlikely places in cyberspace; if we are all looking at the same hip design books we mustn't be surprised if everything we do looks the same as everything else.

Away from the group session how else can we encourage ideas to emerge? I've always found sketching to be conducive to good ideas. And I'm not just talking about mapping out visual ones. I'm talking about the gear that the brain slips into when we draw; it seems to encourage ideas to flow. Aimless sketching works for me but we each have our own technique. Most designers look at books when they want ideas. Others pound through the Internet. This is fine. But we should force ourselves to go to unlikely books and unlikely places in cyberspace; if we are all looking at the same hip design books we mustn't be surprised if everything we do looks the same as everything else.

What about when an idea refuses to emerge? When this happens it is a sign that there's a handbrake on, and we need to take drastic action to loosen it. This kind of 'block' is a common occurrence and we shouldn't punish ourselves for feeling stuck or uninspired, especially

Previous pages
Project: Cabbage Heads
Date: 2008
Art Director: Storm Thorgerson
Photographer: Rupert Truman
(www.rupert-truman.com)
Photograph taken at Bafta, London, during a talk by Storm Thorgerson, as part of paper manufacturer Howard Smith's lecture series. Each member of the capacity audience was invited to place a cabbage in front of his or her face. The resulting photograph by Rupert Truman – who has collaborated on numerous Thorgerson projects – was sold as a digital print at the end of the evening.

if we are under pressure to come up with a great many ideas in a short space of time.

I've always found the confessional approach useful: when I'm stuck I tell someone – a colleague or sympathetic person, even a client – and this often has a dramatic unblocking effect because up until then I've been in denial and refused to believe I was stuck. Owning up often loosens the mental handbrake.

At my old company Intro we used the group session extensively (though not exclusively). In discussions we found that films became a useful trigger point. This was partly because we did a lot of moving image work, but also because movies were a shared enthusiasm that allowed us to trade references to styles and emotions, which in turn led to interesting conclusions about photography, imagery and colour.

But regardless of where ideas come from, the best ones are usually made better by other people. Allowing someone, in an informal conversation or in a more formalized group session, to jump on an idea, to add to it, to remix it, even to trash it, usually means that an idea develops and grows.

Further reading: Daniel Eatock, *Daniel Eatock Imprint*. Princeton Architectural Press, 2008.

1 Hipgnosis was a British design group founded by Storm Thorgerson and Aubrey Powell. They created surrealistic album-cover art for Pink Floyd, Led Zeppelin and Black Sabbath among countless other bands. The group dissolved in 1982.
2 *A Momentary Lapse of Reason*, Pink Floyd (EMI), 1987.
3 Examples of Daniel Eatock's thinking can be viewed at his website: www.danieleatock.com

Illustration

Graphic design and illustration used to sleep in the same bed; today they sleep in separate rooms. This is odd, because many designers crave the freedom of expression enjoyed by illustrators, and many are doing work that looks like illustration. What is illustration today?

As graphic designers, we mostly have to work with the content our clients give us, then – like actors – we are required to slip into a 'role' and convey a message in the style or tone of voice dictated to us by the content. For example, if we are designing a poster for a discount furniture store we will be expected to 'shout', but if we are designing a flyer for our local poetry society we might be asked to adopt a more reflective tone. Most graphic design is about suppressing notions of personal expression in favour of objective neutrality.

Illustrators, on the other hand, are also given a brief but they are encouraged to use their own voices and deploy their own styles. Occasionally, they are asked to work in a particular style, but it is uncommon for them to be asked to adopt one that is not their own. As the American designer Ed Fella noted: 'Whereas graphic design is more anonymous, all illustration is sold for its particular and individual style.'

This seems to me to be illustration's great strength. It's true that some designers sell themselves on their individual stylistic and conceptual approaches – 'I'll do it my way or not at all', they tell their clients – but this is rare and is confined to a handful of designers with the creative flair and muscular personalities

Above
Project: Spirits of the Storm
Date: 2008
Client: Self-initiated
Illustrator: Jasper Goodall
Goodall is an influential British
illustrator. This image is a limited-edition
screen print using gloss UV ink. It is part
of a series of images depicting guardian
spirits or personifications of nature. In
this instance, the poster has an African
theme. www.jaspergoodall.com

required to persuade clients to give them the necessary
licence. When compared to illustrators, graphic designers
are far less likely to be engaged in self-expression.
But for illustrators it's the norm, and in my view this
means the best illustration eclipses most forms of visual
communication. Strange, therefore, that over the past two
or three decades illustration has steadily retreated from
a position of centrality in visual communication to one
of marginality.

This is partly explained by the way graphic designers
have come to own the visual landscape. From the 1970s
onwards, big professionally focused graphic design studios
reinvented design (previously a cottage industry in the
eyes of many business people) as an indispensable aid to
big business. That process accelerated throughout the
1980s with the result that designers are now in control
of corporate images and branding – the places where the
power and money are to be found. They have become their
clients' best friends, and as a consequence it's designers
and art directors who set the pace; it's designers and art

directors who decide whether illustration is appropriate; it's designers and art directors who decide who gets commissioned.

Typography is another factor in the eclipsing of illustration by graphic design. We are supposed to live in the age of image; we do, but most of the imagery we see conveys a commercial message, and very few commercial messages are delivered without words. Look at any televised sporting event. Apart from muscle-bound athletes, what do you see? Advertising billboards with words – brand names, product names, company names. Designers have created all these 'word logos', and they provide clients with the brand-based precision bombing that modern business strategies demand.

The apparent decline of illustration can also be partly attributed to the digital technology and software that in recent decades has enabled graphic designers to effortlessly make images, create collages and montages, and execute numerous visual sleights of hand that were previously the domain of illustrators.

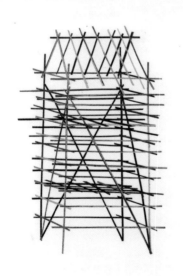

Above and opposite
Project: Tårn series
Date: 2008
Illustrator: Anne Harild
Anne Harild is a Danish artist and a graduate
of the Royal College of Art, London. Tårn
is an ongoing collection of towers, inspired
by vernacular architecture and primitive
structures. It is informed by textures
and materials put to imaginary use.

The final reason for design's overshadowing of illustration is that in the eyes of many clients (as well as art directors) illustration is dangerously imprecise – or to put it another way, it is regarded as less direct than typography and therefore less effective in the delivery of dictatorial branding and marketing messages. Practically, this means clients will trust graphic designers to deliver messages in a way that they rarely grant to illustrators.

Many illustrators have responded to graphic designers' dominance of visual communication by turning away from the fight. This is understandable. Illustrators mainly work on their own, and solitariness can lead to introspection and the development of an inward gaze. Graphic designers, on the other hand, generally work in studios and can hunt in packs. As a consequence, illustration has become the shy introvert, and graphic design has become the pushy extrovert.

This introversion, at least in the field of editorial illustration, has led many illustrators to be content with making 'literal' interpretations of editorial concepts. Under the guidance of art directors and editors, they simply depict an aspect of the text, with the result that illustration rarely rises above the level of decoration. How much better if more illustrators were willing to adopt the Brad Holland approach. In an interview for *Varoom* magazine he said: 'I work from a kind of pre-literary logic. It's like you've locked a writer and an artist in different rooms and given them the same assignment. One of them writes an article, the other draws a picture … I get called by magazines to do pictures for articles that haven't been written yet.'[1] It's this notion of the illustrator being an active rather than a passive contributor to the editorial process that is in danger of being lost as illustrators struggle with their diminished role in newspapers and magazines.

The craft of image-making no longer resembles the old cosy world of illustrators waiting by the phone to be briefed by sympathetic commissioners. Instead, illustration has headed off into new terrain. It is alive and well, and a leading force in pop culture, fashion and commerce.

Furthermore, illustration has not helped itself by its seeming reluctance to have the sort of passionate self-analytical debates that have characterized design in the past two decades. Attempts within the discipline to offer critiques of contemporary illustration are seen as being 'unsupportive'. But in fact the opposite is true. Without critical voices and self-analysis, illustration will continue to be seen as mere 'colouring in'.

Ironically, however, all this is happening at a time when illustration – or perhaps more accurately, image-making – is thriving as never before. Occasionally it finds a brave supporter in advertising. When an advertising campaign is illustration-based, the financial rewards for the illustrator can be generous, and the exposure can be dramatic.

But paradoxically the craft of image-making no longer resembles the old cosy world of illustrators waiting by the phone to be briefed by sympathetic commissioners. Instead, illustration has headed off into new terrain. It is alive and well, and a leading force in pop culture, fashion and commerce. You see it everywhere. Illustration is offering a genuine challenge to graphic design as the creative force most likely to engage people's attention. As mainstream graphic design develops an ever greater dependence on branding strategies, and becomes a sort of super-bland visual Esperanto foisted on to consumers by pushy corporations, illustration flourishes as a creative force people actually want in their lives.

The biggest irony of all is that some of the credit for this rise in illustration's popularity and cultural heft has to go to graphic designers. Pick up any design magazine from anywhere in the world and it will be full of illustration. Look closely, however, and you'll see that people who call themselves graphic designers are doing much of this work.

Today, we see countless examples of illustration and design being united in a way that harks back to the Constructivists and 1960s pioneers of visual communication like Push Pin. We also see illustrators taking control of lettering (see Handwriting/Calligraphy, page 135). The importance of illustration within visual communication is growing, too,

Illustration has not helped itself by its seeming reluctance to have the sort of passionate self-analytical debates that have characterized design in the past two decades.

as more and more clients re-evaluate its power to engage the emotions. With this revival has come a wholesale reassessment of what constitutes illustration. For me, a new expanded definition of the discipline now exists. Illustration is any sort of made image – and by 'made' I mean created by hand, machine or digital sorcery – that isn't pure photography.

1 Jo Davies, 'Pre-literary Logic, an interview with Brad Holland', *Varoom* 06. For a longer version see: www.varoom-mag.com/webonly/index.html

Further reading: Alan Male, *Illustration: A Theoretical and Contextual Perspective*. AVA Publishing, 2007.

In-house working

Working in-house rather than in an independent studio can have many advantages. But there are drawbacks too, and there is also the lingering sense that designers in independent studios are having more fun and getting more and better work. Not necessarily true, of course.

There are three principal types of employment for modern designers: we can work for an independent design studio; we can be freelance and work for a variety of clients; we can work in-house for a corporation, firm or institution. Before we look at the advantages and disadvantages of being an in-house designer, we should be clear about what is meant by the term. In-house designers are salaried employees working for employers in any sector that requires the dedicated services of a designer.

The advantages for designers are easily stated: a regular salary, fringe benefits, paid holidays and other perks of corporate life. But what about the 'spiritual' benefits? Is being an in-house employee beneficial for a designer's development and growth? Well, that depends. The main benefit is that it often gives designers the opportunity to work on a single or limited range of projects and thus refine and develop design skills without the distraction of constantly having to adapt to new conditions, new clients and new demands. It also – although not always – is a less precarious existence than working for a studio. In-house designers often have less anxiety and a more stable workflow than their independent counterparts.

Of course, there are in-house positions that give designers none of the advantages listed above. There are design hellholes that should be avoided in the way we avoid a mad dog in the street. But usually, working in-house provides designers with experiences that make them better-equipped for life in an independent design studio – or for when they set up on their own. In-house working allows novice designers to see how companies function from the inside, an insight that will prove invaluable when they come to deal with companies as clients. Witnessing at first hand the organizational structure of businesses, their chains of command, the way they make decisions, and their attitude to suppliers, can be highly educational. But we also learn that very few companies – and therefore clients – are entirely rational. Most revolve around conflicting egos and elaborate rituals that have to be negotiated and mastered. Working in-house can enable us to gain experience in dealing with the vagaries of corporate life, and can often be an essential step on the way to being a fully mature and competent designer.

In-house working allows novice designers to see how companies function from the inside, an insight that will prove invaluable when they come to deal with companies as clients.

Further reading:
www.aiga.org/content.cfm/guide-careerguide

Installations

Graphic design has traditionally been a 2-D art form, but not any more. Increasingly designers are engaged in making design that is 3-D. They haven't become sculptors – they've become makers of graphic installations. Installations are everywhere – museums, shops, etc.

Above and overleaf
Project: Forever video wall installation
Date: 2008
Client: Victoria & Albert Museum
Creative Direction: Matt Pyke,
Karsten Schmidt and Simon Pyke
Project Management: Philip Ward,
Universal Everything
Floating above the pond in the Victoria &
Albert Museum, London, is an installation
of animations responding to an ever-changing
soundtrack. The bespoke generative design
system at the heart of Forever spawns
unique audio-visual films everyday, forever.
In response to the pond, the sculpture
continually grows upwards from the water,
all movement stems from a central 'spine'
which reacts to the music. Viewable here:
http://universaleverything.com/

Whether it's on screen or on paper, there's something about the flatness of traditional graphic design – its essential 2-Dness – that contributes to the widely held view that it is about the surface of things and therefore, in the minds of many people, disposable and forgettable. Or to put it another way: superficial.

Long ago, the art world realized the limitations of flat, two-dimensional painting, and contemporary art moved into a more substantial world of 3-D installations. Artists made stuff you can walk round; they put sharks in glass tanks filled with formaldehyde; they wrapped buildings in giant tarpaulins; they put unmade beds surrounded by used condoms and bloodstained underwear into galleries. They called it installation art and viewers experienced it by being able to walk round it and touch it.

Exhibition design, museum design, signage and other forms of three-dimensional graphic design have existed for some time now. Creating installations to explain complex factual information, or to create entertaining, interactive or engaging points of reference in retail or gallery environments, has been commonplace since at least the 1950s.

Reviewing a book about the German graphic designer Will Burtin, Rick Poynor noted that Burtin was 'a figure as significant as the handful of heroes we tend to obsess over – Paul Rand, Josef Müller-Brockmann, Wim Crouwel – and in some respects even more interesting'.[1] Burtin fled Nazi Germany in disgust after Hitler repeated Goebbels' invitation that he become design director of the Nazi propaganda ministry. Burtin arrived in the USA vowing never to speak German again. In 1957, working for a pharmaceutical company, he proposed a giant model of a human cell. 'His walk-through model, one million times larger than life,' notes Poynor, 'was built out of plastic – nothing this complex had ever been made in the material – with one mile of electric wiring, and pulsing lights that made it look like the cell was alive. More than 10 million people visited the exhibit and in 1959 it was shown on the BBC.'

Today Burtin's work might be described as not 'interactive' enough. In our high-tech world, the need to explain must always be accompanied by some sort of interaction by the user. No museum or scientific visitor attraction is complete without its own immersive multimedia experience.

In our high-tech world, the need to explain must be accompanied by some sort of user interaction. No museum or scientific visitor attraction is complete without its immersive multimedia experience.

For most designers this means working in screen-based media. It means computer screens, plasma screens and video walls. It can also mean installations made out of more prosaic materials. English designers Why Not Associates created a series of typographic installations in the UK. Their famous Flock of Words moves typography into the third dimension. English designer Quentin Newark designed a fully functioning sundial embedded into the pedestrian area outside the Houses of Parliament in London.

The London-based installation specialists United Visual Artists (UVA) are pioneers of interactive installations that merge visual impact with sophisticated computer programming. They made their reputation by creating work for Massive Attack and U2 in concert venues. Their imaginative use of interactivity can be seen in Paris in Triptych, an installation which, as they say on their website, 'represents the next phase of UVA's explorations in monumental site-specific LED sculpture – three brooding presences that respond to the movements of people approaching them, creating a visceral experience of sound and light.'[2]

Increasingly, the role of the graphic designer is to create design that is tangible, design that can be experienced viscerally, and design that can be interacted within controlled environments. It has often been said that typography is like architecture, but now the link between graphic design and architecture is being cemented. In the entry on interface design in the *Design Dictionary* the following appears: '… media-related aspects of architecture are developed which function as membranes between the inside and outside (and vice versa) and form interactions with systems and products. The areas of application range from trade fairs, exhibitions and museums, to buildings that present processes and, consequently, become interfaces themselves. The interaction can take place using portable equipment (such as cellular phones), or via a person's movement through a room (their position and articulation in space).'[3]

Further reading: R. Roger Remington and Robert S. P. Fripp, *Design and Science: The Life and Work of Will Burtin*. Lund Humphries, 2007.

1 *The Model Designer*, reviewed by Rick Poynor, *Creative Review*, December 2007.
2 www.uva.co.uk
3 Michael Erlhoff and Timothy Marshall (eds), *Design Dictionary: Perspectives on Design Terminology*. Birkhäuser Basel, 2008.

Integrated design

The term 'integrated' has been used in design for some time. Today, integrated communications are the norm. But does it mean the end of specialists and the erosion of craft skills? Or is an ability to work simultaneously across different platforms the sign of a good designer?

In its annual awards scheme D&AD operates an 'integrated' category. It defines the term as a 'communication solution in which a strategic idea will have been applied seamlessly and adapted to a range of appropriate media channels.'[1] The American Marketing Association defines integrated as 'a planning process designed to assure that all brand contacts received by a customer or prospect for a product, service, or organization are relevant to that person and consistent over time'. In the new digital economy integrated communications are the norm.

In recent years it has become increasingly rare for designers to be asked to work on a project that exists only on one platform. Instead they are routinely asked to create work (and ideas) that function and coexist on various platforms. It is not uncommon to be asked to produce work that delivers a message in print and on a variety of screen-based applications; typically this might also involve sound, motion, interactivity and downloadable properties.

I recently worked on a logo project for a mobile phone manufacturer. I presented a range of ideas to my client on paper. I could sense her unease, and when she told me she envisaged no print applications whatsoever for the new logo I realized I'd made a mistake by presenting the work on paper, and that I should have presented it on a screen.

But just how embedded the integrated mentality has become was brought home to me by a conversation I had with a successful director of commercials. It seems that even the high-gloss world of television advertising is feeling the effect of the new integrated culture. My director friend had been hired by an advertising agency to direct a commercial featuring a premiership footballer. The sleek, pouting zillionaire (the footballer, not my friend) was available for one day only, and yet the director had to share him with an Internet film unit, a local radio interview crew, a stills photographer shooting PR shots and a second photographer sent by a book publisher.

What does the demand for integrated communications mean for creative professionals? Does it spell the end of craft and specialization in design, or is it the beginning of a new, fluid era of cross-media versatility?

In the past everything would have been subservient to the television commercial, but not any more. As a forward-thinking director, my friend is aware of the changes that are taking place in advertising and communications, and he embraces the notion of utilizing a variety of media platforms. Yet emotionally – and professionally – he remains wedded to the belief that all creative work should maintain the highest aesthetic and technical standards; but he is worried that these ideals will be eroded by what he calls the 'handheld coup d'état' of YouTube, and the lemming-like rush towards integrated communications.

What does the demand for integrated communications mean for creative professionals? Does it spell the end of craft and specialization in design, or is it the beginning of a new, fluid era of cross-media versatility? Inevitably, in the short term, the insatiable demand for integrated communications will lead to an erosion of standards. There are many advantages to the democratization of media – citizen journalism, and user-generated content have brought many benefits – but high production standards are not one of them. And yet design has been here before: with every new technological advance, with every change in media, designers have had to learn to adapt. And by and large they have done this. When Apple Macs arrived, it was common to see appalling typography. When the World Wide Web appeared, early websites looked as if they had been designed by prehistoric cave dwellers.

In both these cases, the challenge provided the incentive. Most designers knew that in order to improve they had to master new ways of thinking and working. In both the examples I've given, designers got to work and introduced the technical and aesthetic standards we know and relish today. I think the same has happened with integrated communications. Designers know that communications have to work in various media channels and this is sending them back to basics. Rather than causing a diminution of standards, it is actually causing designers to value individual skills, and we are being forced to utilize the talents of different disciplines such as computing and engineering.

Further reading: Robyn Blakeman, *Integrated Marketing Communication: Creative Strategy from Idea to Implementation*. Rowman & Littlefield, 2007.

1 Design and Art Direction (www.d&ad.com).

Interactive design

All graphic design is interactive. But it's only recently become interactive in the sense that users can determine the way content is perceived, arranged, used and generated. Inevitably this involves a new design psychology, and a new way of approaching design tasks.

Interactivity, made possible by ever-advancing technology, is the most important development in graphic design since the arrival of movable type. It has changed the nature of being a designer more profoundly than any other modern development in the craft. Overnight, design went from addressing passive spectators with 'locked down' content, to allowing users to 'use' the content – even generating their own content, as has happened with blogging and user-generated TV channels.[1]

You could argue that ever since handwritten proclamations were nailed to trees in medieval times design has been about interactivity. Readers interact with messages in the sense that they read them and derive information from them. However, short of ripping down the poster and/or scribbling over it, the user can't interact with the poster beyond reading it and acting on the information it contains. This is interaction, but it is of a passive kind. But with the new interactive technology genuine interaction is possible: content can be interrogated and reconfigured in a way that has revolutionized both the way designers think and act, and the way audiences behave.

We only have to contemplate websites that allow social interaction on a global scale (Facebook, MySpace, Bebo); or the broadcast industry's reliance on user-generated content in reporting the news; airline websites that allow customers to check-in online and even choose seats; exhibitions and galleries that allow visitors to participate in exhibitions and displays. These and other interactive possibilities are among the great technological advances of the modern era. Imagine life without the ability to use interactivity to manage our lives – it's unthinkable.

And yet what is the role of the designer in all this? Does interactivity mean the end of authoritatively crafted messages, in favour of complete usability? Or does this new demand for limitless interactivity mean that graphic design has reached its final destination as the selfless delivery medium for every sort of digital message?

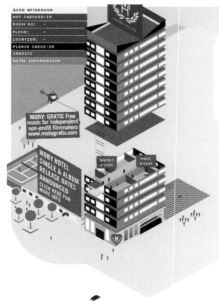

Above
Project: Moby Hotel
Date: 2005
Client: Mute Records
Designer: Studio Tonne
Interactive virtual hotel to support the
release of Moby's album *Hotel*. There is
a variety of interactive features ranging
from tennis on the lawn to one which
allows 'guests' to make their own tracks
using Moby's songs.
www.studiotonne.com/www.mobyhotel.com

1 Current TV is the first 24-hour network
based around viewer-created content.
http://current.com/

The question facing modern designers is how do we ensure the highest standards of presentation when we give control of the content to the users? Product designers and architects have been fighting this battle for decades. Like graphic designers they set the form and the function, but it is nearly always possible for users of products and buildings to change the function, and hence the form. If we don't like a building we can paint it a different colour; if we don't like the design of a car we can customize it. This gives the best product designers and architects humility, and a sense of social responsibility.

Up until now, graphic design has not been this straightforward. We haven't needed much humility, because traditionally we have had control over the content we present. Whatever we serve up (or whatever we can persuade our clients to accept) is what goes. But when we allow the content to be interacted with – shaped, manipulated and used as the user sees fit – we are on less familiar ground. With interactivity, function becomes more complex. Function in the context of interactivity takes graphic design closer to product design and architecture.

Graphic designers are mostly involved in human-computer interaction, which means a person interacting with a screen. But how well-equipped are we to design for this sort of human-machine interactivity? ATM machines are a good example. There are so many things to take into consideration: security, ease of use, colour of screens, typography and branding, not to mention ergonomic considerations such as height from the ground and illumination. Already we have strayed a long way from the designer sitting at his or her desk arranging and rearranging graphic elements to make a pleasing poster or effective leaflet.

Does the demand for interactivity mean that graphic design has finally reached its final destination as the selfless delivery medium for every sort of digital message?

If we are to work as interaction designers we will increasingly have to work with other practitioners from non-design disciplines: cognitive psychologists, sociologists, product designers, engineers and computer scientists. In other words, we have to recognize that interactive design involves other people and other skills. As Bill Moggridge says in his excellent book *Designing Interactions*: 'We are better equipped to face the complexity as an interdisciplinary team, with a collective consciousness, and the ability to create designs as a group or a team rather than as individuals.'

Further reading: Bill Moggridge, *Designing Interactions*. MIT Press, 2006.

Internships

**Internships are now an
established part of the design
landscape. For most graduates
there is no alternative to an
internship as a first step on
the career ladder. But are all
internships good, or are some
exploitative and a waste of time?
And how do we tell the good ones
from the bad ones?**

The AIGA's excellent online guide on the subject of
internships offers this definition: 'A temporary job at a
design studio that is geared toward an upper-level student
or recent graduate. Studios may hire interns to assist on
a specific project or for a set amount of time, such as
the summer or a semester. Students and young designers
often develop their practice by broadening their education
with a mentor, while gaining experience in a professional
design environment. Sponsoring design studios benefit from
each intern's unique approach, perspective and assistance
during the creative process.'

This is the way it should be. But the reality is
sometimes different. As with most things in life, there
are good internships (they follow the model outlined
above), and there are bad ones (unscrupulous studios
see interns as cheap labour, and offer no mentoring or
instruction). I've said elsewhere in this book that there
is no such thing as a bad job in a designer's first few
years of employment (see Employment, page 107). We learn
more from bad experiences than good
ones. But internships are different:
graduates accept them because they
have become an unavoidable step on
the ladder to a career, but the only
internships worth having are ones where
the graduate receives help, advice,
guidance and practical experience.
Not all offers of internships are worth
accepting, and graduates have to learn
to spot the ones that aren't.

**If a studio
is not even
prepared to pay
for an intern's
travel, then
be wary. It
may still be
a worthwhile
opportunity, but
it is much less
likely to be so
than the studio
with a proper
policy towards
internships,
and a commitment
to paying
something.**

Let's look at what we can expect
from a good internship. The internee
should emerge with some direct
experience of working in a professional
environment. They should be given a
place to work, and allowed to shadow
experienced designers. They should be
given some mentoring, and should have
the opportunity to attend meetings and
presentations as an observer and occasional participant.
They should be given insight into professional and ethical
matters. They should be shown the mechanics of studio
life and given a fast-track course in studio etiquette.
They should be given as much practical work as possible
(nothing wrong with a bit of drudgery), and they should
have the opportunity to produce some work they can call
their own. They should also be paid – either travel
expenses or a nominal sum to avoid starvation.

What can we expect from a bad internship? In some
studios interns are dumped in a corner and given menial
tasks that allow full-time staff to do other more

productive ones. I spoke to one young designer recently and asked her what she had done on an internship with a well-known London studio: 'Everything that no one else wanted to do,' was her reply. In studios that view interns as cheap labour, the intern will be ignored and given no practical instruction, and will receive no guidance on professional or ethical matters. Furthermore, the intern in a bad studio is unlikely to be offered remuneration.

For me, this is the acid test. If a studio is not even prepared to pay for an intern's travel, I'd be wary. It may still be a worthwhile opportunity, but it is much less likely to be so **The internee should** than the studio with a proper **emerge with some** policy towards internships, and **direct experience** a commitment to paying something. **of working in** But just as there is a **a professional** responsibility on studios to **environment.** offer meaningful and beneficial internships, there is also a responsibility on interns to perform well. Most studios – big and small – are under pressure from punishing deadlines. They do not have unlimited time to devote to interns. Those interns who recognize this and make themselves available, who show willingness and enthusiasm, will get more attention than those who sit around waiting to be told what to do. I've employed both sorts of interns, and the former are far more likely to receive benefits from an internship.

Further reading: www.aiga.org/content.cfm/a-guide-to-internships

Italics and obliques

Italic and oblique letterforms give variety and colour to text, and provide a way of distinguishing or emphasizing words and sentences. When used large, they can add elegance and drama to layouts. But do we really need italic and oblique alphabets, and what's the difference between them?

Italics first appeared in the fifteenth century, during the Italian Renaissance. The earliest italic letterforms were lower case only and were never mixed with roman ones. It wasn't until the sixteenth and seventeenth centuries that typographers committed the heresy of combining italic and roman letterforms in the same line. Italic typefaces slope to the right, most at around 10 degrees. Their cursive flourishes betray their calligraphic origins.

Italic letterforms (or 'true italics' as they are sometimes called) have been drawn so that they are clearly differentiated from upright roman letters, and shouldn't be confused with oblique typefaces, which are usually sans serif alphabets that have been redrawn in sloped versions. If you look at the oblique and roman versions of a sans serif typeface such as Futura you will see that both versions closely resemble each other. But look at the italic and roman versions of, say, Baskerville, and you will note that both versions are quite different, though

Above
Project: The Italic Poster
Date: 2008
Client: Self-initiated
Designer: Eivind Molvaer
Photographer: Sven Ellingen
Witty poster by designer Eivind Molvaer.
Technically, it should be called The
Oblique Poster. www.eivindmolvaer.com

obviously related. Some modern sans serif typefaces such as Nexus Sans come in customized italic versions.

There's a third sort of italic: today, in the era of computerized typesetting, we can slope any typeface in any direction we choose. But to retain typographic integrity typefaces should not be artificially italicized. Good typographers avoid this like a gourmet avoids shellfish poisoning.

So when is it right to use an italic or an oblique font? Most newspapers and magazines italicize book titles. For example, it can often be hard to know when a film title is being referred to in a sentence unless it is italicized. But house styles vary. The *Guardian* newspaper, for example, doesn't italicize titles. If it wants to refer to a movie called *The Time is Now*, it does so by using initial caps, and only rarely is this confusing. In recent years, due to the stylistic influence of the Internet, it is not uncommon to see titles differentiated by being underlined with a thin rule. Sometimes they are highlighted by blocks of colour.

In general, as typography becomes freer and less bound by tradition, italics and obliques are used with creative verve. Today we are free to use both styles as we see fit. One or two worthwhile rules persist, however. It's rare to see italic typefaces used in all caps. You might get away with it using obliques, but not italics. The other rule is never use software to artificially slope a roman typeface. Far better to chop your hands off and stick your head in boiling oil.

If you look at the oblique and roman versions of a sans serif typeface such as Futura you will see that both versions closely resemble each other. But look at the italic and roman versions of, say, Baskerville, and you will note that both versions are different.

Further reading: http://typophile.com/node/12475?

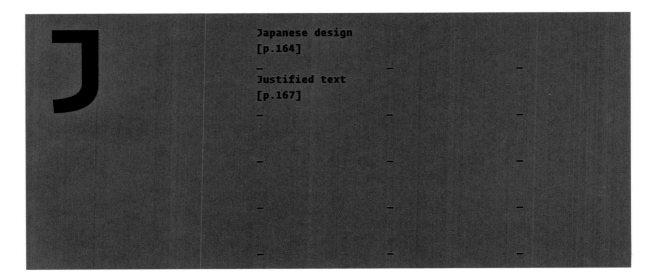

Japanese design

For Western graphic designers Japan is an enchanted land where everything is graphically interesting, and the visual impact is profound and lasting. But what's so special about Japanese design that makes it so compelling to Western eyes? Is it really so different?

All Western designers should be sent to Japan as part of their education. I've never known a designer to return from Japan without having his or her mind blown. 'Mind blown' is a lazy cliché, but it's the only phrase that adequately describes the effect of Japanese graphic culture on Western designers; any designer who visits Japan and doesn't experience this effect should immediately consider a career in pension planning or accountancy.

Arriving in Tokyo is to be assaulted by graphic design. Neon signs, billboards and luminous screens grab us by the retinas and cause us to swoon in wonder. The graphic minutiae of Japanese culture is equally compelling: tickets, till receipts, food packaging, confectionery wrappers and printed ephemera of all kinds instantly become collectable treasure, brought back by the suitcase-full as evidence of a superior visual culture.

But surely this is just the same old visual bombardment by brand owners and ruthless corporations that we encounter the world over? Well, yes. Except there's something so utterly stylish (with a delicious aura of otherness) about even run-of-the-mill Japanese graphic design that we end up being seduced rather than repulsed as we would be by Western equivalents. It is no longer politically correct to talk about the 'otherness' of other races, but in the case of Japan it is unavoidable, and the reason is that although Japanese visual culture is recognizably Western, it is a quixotic Western-ness that makes it simultaneously familiar and unfamiliar; it's the same, yet different.

Japanese artists have always borrowed from other cultures, so it's hardly surprising to find numerous Western influences in graphic design in Japan. But it's

Above
Project: *Idea* magazine, issue 57, front cover
Date: 1963
Cover Design: Paez Torres
Since 1953, the Japanese bi-monthly
magazine has been bringing important
Japanese designers to the attention of an
international audience. It continues to map
both the international and Japanese design
scenes from a Japanese perspective. Issue 57
carries a feature on Argentinean designers.

the way Japanese designers transform these influences
into something uniquely Japanese that grabs our attention.

The best Japanese graphic design has a directness and
immediacy that works even when we don't understand the
written text. Meggs writes: 'The Japanese understand non-
verbal communication, in part because Zen Buddhism teaches
the use of all five senses in receiving communication,
and even states "silence is communication".'[1]

Modern Japanese graphic style evolved from many
sources. Japanese characters are derived from Chinese
characters, which are logograms and represent the entire
word, thus giving written text a highly symbolic and
idiomatic aspect, a feature that can still be seen in
the Japanese graphics of the present day. The designers
of the post-Second World War period were inspired by
the flat, asymmetric compositions of
the masters of Ukiyo-e, or Floating
World, woodblock printmaking.
Another influence was the tradition
of Japanese family crests, known as
Mons. These geometric symbols used by
families as heraldic signs possessed
a graphic purity that predates European
Modernism, and they shaped the
Japanese approach to trademark design
in particular. The Mons heritage can
be seen in the logos of many modern
Japanese corporations. Modernism
and Constructivism were also highly
influential forces in the creation
of modern Japanese graphic design.

As Japan transformed itself into
one of the two leading industrialized
nations of the second half of the
twentieth century, the demand for
graphic communication grew. One of the
leaders of the post-war graphic revolution was Yusaku
Kamekura. Known as 'the boss', he united traditional
Japanese notions of balance and harmony with the bite of
Western Modernism. His poster for the 1964 Tokyo Olympics
combined Japan's national symbol of the sun – as a red
disc – with the Olympic rings and Western typography
in a brutal composition that caused the design world
to take notice of modern Japanese graphic design for
the first time.

Another towering figure in post-war Japanese graphic
culture is Tadanori Yokoo. His work from the 1960s onwards
was to prove influential beyond Japan. His startling
montages melded photography and graphic elements in a
quintessentially Japanese way – seemingly chaotic yet
underpinned by a strong sense of composition and design.

**Japanese
characters
are derived
from Chinese
characters,
which are
logograms and
represent the
entire word,
thus giving
written text a
highly symbolic
and idiomatic
aspect, a
feature that
can still be seen
in the Japanese
graphics of the
present day.**

SEVEN exhibition
APRIL 8–22, 2005 PAO GALLERIES, HONG KONG ARTS CENTRE

Above
Project: Inner rose #01
Date: 2005
Designer: Hideki Nakajima
Work done for 'SEVEN' exhibition
at Pao Galleries, Hong Kong Arts.
Part of a series of three.

His work can be seen in album covers for Miles Davis
and Santana,[2] and in numerous books and articles.

Other important figures include Koichi Sato.
Beginning in the 1970s, he created a body of poetic
work that boasts a Zen-like stillness, and which echoes
the great contemplative traditions of Japanese art.
Igarashi Takenobu studied in Los Angeles before returning
to work in Tokyo. His designs reveal a strong interest
in architecture, and many of his letterforms resemble
three-dimensional buildings.

In the past decade or so, contemporary Japanese
graphic design has lost some of its Japanese-ness. It's
hard to see a figure like Sato emerging in the digital
hothouse of today's Japan. Of the younger generation,
Hideki Nakajima[3] comes closest to matching Sato's poetic
intensity. With his meditative work for the musician
Ryuichi Sakamoto, Nakajima reveals himself to be in the
tradition of great Japanese designers, yet his work has
a Western quality that wouldn't be found in the work of
older Japanese designers.

Other Japanese designers reveal even less of
traditional Japan in their work. Groups like Delaware[4]
and designer/art director Kazunari Hattori[5] show a sharp

digital aesthetic that places them in the continuum of international graphic design. It's also interesting to see how Western designers have been influenced by Japanese design. It's hard to imagine the highly regarded British design groups Designers Republic and Me Company without the Japanese elements they incorporate in their work.

Further reading: Tomoko Sakamoto (ed.), *JPG 2: Japan Graphics*. Actar, 2007.

1 Philip B. Meggs and Alston W. Purvis, *Meggs' History of Graphic Design*, 4th edition. Wiley, 2005.
2 Tadanori Yokoo designed the Japanese edition of the Miles Davis album *Agharta* (Columbia), 1976, and the Santana album *Lotus*, also on the Columbia label, 1974.
3 www.nkjm-d.com
4 www.delaware.gr.jp
5 www.amazingangle.com/7/AD-Hattori.htm

Justified text

Blocks of justified text laid out on a page can look sophisticated and sharp. They appeal to the designer's instinct for order and structure. Ranged left text, on the other hand, can look ragged and scrappy. But for justified text to look good it needs lots of careful attention.

The shape of a block of justified text exerts a powerful attraction for designers. It sits crisply on the page; it looks good; it makes a satisfyingly compact shape. But is it good to read? Eric Gill in his 1931 *An Essay on Typography* noted: '… the merely neat appearance of a page of type in which all the lines are equal in length is a thing of no great value in itself: it partakes too much of the ideas of those who regard books as things to be looked at rather than read.'

As designers we often look at text as graphic blocks that need to be placed on the page with loving care – but without too much regard for their readability. There is no question that they look neat and tidy (when set properly, of course), but as every designer knows, justified text requires lots of manual correction. The hyphenation properties of software can never be relied on. We have to manually intercede, and this is time consuming.

Using justified text in web design is even more problematic. As is noted on the Web Style website: 'The most recent browser versions (and CSS) support justified text, but it is achieved by crude adjustments to word spacing. Fine adjustments are not possible on low-resolution computer displays and are impractical to implement in today's Web browsers. Also, Web browsers are unlikely to offer automatic hyphenation any time soon, another "must" for properly justified text. For the foreseeable future, the legibility of your Web documents will suffer if you set your text in justified format.'[1]

Flush left text allows the designer to make judicious line breaks that actually help the reader, and which allow the text to flow naturally. We should use justified text only when we are sure we have control of spacing and hyphenation.

Blocks of justified text look neat and tidy, but as every designer knows justified text requires lots of manual correction.

Above
Project: *The Drawbridge*
Date: 2009
Client: *The Drawbridge*
Designer: Stephen Coates
Masterly use of justified text by editorial designer Stephen Coates for *The Drawbridge*, an independent quarterly delivering 'thought, wit and reflection through words, photography and drawing'. *The Drawbridge* is a full-colour, broadsheet newspaper.
www.thedrawbridge.org.uk

1 http://webstyleguide.com

Further reading: Eric Gill, *An Essay on Typography*. David R. Godine, 1993 (reprint).

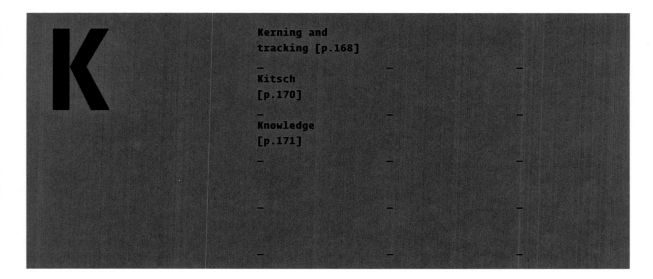

Kerning and tracking

**When non-designers want to poke
fun at graphic designers they
usually mention kerning. To
non-designers kerning and its
sibling, tracking, are nerdish
activities that seem to be of
minimal value. Yet to designers
they are as important as having
wings is to an aeroplane.**

As a young designer I struggled with kerning. I could
see the absolute necessity of it, and I could see that
type that wasn't kerned looked dreadful. My problem,
though, was how to decide what was correct. As a tyro
designer I wanted someone to arbitrate for me. Eventually,
I developed an eye for what was right, and I learnt to
trust my judgement. Despite the reams written on the
subject, and despite the rules and
conventions, typography is mostly a
matter of personal judgement, which
is why I never buy the old nostrum
that it is not art – it is.

Kerning is about adjusting
(increasing or decreasing) the
space between problematical letter
combinations to ensure an even and
consistent look, and to ensure the
eyes of the reader are not distracted
by gaps and collisions within words.

The term 'kerning' comes from
hot-metal typesetting, where certain
letters (typically lower-case 'l's
and 'f's) extended beyond the metal
block the letter sat on, thus creating
unsightly combinations of letters.
Kerning pairs are letter combinations that produce
unattractive gaps unless they are kerned. 'AT', 'AV' and
'WA' are typical combinations. Digital typefaces control
the space between letters by a table of kerning pairs,
which specifies the spaces between letter combinations.

Conventional wisdom dictates that the bigger the
point size, the greater the need for kerning. This is
true, but it's dangerous to assume that many fonts

**Tracking is
often confused
with kerning.
Tracking refers
to the control
of all the
spaces between
all the letters
in a given
text block.
When tracking
commands
are applied
they affect
all interletter
spaces equally.**

Above
Project: *Idea* vs The Designers Republic
magazine cover
Date: 2002
Publisher: *Idea* magazine
Designer: The Designers Republic
The cover for this special edition of the
Japanese magazine shows Designers Republic's
trademark negative kerning. Letters overlap
yet legibility is retained. The publication
features a feast of TDR work including
Wipe Out Series, Emigre, Satoshi Tomiie,
Funkstorung, Warp, Gatecrusher and Towa Tei.
Exclusively available on the *Idea* website.
www.idea-mag.com/en/publication/b013.php

don't need kerning when they are used small. Futura,
for example, even at small sizes, needs constant
vigilance, especially where numerals with two or
more digits are involved.

Tracking is often confused with kerning. Tracking
refers to the control of all the spaces between all the
letters in a given text block. When tracking commands
are applied they affect all interletter spaces equally.
We can isolate a word, a line or an entire block of text,
but when we apply plus or minus tracking everything we
have highlighted is affected uniformly.

Tracking affects the 'colour' of text. Even small
amounts of negative tracking can make text look dark and
bunched; too much positive tracking, and it starts to
look grey and gappy. We are sometimes tempted to resort
to tracking to get out of sticky line-break problems;
we think if we crunch (or open up) the occasional line in
a body of text, no one will notice. Our clients probably
won't, but it's a design truism that
properly kerned and letterspaced
type – whatever the size, whatever the
typeface – has a whiff of perfection
about it that even non-designers
recognize. Look at any great piece
of formal typography and you'll find
that faultless kerning and tracking
are ingredients.

Of course, as designers become
older and grander, they find kerning
and tracking a chore and hand them
over to studio juniors. Studio juniors might complain
about this, but there are few better ways of learning
the art of kerning and tracking than spending hours
kerning and tracking a lazy creative director's layouts.
Trust me. I'm a creative director.

> **Futura, for
> example, even
> at small sizes,
> needs constant
> vigilance,
> especially
> where numerals
> with two or
> more digits
> are involved.**

**Further reading: Ellen Lupton, *Thinking with Type:
A Critical Guide for Designers, Writers, Editors, &
Students*. Princeton Architectural Press, 2007.**

Kitsch

When designers use kitsch
elements in their work it is
mostly done to signal superior
taste, or to demonstrate
sufficient confidence and
self-belief to be able to
embrace the unlikeable without
being tainted by it. But what
is kitsch and does it have
a place in graphic design?

Kitsch is a word of German or Yiddish origin that was originally used to identify a poor copy of an existing artwork. Today, in the twenty-first century, kitsch means bad taste and defines any mass-produced lurid or sentimental item. The American art critic Clement Greenberg believed kitsch was the opposite of avant-garde (see Avant Garde design, page 25).

Essential ingredients of kitsch are fakery, pretentiousness and cheapness. The fakery can be seen in the inept aping of a serious work of art, or in the exaggerated depiction of emotions such as sentimentality and self-pity. The pretentiousness usually takes the form of feigned seriousness. And the cheapness is found in impoverished manufacturing techniques – although kitsch can sometimes be expensive. Kitsch paintings often show faces with tears rolling down their cheeks. Kitsch statues are rustic ladies in crinoline dresses, with parasols and twittering bluebirds. Garden gnomes are kitsch. Today, kitsch is anything that is not good taste.

But kitsch is losing its special status in matters of taste and art appreciation. Jeff Koons' supporters tell us his sculptures of puppies and Michael Jackson as a porcelain milkmaid are works of aesthetic delight. There is no irony in Koons; he asks us to enjoy his Balloon Flowers, a sculpture of twisted balloons made out of stainless steel with a reflective surface, as pure art.[1] When talking about it, he uses words such as 'joyous' and 'transcendence'. It would seem that contemporary art has no difficulty assimilating kitsch.

It could be argued that vast amounts of commercial graphic design are kitsch – the cheesy depictions of 'freshness' we see on air-freshener cans or on packaging for toilet paper, for example.

For designers, kitsch poses a subtler problem. It could be argued that vast amounts of commercial graphic design are kitsch – the cheesy depictions of 'freshness' we see on air-freshener cans or on packaging for toilet paper, for example. As a consequence, most graphic designers avoid kitsch for fear of aligning themselves with the world of airfresheners and toilet-roll packaging. Austere Modernism and geometric rigour are much safer territories. But there's another sort of graphic designer who knowingly uses kitsch elements in his or her work. They do it as a way of signalling their confidence in, and command of, the image world. Kitsch and bad-taste imagery have become a way of saying – I'm about more than good taste. It's a way of saying – I know what I'm doing and I have enough confidence in my ability as an image-maker to stick a fluffy kitten or a diamanté pistol into my design. It's a way of saying: unlike the designer who designs air-freshener and toilet-roll packaging I have the freedom of self-expression.

Further reading: Stephen Bayley, *Taste*. Pantheon, 1992.

Opposite
Project: *Andy's Big Book of Shite*
Date: 2009
Client: Self-initiated
Designer: Andy Altmann, Why Not Associates
The design company co-founded by Andy Altmann – Why Not Associates – has a track record for the inclusion of wit in their work. Often this takes the form of dabbling with kitsch. Altmann has always been a connoisseur of kitsch: 'I love kitsch. My college library used to have a book on the subject. I remember the Nazi tea service. Beautiful china with swastikas! I have been working on a book for years – *Andy's Big Book of Shite*.'

1 www.wtc.com/media/videos/Jeff%20Koons

Knowledge

An obsession with our craft often means that designers lack knowledge of the wider world. Yet knowledge is power, and the more we know the better equipped we are to be effective designers, and the less likely we are to be treated as brainless lackeys.

I was talking to a designer recently. The word 'obelisk' came up in conversation. The designer said he didn't know what an obelisk was. This seemed a strange omission in a designer's knowledge bank. Obelisk is an established term in the visual lexicon; surely anyone with an interest in the visual world would have come across this term before? Yet why should it matter? Not knowing what an obelisk is doesn't prevent someone being a good designer. Or does it? Well, yes and no. One of the best things about being a graphic designer is that we never know what project is going to land on our desks next. We never know who is going to walk through our door. We never know what unfamiliar world we are going to have to become acquainted with. Every client wants its designers to know about its world.

Designers need two sorts of knowledge: the first is technical/ professional; the second is cultural/ political.

In an essay entitled 'Why Designers Can't Think', Michael Bierut writes: '… how can a designer plan an annual report without some knowledge of economics? Lay out a book without an interest in, if not passion for, literature? Design a logo for a high-tech company without some familiarity with science?'[1]

In fact, so great are the demands clients make on designers for high levels of knowledge and expertise that design is becoming increasingly – and irrevocably – compartmentalized. Food companies only want to work with food-packaging designers; movie companies only want to work with movie specialists. There's a grim-faced logic to this: why would clients work with designers who don't know the formulae and conventions of disciplines such as food packaging and movie posters? Yet the danger with this sector-based thinking is that everything ends up looking the same. No one risks breaking the rules and customs, and so designers become stale and formulaic.

But for designers who offer a general design service, there is always the thrill of new clients from new areas, bringing with them the excitement of a new challenge. And to meet these challenges we need talent, skill and professionalism; but more than this we need knowledge. We need to know stuff.

Designers have always cited the importance of research. When we are given a new job we study the subject, and it's vital that we do this. But I often think about what the British writer Iain Sinclair said about research. He was asked if he had done a lot of research for his latest book. 'Research?' he said, 'my whole life is research.' I can't think of a better motto for the modern graphic designer.

It's common for clients who are fishing for new designers to visit a number of studios before making a final decision. This is a critical moment in the hiring process. It's the moment when we need to demonstrate knowledge and understanding.

Project-generated research is no longer enough. We also need a wider understanding of the world. In fact, designers need two sorts of knowledge: the first is technical/professional; the second is cultural/political. Most of us manage to keep up with the technical and professional demands of being a designer: we need to know about everything from software developments to health and safety legislation; we need to know about IT breakthroughs and copyright laws. These demands should not be underestimated; keeping up-to-date with technical and professional matters is hard work, but most of us manage it.

By cultural/political knowledge I mean knowledge of the world around us. I mean an understanding of how the world works. Designers often shout about the need to be taken more seriously and to be involved earlier in projects, but this won't happen if all we know about is our own craft. How can we be expected to function in the complex spheres of communication, information and entertainment if we know nothing about how the world works?

Today, smart clients will pay more for thinking and knowledge than they will for design. Many big design groups put all their intellectual muscle (and resources) into strategy and planning with the result that, for them and for their clients, design has become 'look and feel' – something that is sprayed on with an aerosol at the end so that most corporate design has a dull uniformity (see Look and feel, page 182).

What I'm advocating here is specialist design knowledge infused with experience and understanding of the wider world. To acquire this 'additional' knowledge we need to be on a mission to accumulate it: we need to speak to people from other disciplines; we need to watch and study; and once we've done all these things we need to keep doing them. But most of all we need to read. As Jessica Helfand wrote about her time as a student of Paul Rand: 'I don't remember talking about design so much as just talking – about life, about ideas, about reading. "You will learn most things by looking," he would say, "but reading gives understanding. Reading will make you free."'[2]

Designers often shout about the need to be taken more seriously and to be involved earlier in projects, but this won't happen if all we know about is our own craft.

If we only do research after we've secured a job, we are disadvantaging ourselves at a crucial stage in the design process. Clients like to meet designers before commissioning them, especially if it is a new relationship. It's common for clients who are fishing for new designers to visit a number of studios before making a final decision. This is a critical moment in the hiring process. It's the moment when we need to demonstrate knowledge and understanding. It's the moment when we must avoid appearing wrapped up in the technical and professional concerns of being a designer. If we can do this, we become a much more attractive proposition for clients.

Further reading: Paul Rand, Thoughts on Design. Van Nostrand Reinhold, 1972.

1 Michael Bierut, 'Why Designers Can't Think', in Seventy-nine Short Essays on Design... Princeton Architectural Press, 2007.
2 Jessica Helfand, 'Remembering Paul Rand', January 2008. www.designobserver.com/archives/entry.html?id=27852

Leading

The horizontal space between lines of text is as important as the text itself. Get it right and text becomes inviting. Get it wrong and we run the risk of rendering text unreadable. Too much space can be as damaging as too little space. So how do we know what's right?

Opposite
Project: 50 Years of Helvetica poster
Date: 2007
Client: Blanka/Longlunch
Designer: Andrew Neely
A poster designed to promote two Helvetica events running simultaneously at the same venue. Both functions had to be promoted equally while still presented as two separate entities. This idea is reinforced visually by the absence of leading and allowing ascenders and descenders to overlap.

Leading – there's a clue in the name – comes from the strips of lead used in hot-metal typesetting to keep lines of text apart. Unless typesetters inserted these strips, ascenders and descenders would touch, creating unpleasant collisions. Text was either 'set solid' (no leading) or set 'with leading'. Today's typographer controls the space between lines by using sophisticated software to specify a point size.

The longer the line of text, the more leading is needed to enable the eye to locate the next line. But introduce too much space and the lines become isolated and hard to read in sequence. How do we decide on the correct amount of leading? By intuition mainly, and by endlessly studying examples of well-formatted – and badly formatted – text. And also through constant experimentation. In the digital era there is no excuse for not looking at what happens when we alter leading even by tiny amounts. And we must always read what we create. As designers, concerned with the visual appeal of our work, we tend to squint at text and see it as blocks or shapes to be arranged on a page or on the screen. But it has to be read, so as well as squinting to see how it sits in relation to other graphic elements we need to open our eyes and read the words we are formatting. What looks good to the designer's eye as a block of text might be uncomfortable to read. We'll only know this by reading it.

Leading is a matter of individual judgement and, like all other aspects of typography and layout, it is subject to fashions and fads.

Leading is a simple matter when we are faced with judging the appropriate horizontal space in a block of

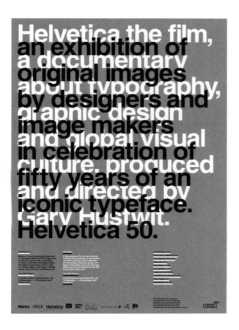

text. It becomes more complex when we are required to mix lots of different sizes of text, or when we have to align columns of different-sized text, such as a sidebar, or insert a footnote. It is not possible to use the same leading throughout, and we have to vary it. But it is usually desirable to look for some sort of harmony. Different amounts of leading work best when they are increased or decreased incrementally in regular proportions.

Yet leading is a matter of individual judgement and, like all other aspects of typography and layout, it is subject to fashions and fads. The legacy of Modernism dictates that lines of text look and function best when they are closer together, but in the 1980s it was common to see widely spaced lines of text. In the past two decades, though, a combination of fashion and the pressure on graphic designers to serve up instant typographic solutions and avoid wasteful uses of space, has meant that deep leading has fallen into disuse. Today, like wearing a bow tie, it looks like an affectation, and is best avoided. Paradoxically, we are far more likely to see negative leading: the clashing of lines of text is seen as chic and daring.

Further reading: Gavin Ambrose and Paul Harris, *Basic Design: Typography*. AVA, 2005.

Legibility

When clients moan about design they are often complaining about a lack of legibility. Their solution is usually to request that the type is made bigger. Designers tend to resist this on the grounds that it can destroy balance and harmony. But what if the clients are right?

The importance of legibility increases with the importance of the message being delivered. If designers make road signs illegible they run the risk of killing people; we wouldn't want a railway timetable – or our bank statements – to be illegible, but no one minds if a rock band's name on a CD cover is hard to decipher. Radical designers have always tested the limits of legibility. Generally, when designers dispense with legibility it is because they are atrocious designers, or they do so with revolutionary or contrarian aims.

In the 1990s, design had its famous 'legibility wars'. Graphic designers discovered that the new computer technology made it easy to manipulate type and to layer text upon text, and text with imagery. This period of graphic exploration coincided with the newly fashionable theories of deconstruction that had taken hold in certain influential design schools in the USA. These French-derived theories encouraged designers to 'deconstruct' conventional and established practices through interrogation of rules and conventions, and one of the first conventions to be assaulted was that of legibility. For some designers this led to creating new and exhilarating works of complex beauty as they

tested the extent to which meanings could be grasped when messages were wilfully distorted. For others it led to infantile posturing and 1990s grunge style.

Much of the discourse surrounding legibility was conducted in the pages of *Émigré*, the magazine founded by Rudy VanderLans and Zuzana Licko. Many designers saw legibility as part of graphic design's servility to corporate culture, and its increasing anonymity as a tool of communication. As VanderLans pointed out: 'There existed, at the time, and perhaps still today, a very strong feeling that for texts and information to be easily readable it had to be presented "neutrally". We argued that there was no such thing as neutrality or transparency in design, that all graphic gestures are loaded with meaning. Also, we weren't interested in addressing the needs of multi-national corporations and lowest common denominator audiences.'[1]

In recent years, graphic design has been marked by both the continuing dominance of Modernist principles of clarity, and increasing financial pressure to ensure legibility – and readability – in all commercial communications: brand owners don't want their 'target markets' struggling to comprehend their messages. Furthermore, the rise of the Internet has been mirrored by the rise of usability experts less concerned with legibility than readability. What is the difference? Legibility concerns clarity of texts as determined by fonts, point size, column measurement and layout, and is not concerned with content or language. Readability is as much about the use of language as it is about presentation. Our ability to read a piece of text is affected by the length of sentences, the use of punctuation, and the precise and engaging use of language. For clients, however, legibility and readability are two sides of the same coin. They want their audiences to read texts with ease, and for this they demand that designers give them legibility. For most clients that means making text 'big'. No client ever told a graphic designer to make type smaller.

Yet legibility is affected by dozens of factors outside of the technical aspects of graphic design. Any sort of visual impairment can make the simple act of reading difficult; as we get older our eyes become less effective; are we reading ink on paper or are we, as is increasingly likely, reading text on a screen? (see Accessibility, page 8).

A newspaper from the 1930s is almost unreadable today. How would a scholarly medieval monk cope with a 1960s psychedelic poster? How would a Victorian typesetter accustomed to woodblock type cope with scrolling text on a web page?

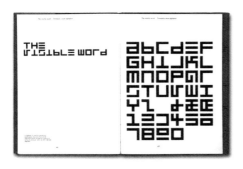

Type designer Zuzana Licko states: 'Typefaces are not intrinsically legible. Rather, it is the reader's familiarity with faces that accounts for their legibility. Studies have shown that readers read best what they read most. Legibility is also a dynamic process, as readers' habits are ever changing. It seems curious that black letter typestyles, which we find illegible today, were actually preferred over more humanistic designs during the eleventh and fifteenth centuries. Similarly, typefaces that we perceive as illegible today may well become tomorrow's classic choices.'[2]

Historically our assessment of legibility has changed over time. When we look at medieval manuscripts they seem to us impenetrable; more like a code than readable text. Even when we try and read text designed in the modern era – work connected with the Bauhaus, for example – we are often struck by how hard it is to read. The densely-packed lines of a newspaper from the 1930s is almost unreadable today. By the same token, how would a scholarly medieval monk cope with a 1960s psychedelic poster? How would a Victorian typesetter accustomed to woodblock type cope with scrolling text on a web page? Theories about fonts, number of words per line, sans serif type versus serif type, and the optimum column measure, are all subject to revision. Today, our concept of what is legible is flexible. The ordinary person is confronted daily with myriad different typographic styles and copes with them admirably.

In recent years, graphic design has been marked by both the continuing dominance of Modernist principles of clarity, an ever increasing financial pressure to ensure legibility in all commercial communications: brand owners don't want their 'target markets' struggling to comprehend their messages.

In an article in *Eye* 67, Kevin Larson (researcher for Microsoft's advanced reading technologies) and Jim Sheedy (Dean of the College of Optometry at Pacific University, Oregon) investigated the workings of the human eye, and the operation of its complex muscle system in the act of reading: 'Reading is a very stressful task,' they point out. 'When people read, their eyes need to make roughly four movements every second – that is 15,000 eye movements every hour they spend reading.' Designers, they stress, must do everything possible to make this complex ocular activity as comfortable as possible. Their concluding advice is revealing: 'Designers usually try to use high quality text when readers are expected to read for any period of time, but using a comfortable text size is not always possible. In print, there is a trade-off between type size and the

Opposite and above
Spreads from *The Visible World. Problems of Legibility* by Herbert Spencer. Published by Lund Humphries in association with the Royal College of Art, 1969. The detail opposite shows an alphabet designed by Brian Coe – part of an experiment to see how much of each lower-case letter could be eliminated without affecting legibility. The detail above shows a typeface developed by Epps and Evans at the UK's National Physical Laboratory (Division of Computer Sciences). All curves and diagonals have been removed to facilitate mechanical optical recognition.

amount of text that can fit on a page. Nine-point type may be chosen because it is cost effective, whereas 11-point would be easier to identify visually and would reduce eye strain. Twelve-point may be needed for good character definition on computer screens, because readers frequently sit further from a screen than from a printed page, but many Web pages specify small point sizes despite the fact that it costs no more to create additional or longer pages. Designers need to argue for larger text sizes to reduce the effects of eye strain.'[3]

So, making the type bigger means less eye strain and therefore increases legibility. Proof – perhaps – that clients have been right all along.

Further reading: http://legibletype.blog.com/

1 Toshiaki Koga, interview with Rudy VanderLans, *Idea* magazine (Japan), 2005.
2 Interview with Zuzana Licko, *Émigré 15*, 1990.
3 Kevin Larson and Jim Sheedy, 'Blink: The Stress of Reading', *Eye 67*, 2008.

Letterspacing

Wide letterspacing is highly unfashionable. Since Modernism decreed that letters should be tightly spaced it has been a crime to space them widely in words. But is there a place for letterspacing? Or is it a typographic no-go area – a sign of weakness and vapidity?

Most typographic fashions are periodically recycled – but not letterspacing. Letterspacing has been a graphic design crime for the past few decades. The last occasion when it was used with conviction was in the work of the Swiss designer Wolfgang Weingart in the early 1970s, and in the typographic offerings of his pupils Dan Friedman and April Greiman. Weingart went further than mere letterspacing and introduced variable or incremental letterspacing; in his intense black-and-white graphic explorations it was common to find words where it doubled between each letter.

Letterspacing became a common feature in the Art Deco and Memphis-inspired post-Modernism of 1980s graphic design, and also enjoyed extensive utilization in the American New Wave graphics of the same decade. As Dan Friedman said in a 1994 interview with Ellen Lupton: 'Type in the 80s was about excess; type in the 90s is about restraint.'[1] To contemporary eyes, New Wave design looks cheap and faddy.

Today, widely letterspaced words and phrases are rare. Clients demand the instantaneousness of conventionally (that is, tightly) spaced words. Personally, I'd like to see letterspacing revived. When used with confidence it can be invigorating, as Weingart proved with his early experimental work. But while trendsetting graphic designers and typographers remain wedded to Modernist dogma, wide letterspacing is unlikely to make a return.

1 Ellen Lupton interviews Dan Friedman, 15 June 1994. www.elupton.com/index.php?id=23

Further reading: Wolfgang Weingart, *Wolfgang Weingart: My Way to Typography*. Lars Müller Publishers, 2000.

Ligatures

The ability to use ligatures with style and purpose is one of the ways designers demonstrate typographic sophistication. Recently these have become fashionably ubiquitous and are in danger of turning into a sort of upmarket drop shadow. When and where is it desirable to use them?

LA NT KA TH
UT EA EA HT
CA FR RR GA
TU RA ST M

Above
Series of ligatures for the typeface Avant Garde designed by Herb Lubalin, with assistance from Tom Carnase. The typeface was initially designed in the 1960s. It enjoyed a huge vogue in the 1970s and became one of the defining typefaces of the decade. It is enjoying a revival today. It is greatly prized for its geometric look and its variety of ligatures.

1 www.markboulton.co.uk
2 www.markboulton.co.uk/journal/comments/five_
simple_steps_to_better_typography_part_3/

Ligatures are specific combinations of letters that are joined together to prevent gaps and unsightly collisions. There are five common ligatures – fi, ffi, fl, ffl and ff – and when these letter combinations are redrawn as a single combined character they sit elegantly alongside other letter combinations. They are a typographic detail that can add refinement to text – especially headline text. But they can also add a hint of pedantry and fussiness, which means they should be used sparingly and with care.

Ligatures are mainly found in serif typefaces, although some sans serif fonts – such as Gill Sans – have them, too. The Émigré typeface Mrs Eaves (named after Sarah Eaves, the wife of John Baskerville) is a modern font that comes with a full complement of elegant ligatures, yet still manages to exude modernity. It is based on Baskerville, and was designed by Zuzana Licko.

The decision to use or not use a ligature varies from project to project. If we were preparing a headline for a magazine article that reads, 'Fluff is everywhere' we probably wouldn't bother to use ligatures for the Fl and ff combinations. But if we were creating the logo for a company called the Fluff Company we might well choose to use ligatures. Increasingly, we are seeing them used as purely decorative elements.

Ligatures become more problematical online. HTML has trouble handling them. As designer Mark Boulton notes on his website,[1] 'I tend to only use ligatures for on-screen use if I'm creating logotypes, or graphical headers or elements that require them. In this instance all use of ligatures is fine. There are many people who disagree, stating that ligatures are a relic of a by-gone age. I disagree. The use of ligatures in your typesetting, for print or on screen, shows a typographic maturity and an understanding of the craft.'[2]

The Émigré typeface Mrs Eaves is a modern font that comes with a full complement of elegant ligatures yet still manages to exude modernity.

Further reading: www.fonts.com/aboutfonts/articles/fyti/ligaturespartone.htm

Logos

Clients understand logos. They get the point of them. They see the benefits of a well-designed logo. In commercial terms, a good logo means brand recognition. But woe betide any designer who produces a logo that no one likes, or worse, changes one that everyone loves.

Above and opposite
Project: Rotterdam City of Architecture logo series
Date: 2006
Client: Rotterdam Marketing, the Netherlands
Designer: 75B
Logo series for the Rotterdam City of Architecture campaign. Used randomly in different media, the logos show how it is possible to create a diverse and varied identity while retaining a high recognition factor.

No commercial body can exist without a logo. No benevolent institution, rock band, consumer product or religious body can manage without one. Everyone and everything has a logo – even cities and nations have them. Which is just as well for designers, because without logos our profession would be even more anonymous than it already is. Logos give designers kudos: they are one of the few end products of graphic design that register on the public's radar. Of course, this visibility means that when we produce logos that are not liked – or tamper with ones that are loved – the response is often ferocious, with damaging consequences to the status of designers. The tabloid press relishes a logo scandal – especially when, as was the case with the notorious London 2012 Olympics logo,[1] public money is involved. The faux outrage of the British press (tabloids and broadsheets) was spectacular. The logo was front-page news, and its designers, the British firm Wolff Olins, were vilified. Their fees were subjected to scrutiny and ridicule; reporters even camped outside the house of the creative director, subjecting him and his family to unacceptable harassment. All because of a logo.

And yet, in our brand-obsessed culture we shouldn't be surprised if non-designers are logo aware. At a time when people seem perfectly happy – even proud – to wear the logos of shops and consumer products on T-shirts, caps and bags, it is perhaps inevitable that there will be strong interest in logos. They are, after all, the tribal markings of a modern consumer society. They are the badges by which we allow ourselves to be aligned with social and subcultural groups.

The era of the monolithic, static, un-changing logo is over. In our visual culture we want variety and stimulus. Accordingly, the logos of the future are likely to be ever changing and malleable.

Logos come in two main varieties. Most are typographic. These are called logotypes: the name of the company or product is rendered in a fixed style of lettering. Coca-Cola is perhaps the best-known example. Other logos are purely symbolic: the Mercedes badge, the McDonald's arches and the Apple symbol don't need to be accompanied by the company name. Our brand literacy means we recognize them instantly. Most logos are, however, a combination of symbol and typography.

So what are the rules of good logo design? The vast changes that have taken place in our culture – and specifically in the business arena – have meant that the logos of today are different from the ones of 50 years ago. Logos once strived to express the nature of an organization or product; today they are more likely to

be abstract shapes that strive for memorability rather than inviting interpretation. When designers or clients try to tell me what their logos represent, my instinct is usually to reach for the sick bag.

Paul Rand, who designed more enduring logos than most designers, was a pioneer of the 'abstract' logo. He wrote: 'Surprising to many, the subject matter of a logo is of relatively little importance, and even appropriateness of content does not always play a significant role. This does not imply that appropriateness is undesirable. It merely indicates that a one-to-one relationship between a symbol and what is symbolized is very often impossible to achieve and, under certain circumstances, objectionable. Ultimately, the only mandate in the design of logos, it seems, is that they be distinctive, memorable and clear.'[2] Not only is it wise to avoid the baroque and pretentious rationales, it is increasingly unwise for designers to create logos that are too specific. Today, businesses and products change their functions with dizzying speed: why saddle them with an identity that locks them into a particular message.

Yet perhaps the biggest task facing the designer is the fact that logos have to work in a variety of media; the great ones of the past nearly always did this by default. In the days of poor reproduction logos had an intrinsic robustness that meant they were equally effective on vans and the sides of buildings. Today, a logo will have to work on numerous platforms – mobile phone screen, website, T-shirt, and at the end of a television commercial. Increasingly, too, logos have to move. The days of the static unchanging logo have gone. Today our logos are expected to be mini movies that tell us stories.

The final development in logo design that designers have to take into consideration is that the era of the monolithic, unchanging logo is over. In our visual culture we want variety and stimulus. Accordingly, the logos of the future are likely to be ever changing and malleable. The London Olympics logo was a brave but flawed attempt to achieve this. A much more interesting manifestation of this approach can be found in the Dutch design group 75B's approach to logo design. Their Rotterdam City of Architecture is a triumph of memorable yet fluid logo design.

Further reading: Michael Evamy, *Logo*. Laurence King Publishing, 2007.

1 I have written about the London 2012 Olympics logo on two occasions: 'The 2012 Olympic Logo Ate My Hamster' (www.designobserver. com/archives/025852.html) and 'Wolff Olins: Expectations Confounded' (www.creativereview. co.uk/crblog/wolff-olins-expectations-confounded).
2 Paul Rand, *Design, Form, and Chaos*. Yale University Press, 1993.

Look and feel

The term 'look and feel' first appeared in the early days of web design. It was used to define the way computer interfaces both 'looked' and 'functioned'. Today it is widely used by commissioners of design to describe the act of giving visual expression to content, ideas and strategies.

Is 'look and feel' a useful piece of verbal shorthand that emphasizes the importance of appearance and usability in modern strategy-driven communications? Or is it a babyish term that reduces the designer to the role of decorator – someone who gets asked to 'colour in' strategic plans made by smart marketing wonks who think design is the easy bit at the end?

The term achieved notoriety when Apple used it in their 1980s lawsuit against Microsoft for 'stealing the look and feel of the Mac OS'. The website Usability First defines the term as: 'The appearance (look) and interactive style (feel) of software whose uniqueness to a particular platform or application defines the aesthetics and values of the application and how users subjectively respond to it … The look-and-feel is often considered to incorporate the copyrightable aspects of the user interface ...' Surprisingly, the phrase doesn't show up in a glossary of terms on the US Copyright Office website, or on the USA Patents and Trademarks Office site.

Virginia Postrel, author of *The Substance of Style*, has a fondness for the phrase. In her book she makes a persuasive case for the dominance of aesthetics in modern commercial life, and uses the term 'look and feel' throughout the text. On the *Design Observer* blog she wrote: 'The original title of *The Substance of Style* was in fact *Look and Feel*. It got as far as a great cover design before the sales people at HarperCollins nixed it because, they said, no one knew from the title what the book was about.' She continued: 'I use it and "aesthetics" interchangeably in the book, not as a synonym for "design" but specifically for aspects of design that appeal to the senses and that are not, in the normal use of the word, strictly functional.'[1]

Jason Tselentis, the interactive designer and keen blogger, first heard the phrase when he worked at Intel in 2002. 'I was hired to be a user-interface designer with Intel Labs,' he notes, 'and was told I'd be working on software "look and feel". At that time I'd been a designer/programmer since 1997, but was unsure of this new phrase. Did they want me to do something new? Feel? Did this mean I'd be working on touch-screen technology?' Tselentis continues: 'The term struck me as odd and eventually annoying. Most of what I heard through the computer science, human-computer interaction, and heuristical meetings was this term being used in a "graphic design" context. And whenever I showed CompSci folks my work in progress (icons, menus, data flow, user

The term 'look and feel' confines designers to the form part of the equation only, whereas all great design gives both form and function equal status.

interfaces), all they kept saying was, "I like the look and feel" or "That's not the look and feel we're going for. Have you seen how Office lays things out?" So I took look and feel to be synonymous with interaction design, which others call graphic design for the computer.'

The British designer Michael Johnson, a perennial favourite with international design juries, has noted an increase in usage of the term: 'Yes, people use it a lot,' he says. 'I've always mistrusted it as a phrase – apart from sounding vaguely pornographic, I think when you succumb to "look and feel" you're only a hop and a skip away from mood boards, and that really is the end of design as we know it. It's the kind of phrase that researchers love to throw around in focus groups, a process almost always destined to remove the last hints of creativity from a project.'

Ever since W. A. Dwiggins[2] coined the term 'graphic design' designers have agonized over the nomenclature of their trade. In recent decades we have been dumping the word 'design' as fast as we can in favour of more business-friendly terms such as 'corporate image', 'corporate identity' and, most recently, 'branding'. But oddly we are in a period when the 'd' word seems to be in vogue with influential commentators and business theorists like Bruce Nussbaum,[3] so this hardly seems the time to be dumping 'design' (as both verb and noun) in favour of 'look and feel'.

For many designers, any terminology that allows clients to feel comfortable with the language of design is useful, and for those working in branding 'look and feel' adequately captures the notion that design is about more than logos and layouts: to branding people, 'look and feel' conveys the full extent of a brand's presence – its colour, its tone of voice and its flavour.

It's hard to object to this. Yet, I can't help thinking there's something damaging in the way clients (and designers) are using the term. The effect of replacing 'design' with 'look and feel' is to separate the design process from the content, or the underlying strategy behind a piece of communication. It takes us back to the oldest argument in graphic design: the question of form vs function. The term 'look and feel', with its overwhelming emphasis on the appearance of things, confines designers to the form part of the equation only, whereas all great design gives both form and function equal status.

1 www.designobserver.com/archives/032084.html
2 www.adcglobal.org/archive/hof/1979/?id=264
3 www.businessweek.com/innovate/
  NussbaumOnDesign/

Further reading: Virginia I. Postrel, *The Substance of Style: How the Rise of Aesthetic Value is Remaking Commerce, Culture, and Consciousness*. HarperCollins, 2004.

Lorem Ipsum

Lorem Ipsum is 'filler text' which allows graphic designers to mimic the effect of real text in dummy layouts. This process is sometimes known as 'Greeking', which is odd, because the text is clearly Latin, although the word 'lorem' doesn't exist in my Latin dictionary.

More useful than a Swiss Army knife to a boy scout, Lorem Ipsum 'filler text' allows busy designers to format dummy text to replicate the effect of real text. Its appeal is that the frequency of letters mimics the frequency with which the same letters appear in real text. In the pre-digital era it was available as rub-down transfer sheets, but with the advent of Macs it was included in early publishing software. Today, designers go to websites where any amount of Lorem Ipsum can be generated, then taken and formatted and used in documents.

Before and After magazine[1] quoted a professor of Latin, Richard McClintock, who claimed to have found the phrase Lorem Ipsum in a treatise on the theory of ethics written by Cicero in 45 BC. He recalled having seen it in a book of early metal type samples, which commonly used extracts from the classics. 'What I find remarkable,' he said, 'is that this text has been the industry's standard dummy text ever since some printer in the 1500s took a galley of type and scrambled it to make a type specimen book; it has survived not only four centuries of letter-by-letter resetting but even the leap into electronic typesetting, essentially unchanged.'

But when the website Straight Dope[2] spoke to McClintock he said he'd been unable to locate the old type sample in which he thought he'd seen Lorem Ipsum. The earliest text he could find was on Letraset sheets from the 1970s.

1 www.bamagazine.com
2 www.straightdope.com/columns/010216.html

Further reading: www.loremipsum.de

Lower case

Is all-lower-case typography a sign of coolness? Or a sign of illiteracy? When we get an email from a friend without capital letters, it looks intimate and friendly; but what do people think when they see commercial messages in lower case only?

Among many designers the use of only lower-case letters is commonplace. Undoubtedly, this can look cool, stylish and modern. But we have capital letters for a reason, and without them meaning is not always clear. To understand the effect of text rendered in all lower case here's a revealing (and painful to recount) anecdote. I was asked to write an essay for a catalogue. It was a subject that interested me so I accepted the invitation. When I got my copy of the printed document the designer had rendered all my text in lower case; he had further complicated matters by using a small text size, tight leading and a too-wide column measure. It would have been hard to read if it had been set in upper and lower case, but set only in lower case it was unreadable. Two thousand words of grey, bilge-water soup. I was devastated.

It's something all designers have done – laid out an author's text in a style that suits their aesthetic tastes but which has no regard for readability. To render 2,000 words of text in lower case only is to slap the writer (and the reader) in the face with a wet towel.

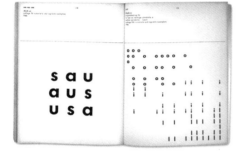

Above
Project: *Edition Hansjörg Mayer*, front cover and spreads
Date: 1968
Publisher: Hansjörg Mayer, Germany
Designer: Hansjörg Mayer
Typographer, printer, publisher and lecturer Hansjörg Mayer (b. 1943), concerns himself with 'both functional and autonomous typography'. He defines autonomous typography as 'materials with which an object can be made. Containing its own determined structure and its own density.' Mayer's consistent use of one typeface – Futura – and his insistence on only ever using lower-case letters and leaving out all punctuation marks, makes his work remarkable.

Lower-case letters first appeared in AD 800. Prior to that, lettering was only ever rendered in capitals. During the Renaissance (fourteenth to sixteenth centuries) capitals (majuscules) and lower case (minuscules) were mixed for the first time, and the two-tier alphabet we know today was developed. Designers and typographers have regularly challenged this system of mixing upper- and lower-case letters. Words and phrases rendered in capitals only have been used in design and advertising since the first clients with messages to get over urged designers to shout. But lower-case letters have had their advocates too: in *Pioneers of Modern Typography*, Herbert Spencer wrote: '[Herbert] Bayer argued strongly in favour of a single alphabet – "why should we write and print in two alphabets? We do not speak a capital A and a small a".' Well, we do in fact speak in capital letters. We use emphasis and pauses to indicate new sentences.

So what am I saying? We can never use only lower-case letters in formal communication? Not at all. There are many instances when the use of lower-case only is effective, readable and stylish. However, there are many more cases where it is downright unhelpful. For a start, navigating through big chunks of text is difficult without the signposting of capital letters at the beginning of sentences and where proper names are used. There is also the likelihood that if we omit capital letters the message is viewed as fundamentally unserious – frivolous even. There are many other places where all-lower-case letters are a mistake.

For example, it has been fashionable for designers to design their stationery (business cards, letterheads, etc.) using lower-case letters only. This can look stylish and can signal typographic adroitness. But most addresses contain numerals (zip codes, postcodes, etc.) and when lower-case letters are combined with lining numerals (see Numerals, page 217), which are designed to match the cap height of the alphabet, the result is gross. The solution is to use non-lining numerals (see Numerals), or the small caps version of numerals. Small caps are upper-case letters drawn to match the x-height of the lower-case version of the alphabet. Not all typefaces have small-caps versions, and while it is never acceptable to 'shrink' numerals to the x-height, since the weight of the numerals will not match the weight of the letters, it is sometimes acceptable to reduce the size of lining numerals to make them less noticeable.

If all-capital letters is shouting, all lower case is whispering. Both types of voice are useful, but mostly we want to speak in normal, well-modulated tones. And for this we need upper- and lower-case letters.

Lower case can be effective in striking a note of intimacy or softness. But if all-capital letters is shouting, all lower case is whispering. Both types of voice are useful, but mostly we want to speak in normal, well-modulated tones. And for this we need upper- and lower-case letters.

Further reading: Herbert Spencer, *Pioneers of Modern Typography*, revised edition, foreword by Rick Poynor. MIT Press, 2004.

M

Magazine design

In the best magazines we can map a micro-history of typography, art direction, illustration, photography and the expression of editorial content through visual design. At the same time, the modern mass-market magazine shows what happens when design is used as a battering ram.

For the general public, magazines are one of the most noticeable manifestations of the art of graphic design. When a magazine changes its design, readers take notice. Hardly surprising, perhaps, since magazines occupy a cherished place in the lives of millions of readers. Successful mags (both mass market and niche) inspire tribal loyalty, and influence the way their readers live and think.

In many niche and specialist magazines, design is used by art directors, designers and editors to create a compelling visual and editorial experience. The effect is to create an intimate 'voice' that, over time, becomes the voice of a well-liked friend.

The role of design in mass-market magazines is different: design is instead used to cajole and direct. Readers are encouraged to approach printed mass-market magazines in the same way that they zap through television channels and web pages. In a desperate attempt to ape the notion of multi-channel TV, and the hyperlinked, hurly-burly of the web, modern magazine editors and publishers ask designers and art directors to give them 'interactive'

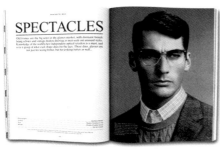

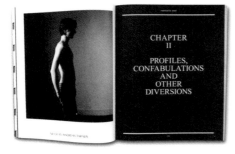

Above
Project: *Fantastic Man* No. 8
Date: 2008
Designer: Jop van Bennekom
Described as a 'fashion magazine for guys
who hate fashion magazines', *Fantastic Man*
is the product of a collaboration between
designer Jop van Bennekom and journalist
Gert Jonkers. The magazine's cool restraint
is at odds with the visual freneticism of
most current magazines.

spreads full of frenetic activity, standfirsts, shout outs and sidebars.

Modern mass-market magazines make few demands on their readers. Many of the most commercially successful ones also contain some of the most garish, patronizing and hideous layouts you'll find anywhere in visual communication. Sophisticated design is of no interest to publishers absorbed in the task of getting their magazines on to the shelves of the supermarkets; if this means Neanderthal layouts and every magazine looking the same, then that's what readers will get. Thousands of magazines are published regularly around the world. New ones appear constantly. This is surprising at a time when the Internet is assuming cosmic proportions, and when the allure of social media sites is exerting an irresistible pull on millions of traditional magazine readers.

Today few magazines exist as print-only entities. Commercial publishers see online advertising revenues soaring. They see consumers accessing online content via hand-held devices. Some of them even notice that web publishing is greener than print publishing. And were it not for the fact noted by the media commentator Jeff Jarvis that 'All online is a freesheet',[1] it would be hard to imagine, in the current climate, a publisher bothering to produce a printed edition of a planned new title. If this sounds far-fetched, look at what's happening to the record business: it is being transformed by the move to digital.

But the fate of commercial printed magazines is not in the hands of publishers. It is the advertisers and big brand-owners who dictate the future, and they are already moving their millions online. When they decide that printed magazines are no longer an effective way to 'capture eyeballs', mags will lose their main source of income. For designers the consequence is that tomorrow's magazine designer needs to be adept at designing content that can be delivered on multiple platforms. The static page of the magazine – the canvas for many of graphic design's finest moments – is slowly becoming a relic of another era: a pre-electronic era when print was the pre-eminent medium.

Oddly, however, radical magazine design has never been more influential among progressive designers than it is now. There was a time when record covers set the pulse rate for graphic design: the album covers of the 1970s and 1980s inspired a generation to study graphic design and forge careers in design. Today, it is far more

There was a time when record covers set the pulse rate for graphic design. Today, it is far more likely that young idealistic designers will be inspired by the experimental layouts of magazines.

Above
Project: *File* magazine, issue 1
Date: 2009
Designer: Thorbjørn Ankerstjerne/Fabio Sebastinelli
File is a magazine focusing on graphic design, art and visual communication. As the viability of printed publications is threatened by the Internet and the changing media landscape, *File*'s response is to include a DVD and a limited-edition print with each issue. The DVD features over two hours of short films, music videos and interviews. Issue 1 features a poster by Geoff McFetridge.

likely that young idealistic designers will be inspired by the experimental layouts of magazines such as *032c*, designed by Mike Meiré,[2] or the Day-Glo, MySpace-like anarchy of *Super Super* under Steve Slocombe's creative direction,[3] or the magazines designed by Dutch designer Jop van Bennekom: *Re-Magazine*, *Butt* and *Fantastic Man*.[4] These last three publications have inspired designers with their stark brilliance. But van Bennekom is not like other magazine designers. Along with journalist Gert Jonkers he is also the editor and publisher of his magazines, a fact that takes us to one of the secrets of effective magazine design: designers need to be more like editors.

The British magazine designer Jeremy Leslie runs a blog devoted to magazine and editorial design.[5] He has also published two books on the subject. Leslie defines the design of magazines as a 'process of collaboration between editors and designers. The chemistry between these two disciplines is a central part of the process – a good magazine designer will always have a good grasp of journalism, a good editor will always understand the importance of design.'

This may seem self-evident, but it is surprising how rare this chemistry is. Yet the simple fact is that you only get good magazines when you get genuine collaboration. The British editorial designer Simon Esterson (*Eye* magazine art director and proprietor)[6] advises magazine designers to 'learn to edit'. He says: 'Most of the time you are creating by distilling the best from other people's raw material, so learn to edit your ideas, other people's ideas, pictures and words. Appreciate words and pictures and how they can be used in different ways and combinations on a page to tell stories and hold the reader's attention.' He adds: 'Curiosity is essential, you need to engage with a magazine's content. Go native and think like a journalist, not just somebody making arbitrary patterns on the page. Ask yourself: what's the story here? How can we tell it? Also collaborate. Find the photographers, illustrators, editors, type designers, printers you like to work with.'

For the designer working on the launch of a new magazine, or the redesign of an existing one, there is a complex dance to be done. Keeping editors, advertising sales departments and publishers happy, with all their conflicting requirements, is a tough job. The task will include balancing the need to ensure reader engagement with making provision for advertising and shelf impact, and a dozen other sometimes conflicting demands. New launches and redesigns also have to contend with focus groups and direct input from advertisers.

Yet even when the designer has jumped through all these hoops there is often one last barrier to contend

Above
Project: *Super Super* magazine spread
Date: 2009
Creative Director: Steve Slocombe
Fashion spread from *Super Super* magazine
showing the magazine's refreshingly
unstructured approach to type and image.

1 Jeff Jarvis, 'Review of the year: New media:
  Facebook climbs the social scale', *Guardian*,
  17 December 2007. www.guardian.co.uk/
  media/2007/dec/17/facebook.yahoo
2 www.meireundmeire.de
3 www.myspace.com/thesupersuper
4 http://calendar.walkerart.org/event.
  wac?id=3690 http://magculture.com
5 http://magculture.com
6 At the time of writing, Simon Esterson
  had just become one of the owners of *Eye*
  magazine.
7 In Meggs' *History of Graphic Design*, Philip
  Meggs writes: '[Alexey] Brodovitch taught
  designers how to use photography. His
  cropping, enlargement, and juxtaposition
  of images and his exquisite selection from
  contact sheets were all accomplished with
  extraordinary intuitive judgment.'

with. When an independent magazine designer is called in to redesign or launch a title, he or she is required, in most cases, to create a template for others to implement in the future. The designer designs the publication's new look, then hands over grids, style templates, colour schemes and the instructions needed to enable an in-house team to produce the magazine. Many of these teams are competent and committed to faithfully implementing the new design. But sometimes in-house designers resent the intrusion of an outsider, and take every opportunity to alter and dilute the new design. Sometimes publishers and editors start tinkering with it the minute the designer's back is turned. It's a galling business.

So does this mean the end of innovative magazine design? Could a new Alexey Brodovitch[7] emerge today? Will there be a new generation of van Bennekoms, able to deal with the realities of online publishing? 'I hope so,' says Esterson. 'Small magazines give designers lots of freedom and responsibility, but usually have limited resources. Big magazines give you less freedom, shared responsibility and lots of resources. Try both and decide what structure works best for you.' The magazine designer of the future, in the view of Esterson, will need to have web-design skills in order to deal with the increasing trend for magazines to be available in both printed and online versions. 'And it might be a good idea,' he says, 'to learn how to use a video camera.' He adds: 'But the best design tool you have is still your brain.'

Further reading: http://magculture.com/blog/

Marketing

Marketing people are often unsympathetic to design. Conversely, design people are often dismissive of marketing. But marketing controls design because marketing is about strategy and planning, and design is about intuition. Clients are happy to pay for strategy, but less keen to pay for intuition.

In the United Kingdom Domino's, the home delivery pizza company, sponsors *The Simpsons*. Every time an episode is broadcast the chain experiences what it calls 'the Simpsons rush'. As soon as the Domino's sponsorship stings appear on the television screen, vast numbers of people suddenly develop a pizza craving and Domino outlets around the country go into overdrive to meet the demand.

There are two ways of looking at this. In business terms it is a hugely effective piece of marketing: by the simple device of attaching Domino's name to a hit television programme, orders for pizzas soar. It's a good fit – food features prominently in episodes of *The Simpsons*; the early evening time-slot is well timed; *The Simpsons* is watched by children (adults too), and children like pizzas. This act of marketing genius allows the Domino's chain to give employment to lots of people, and it also benefits the suppliers of pizza ingredients.

Yet looked at from a societal viewpoint it seems like a cynical act of manipulation. By saturating the programme with seductive advertising for their products, Domino's plays on the desire for instant gratification among children (and adults). It puts pressure on parents to pay for products for which there are cheaper alternatives, and it encourages the consumption of processed food at a time when it is being blamed for high levels of obesity. So, is Domino's the smartest marketer on the block or an exploitative corporation foisting its wares on people who would be better off – in more ways than one – without them? When I see smart and unpatronizing marketing that deploys clever imagery, good copy and original strategic thinking, I'm seduced by it – although my natural inclination is usually to spurn attempts to sell me things. Honest marketing leaves me with the feeling that I'm exercising free choice, while deceitful marketing makes me feel I am being controlled and patronized.

As in all instances where design is at loggerheads with its paymasters, it is up to designers to resolve the matter. No one is going to do it for us.

If this seems like an over-reaction, think about breakfast cereals, which are sold as being 'good for you' but which contain huge amounts of salt; think of fizzy drinks that are sold as 'energy drinks', but which contain dubious chemicals and come with excessive sugar content. This is deceitful marketing: it assumes that if you tell people a product is good for their hearts they won't bother to ask whether it will harm any other part of their bodies. It is marketing based on the arrogant assumption that it can dictate how people will think; and the more a product is designed to appeal to a mass market, the more dictatorial marketing becomes.

THINK (TA
'VISIBLIZE
YOURSELF,
MY TINY FRIEND

Most marketing isn't dishonest; it's just dumb. The dumbness is usually caused by marketing wonks trying to speak to so many people at once that they end up adopting a tone of epic blandness. As a designer I've often worked with bright marketing professionals who treat their audiences as intelligent and discriminating human beings – people who need facts rather than hype, who need the truth rather than deceit. I've worked on projects where marketing teams have seen the benefits of good design and treated designers as valued collaborators. They know their idea will be better communicated by effective design.

But the simple reality is that, in most cases, marketing leads and design follows. Marketing hires designers to put flesh on their plans and schemes, result in design that is generally subordinate to marketing whereas it should be an equal partner (see Look and Feel, page 182). By the time the designer gets involved all the thinking is done. The big design groups understand this, and have developed strategic and marketing skills. For the rest of us, we have a stark choice to make: do we accept our role as the servant of marketing and get on with it, or do we also develop the skills that enable us to offer ourselves as more than mere form givers?

As with the Domino's example, we also have to consider the ethical questions inherent in marketing; each of us must decide where we stand on this matter. If a landmine company asked me to design its sales brochure, I'd say no. But if a breakfast cereal manufacturer asked me to design a website that promoted the cereal as fun for kids, I might do it on the grounds that I was not being asked to say it was healthy. Other designers will take different positions in both these cases. Each of us must make our own decisions.

But let's assume we have dealt with the ethics of the task in front of us – what, then, is the best way to develop a relationship with marketing? Well, it's not going to be easy: design is often undervalued by marketing people (just as it can often be overvalued by designers). When we encounter clients who have an unreasonable or dismissive attitude to design, we have a choice: we can walk away or we can decide to engage with the problem. But as in all instances where design is at loggerheads with its paymasters, it is up to designers to resolve the matter. No one is going to do it for us.

> **If a landmine company asked me to design its sales brochure, I'd say no. But if a breakfast cereal manufacturer asked me to design a website that promoted the cereal as fun for kids, I might do it on the grounds that I was not being asked to say it was healthy.**

Above
Drawing by Paul Davis, 2009

In the case of marketing, we have to learn, and constantly adapt to, its rules, its conventions and its mechanics. This can often be surprisingly easy for designers: with our ability to be objective, and capability of seeing the other person's point of view (see Empathy, page 106), we frequently have an aptitude for, and an instinctual grasp of, marketing tactics and strategies. However, the designer's intuitive grasp of communication is increasingly at odds with the current trend towards a more mechanistic approach within marketing circles. In contemporary marketing questions of both judgement and intuition are replaced by tools such as business metrics, market research and consumer behaviour analysis. David Ogilvy, the advertising guru, wrote: 'I notice increasing reluctance on the part of marketing executives to use judgment; they are coming to rely too much on research, and they use it as a drunkard uses a lamp post for support, rather than for illumination.'[1]

So if we are to live in harmony with our marketing clients, we have to become as well-versed in their craft as possible. This is doubly relevant today, as marketing is going through a profound change. As with many aspects of commercial life, it has been turned on its head by the Internet. In the new digital world the consumer is in charge. Giant corporations with previously abysmal records of communicating with customers now use the Internet to speak directly to them. I just tapped the phrase 'contact us' into Google and got 3,320,000,000 hits. This is the new marketing: thanks to blogs and chat rooms the relationship between customer and supplier is now a conversation, and this 'two-way' marketing means the death of the traditional dictatorial approach.

Further reading: Sam Hill and Glenn Rifkin, *Radical Marketing: From Harvard to Harley, Lessons From Ten That Broke the Rules and Made It Big*. HarperCollins, 1999.

1 David Ogilvy, *Confessions of an Advertising Man*. Atheneum, revised edition, 1988.

Modernism

For some graphic designers Modernism is the gold standard, and provides an ethical and stylistic 'solution' for all design tasks. For others it is a sterile, arrogant and rhetorical visual style used by designers who claim to know what is best for their audience.

In 1908, the architect Adolf Loos wrote an influential essay entitled 'Ornament and Crime' in which he repudiated the florid styles of the time and advocated an adornment-free approach to architecture and the manufacture of objects. Modernism in graphic design might be said to have begun with the establishment in Germany of the Bauhaus school. It was founded by the architect Walter Gropius who believed in the merging of crafts and the fine arts, and who wanted to revitalize design by putting an end to the imitation of old 'naturalistic' styles, and allow design to embrace the new age of mass production. The Bauhaus fought to develop a truly modern machine aesthetic, but by 1933 it had succumbed to Nazi pressure and was closed.

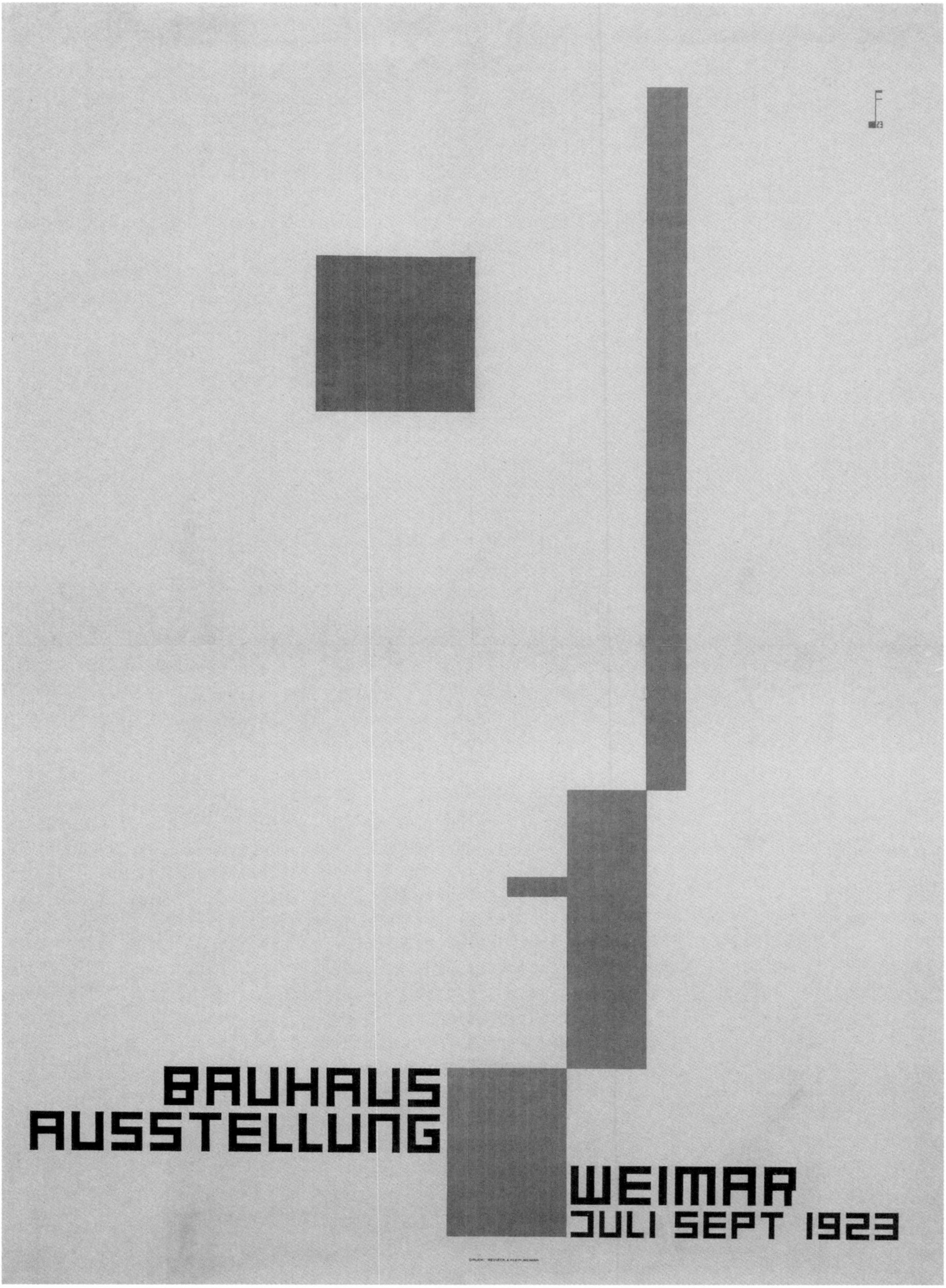
BAUHAUS
AUSSTELLUNG
WEIMAR
JULI SEPT 1923

Today, reaction to the utopian dream espoused by the Bauhaus, and its followers, ranges from wide-eyed acceptance to the outright dismissive. Writing in the *Guardian* in 2006, the art critic Robert Hughes adopted a sniffy tone: 'When Gropius in 1919 wrote a programme for the first state Bauhaus, which was set up in Weimar, he invoked the images of a cathedral, a crystal edifice, a new community of faith expressing itself in craft. At the root, there was always something penitential about modernism, with its stern abjuration of the world's sensuous pleasures in the interest of higher ones. You were never left in any doubt that the monk's cell was a better place to be than the capitalist's study, let alone his wife's boudoir.'[1]

Writing in the same newspaper in 2007, the design writer Fiona MacCarthy espoused the alternative view: 'I have always loved Bauhaus's peculiar combination of solemnity and regimented craziness … But it was not until last spring that I saw the Dessau buildings, which had for many years been marooned in communist East Germany. I now understand what Reyner Banham meant when he called the Bauhaus at Dessau "a sacred site". What made it so moving? Not just the architectural coherence of the school and the masters' houses nearby in the pine woods, but the weight of its history. Bauhaus ideas survived to shape the modern world.'[2]

Despite the sheer functionality of Modernist styles and Modernist thinking, today's clients are not always sympathetic towards it. It's customary for them to say layouts that use the Modernist ethos are 'cold' and 'unwelcoming'.

From the contrasting views of Hughes and MacCarthy we sense that Modernism is the designers' and not the public's style – a recurring theme when it is evaluated. But if Modernism stood for anything it stood for newness, and it is inevitable that a typographic style would emerge that reflected the new machine aesthetic. The writer L. Sandusky noted: 'The Bauhaus was in the right place at the right time to catch the influence of constructivism and De Stijl and transmute them into utilitarian functionalism which in printing and advertising design was to become known as the new typography.'[3] Bauhaus typography was to mutate over the post-war years into the International Style or Swiss Style, and by the 1960s it had become the major stylistic force in world graphic design, largely due to its dominance in American commercial culture. Even in 1938, Sandusky could write: 'The story of the Bauhaus is the story of how a considerable body of contemporary American printing and advertising came to be what it is.' Today, the Modernist approach to design and typography is

Previous page
Project: Bauhaus Ausstellung
Date: 1923
Designer: Fritz Schleifer
Lithographic poster. An exquisite example of high Bauhuas Modernism showing the use of geometric shapes used to create poetic tension. From the Bauhaus-Archiv, Berlin.

everywhere. But what does it mean to be an adherent of Modernist design principles today? Modernism was never just a style – it was an ideology and, ideologically speaking, it is making a cautious return. We can see it in the way design – and design thinking – is being brought back into areas like social housing, issues relating to sustainability and the management of change in society. 'Design' is now a buzzword used in the social sphere in a way not seen since the 1960s. In 2005, Stanford University in California launched its d.school, an institution that proclaims itself the home of the interdisciplinary vanguard, set to unlock the potential of 'design thinking'. It states: 'The d.school is a place for project teams to tackle difficult, messy problems. The prototypes produced in the d.school include objects, software, experiences, performances, and organizations. They are imperfect and ever-evolving solutions. We use design thinking to tackle hard social problems: Stop drunk driving. Build better elementary schools. Develop environmentally sustainable offerings.'[4] If that isn't a Modernist manifesto, I don't know what is.

Clients prefer more actively grabby and punchy graphics: for them, paradoxically, Modernism is seen as elitist and rarefied.

For the precise and aesthetically pleasing transmission of information, there is nothing better than Modernist design principles. We can call it sterile and dictatorial, but for the effective conveying of information, it has never been bettered.

In the 1990s, under the influence of the Swiss masters, and as a reaction to the Deconstructionist tendencies of radical American designers, Neo-Modernism enjoyed a strong following in the United Kingdom where, traditionally, Modernism had never held much sway. But a host of young design groups showed that an updated Modernism had the conceptual and stylistic weight to function in the diverse and clamorous final years of the twentieth century.

Despite the sheer functionality of Modernist styles and Modernist thinking, today's clients are not always sympathetic towards it. It's customary for them to say layouts that use the Modernist ethos are 'cold' and 'unwelcoming'. They prefer more actively grabby and punchy graphics: for them, paradoxically, Modernism is seen as elitist and rarefied.

Further reading: Robin Kinross, 'The Bauhaus Again: in the Constellation of Typographic Modernism', from *Unjustified Texts. Perspectives on Typography*. Hyphen Press, 2002.

1 Robert Hughes, 'Paradise Now', *Guardian*, 20 March 2006.
2 Fiona MacCarthy, 'House Style', *Guardian*, 17 November 2007.
3 L. Sandusky, 'The Bauhaus Tradition and the New Typography', *PM*, 1938. Reprinted in Steven Heller and Philip B. Meggs (eds), *Texts on Type: Critical Writings on Typography*. Allworth Press, 2001.
4 www.stanford.edu/group/dschool/

Money

Clients are often sophisticated financial operators, while designers are often financially unsophisticated. But although many designers regret the way design is compromised by financial considerations, there isn't much to be gained by financial ineptitude. Is it possible to combine design integrity with financial competence?

Graphic designers rarely talk about money. Anyone reading the literature of graphic design might imagine that designers live on air. Why the coyness? Lots of designers – although by no means all – appear to be in thrall to dreams of artistic purity where the mention of cash is taboo. Yet anyone who runs a studio or works as a freelance designer, needs a high degree of sophistication in the way they manage money. But where are designers supposed to acquire financial skills? Most of us have to find out the hard way, by making mistakes.

Of course, not all designers have problems with money. There are many who are financially savvy, possess business acumen and know how to negotiate fees, manage their cash flows, and run profitable businesses. And there's another – much rarer – kind of designer who will have nothing to do with the profit-driven treadmill: these are designers who reject the kill-or-be-killed world of capitalism, and do pro bono work, or work for non-profit-making organizations.

But for the rest of us, with bills and taxes to pay, we can't avoid wrestling with the daily realities of finance. An accountant I once employed – a clever man with a lump of granite where other people have a heart – identified the root of the problem. 'Trouble with you designers,' he said, 'is that you earn a living doing something you love, and when you are in love with your work you aren't rational about it. You are emotional about it, and this clouds your judgement. Emotion and business don't mix.'

My granite-hearted accountant had a point. For instance, when asked to take on a new project a designer's first consideration is usually not how much is this job worth but is it the sort of work I want to do? If it's an enticing brief with the potential to create a first-rate piece of work, many of us will jump at it regardless of the remuneration involved. Some of us will even take on work with no remuneration because we like the project. And yet, it has always been my contention that it is possible for designers to combine this emotional attachment to their work with the most basic financial skills. I've also noticed that some of the most high-minded and idealistic designers are extremely sharp when it comes to money; they insist on being paid promptly, have a clear idea about their value and get the best rates for their labours.

If a designer's primary objective is to earn a lot of money, he or she is unlikely to achieve their goal. The only way to make money as a designer is to be an exemplary designer. And the only way we become exemplary designers is by making this our primary ambition.

¥ ЛВ Rs

£ đ kr

₵ zł ₪

₵ ден S/.

For sophisticated financial advice a good accountant is essential. But there are basic financial principles concerning the way we run a design studio – or conduct our affairs as a freelance designer – that are no more than simple common sense. The designer Marcello Minale, in *How to Keep Running a Successful Design Company*, writes: 'The procedure is simple, calculate your overheads – how much is it costing to run the company in wages, rent, and so on. Then collect all your invoices for that month, subtract the costs and add up all the fees charged. If your fee income exceeds your outgoings then you are in profit. Hooray! If your outgoings outstrip your fee incomes, you are making a loss, and you must take corrective action if you want to survive.'[1]

Minale's blunt pragmatism cuts to the heart of the matter. If our outgoings exceed our incomings, we are in danger. Yet, even when we have more money coming in than we have going out, we are still obliged to contend with cash flow. Cash flow is the single most treacherous financial element that a small business has to deal with. It is the most important measure of a company's, or an individual's, solvency. Cash flow has various technical meanings within financial accounting, but for the hard-working designer living on fees and trying to keep a studio afloat it means cash receipts minus cash payments over a given period of time. Or to put it another way: money in versus money out. Mastering cash flow requires financial discipline (controlling money out) and a robust approach to getting it in (debt chasing). (See Debt chasing, page 86.)

But cash flow aside, the most common financial question I hear designers asking is: 'How much should I charge?' Knowing how much to charge is based on how much income is needed to stay solvent and to make a profit. To make this possible, all designers need a rate card of charges. This menu of costs should show hourly or daily charge-out rates. It is a set of figures we can quote to clients without feeling embarrassed or apologetic. But how do we arrive at these figures?

We calculate our charge-out rates by adding up all our costs, just as Marcello Minale advises. This enables us to arrive at the break-even monthly figure that allows us to stay in business. We must include everything from

For the hard-working designer living on fees and trying to keep a studio afloat it means cash receipts minus cash payments over a given period of time. Or to put it another way: money in versus money out. Mastering cash flow requires financial discipline (controlling money out) and a robust approach to getting it in (debt chasing).

Above and overleaf
Range of international currency symbols taken from various typographic alphabets.

salaries to the cost of toilet rolls, and it is important to include a sum for contingencies (for example, if a computer suddenly fails and needs to be repaired or replaced).

Yet even when we've done this, we are still missing a vital element: as my accountant never failed to remind me, breaking even isn't enough; we need a profit margin. So we must also add, say, 30 per cent – and by doing this we finally arrive at a figure that is our monthly target. This is the sum we have to invoice each month to remain solvent. Let's call this monthly target 'x', and with this figure we can now calculate our hourly charge-out rates – in other words, our fees. To do this we simply divide 'x' by the number of hours we work each week (say 40), and to arrive at a daily rate we divide 'x' by the number of days worked each month.

So, equipped with these basic charge-out rates we can tell our clients what any task will cost them in fees and, just as importantly, we can constantly monitor our own performance: if, for example, we've quoted ten hours for a project and taken 20 hours to complete the task, we know we have underquoted.

All this takes us closer to being able to answer the question 'How much should I charge?' But before we can come up with a figure we have to consider the external costs generated by undertaking a particular project. If we have to buy images from a picture library, or commission photography, or pay for web coding, we must add these to the figure we quote to our clients. This is a fraught and contentious area for small studios and solo designers. If we are incurring costs on behalf of a client, it is perfectly legitimate to add a sum to cover the expense of doing so: it's called a mark-up. Most clients will accept this as long as the mark-up is 'reasonable', and we should be prepared to state, if asked, what it is. But if, as happens frequently nowadays, clients challenge the mark-up, we should ask them to accept the bill directly from the supplier.

A big fat print bill, or a hefty photography fee, can inflate the amount we bill our clients for. This looks good. It gives us the feeling we're making money. But it is a potential snake pit.

A big fat print bill, or a hefty photography fee, can inflate the amount we bill our clients for. This looks good. It gives us the feeling we're making money. But it is a potential snake pit. What happens if the client decides not to pay our invoice because they don't like the quality of the printer's work? Do we still have to pay the printer? What happens when a photographer submits a final invoice for more than his or her original quote?

₭ ﷼ ₩

ƒ руб ฿

$ ٯ €

₴ ₮ Kč

Are we obliged to pay the new amount? In both these instances, we are at risk unless we have been vigilant in the commissioning of our external suppliers. Carrying suppliers' bills requires discipline (see Commissioning creatives, page 68). If we don't control and manage external costs we are in peril.

When I became a graphic designer I was warned that I was entering a profession where it wasn't possible to earn much of a living, but by the time I started my own studio in 1989 this had changed. I set up a studio because I craved the creative freedom that would come with being in charge of my own destiny, but I also did it because I needed to make money. To do this in those days, designers had to be prepared to work very hard, and had to develop a quick instinct for negotiating fees and spotting opportunities to do things for clients, like print buying and purchasing additional services such as retouching and producing photoshoots, all of which earned valuable additional income. But today, the simple truth is that designers have lost control over the way they earn fees, and the art of negotiating fees is a dying skill. In my experience, even when clients ask us to prepare elaborate and detailed quotations they usually know how much they have to spend. The designer's task is to come up with a fee that is close to this unknown figure, or one that is lower.

What this means in practice is that today the buyers of design services call the shots, and the bigger clients are, the more control they want to have over what they spend.

For the New York-based designer and Pentagram partner Michael Bierut, the modern trend of clients dictating fees needn't be a problem. He notes: 'Occasionally a client will simply pick a firm on merit and say "We want to work with you. We have this much to spend. Is that okay?" This is actually my favorite situation. I have never said no, no matter how low the number. I suspect this is true for other designers as well.' He goes on to say: 'It is increasingly rare to find clients willing to enter into an open-ended arrangement with designers. Very rarely (in my experience) will a design firm be on retainer to a client and work on an hourly basis, simply sending invoices for work performed, based on how long it takes and with no advance estimating. This arrangement is nice – lawyers seem to do quite well with it.'

Pentagram's international spread of offices gives Bierut an eagle-eyed view of the way clients set fees: 'In my experience, some clients will ask a variety of firms to submit fixed fee estimates for a set scope of work, and will select one they like based on various criteria. In the public sector, sometimes they have to pick the lowest bid. Other times they'll say you can have the job if you adjust your fee to match the lowest. Sometimes they appear to have an idea beforehand what the budget is. Other times they use the bidding process to establish the "going rate".'

What this means in practice is that today the buyers of design services call the shots, and the bigger clients are, the more control they want to have over what they spend. Most large firms have sophisticated procurement practices: they know how to buy print and other communication services, and they know they want to avoid a designer's mark-up. The result of all this? Despite the massive growth in demand for design services it is tougher than ever to make money.

Another problem area is estimating the number of hours a project will take. It's no comfort to know that nearly every project in the entire history of graphic design has taken longer than was initially estimated. If we quote 25 hours, we can be sure it will take longer. But we have to estimate something, so we have to make an intelligent guess; and this intelligent guess needs to be as realistic as possible if we are to monitor the performance of our business accurately, and if we are to be able to look a client in the eye and tell them what a particular project will cost. But estimating the amount of time a project will take is fraught with danger: if we guess too high, we will arrive at an amount that will scare the client away; if we guess too low we will arrive at a figure that means we lose money.[2]

It is therefore common for a client to have already determined what they want to spend long before they ask a designer to specify his or her charges. Some clients will tell us what their budget is, and then it's a simple matter of deciding whether it is reasonable or not.

But this still leaves us with one last matter to contend with: clients ask designers to prepare quotations for work, yet most clients know exactly how much they want to spend when they approach a designer. No modern business allows itself to enter into a new project without first setting a budget. It is therefore common for a client to have already determined what they want to spend long before they ask a designer to specify his or her charges. Some clients will tell us what their budget is, and then it's a simple matter of deciding whether it is reasonable or not. We do this by applying the above formula to the job.

Some clients will ask us to quote and then tell us how much they have to spend. They do this in the hope that we will name a price lower than their allocated budget.

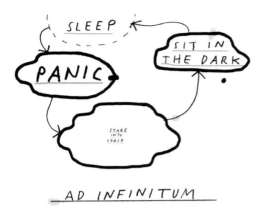

SLEEP

PANIC

SIT IN
THE DARK

STARE
INTO
SPACE

AD INFINITUM

Above
Drawing by Paul Davis, 2009

1 These figures should be subject to constant revision as circumstances change. As a studio grows, as it employs more people and acquires new equipment, it needs to reflect these increased costs in revised charge-out rates.
2 This brings us to yet another part of the answer to the question 'How much should I charge?': psychology. What's psychology got to do with professional fees? Well, I'm tempted to say everything, but that wouldn't be quite right. What I will say is that informing clients of costs requires almost as much skill as calculating those costs in the first place. This important aspect of charging is dealt with elsewhere (see Negotiating fees, page 208).
3 Terms and Conditions are a dull and tedious detail that many designers would rather avoid. But it is not wise to do this. An accountant – the granite-hearted kind are the best – will advise on all the details.

It figures, therefore, that before we prepare elaborate costings the first question to ask a client is: 'How much have you got to spend?' Some clients will tell us, but most will say: 'I'm asking three studios to quote. Let me have your quotation and I'll decide.' In this case we have to prepare a quotation itemizing our costs in the normal way.

As we have seen, there is no easy answer to 'How much should I charge?'. But it is never wise to guess, or name a figure and hope the client will accept it. Modern business demands transparency, so there is really no way to avoid establishing a proper scale of charges and sticking to it. The simple rule of all finance is that the more professional we are the less likely we are to have problems.

For many designers the protocols of financial management are tedious, but there's nothing more tedious than dealing with a bankruptcy or coping with financial collapse. By always preparing detailed and honest job-costings; by always putting quotations to clients in writing; by never sending an invoice until we have agreement on the final price, including extras; by ensuring we have a purchase order for even the smallest job; and by establishing professional Terms and Conditions,[3] we can avoid many of the problems that harass designers.

In the new ultra-professional climate in which most designers operate, they can no longer plead financial naivety. We all have to be financially savvy; the more disciplined and the more vigilant we are about our finances, the more likely we are to make money. And yet there's a paradox here: if a designer's primary objective is to earn a lot, he or she is unlikely to achieve their goal. The only way to make money as a designer is to be an exemplary designer. And the only way we become exemplary designers is by making this our primary ambition. Making money has to be ranked less highly in our scale of priorities.

Further reading:
www.aiga.org/content.cfm/standard-agreement

The most common financial question I hear designers asking is: 'How much should I charge?' Knowing how much to charge is based on how much income is needed to stay solvent and to make a profit.

Motion design

Most students emerge from design school with the ability to make images and text move. Inexpensive software enables anyone to produce moving image sequences, but it takes more than software to create convincing motion.

There's a sense in which graphic design has been on a long search to find its most potent, engaging and effective form: for many, that form is motion graphics. Like many designers, I got into motion design around the time the digital transformation of design was beginning to get under way. For designers in the late 1980s and early 1990s, there was a growing feeling that anything was possible – even motion. And when I co-founded my design company Intro in 1989, we combined print and motion design at a time when it was rare to find both disciplines under the same roof.

Back then we were still dependent on traditional, non-digital film-craft skills such as shooting on film stock, film and video editing, paint and trace animation, etc. Desktop editing and animation were still a year or two in the future, but the move towards a screen-based design culture was under way, and many designers came to realize that graphic design was no longer static, and no longer fixed in time. It was possible to make type move, and to extend design's frozen moment across time. This profoundly changed the way designers thought about visual communication. For me the catalyst for this transformation from static graphic design to moving graphic design was the arrival in the United Kingdom of MTV. It had been established in the United States since 1981, but when it splash-landed into the UK media scene in 1987 its impact was seismic.

Looking at MTV today, with its slick production values and its status as a global media brand, it's hard to believe it once had some of the spirit of punk about it: there was a sense – at least for graphic designers and video directors – that here was a broadcast medium, that 'anyone can contribute to'. And when MTV offered young British video directors and designers the opportunity to make idents for the new channel by committing acts of graphic violence to its logo, it felt like a brave new world opening up. MTV didn't pay much – their budgets were paltry – but it offered a platform for motion graphics that had not previously existed, and it offered the kudos of television exposure to designers who normally wouldn't get as much as a sniff of a cathode ray.

By the final two decades of the twentieth century, motion graphics had became a bona fide design activity.

Digital technology allows the modern filmmaker to make a different sort of film: it allows the creation of a new, hybrid, non-linear, audiovisual cinematic bloodline that contains animation, the sampling of sound and vision and the creation of graphic effects.

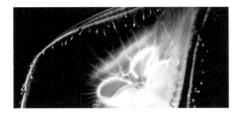

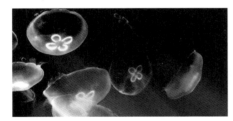

Above
Project: *The Mast*
Date: 2009
Client: Araya/Benbecula Records
Designer/Director: Sean Pruen
Short film shot at the Horniman Museum, London, studying the effect of light and colour on a school of jellyfish. *The Mast* was directed, photographed, designed and edited by designer and filmmaker Sean Pruen for experimental electronic musician Araya on Benbecula Records. This stylish and hypnotic film can be seen at: www.seanographic.co.uk

Design houses specializing in motion graphics sprang up, and others added motion design to their list of services. To deal with the new branded TV landscape, designers started to specialize in television graphics, and offered the sort of sophisticated design services that had long been available in print communications (see Broadcast design, page 56). Of course, there had always been designers who worked in motion. Saul Bass might be said to have invented the genre in the 1960s, but although he had a genuine graphic design sensibility – he designed print graphics as well – he was also versed in film technology and could call on the services of Hollywood's finest filmcraft people.

Even further back, avant-garde filmmakers bequeathed a legacy of visionary motion graphics: among others, László Moholy-Nagy, Oskar Fischinger, Harry Smith, Norman McLaren, Stan Brakhage and Len Lye added to the syntax of visual communication with techniques that bypassed those of traditional film and used manual processes – drawing on to film stock and exposing objects placed directly on it – that allowed films to be made without a camera. Today, motion graphic designers make films without a camera – it's called using a computer.

For the modern graphic designer, working with motion is the norm. All that is needed is a powerful computer and some smart software. Digital technology allows the modern filmmaker to make a different sort of film: it allows the creation of a new, hybrid, non-linear, audiovisual cinematic bloodline that contains animation, the sampling of sound and vision and the creation of graphic effects.

In conventional cinema, when a print is made that's it; you can only change it at vast expense. But a digital film can be easily changed. When a sequence is constructed from binary information, it can be endlessly remixed.

At the digital frontier, the camera has been replaced by the computer as the principal tool of the filmmaker, and the processing power of the microchip has replaced light as the primary component in making images move. But most critically, digital technology has put the ability to make time-based media into the hands of individuals unversed in traditional film craft.

The notion of film-less films – of movies made in computers – opens up numerous avenues of exploration, and offers a set of intriguing possibilities not available to the conventional filmmaker. The all-digital realm is different. Take, for example, the traditional notion of a work of art being 'finished': this is an alien concept to the digital filmmaker. In conventional cinema, when a print is made that's it; you can only change it at vast

Above top
Project: Yell.com cinema commercial
Date: 2006
Client: AKQA
Director: Julian Gibbs, Intro
Commercial presenting the endless
possibilities of using the yell.com directory
to search for everything from karate lessons
to wine bars. Intro directed, edited and
completed all the post-production in-house.

Above
Project: *The Snow Queen* film
Date: 2005
Client: CBBC
Director: Julian Gibbs, Intro
An hour-length film adaptation of Hans
Christian Andersen's classic fairytale,
made by compositing blue screen footage
with animated and photo-collaged backgrounds.

Opposite top
Project: 00sieben.19.01.00
Date: 2000
Label: Synchron
Designer: Ralph Steinbrüchel

Opposite bottom
Project: End5.29.09.99
Date: 1999
Label: Synchron
Designer: Ralph Steinbrüchel
7" vinyl inserts by Swiss-based musician,
label owner and designer Ralph Steinbrüchel.
Part of the granulat_live_series.
www.synchron.ch

1 I worked with Julian Gibbs at Intro, the
design company I co-founded in London.
He ran the Intro moving-image team making
music videos, TV commercials and broadcast
graphics. He was a pioneer of the use of
desktop computers in motion graphics. In the
early nineties he directed a TV commercial
for Q magazine, which as far as we could tell
at the time, was the first example of a TV
commercial made entirely on an Apple Mac.

expense. But a digital film can be easily changed. When
a sequence is constructed from binary information, it can
be endlessly remixed. In the digital world the notion of
a 'finished' work has become redundant: think of digital
music – tracks are reconfigured endlessly by remixers
to the point that the notion of an 'original' is almost
irrelevant. As a result, music can now be said to exist in
a state of constant flux and impermanence. Of course, this
new fluid meta-universe of change doesn't always guarantee
better 'art' – but it gives us a new syntax for moving
images (and the arts in general) that the great artists
of the past could not have envisaged.

What does all this mean for graphic designers?
It means that design is no longer static: it exists
in time as well as space. It means that designers
have to learn to make movement that is convincing and
narratively compelling. It means that
designers can make title sequences,
advertisements, music videos, trailers
and presentations using basic software
(mainly After Effects and Final Cut
Pro). It means that designers need to
study the great animators and the great
live-action directors.

For the filmmaker Julian Gibbs,
a designer/director who trained as
a conventional animator, but who was
among the first to adopt digital
technology, the new democratic world
of motion graphics is a minefield:[1]
'Watching YouTube confirms that yes, indeed, anyone
can do it, there is no longer any complicated science
accompanying the process, no chemistry or alchemy or dark
magic that first bought us colour film like *The Wizard of
Oz* or the massive spectacle of Kubrick's *2001* in 70mm,
now it can all be done with our camera phones and bashed
out to billions in about half an hour by a 12-year-old,
job done.' But he advises against an over reliance on
technology: 'Human touch is critical. Computers are dead
things, they can't cook like us, they have no dreams,
although oddly enough they have huge memories but no
facility to reminisce. This lack of ability to indulge in
past experience makes our role what it is. As the artist
we are the magic element in the equation, we input our
collections of psychology, associations and conditioning,
our neurotic meanderings, bits of fluff and sentient
shite, the stuff that makes us human.'

**Design is no
longer static:
it exists in
time as well
as space. It
means that
designers have
to learn to make
movement that
is convincing
and narratively
compelling.**

**Further reading: Shane R. J. Walter, *Motion Blur:
Multidimensional Moving Imagemakers: v.2*, DVD edition.
Laurence King Publishing, 2008.**

Music design

Despite the widespread practice of downloading music from the Internet, and despite tumbling record-company budgets, designers still want to design record covers. But is there still work for designers, and are record companies still willing to pay to have evocative artwork?

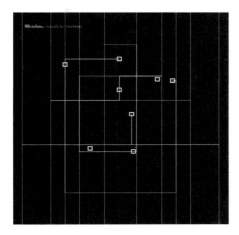

Mainstream graphic design had kept album cover art at arm's length. This was because record sleeves mainly eschewed design formalism in favour of a less structured approach. The great covers of the 1960s and 1970s – the golden age for cover art – are vivid explosions of type and image. But they rarely boasted sophisticated typography or adhered to the prescribed codes of graphic design. There were exceptions but, as a general rule, record-cover art was insufficiently formal to be considered 'real design' by educators, design's professional bodies, or the design elite.

One of the best routes into music design is via musicians, bands, DJs, producers, etc. There can't be many people who don't know someone in a band, and bands tend to be enthusiastic about their cover art and their visual identity.

To mainstream designers, record-cover design appeared a free-for-all – anything goes, or so it seemed. They were concerned with strict commercial issues: they had sophisticated briefs and worked within their restraints. Record-sleeve designers were just 'playing at it'. But in the second half of the 1970s a group of British designers, born into the pop culture era, found ways of combining record-cover art with Modernist design principles. The English duo of Peter Saville and Malcolm Garrett discovered Herbert Spencer's *Principles of Modern Typography*, and the result was the increased graphic sophistication of cover art, and its gradual, but by no means complete acceptance within 'grown-up' design. In the 1990s, the process of integration accelerated. Groups like Farrow, Blue Source and my old studio, Intro, proved that you could create iconoclastic cover art but still apply sophisticated graphic design thinking. Ironically, the record industry had, for the past two decades, been as commercially demanding as any other consumer-orientated business. Since the 1990s, record covers have been subjected to market research, and record company people are not usually trained at Proctor & Gamble or Coca-Cola.

Yet within graphic design interest in cover art remains high. It is still a frequent subject for a final thesis, and for many young designers record-sleeve design remains a valuable and fulfilling activity. The reality, however, is different. The record cover is dead – and if it's not dead, then, as Frank Zappa once said about jazz, it smells funny.

This demise of the record cover has been under way for some time. Ever since the arrival of the music video, followed by the shrunken canvas of the CD, cover art has been diminishing in importance. Once the most essential visual element in the marketing and promotion of bands,

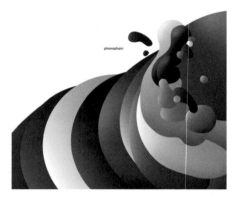

Above
Projects: Maja Ratkje – Voice;
Phonophani – Phonophani
Dates: 2002/2006
Label: Rune Grammofon
Designer: Kim Hiorthøy

the album cover is now just one of a dozen requirements for the successful marketing of music. There are good reasons for its loss of status: in the 1960s and 1970s it was pretty much all there was; there was no MTV, no glossy colour magazines, no Internet. Consequently, record sleeves represented the major part of a band or a musician's visual identity. Today, the album cover is just one of many surfaces to be filled, no less and no more important than any other.

All this means that it has never been tougher to be a record-cover designer. The big record companies view sleeve design as a marginal activity, and those independent labels that still value it only have tiny budgets. But it's hard to be critical of this development: record covers are not as commercially important as they once were. In the golden age of sleeve design – the 1960s and 1970s – they were often the only platform bands had for a visual identity. Now, in the digital age, there are countless ways for bands and musicians to present themselves. On top of all this, legal (and illegal) downloading is steadily eroding the need for printed and manufactured packaging. It's hardly surprising therefore that the big labels don't give a hoot about record-cover design. If you want to be treated with respect as a designer, you'd be better off working for an insurance company. They pay more, too.

But, designers love music. And designers love record covers. Whenever I go to art schools, or give talks to designers, I'm astonished at how strong the interest in record covers is. And I'm often asked the question: 'How do you break into music design?'

It's not easy; even getting appointments to see labels requires hard graft. Unfortunately, the direct approach – calling up or sending mailers – is almost worthless. The grim reality is that the record business (at every level) works on the 'who you know' rule. Occasionally, some enlightened person within a label will spot a piece of work and track down the designer. This used to be common practice; today it is rare.

One of the best routes into music design is via musicians, bands, DJs, producers, etc. There can't be many people who don't know someone in a band, and bands tend to be enthusiastic about their cover art and their visual identity. These are usually high on their list of priorities, so it's worth badgering them to let you design for them.

There are two sorts of bands: unsigned and signed. Assuming you are looking for a first foothold on the music industry ladder, it's worth offering to do artwork for unsigned bands. It's rare for them to have any money, therefore you have to be prepared to do the work for

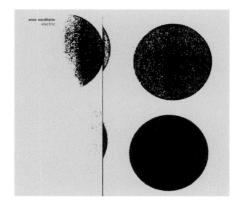

Above
Projects: Arne Nordheim – Electric
Shining – Grindstone
Dates: 2002/2007
Label: Rune Grammofon
Designer: Kim Hiorthøy
The Norwegian designer has created a
compelling and idiosyncratic house style
for Oslo-based record label Rune Grammofon.
Hiorthøy uses a vast array of techniques
and graphic effects, yet manages to retain
a distinctive and readily identifiable
house style.

nothing. I'm never keen on advocating working for no money (unless it's for a charity) but in this instance there really is no choice. However, try and get an agreement that if and when the band is signed you will be employed to create the artwork. Most signed bands have contractual control over their artwork (they should, they pay for it!), and most bands are keen to have the final say on who designs their album covers. Many famous record-cover designers received their first sleeve-design commissions from bands. It's one of the best ways of breaking into music design.

Of course, once you have a successful job to your name the situation changes. The record industry understands only one language: the language of success. If you design a cover for a successful band, labels keen to replicate the success of your project will track you down. But don't sit about waiting for this to happen. You must move fast to take advantage of your success; send details of your project to the product managers for the big labels.

Small independent labels are more approachable than big ones. They also have a deeper interest in design. But be aware that indie labels tend to concentrate on one style of music, so before you approach one ask yourself if your work is appropriate. If the answer's no, don't waste your time. Offering to undertake the design of some of the less glamorous aspects of a label's activities can sometimes prove a good way to get a foot in the door. I'm thinking of flyers, mail-outs, stickers, updating web pages and designing labels for advance promo copies of new releases.

Most importantly, don't be starry-eyed about the music business. The days of the coke-snorting designer turning up at a rock star's mansion to discuss million-dollar art-direction ideas are a thing of the past (it used to happen!). Reliability is vital. The tight economics of the modern record industry demand professionalism. Naturally, flair and originality are valued, but they have to be matched with efficiency and accuracy.

The record industry understands only one language: the language of success. If you design a cover for a successful band, labels keen to replicate the success of your project will track you down. But don't sit about waiting for this to happen. You must move fast to take advantage of your success.

Further reading: Adrian Shaughnessy, *Cover Art By: New Music Graphics*. Laurence King Publishing, 2008.

N

Negotiating fees

We often have to jump through burning hoops to convince clients to hire us. But even when they are persuaded by our design skills we still have to negotiate our fees. It's a vital part of the design process, yet unlike our clients few of us have any training in this area.

I once had a client who was a zealous negotiator of fees. One day he asked me to give him a price for a project. I prepared a costing based on the number of hours needed to complete the job, I added all external costs and I included a profit margin. I then reduced the total because I knew he was a hard-nosed negotiator who squeezed my budgets until my eyes watered.

I called him up to give him the figure. I called him rather than emailing him because it is easy for clients to bounce back an email saying no, but much harder to argue with a real live human being. When I named my price my client was silent. And stayed silent. My instinct was to blurt out a lower fee – anything to fill the silence. But I held out just long enough to hear him muffle a laugh. 'Sorry,' he said, 'can't keep this up. I've just been on a training course to learn financial negotiation techniques. I was told to say nothing when someone gives me a price. Nine times out of ten, they give you a lower price straightaway.' I laughed a weak laugh and reduced my price.

Just as there is an 'art' to receiving a quotation, there is also an art to giving one. The people who are good at delivering a cost to a client do it in a deadpan, matter-of-fact manner, with no hesitation or diffidence. They just come right out with it. They deliver it confidently, professionally and without apology. It's a beautiful thing to see. I've never mastered it myself. I bluster. Get irritated, and take everything much too personally. I always allow a hint of desperation to enter

Professionalism in negotiating fees is equally important. If we appear amateurish or too casual, our clients, like lions who see a lame antelope, will pick us off with ease.

ADVICE # 1726

FEES:
AIM HIGH, ACCEPT HALF,
NEARLY EVERYONE HAPPY.

my voice, and you can bet my clients spot this (even if they haven't been on courses that teach them how to kill designers with their bare hands).

There's a psychology to delivering a cost, and as soon as my studio grew to an appropriate size I employed brilliant professional people who were able to get clients to agree to budgets simply by being super-efficient, reassuring and confident. Negotiating budgets involves a complex ritual, and the most important part of that ritual is confidence. But more than just confidence is needed. The three key elements – besides confidence – are market intelligence, professionalism and flexibility.

1. Market intelligence means understanding and knowing our clients and their businesses, and asking questions such as: are they in a business sector where design is valued? Have they got a track record for working with recognized design groups? Are they likely to pay market rates? Do they have a reputation for cost cutting? If we can gather answers to these questions (over time we develop an instinct for this stuff) we can formulate a way of approaching clients with an appropriate budget. This requires keeping eyes and ears open for the tiniest of clues; for example, the client who moans about the charges levied by a previous supplier isn't going to be sympathetic to a high cost.
2. Professionalism in negotiating fees is equally important. If we appear amateurish or too casual, our clients, like lions who see a lame antelope, will pick us off with ease. To be professional means preparing costs in a way that reflects a properly worked out scale of hourly or daily charges. It means showing as much transparency as possible. And it means believing in what we are charging – so no guesses or fingers held up to the wind: prices must be real and relate to the amount of work involved. The worst thing we can do (as I did with my client

Above
Drawing by Paul Davis, 2009

above) is to suddenly drop our prices: this tells clients we are fundamentally unserious and our costings are made out of whims and guesses. If we are obliged to drop prices, we need to explain why we are doing so and what this involves – usually some aspect of the budget has to be cut, or some concessions given.

3. How does flexibility square with being resolute about not dropping prices? In the new world of cost-cutting finance we have to have a flexible and open mind when it comes to costing. The English designer Michael Johnson describes a revealing incident: 'Once, in the late eighties, I spent nearly £20,000 on just the photography for a bank leaflet. Admittedly, it was an important leaflet (for the student market) and leaflets and posters were then the key ways to approach the market. But still, 20 grand? Only last week a client asked me to expand the scope of their annual report but then revealed their photography budget to be a princely £1,000. We gulped a little, but it didn't come as a huge surprise.'[1] What Johnson is showing here is that unless we adopt a negotiating approach to our fees and costs that takes into account the way clients think about, and purchase, design we will have problems. Johnson is clearly surprised at the drop in budget, but he knows why – he is flexible. Adopting a 'this is the way we always do things' approach is to write a commercial suicide note. We must have professionalism and integrity in the way we present our fees, but we must also be adaptable and sensitive to market changes and clients' needs.

As has been noted elsewhere in this book (see Money, page 196), most clients set their own budgets. They know exactly how much they want to spend before we even give them our costings. So what do we do in this situation? I always assume clients know how much money they have for a project, so I always ask them to tell me. They don't always do so, and usually insist on me submitting a price, but occasionally a great deal of work is avoided by a client stating their budget. Inevitably, this usually means settling somewhere in the middle (though generally nearer to the client's figure than our own). But by being confident, professional and flexible, and by using market intelligence, we can at least attempt to negotiate a fee that is realistic and acceptable. And one that doesn't make us look like rank amateurs.

1 Michael Johnson, 'Which way now?', March 2007. www.johnsonbanks.co.uk/thoughtfortheweek/index.php?thoughtid=162

Further reading: www.creativepro.com/article/the-art-of-business-negotiating-fees

New business

Ask designers what they want from the design fairy and most would say: a steady flow of new work. But how do we find new work? And how do we find the right sort of work? Is there an alternative to touting around our creative skills like a snake-oil salesman in the Wild West?

All designers look for ways to attract new clients and new work. Some individuals and some studios are in the happy position of attracting a steady flow of new projects. They have plenty of work and seem never to have to go hunting for clients. Yet we can be sure this is not an accident. It is the result of various factors, and paramount among them will be the fact that the individual or studio has a good reputation and does good work. Nothing attracts new clients like a glowing reputation and a body of successful designs, and designers need have no more sophisticated sales strategy than continuously to produce good work.

But for the vast majority of designers clients have to be searched for, fought over, and wooed in competitive tendering procedures. In other words, clients don't come to us; we have to go to them. So what's the best way to do this? Is it wise to try to sell design skills like any other business-sector service? Or is design inimical to conventional sales techniques? And while we're on the subject, I wonder whether it's feasible today for any

Is it wise to try to sell design skills like any other business-sector service? Or is design inimical to conventional sales techniques?

business-sector services to be sold successfully using conventional sales tactics. Consumers seem increasingly resistant to modern selling strategies. Cold-calling, most forms of direct mail, and the ubiquitous spam are imprecise, intrusive, wasteful, but, most of all, resented. Anyone who has had a call at home at 8.00 p.m. from someone selling double glazing or financial services, or has had to clear out dense clusters of unwanted emails, will tell you just how annoying these tactics can be. And if the general public doesn't like them, we can be sure they won't be any more popular in the business sector. In the context of selling design, most sales activities have the effect of saying 'I'm desperate', and are rarely successful.

But freelance designers, and people who run studios, have to find new clients. Even when business is buoyant this is never an easy job. And it's especially difficult today when the buyer is nearly always king, and competition has reached new peaks of intensity.

Big, well-upholstered design companies with the funds – and personnel – can use all the latest sales and marketing strategies. New-business people will operate a sophisticated database of 'hot' and 'cold' contacts. Their bedtime reading will be fierce-looking documents with titles like 'Customer Value Maximization'. They will host seminars, give lectures, publish research, get written about in *The Economist* and maintain an ultra-slick, client-focused website.

Above
Project: *Studio Brochure #2*
Date: 2009
Client: Emmi
Designer: Emmi Salonen
Emmi is a small graphic design studio in London specializing in identity and print. The *Studio Brochure* is a 36-page document designed to inform potential and existing clients about the studio's work. It is available to buy on the studio website, www.emmi.co.uk

The rest of us have to rely on less sophisticated methods. We might have a brochure and a website. We might send out email newsletters, and every so often we might get around to sending out an eye-catching mailshot. We enter competitions in the hope of being able to append the words 'award-winning' to our designs. We send work to the design press in the expectation of attracting the camera-flash of media attention. And occasionally we spruce up our portfolio, call existing or potential clients and ask them if we can show them our latest work.

Occasionally, just occasionally, these tactics succeed. But regardless of our best efforts – sophisticated or unsophisticated – most new-business opportunities for designers are created in one of two ways: the first is via word-of-mouth, and the second via random encounters in the business and social nexus that most of us live in. In other words, we get most of our new business from people who've heard good things about us, and about our work, and through attending social events such as weddings and parties.

The best way to win new business is to win it from existing clients. Making sure clients we've worked with before still love us and still want to work with us is an essential part of any designer's new-business activities.

Now, I'm not advocating a do-nothing policy here. What I am saying, however, is that the secret of new business is to get clients to call us. A call from a potential client with a nice project and a bit of cash to spend is the multiple orgasm of new business. But how do we attract those calls? Well, by doing work that gets people talking, and by shamelessly exploiting the chemistry of human relationships.

Each of us finds a way of attracting clients; some of us do it zealously, and some of us do it half-heartedly and apologetically, but the only real mistake we can make is to do nothing. In the early days of running a studio I'd ring up companies I wanted to work with. I hated doing it and this obviously showed because I never got anything. But I managed to attract clients by going to events and cultivating as many professional relationships as I could with the people I met. These people became contacts, and I sent them mail-outs and kept in touch with them. Gradually, I built up a database of contacts and set about systematically keeping in touch with them. I also set myself a target: to get to see people. I reasoned if I could sit down with a potential client I could persuade them to work with me. Even better, if I could get people to come to the studio I felt certain I'd be able to get commissions.

Above
Project: Red Bulletin 01
Date: 2008
Designer: Red
Brighton-based design group Red mails out
limited-edition posters to existing and
potential clients. One side features current
work; the reverse contains artwork specially
made for the poster.

Over time, I learnt another thing: I learnt not to compartmentalize my new-business activities. I learnt that if we viewed every action as having a new-business aspect, and if everyone in the studio realized they too had a new-business role, we greatly increased our flow of new work. It starts with the receptionist (or whoever answers the phone), and goes all the way to the studio heads. Even suppliers and professional advisers can be harnessed into performing a new-business role; treat them right and they become powerful advocates of your company. Then just sit back and wait for the phone to ring. The first call will be from someone selling time-share apartments in Florida, but the next one …

There's another important law governing new business. The time to look for it is when we are busy. Generating new projects always takes time, so chasing up potential clients when we have no work is not smart. We need to be looking for new business while we are busy – which for most small and medium-sized design groups, and of course solo designers, is not easy. But we have to do it if we want to keep a steady flow of work, and this means putting aside time each day (or week) for keeping in touch with current clients, sending promo material to potential clients and following up any hot leads. With modern communications this needn't be onerous but, paradoxically, it is one of the first activities to be dumped when we get busy.

'Keeping in touch with current clients' is an innocuous phrase – but it is the key to good new-business activity. On his website, Win Without Pitching,[1] the Canadian sales strategist Blair Enns offers sales-consulting to marketing communication agencies. Enns advocates nurturing clients as an essential part of the sales process – talking to them when they are not necessarily in a commissioning cycle, paying them attention when there is no immediate reward in sight. Of course, there is a fine line between 'keeping in contact' and being a pest, but most designers know the difference.

I would add one final suggestion to the above. The first will be alien to most designers: take ideas to clients. It's not an approach I'd previously adopted, but lately I had my eyes opened to its potential. I recently worked with two people (both non-designers) who run a creative business and who increasingly adopted a 'take ideas to the clients' strategy. This proved remarkably successful, and as competition grows it is no longer an option to wait passively to be invited to pitch. Taking

The time to look for new business is when we are busy. Generating new projects always takes time, so chasing up potential clients when we have no work is not smart.

ideas to clients (for new strategies, utilization of new platforms, etc.) involves as much work and research as an unpaid pitch. But this is where the comparison ends. Why? Because even if you fail to persuade a client to adopt an idea you've proposed, you own that idea and can pitch it to someone else – strictly 'on your own terms', of course.

Further reading: Linda Cooper Bowen, *The Graphic Designer's Guide to Creative Marketing: Finding & Keeping Your Best Clients*. Wiley, 1999.

1 www.winwithoutpitching.com

Newspaper design

Newspapers are not about news any more. By the time they hit the streets the news they carry is not news, it's history. So what is the role of the newspaper designer in a world where the real-time, always-on electronic media does the job of disseminating news better than newsprint?

Despite the rise of 24-hour news channels on television, numberless radio stations and the Internet, newspapers haven't vanished from our cultural lives. We still like the wood-pulp-and-ink technology of our favourite daily papers. Advertisers may be moving their money online, but newspapers still have a loyal if perhaps dwindling readership; broadsheet readers value sober analysis, informed opinion and incisive writing, while an even bigger group relishes the lurid outpourings of the tabloids. And despite the clatter of laptop keyboards that forms the soundtrack to most train journeys, it's much easier to read a newspaper during the morning commute than it is to log on to the Internet and read the news from a computer screen.[1] Newspapers don't cut out when you go into a tunnel either.

Regardless of our appetite for newsprint, the daily papers (big or small, serious or frivolous) have a fight on their hands to stay in contention in the always-on, electronic-media environment. One of the ways in which newspapers are retaining their special status in the eyes of many is by their careful and sophisticated use of graphic design. The designer may not be as important as the editor or star columnists, but no newspaper can neglect its appearance or its graphic functionality; and it has become increasingly common for newspaper editors to crow about their paper's redesign as much as when they sign a new columnist. Newspaper design is no longer invisible.

This hasn't always been the case. Even within graphic design, newspaper design has been a neglected art: among designers it hasn't enjoyed the same prestige as magazine design or more general forms of design – identity, branding and brochure work, for example. 'Because of the technology, and because of the daily deadlines,' explains

The new *Guardian* is a triumph of seemingly effortless style and disciplined editorial control. But the newspaper manages to maintain its remarkable elegance and clarity only because design and editorial intent walk arm-in-arm.

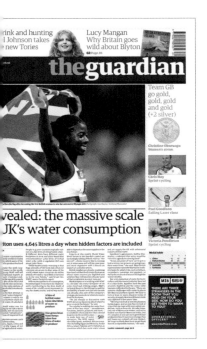

editorial designer Simon Esterson, 'newspaper design is different from other kinds of design. When I design a format for a newspaper, I'm building a kit of parts; it's a bit like building with Lego. Most of what I do is about "if" – "if" you had a headline here it could look like this: "if" you did this here it could look like that. And the papers that get this right are the ones that have a look and a spirit that serves them well; and the ones who are constantly reinventing themselves are the ones who quickly lose their style and spirit. Now, many designers don't like this. They don't like the fact that they can't control every aspect of the design.'

The *Guardian*'s redesign in 2005 has been described as 'one of the most important pieces of publishing design work in recent years'.[2] The new *Guardian* is a triumph of seemingly effortless style and disciplined editorial control. But the newspaper manages to maintain its remarkable elegance and clarity only because design and editorial intent walk arm-in-arm. To see what I mean, look at the way the paper retains its discipline throughout the entire publication – and throughout all its supplements and, most importantly, on its much-visited website. Headlines and subheadings, captions and pull quotes, are all executed with the same control and attention to detail. There are no lazy sub-editors saying they want 20 words when there is only space for ten; there are no flighty designers ignoring the paper's typographic rules and its carefully gridded structure. Instead, what we get

Above and overleaf
Project: the *Guardian* newspaper
Date: 2009
Designer: the *Guardian*
Creative Director: Mark Porter

is textbook integration of editorial content and design. It's a staggering achievement – and never dull, despite having far more structure and discipline than is normally found in newspaper design.

Yet one of the oddest things about the *Guardian* redesign is that the paper was already among the best-designed newspapers in the world. David Hillman,[3] an editorial designer of distinction, created it in the 1980s and his design, although beginning to show signs of age, was still widely regarded as exemplary. On his blog, the editorial designer Jeremy Leslie reports a lecture given by Mark Porter, the creative director of the *Guardian*, and the man who led the current redesign. Leslie quotes Porter saying the David Hillman redesign was 'purely a design project'. Porter backed up this observation with slides showing there was no journalistic advance or change in conjunction with the design, and pointed out that the recent redesign was far more extensive, with both the content and presentation being overhauled.

That nails it for me. Newspaper design can't be done in isolation from the content. This may appear glaringly obvious, but the people it rarely seems to occur to are the editors and publishers of newspapers, who seem to want design to 'react' to content whereas, as the new-look *Guardian* proves, both have to advance simultaneously.

Of course, there is another element in all this: electronic media. It is now no longer possible to produce a newspaper without also publishing on all available electronic platforms. The United Kingdom's best-selling tabloid, the *Sun*, a newspaper that thrives on the scandalous lives of TV soap stars, footballers' wives and Hollywood starlets showing too much underwear, advertises extensively on television. It does so with the tagline Paper Online Mobile.

These three words map out the terrain for the newspaper designer of the future. The disciplined layout of text and imagery on paper must be matched by the way content is presented in electronic media – everything from the paper's website to the reduced canvas of the mobile phone. Yet again the *Guardian* leads the way: its integration of a daily newspaper with a content-driven website is successful and highly usable. Other examples, of which there are myriad, seem to confirm the suspicion that newspapers haven't

The United Kingdom's best-selling tabloid, the Sun, a newspaper that thrives on the scandalous lives of TV soap stars, footballers' wives and Hollywood starlets showing too much underwear, advertises extensively on television. It does so with the tagline Paper Online Mobile.

1 Mark Porter, the creative director of the *Guardian*, which recently went through a dramatic transformation from 'broadsheet' format to the smaller and more manageable 'Berliner' format, pointed out: 'When I give talks about the *Guardian* redesign I usually touch on the fact that a lot of our readers are in urban centres and use public transport, which was a strong factor in leading us to question the broadsheet format.' www.markporter.com

2 Taken from 'Newspaper Design Day'; essay by Jeremy Leslie. http://magculture.com/blog/?p=50

3 In the 1960s, David Hillman was art editor of the *Sunday Times*, and then art director and deputy editor of *Nova*, one of the most influential magazines of the period. He was a Pentagram partner for 29 years and left in 2007 to form his own practice, Studio David Hillman. www.studiodavidhillman.com

4 www.nytimes.com/indexes/2007/12/02/style/t/index.html#pageName=Home

found a visual and editorial language that allows for seamless integration. The *New York Times* style website,[4] an offshoot of its well-designed printed supplement, is a good example of overcooked web design, and is further marred by intrusive advertising. The site is elegant and oozes upscale chic, but you have to be obsessed with its content to want to wrestle with its fussy interface. Stick to the print version.

Further reading: www.newsdesigner.com

Numerals

Few aspects of typography tax graphic designers as much as numerals. Ill-judged, they can ruin typographic layouts as surely as poor kerning or bad tracking. But what are the rules, and what's the difference between non-aligning and lining numerals, and does the difference matter?

There are two kinds of numerals: old style and lining. Old-style numbers project below the baseline and above the x-height. They are also called hanging or non-aligning numerals and are usually thought of as lower-case numbers. When we need to give dates and numbers within text, old-style numbers are best suited to the task. They fit in better. They are found in typefaces such as Sabon, Baskerville and Bodoni. Many serif typefaces carry both sorts of numerals – old style and lining – whereas sans serif fonts tend to have lining numerals only.

Lining numerals, on the other hand, are aligned to the baseline and are usually equal to the cap height of most typefaces. They are generally found in sans serif fonts, and we think of them as upper-case numbers. They are also monospaced, which means they are ideally suited to tabular layouts, such as financial reports and the presentation of numerical information. When they are used with upper- and lower-case text, as in a block of text, they tend to look oversized. We often see this in address blocks on letterheads and business cards.

One of the best ways to deal with lining numerals in text is to use small caps. It's never a good idea to fake small caps by reducing normal numerals – they are invariably out of proportion. If old-style numbers – or small caps – are unavailable in a typeface it is usually wise to reduce the point size of lining numerals slightly. A reduction of 10 per cent or so (it will vary from font to font) will make the numerals less conspicuous.

Further reading: Robert Bringhurst, *The Elements of Typographic Style*. H&M, 1992.

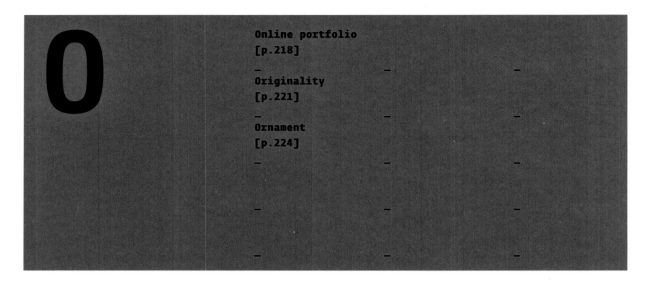

Online portfolio

Designers without websites are like hikers without boots: they aren't going to get far. Today, any designer looking for employment – or clients – has to have a website. But if there are as many 'hire me' sites as there are designers, how do we know what makes a good online portfolio stand out?

When I wrote *How to be a graphic designer without losing your soul*, I provided a comprehensive list of the essential requirements for the job-hunting or client-seeking designer.[1] I wrote the book in the summer of 2005, and I barely mentioned the need for designers to have their own websites. Back then, you could get by with a black vinyl portfolio and a few printouts of your best work. But not any more. It is now obligatory for freelance designers, studios and designers looking for employment to have their own online portfolios.

Today, it's a rare designer who doesn't have a website displaying his or her work. Yet it's equally rare to find a designer's 'hire me' portfolio site that avoids the usual pitfalls of self-indulgence and self-absorption. In fact, the best that can be said about most online portfolios is that they suffer from the affliction that we designers often possess: namely, we are good at communicating our clients' intentions but less good at communicating our own.

So, what makes a good online portfolio? It is perhaps easier to say what makes a bad one: the most common failing in designers' personal sites is a tendency to make them appeal to other designers – or worse, self-regarding. Autobiographical self-absorption is fine if the intention is to have a personal site for like-minded individuals. But it is highly unlikely to attract clients. To attract clients, we need to set about the task with professional objectivity. And the best way to be objective is to write a brief. We wouldn't design a website for a client who refused to give us one, so why treat ourselves any differently?

Let's define the purpose of the online portfolio as a site targeted at potential employers – or, in the case

Opposite
Project: www.keepsmesane.co.uk
Date: 2009
Designer: Darren Firth
The online portfolio site of designer and art director Darren Firth.

of freelance designers, at potential clients. Let's also decide that the site should: (1) say who we are and what we want; (2) what we do; (3) show some work; (4) make it easy to get in touch with us.

Explaining 'who we are and what we want' is easy, as long as we remember who we're speaking to. Clients and employers don't need long rambling statements about our innermost feelings; they need the facts, stated in a clear and precise manner. We need to supply details of age, education, previous experience, current situation, and a statement of what we are looking for – full-time employment, part-time work or freelance work, for example. 'What we do' is a list of skills – but only those skills that are of interest to potential employers and clients. No need to mention the swimming certificate we won at school. If we offer typography, web design and illustration, we should say this. If we can turn our hand to anything, we should state this. We should also be honest about our skills. Employers have a nose for deceit. They are on the lookout for it.

I once did some ad hoc research and asked half a dozen clients what they looked for in a designer's website: most of them said they went straight to a client list.

'Show some work' is the most problematical area. How much do we show, and in what format? Are 3-D objects carefully lit and photographed, or do we show them as flat, cropped images? How much explanatory text should we provide? The answers to these questions will vary depending on the individual concerned. But here are a few rules gleaned from long hours spent slogging through portfolio sites when I've been hiring designers. Keep examples of your work to a minimum: five or six are enough. Only show more if a design merits it. Don't just show 'cool' work. Too many sites I visit show what the designer likes best. It is usually done for friends and imaginary clients. No problem with this if the work shows a particular skill, but in reality most employers want to know how a designer will shape up when asked to design a website for the local garden centre.

How the work is displayed – photographically or as cropped digital files – depends entirely on the work. My own strong preference is to have examples of design work presented so that I can see details such as typographic accuracy: this usually means that I want to be able to enlarge images for closer inspection when necessary. What I don't want is excessive information about the work. It is normally sufficient to provide the client's name, an outline of the brief and a short project description. And always remember: when clients sit down to look at sites they are probably looking at a bunch of them, so only the distinctive and the incisive will stand out.

'Make it easy to get in touch with us' is vital information. The potential client or employer shouldn't be penalized by having to hunt down contact details. An email address and telephone number is usually enough. These should be prominently displayed on the home page.

One last thought on content. I once did some ad hoc research and asked half a dozen clients what they looked for on a designer's website. Most of them said they went straight to a client list. For tyro designers just starting out, not having a client list is a disadvantage. But pretty much everyone started out without a client list, and even if you've only got one client, list them with pride. For designers with a long list of clients, display it prominently.

Keep examples of your work to a minimum: five or six are enough. Only show more if a design merits it. Don't just show 'cool' work.

As well as the content of the website, we need to think about its design and the language we use on it. Unsurprisingly, we are as likely to be judged on our web design and presentation skills as on the content of the site. A smart design with low file sizes and fast action is always desirable. Long download times are likely to encourage time-poor employers to go elsewhere. And the only thing more off-putting than a poorly designed site is poor language. Keep it simple. Short sentences. Clear expression. Honest expression. The web designer and blogger Jason Kottke shows how to do it properly. He is clear and concise, but suggests someone with a personality and opinions: 'Hi there. I'm Jason Kottke, a NYC-based web designer, and this is my design portfolio. I dislike portfolios somewhat because they offer such a flat view of the rich process and product of web design. As such, I consider this an introduction to a conversation about the work I do and how I do it. If you'd like to hear more, please get in touch.'[2]

Further reading: www.smashingmagazine.com/2008/03/04/ creating-a-successful-online-portfolio

1 Adrian Shaughnessy, *How to be a graphic designer without losing your soul*. Laurence King Publishing, 2005.
2 www.kottke.org/portfolio/portfolio.html

Originality

Does originality matter when, as far as most clients are concerned, the only thing that counts is achieving the end result? And how is originality possible when most of the time our clients are paying us to deal in a universal visual language that everyone understands?

Originality is important because honesty is important, and plagiarism for commercial or personal gain is dishonest. But in graphic design the water gets muddied very quickly. If a graphic designer includes a photograph of a succulent plate of food on the packaging of a frozen ready-meal – just like every other ready-meal in the supermarket freezer – is this plagiarism, or someone following an acceptable commercial convention? When Peter Saville 'lifts' a Müller-Brockmann typographic styling for a New Order record cover, and then makes no secret of it, is this brazen theft or inspired appropriation? Has Milton Glaser's 1976 logo for New York (I♥NY) passed into communal ownership, or should Glaser feel aggrieved when it is adapted by a Boy Scout troop to advertise a fund-raising barbecue?

As Picasso demonstrated when he used African masks in his work, it is acceptable to borrow from others as long as we make something new out of what we borrow. It is also essential that we are willing to acknowledge our sources. Copyists never own up to copying.

These problems exist in all areas of creative endeavour: art, films, writing, music and advertising. Look at record reviews of new bands: today's music critics often confine themselves to merely listing a band's influences and reference points ('… early-Beatles mixed with mid-period Judas Priest and a smidgen of post-punk Gang of Four angst'). Take advertising: Honda UK's award-winning 'Cog' commercial was said to copy key elements of a film made in 1987 by artists Peter Fischli and David Weiss.[1] And in art Turner Prize nominee Glenn Brown replicated science-fiction book covers by illustrators Chris Foss and Anthony Roberts on a vast scale, with unembarrassed accuracy.[2]

Examples of designers' obsession with originality turn up regularly in the pages of the design press and on blogs. Designers point out, usually good-humouredly, although you suspect through gritted teeth, instances where they feel their work has been intentionally or accidentally copied, or where they want to assert that they 'got there first'. A recent letter pointed out the similarity between two pieces of printed work, both showing a fork spearing – in one case a map of Australia and in the other a scrap of biblical text. In both this facile visual gesture appears to do the job for which it was intended. But did the writer of the letter really think these were the first times this idea had been used? Rather, it seems to be part of a generic pool of visual tropes to be used, like all tropes, when appropriate.

This is not to say that plagiarism doesn't exist in graphic design. But real barefaced theft is rare and

Above top
Project: New Order – Movement
Date: 1981
Designer: Peter Saville & Grafica Industria
Label: Factory
This design is based closely on the work of
Italian Futurist Fortunato Depero. Depero's
original design was created in 1932 as the
cover of the publication *Futurismo*.

Above
Project: New Order – Low Life
Date: 1985
Designer: Peter Saville Associates
Photography: Trevor Key
Label: Factory
This design is based on a famous poster
(Der Film – 1960) by Josef-Müller Brockmann,
which also used overlapping typography.

is invariably recognized and dismissed as such. It is
unlikely, for example, that a piece of blatant copying
would ever win a design award: vigilant jurists would
chuck it out. And as designers we are obliged, partly
by morality and partly by law, not to take the work of
others for our own gain.

But digital technology has given designers the
ability to work in ways that automatically lend themselves
to cloning and sampling. We can grab images in seconds;
we have manipulation tools that allow existing forms to
be distorted and reformulated unrecognizably. Technology
has opened up new, unimagined possibilities, and with this
has come the need to evolve a new critical vocabulary
to accommodate these changes: shouting 'rip-off' is no
longer good enough, and narrow, outdated definitions of
what constitutes originality need to be re-examined. In
our image-laden world originality is nigh on impossible.
Creative people today are synthesists. Some are good at
it, others less so, while others are forced into formulaic
responses by clients terrified of doing anything new.
Yet the biggest problem relating to questions of
plagiarism and originality in design is that most of
the graphic design we see around us is dealing with
the universal visual language of symbols and signs.
This universal language occasionally
causes designers to get upset over what
they think is a case of plagiarism.
If two designers elect to use similar
illustrations of fruit on the labels
they stick on their respective fruit-
drink bottles, should we assume that
one is guilty of copying the other, or
are we simply looking at the lingua
franca of modern commercial design?

If a designer is asked to design
the male and female symbols for a
public toilet, it is perfectly natural
that he or she might attempt to bring
some fresh thinking to the task. They

**Talking about
originality in
graphic design
is a risky
business, and
when we accuse
others of
ripping us off
or plagiarizing
us we need to
be sure of our
definition of
originality.**

might experiment with these archetypal gender pictograms
and try and create a new graphic twist. In trendy bars
and clubs there are sometimes examples by designers who
have decided to mess around with the simple iconography,
but this often makes for embarrassing confusion and it is
advisable to stick to trusted formulae, even if it means
being accused of a lack of originality.

In the minds of many clients, if design is to do its
job it needs to deploy familiar and well-worn symbols
and metaphors. Nothing suggests approval more instantly
than a graphic tick in a box, or conveys the notion of a
bright idea more explicitly than a light bulb. But if we

use these symbols are we guilty of copying? Of course not. We are simply dipping into design's dressing-up box and pulling out the most appropriate costume. This is not to say that we should never look for fresh ways to present familiar concepts – we just shouldn't beat ourselves up over the use of instantly recognizable symbols.

Digital technology has given designers the ability to work in ways that automatically lend themselves to cloning and sampling. We can grab images in seconds; we have manipulation tools that allow existing forms to be distorted and reformulated unrecognizably.

Talking about originality in graphic design is a risky business, and when we accuse others of ripping us off or plagiarizing us we need to be sure of our definition of originality. Every great movement or school in design has its roots in previous movements or schools. Even revolutionary eruptions like Punk and Psychedelia can be traced back to, in the case of Punk, Situationism, and in the case of Psychedelia, Art Nouveau. Yet despite revealing their historical antecedents, both these movements are utterly distinctive. The great designer Derek Birdsall said in an interview: 'If a design works then there is every reason, whether it is your own or someone else's, to use it again.' Birdsall's work is as fresh and distinctive as any in graphic design. As Picasso demonstrated when he used African masks in his work, it is acceptable to borrow from others as long as we make something new out of what we borrow. It is also essential that we are willing to acknowledge our sources. Copyists never own up to copying. That's the difference.

Further reading: Michael Bierut, 'I Am a Plagiarist', November 2006. www.designobserver.com/archives/entry. html?id=14444

1 http://commercial-archive.com/node/104352
2 Rian Hughes, 'Meanwhile, in the weird world of art', Eye 38, Spring 2001.

Ornament

After two decades of Helvetica-driven minimalism and the bitmapped excesses of digital brutalism, a growing band of graphic designers has challenged the no-deco orthodoxy, and turned to both traditional and newer modes of ornament and decoration to create a sort of post-Modern baroque.

Since the rise of Modernist functionalism, ornament and decoration have been dirty words in graphic design. But as the Victorian architect and designer Owen Jones wrote in *The Grammar of Ornament*, his definitive 1856 study of the subject: '… it would appear that there is scarcely a people, in however early a stage of civilization, with whom the desire for ornament is not a strong instinct. The desire is absent in none, and it grows and increases with all in the ratio of their progress in civilization.' Ornamentation is linked in the modern mind with bling, and other forms of showy excess and wealth flaunting.

The stand against decoration in graphic design can be traced back to the Bauhaus and to the rise of Modernist graphics from the 1920s onwards. The Bauhaus began with the intention of not propagating 'any style, system, dogma, formula, or vogue, but simply to exert a revitalizing influence on design'. Its founder, Walter Gropius, wanted to embrace the machine; he welcomed mass production, and saw the veneration of the handmade and the dignity of manual labour as pointless idealism in the face of machine age reality. Gropius wanted a pure and futuristic machine aesthetic befitting the modern era. He also envisaged a future where all design disciples were united under a single philosophical premise. In the Bauhaus' vision, typography, furniture and architecture all came together from a single wellspring of rational thought, and superfluous decoration played no part in this vision.

In his seminal book *The New Typography*,[1] Jan Tschichold, the high priest of Modernist asymmetrical typography, wrote: 'The ornate yet corseted ugliness of European typography at the beginning of the twentieth century needed vigorous cleansing and exercise, and functionalist modernism appeared to be the goad and caustic required.' He also pronounced his typographic creed: 'None of the typefaces to whose basic form some kind of ornament has been added (serifs in roman type, lozenge shapes and curlicues in Fraktur) meet our requirements for clarity and purity. Among all the types that are available, the so-called 'Grotesque' (sans serif) or 'block letter' ('skeleton letters' would be a better name) is the only one in spiritual accordance with our time.'

As designers become increasingly dependent on digital technology for graphic expression, so it becomes necessary to maintain a link with the handmade, and the sort of aesthetic creation that can be seen as the work of human beings rather than the pixel-based assemblages of invisible digital codes.

Opposite
Project: Design Ignites Change poster
Date: 2008
Client: Academy for Educational Development
Designer: Marian Bantjes
Graphic designer Marian Bantjes is at the forefront of the ornamental movement in graphic design. Her poster was created for the Academy for Educational Development, a Canadian-based international non-profit organization. It was part of a series of posters promoting the importance of design in development work. The poster was available for sale and the proceeds went to provide assistance to children orphaned by HIV/AIDS in Kenya.

But a love of ornamentation is fundamental to human beings. It is apparently not something we learn, or a taste we acquire over time; rather it comes hardwired into our systems. Given a choice, we prefer the lovely to the gross; the elegant to the malformed; the beautiful to the downright ugly. The writer Virginia Postrel, in *The Substance of Style*,[2] makes the point that a desire for aesthetic satisfaction is woven into every aspect of modern life. Her book is subtitled 'How the rise of aesthetic value is remaking commerce, culture and consciousness', and designers, she argues, are on hand to reap the benefits. Or are they? For many graphic designers the notion of gratuitous beauty is hard to take. For these pragmatists, graphic design is about the communication of commercial messages. Why would anyone, they argue, want to interfere with design's practical and functional aims by introducing the distraction of superfluous decoration? Paul Rand expressed the professional designer's view when he wrote: 'A design that is complex, fussy, or obscure harbours a self-destructive mechanism.' But Rand was no philistine; although he was quick to dismiss much contemporary design as 'squiggles, pixels and doodles' and as damaging as 'drugs or pollution', he advocated the need for beauty in design; for him this was best achieved by eschewing decoration in favour of purity of line and balance of form.

For many graphic designers the notion of gratuitous beauty is hard to take. For these pragmatists, graphic design is about the communication of commercial messages. Why would anyone, they argue, want to interfere with design's practical and functional aims.

Yet, as Virginia Postrel notes: 'For designers, embracing the age of look and feel means dropping their defensiveness about the pleasure their work creates. Making things beautiful or interesting is as valuable, and necessary as making things work.' As heavy-duty back-up, she quotes usability guru Donald Norman's stark observation: 'Attractive things work better.' For Postrel, the argument is clearly stated: 'When we decide next how to spend our time, money, or creative effort,' she writes, 'aesthetics is increasingly likely to top our priorities.'

Yet the urge to avoid the needlessly decorative runs deep in graphic design culture. This stands at odds with Modernism because it breaks nearly every rule the Modernists hold dear. And as with all modes of contemporary design, in this age of eclecticism and plunder it steals indiscriminately from many areas: heraldry, Victoriana, rococo, neoclassicism, gentleman's club style, country-house furnishings and the decorative lexicon of flourishes, cartouches, embellishments and floral patterns. This new decorative approach to design has entered the mainstream. It can be found in interior design, product design and even advertising, where whiplash tendrils accompany everything from holidays to face cream.

The ornate can be viewed as an attempt to introduce emotion into the otherwise frequently arid world of graphic communications.

In a series of articles under the title 'The Decriminalization of Ornament' in *Eye* magazine, writer Alice Twemlow quotes designer and academic Denise Gonzales Crisp: 'I come from an illustration background, so the idea of being able to make pictures is more allowable to me. I actually approach typography from that perspective … It's in typography that you find the deepest tradition of the decorative within graphic design: type designers made decorative borders and ornaments that were integrated conceptually with a type family.'[3]

But what is the new graphic ornate saying about modern visual culture, and why has it appeared now? It can be seen as a reaction against the escalating technological complexity of modern design: as designers become increasingly dependent on digital technology for graphic expression, so it becomes necessary to maintain a link with the handmade, and the sort of aesthetic creation that can be seen as the work of human beings rather than the pixel-based assemblages of invisible digital codes. Furthermore, as graphic design becomes something that everyone can do (or at least everyone who has access to a computer with graphics software), designers need to reassert their skills. They need to remind everyone (for personal reasons as much as for business reasons) that they are the best people to do design.

The ornate can be viewed as an attempt to introduce emotion into the otherwise frequently arid world of graphic communications. Clients often claim to want 'emotion' in the work they commission ('make it warm'). But when it comes to it they pull back and restrict emotional expression to a narrow band of minor chords, suppressing any attempts to raise the emotional temperature. Among most serious designers the normal mode of expression is cool detachment. So it is hardly surprising if other designers – and some clients – want to inject raw and genuine emotion into the contemporary graphic landscape. What better way to do this than reintroduce the graceful, the elegant and the beautiful.

Further reading: Alice Twemlow, 'The Decriminalization of Ornament', *Eye* 58, 2005.

1 Jan Tschichold, *The New Typography*. University of California Press, 1998.
2 Virginia Postrel, *The Substance of Style*. HarperCollins, 2003.
3 Alice Twemlow, 'The Decorational', *Eye* 58, 2005.

P

Packaging graphics

There's a sense in which nearly all graphic design is about packaging. Graphic design is the art of 'visual presentation', and nowhere is this more plainly revealed than in the packaging of consumer products. Once the crowning glory of the graphic designer's craft, package design is now widely demonized as a black art.

Take a trip to your local supermarket and look at the banks of packaged goods on display. What do you see? Vast amounts of creative energy devoted to dressing up products that are often identical, and which are often no more essential to our well-being than the fluff we sweep up from the floor.

The argument in favour of good packaging graphics is expressed in an article on the UK Design Council's website, The Business Case by Jonathan Sands, the CEO of design company Elmwood. Sands notes that: '… packaging can often end up becoming the thing of real value above and beyond the actual product itself — the packaging becomes the brand. Just think about a Cadbury's Dairy Milk chocolate bar and a supermarket own brand equivalent. If both are unwrapped how would you tell the difference? The purple wrap of Cadbury's Dairy Milk is the emotional reason why you'd pay more although there may be seemingly little difference in product delivery.'

We see evidence of this when consumer products — usually foodstuffs — are advertised on TV, and the fact that they now have 'new packaging graphics' is trumpeted as a major selling feature.

But there's a counter-argument that sees packaging in a different light. To sneer at graphic design, all you have to do is mention soap powder boxes, baked bean cans or confectionery wrappers. Here are goods that would be better — and cheaper — if sold in plain wrappers. If you wanted to be even more damning, you could mention that packaging is often cited, along with television commercials, billboards and press advertisements, as part of the corrosive system of commercial hype and spin that governs our lives as consumers. And you could go even further and point out that today, at a time when awareness

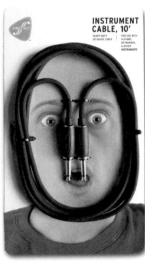

Above
Project: Instrument Cable packaging
Date: 2006
Client: First Act, Boston
Art Direction: Stephen Doyle
Designer/Photographer: Brian Chojnowski
Studio: Doyle Partners
These witty and economical packages were
inspired by the set of 12 magic markers that
Stephen Doyle had when he was in sixth grade;
called Doodlers they were packaged in a flat
white box, like crayons. A black marker
drawing of a smiling face on the cover gave
way to a big smile-shaped die-cut, revealing
the dozen markers as coloured teeth. Models
are Stephen Doyle's graduate students.

of green issues has reached a critical point, packaging is frequently wasteful, and in many cases downright damaging to the environment.

For designers, there is yet another consideration. As designers we are compelled to make everything we touch look good and be as effective as we can make it. It's part of our DNA. Why shouldn't shower gel, toilet cleaners and toothpaste come in well-designed packaging with attractive graphics? Like a lawyer asked to represent a criminal, we are professionally obligated to make these products look as attractive as we possibly can. And, of course, as consumers we demand attractive packaging – and also want packaging that is robust and hygienic. I recently found myself staring at a display of 'environmentally friendly' household cleaning products in my local deli. The brand is reasonably well known in the UK, but the packaging is dull and lifeless. Compared to the exquisite graphics on the exotic foodstuffs that surrounded me, the 'green' products had a dismal, 'hair shirt' appearance that made them unappealing. I checked myself: what had I been thinking? Here was a worthwhile and necessary product, but I was put off buying it because it has dull graphics.

Designers are compelled to make everything look as good, and be as effective, as possible. So why shouldn't soap powder and toothpaste come in well-designed packaging? Like a lawyer asked to represent a criminal, we are professionally obligated to make these products look as attractive as possible.

This is the dilemma facing designers. The taste for heavily aestheticized packaging is now so ingrained in consumers that when it isn't well designed and seductive the product is unlikely to sell. But perhaps the green question holds the key to the future direction of packaging. Legislation in Europe promises to outlaw any that is wasteful and excessive, and as consumers become more green-aware a natural demand will set in for more restrained, economical and recyclable packaging. We can already see this in the way free plastic supermarket bags have been demonized, and how even the biggest supermarkets are turning – slowly – to more durable and reusable alternatives.

NetRegs[1] is a UK government website that provides free guidance to help small businesses to comply with environmental legislation and protect the environment. In a section called Packaging Waste Reduction and Regulation it offers the following advice:

Use the minimum packaging required for safety, hygiene and consumer acceptance.

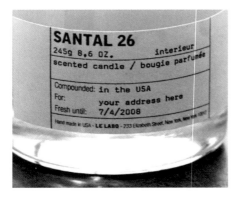

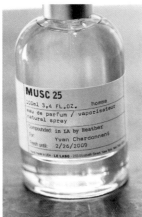

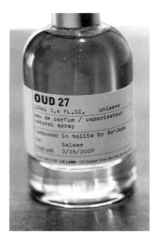

Above and opposite
Project: Le Labo packaging
Date: 2009
Client: Le Labo Fragrances, Grasse & New York
Designer: Olivier Pascalie
Ultra chic, and at the same time ultra
functional bottle and label designs that
avoid the usual faux-sophisticated graphic
twaddle of most fragrance packaging. All
bottles are reusable, and the company
actively promotes refilling. Labels
are one colour.

Where possible use packaging that can be reused, recycled or recovered.

When designing and manufacturing packaging, if it cannot be recovered or reused make sure it will have a minimal impact on the environment. If packaging waste has to be incinerated or disposed of at a landfill, make sure any hazardous substances are minimized.

Wherever possible, design packaging so that it can be reused several times.

The end of lavish physical packaging should not be the end of good packaging graphics, however. There are many examples of restrained and honest packaging that does not 'over promise', and which is not excessively wasteful. Apple's iPod and iPod-related products provide a masterclass in good packaging design. The boxes have a graphic simplicity that makes them highly desirable. And yet almost any other consumer electronics company would have used a photograph of a swooning teenage girl with headphones clamped to her ears, and a dorky illustration of musical notes and naff imagery wafting around her head. Apple demonstrates that this sort of gratuitous hype is unnecessary.

For designers working in the packaging sector the future is uncertain. New consumer legislation relating to food labelling, and growing demands to use sustainable resources, has made the job increasingly complex. And yet for many, this is what being a designer is all about: negotiating restraints and navigating competing demands. There has never been as much beautifully designed packaging as there is today, and when designers get it right, environmentally, ergonomically, and functionally, the results can add greatly to the success of products. Designers are full of stories that reveal the power of good packaging to fuel the success of products. My favourite packaging 'urban myth' concerns the English designer Michael Peters. Peters ran one of the first design groups to combine design and business strategy. He was a pioneer in this area. In the late 1970s, his studio redesigned the graphics for the external packaging for a range of coloured bottled inks for Winsor & Newton, the leading ink manufacturer. He packaged the inks in little cardboard cubes, and decorated them (and the labels on the bottles) with illustrations by many of the leading illustrators of the day. The effect was delightful, and appealed strongly to the sort of people who bought inks. The design was an instant success with the buying public, so much so that Winsor & Newton succeeded in increasing the size of the ink market. In other words, they sold more inks than they had ever sold before, which seems to suggest that they were succeeding in selling to people who

normally didn't buy coloured inks but who were attracted by the packaging.

I hope this is not just packaging mythology, because I've told this story to clients on many occasions as a way of making the point that good design – brave design – can have a direct monetary benefit. It's a crass argument, but it's often the only one clients understand.[2]

Further reading: Publications Loft, *Unique Packaging*. Collins Design, 2007.

1 www.netregs.gov
2 Shortly after writing this I met Michael Peters and he confirmed that the story was true.

Paper

Specifying paper used to be fun. Today, choosing paper stock involves juggling issues relating to cost, technical matters and sustainability, and that's before we even start thinking about appearance and texture, or the role of electronic paper.

I've always admired connoisseurs of paper who spend hours studying a paper merchant's stock books. I see them sniffing, stroking and inspecting sheets of paper like detectives looking for fingerprints. Can't do it myself. Every time I've asked a printer to use a paper stock they've not previously used, I've been disappointed with the outcome, and this has made me timid and unadventurous. I find myself relying on a few trusted stocks, and on the good sense of printers. No printer ever recommended a stock they couldn't vouch for. So trust your printer when choosing paper stock.

Paul Hewitt runs a well-respected print shop called Generation Press.[1] He has a loyal following among picky designers who have come to value and trust his wisdom when dealing with the vagaries of paper stock. I asked him to describe the process for choosing paper successfully.

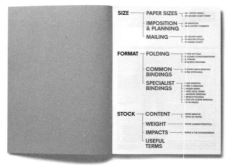

Above and opposite
Project: *Size, Format, Stock*
Date: 2009
Client: Fenner Paper
Designers: Matt Willey, Zoë Bather,
David Hört
A practical guide to using paper in design,
which was available as a supplement in
issue 171 of *Grafik* magazine. Published
in collaboration with Justin Hobson at
Fenner Paper, the manual covers areas
such as pagination, binding techniques
and environmental considerations.

'Firstly you have to think about the surface of the paper. The general rule would be that the smoother the paper the better it would hold an image. If you decide that a coated stock is going to be best for your project, it's worth considering the variety of coated stocks that are available, and the effect they will have on your images. If you choose a particular coated range of paper they will most likely have a gloss, silk and matt sheet to the range. Coated stock is "calendered".[2] Matt stock is calendered once, leaving the fibres quite random, which gives the matt effect. When we print on matt stock, a sharp dot goes on to the surface, but the dispersion of the printed dot into and around the fibres would make the dot slightly fatter and slightly weaker looking. A silk finish means the paper has been calendered again, which makes the fibres a little more aligned giving a silky effect. When this paper is printed on, the dot remains fairly sharp but with some dispersion. Finally, when it is calendered again and the fibres are much more uniform this gives a glossy shiny surface, which is the best surface to put an ink dot on to. You put a sharp dot on to the surface and it stays sharp. It also gives the effect of more colour so the image is brighter and sharper.'

Of course, many projects demand the more 'organic' qualities of uncoated stock. Designers and paper enthusiasts talk about its 'personality', 'tactility' and 'warmth'. Uncoated stocks offer a far greater range of effects and colours. 'The colour of an uncoated sheet is a big factor in choosing the right sheet for the project,' notes Hewitt. 'The sheets range from bright white to different types of whites (warm off-whites, cold grey-whites, etc.), plus a myriad of colours. The colour or shade is more important if you are printing images, as it will have a global effect on the colours you are printing. If you have a photographic project the colour of the paper is important but the quality of the surface is also very important. The better the quality, the better any image will be reproduced. If you are using images that are not that great, the rougher the surface the more forgiving it is to poor photography. The better the images are, the more important it is to choose a good-quality uncoated stock.

No good printer ever recommended a paper stock they couldn't vouch for. So trust your printer when choosing paper.

'The most common mistake designers make is that there is a particular stock they have always wanted to use, so at the first opportunity they choose it. Only to find out later that it was not the best choice for reproducing the style of graphics or images used.' But surely a good printer will spot this and advise on

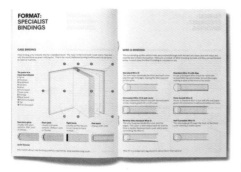

alternatives? 'Problem is,' explains Hewitt, 'it often happens that designers don't show images to the printer in advance. I would suggest that when asking for prices designers should also give an idea of what the final artwork might look like, and engage the printer in the project at an early stage. By talking to your printer it is possible to be alerted to the dangers involved in certain sorts of paper. If a "difficult" paper has been chosen, different factors may come into any advice given. For example, speed of turnaround from receipt of artwork always has a bearing on what stock could be used; if large amounts of colour are involved, it may not be advisable to use solids and saturated images on certain stocks.'

Hewitt gives an example of how a designer's choice of paper encouraged him to offer advice to ensure a satisfactory outcome. The designer came to Hewitt with a magazine project. He wanted to use Bible paper for the text and a 34 gsm onion-skin for the cover. 'From the outset I advised that too much ink would have an adverse effect on the papers chosen. For such a technically difficult project, I asked that he show us his ideas as he went along, so that I could advise whether or not I felt they were appropriate for the paper he had chosen. So began an exciting and engaging experience that meant we were both committed to the best possible outcome. 'One of the spreads the designer showed me had a very saturated vignette across a double-page spread. It struck me that this would not only be difficult to print, but it was also expecting too much from the stock. So, it was decided that the vignette was unnecessary and detrimental. I advised that he shouldn't allow the boldness of his initial concept to be diluted by trying to overdesign the project. I wasn't sure whether this advice was going to have a good or bad effect on him, but not only did he come back with a far superior design, it was also completely appropriate to the material being used. For me, this story illustrates the value of printers and designers working together to get the most out of a chosen stock. I see my job as more than just warning designers about the dangers of certain papers. Helping them to get the most of the desired paper is critical.'

Every time I've asked a printer to use a paper stock they've not used before, I've been disappointed with the outcome. I find myself relying on a few trusted stocks, and on the good sense of printers.

As if wrestling with the technical complexities of paper wasn't onerous enough, modern designers also need to consider sustainability. When we think of 'green' paper we naturally think of recycled stock, which in turn makes us think of poor-quality reproduction. If a job demands slick production standards we might feel hesitant about specifying recycled paper. Is this justified? In an essay taken from *Green Design* the writer Colin Berry[3] examines the use of recycled stock by American designers. He writes: '… recycled paper is better than ever. Dozens of mills and manufacturers are creating new lines of superior options for the working designer. New Leaf, Mohawk, Neenah, Domtar, Fox River and more than a dozen other companies sell a range of coated, uncoated, copy and specialty papers in a variety of weights — all with sizeable percentages of recycled fiber. High-quality recycled paper is plentiful, and dropping in price.'[4]

But many clients still demand super-sharp images; they want to give their products and services the seductive allure that only comes from brilliant reproduction on high-quality virgin print stock. And yet, increasingly, other clients recognize the benefits – and kudos – of recycled stock. Designers can no longer remain passive in this matter. Not only is it morally incumbent upon us to take a stance on environmental issues, but it is also increasingly likely that our clients will demand it.

Further reading: www.paperonline.org

1 www.generationpress.co.uk
2 Calendered: paper stock made smooth and glossy by being pressed between rollers.
3 www.colinberry.com
4 Colin Berry, 'Paper As Progress: Where Recycled and Alternative Papers Meet High Design', July 2006 (adapted from Buzz Poole [ed.], *Green Design*. Mark Batty Publisher, 2006). www.graphics.com/modules.php?name=Sections&op=viewarticle&artid=395

Personal work

For many designers, doing self-initiated projects and personal work is an essential part of being a designer. It's a way of staying motivated. For others, it's a waste of time and a denial of the true role of the designer as someone who responds to external briefs. Which is it?

A few years after setting up my studio I was invited to give a lecture about its work. It was the first time I'd been asked to do this. It was a proud (and nervy) moment. The presentation seemed to go well (though thinking back, I doubt it would have been much good; I made the classic error most inexperienced designers make and talked about myself in the self-absorbed way that we mistake for insight). At the end of the presentation someone asked me why I'd shown no personal work. This threw me. I wasn't sure how to reply. I realized there was a rebuke in his question. I mumbled apologetically that I had none to show because we didn't do any personal work. My interlocutor was unimpressed.

In the last two decades the notion of undertaking self-initiated projects has become a big talking point among design's commentariat. There are many who see it as an essential part of a designer's mental hygiene. They see it as transporting graphic design to the higher plane of authorship. They see it as a rejection of the designer's role as silent servant of the client's message. There are others who regard personal work as self-indulgent onanism. Perhaps we need to make a distinction between self-initiated projects and personal work. Self-initiated projects are projects where we write our own brief. We

might start a T-shirt company selling our own T-shirts. Or we might stage an event, requiring us to make flyers and e-cards. Personal work, on the other hand, is work that need have no purpose other than to satisfy an instinct a designer has. He or she might design a typeface without any purpose in mind. Or they might create a CD cover for a favourite music compilation. Personal work needs no external reason to bring it into being other than the designer's desire to create it.

It took me a few years to formulate how I'd like to have responded to the guy who asked me the question at the lecture. Back then, I couldn't be sure of my response, but now I'd say to him that personal work is absolutely fine if that's what the individual wants – or needs – to do. But for me, all my work is personal anyway. The fact that it's not self-initiated doesn't mean it's not personal; the fact that I have a client with a brief and a deadline and a budget, and a sackful of prejudices, restrictions and limitations, doesn't stop me trying to do personal work. It's all personal.

But I have another, more pragmatic reason, for thinking this way. When designers start to see their professional work as somehow inferior to the work they do for themselves, they start to think about it in an inferior way. If we only see self-initiated work as freedom, and commercial work as restrictive, we will end up doing second-rate commercial work.

For designers stuck in dead-end jobs personal projects can be a way of keeping their spirits alive. Without a self-directed approach designers might otherwise stagnate. Self-initiated projects allow us to experiment and pursue avenues of discovery. But, wherever possible, designers should try to find live briefs because being a designer is never just about doing good work; it's about clients, deadlines, budgets and a thousand other mundane restrictions.

Further reading: Kevin Finn (ed.), *Open Manifesto {3}: What is Graphic Design?*, 2007. www.openmanifesto.net

Above
Project: Memory and Autopsy
Date: 2007
Designer: Adrian Shaughnessy
64-page book designed, photographed and written by the author of this book. Unpublished.

Photography

As graphic designers we work with photography in different ways. We art-direct photographers to give us the images we want; we use pre-existing photographs; we manipulate images to say anything we choose; we can even take our own pictures. Photography is part of the DNA of graphic design.

I once asked some designers – typographers with a Neo-Modernist style – whether they were interested in working with me on a project involving illustration. They declined. 'If it was photography,' they said, 'we'd be interested.' This preference for the photographic image over the hand-rendered image is common among modern graphic designers. The mechanistic sheen of photography – and its malleability – seems to dovetail with modern design better than the more organic – less malleable – types of illustration.

Within visual communication, photography is the default setting: when did we last see a car advertisement that didn't use a gleaming, glowing photograph of a car? Show me a magazine that doesn't have a photograph on the front cover. Most food packaging uses carefully manicured photographs to reveal its edible contents. The photographic image reigns supreme. Clients and consumers trust its apparent honesty.

It's odd, then, that as designers we should spend so much of our time making photographs into simulacra of the truth. Odd, then, that most of the commercial photography we see has been transformed in Photoshop. Odd that the photographic image is – for many design tasks – the start point, not the end point.

The modern graphic designer is required to be adept at art directing, choosing, retouching and cropping images. The modern designer has to know how a photographic image can be made to work in a variety of formats and spaces – a single image might be required to work as a web banner and a billboard. Photographs have to be as malleable as fresh clay, and this changes fundamentally the way we look at pictures. When we scrutinize photographs we gauge them for their potential to be changed. When we are art-directing shoots we usually ask the photographer to give us images that we can adapt. When we examine pictures we look for opportunities to move and reposition key elements, and we search for opportunities to change colours and tonality. In other words, the modern photograph is rarely complete; it is always in a state of flux.

When we examine pictures we look for opportunities to move and reposition key elements, and we search for opportunities to change colours and tonality. The modern photograph is rarely complete – it's always in a state of flux.

There are more theories about photography than there are theories about dieting. Writers such as Susan Sontag,[1] Walter Benjamin,[2] and Vilem Flusser[3] have expounded on the photographic image in the modern world. For the designer, it's usually about the potential of an image, not the image itself.

It's worth studying the work of the great magazine art directors of the twentieth century to see the alchemical magic of photographic images in the hands of a master. Look at the work of Alexey Brodovitch (*Harper's Bazaar*), Henry Wolf (*Harper's Bazaar*, *Esquire*), Cipe Pineles (*Seventeen*), Willy Fleckhaus (*twen*), Fabien Baron (*Vogue*, *Interview*) and Neville Brody (*The Face*), to see how they use photographic images with organic directness. They handle photography with such consummate ease that we take this fusion of type, layout and photographs as entirely natural. In fact, after a while it becomes difficult for designers to view a photograph without wanting to see it merged with text and positioned judiciously on a page.

The English designer Quentin Newark told me he once presented Paul Rand with a photographic book he'd designed. Rand looked at it and said: 'I don't like designing photography books, someone else has done all the work.'[4] We know what Rand is talking about. To be handed a batch of great photographs means all we have to do is lay them out with care. What could be easier? And yet we still see appalling layouts – especially in the pages of modern magazines where editors think ramped-up freneticism guarantees engagement.

By far the most important aspect of grouping photographs on a page is the need to maintain the narrative flow of the images. To do this, designers need to act and think like journalists telling a story.

By positioning and juxtaposing images, by manipulating their relative sizes, and by cropping them with an eye for balance and impact, it is possible to group photographs together in a way that is coherent and engaging – and which doesn't look like an explosion in a picture library. But by far the most important aspect of grouping photographs on a page is the need to maintain the narrative flow of the images. To do this, designers need to act and think like journalists telling a story. They must ask themselves: What are these pictures telling us? How can we bring out their inherent qualities? As designers, we are often seduced into dealing with photographs as blocks of form, but 'every picture tells a story' so we are really handling chunks of narrative.

There are many small rules and tricks to help us. The most important of which is the rule of thumb that when there are a lot of headshots it is best to scale all the heads to the same size. Also, when a number of different images are grouped side by side it is advisable to set as few sizes for picture boxes as possible, and then repeat them as often as possible. Dynamic contrast is equally important. Big images next to small ones can

1 'To collect photographs is to collect the world. Movies and television programs light up walls, flicker, and go out; but with still photographs the image is also an object, lightweight, cheap to produce, easy to carry about, accumulate, store.' From Susan Sontag, *On Photography*. Picador, 2001.
2 In his 1931 essay 'A Short History of Photography' the Marxist critic Walter Benjamin quoted László Moholy-Nagy: 'The illiteracy of the future will be ignorance not of reading or writing, but of photography.'
3 Vilem Flusser, *Towards a Philosophy of Photography*. Reaktion Books, 2000.
4 Quoted in Adrian Shaughnessy, 'The Order of Pages', *Eye* 51, Spring 2004.

MARGARET
HOWELL

NOVEMBER

M	02	09	16	23	30
T	03	10	17	24	
W	04	11	18	25	
T	05	12	19	26	
F	06	13	20	27	
S	07	14	21	28	
S 01	08	15	22	29	

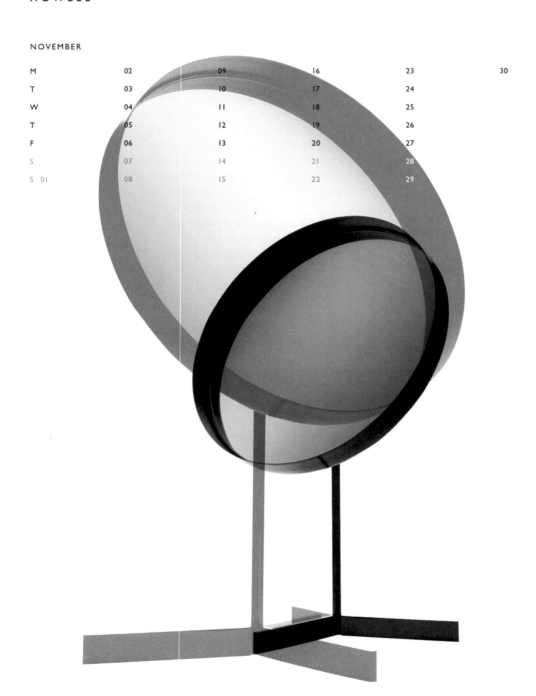

Opposite and above
Project: A Selection of
Modern British Design — Calendar
Date: 2009
Client: Margaret Howell
Designer: Small
Photographer: Lee Funnell
Stylish combination of photography and
graphics for a calendar for fashion retailer
Margaret Howell. The graphic precision of
photographer Lee Funnell's work is greatly
in demand by designers. Her work can be seen
at www.graphicphoto.com

create tension — but only if there is a reason for doing this. The small image must supply information that the larger image doesn't give. There has to be a reason over and above the purely aesthetic for the juxtapositioning of two boxes. A problem that makes dealing with lots of different photographs difficult is that each image has its own internal composition. Most photographs are centrally composed, but others are asymmetrically structured. Getting these images to sit in harmony can be tricky, and only trial and error, and an eye for internal balance, can resolve this.

The best way to learn about photography is to take photographs. In the digital era, this has never been easier and even more importantly, it has never been easier to publish them. Look at Flikr or the countless blogs that carry photographs and we see an unending stream of photographic images that are technically accomplished and compositionally sophisticated. Everyone knows how to take pictures now, the technology makes it hard to fail, and we have surely reached a point where there is no such thing as a bad photograph. But the sheer cosmically proportioned volume of photographic images has a numbing effect; it makes us lazy and uncritical. When everything looks good, nothing looks good. And so the designer is forced to approach photography with a sharper eye than other people. Designers have to be aware that the stakes are higher than before. If we want photographs to have an effect, we have to learn to distinguish between photographs that are mere data, and photographs that tell us something new.

It's worth studying the work of the great magazine art directors of the twentieth century to see the alchemical magic of photographic images in the hands of a master.

Further reading: Stephen Shore, *The Nature of Photographs: A Primer*. Phaidon, 2007.

Pitching

Nothing raises a designer's blood pressure more than 'pitching'. Why? Pitching's part of normal business life – everyone does it. In design it usually means doing the job for nothing in the hope of winning the job. In the USA it's called 'spec work', and designers agonize over the correct response.

Today, clients with design projects will almost invariably invite a number of studios, or individual designers, to take part in a competitive 'tender'[1] with the aim of winning their business. The bigger the project, the more likely this is to happen.

Pitching has become a fact of contemporary commercial life. Everyone pitches: advertising agencies pitch for new accounts; freelance writers pitch ideas to editors; pension companies pitch retirement plans to the public. Life's a pitch, as someone once said.

It's easy to see how this situation has arisen. In a service-based economy where clients (in all sectors) have dozens, sometimes hundreds of potential suppliers to choose from, the competitive pitch is the favoured method for sifting through the options and coming to a decision. Appointing suppliers of any kind is a risky business. And when it comes to design – an area where few clients are ever entirely confident about the outcome – the risk factor is high, and inviting hungry designers to compete against each other therefore seems to be an effective way of reducing that risk. On top of this, the Darwinian business view is that if designers have to compete for every assignment they will be incentivized to do their utmost to win, thus ensuring that clients get the best possible response. Looked at from a purely commercial perspective this reasoning is hard to argue with, and if designers are willing to expend creative energy and time (not to mention cash) trying to win assignments, it would be an odd business that declined to take advantage of their 'generosity'.

Politely refusing invitations to free-pitch on the grounds that we don't believe our client's best interests are served in this way need not be commercial suicide. It's surprising to discover how often clients I've said 'no' to have come back with offers of work.

Even when clients might wish to dispense with the pitching process and appoint the designer, or designers, they think best for their assignment, they can't. For many commercial bodies, the competitive pitch process is embedded into their operating rules. This is especially true of the public sector where, ironically, fairness, even-handedness and the desire to root out favouritism and corruption are paramount.

But there's an aspect to pitching that we haven't discussed yet, and it's the part that vexes designers the most. To put it as bluntly as possible: most pitching is unpaid. Free pitching – the winner takes everything, the losers get nothing – is depressingly common in design, and even the most pragmatic and business-minded designers

AND THEN WE CAN KIND OF SORT OF LIKE EXTRAPOLATE IT?

see it as a fundamentally unfair and ethically dubious practice.[2] The argument against unpaid pitching goes like this. Pitching usually requires designers to submit a full creative and strategic response to a brief. This might involve submitting visual designs, strategy proposals, production schedules, technical specifications and detailed costings. In other words, it requires designers to do the job in order to win it.

Designers argue that the client's interests are not best served by forcing them to function in the artificial circumstances of an unpaid pitch, and that designers cannot be expected to offer effective proposals without the research, strategic thinking and client contact that is essential in modern visual communications. The unpaid competitive pitch reduces design to a beauty parade and a lottery. In the view of most designers, it stinks.

Yet clients don't see it like this. They see only benefits. And what benefits! They have eliminated nearly all the risk involved in choosing a supplier, and as they have the luxury of numerous submissions to choose from, each done by different designers (I've heard of pitches involving 15 competing studios), they can be reasonably sure the option they finally choose will be the correct one. Look at it this way: if you wanted your house painted but were unsure which colour to use, think how beneficial it would be if a skilled house-painter did the job at no cost, and you only paid up if you liked the result.

This is the gift we give to our clients when we free-pitch. What's more, when designers submit creative proposals, clients can show the results to the intended audience to gauge their likely success;[3] they can market test them; they can discuss them among themselves – all quantifiable commercial advantages for which they pay nothing.

Of course, there are still clients with enough savvy to choose a studio and award them a project without the hoop-jumping of an unpaid competitive pitch. Some clients allocate a pitch fee:[4] it is never enough to cover costs, but it is a helpful gesture and indicates commitment on their part. There are also ethically minded clients who choose designers based on a credentials presentation. In this situation, designers present their skills and attributes. The iniquities of free pitching lead to a sense of inertia. But we are not helpless; there are things we can

If you wanted your house painted but were unsure which colour to use, think how beneficial it would be if a skilled house-painter did the job at no cost, and you only paid up if you liked the result. This is the gift we give to our clients when we free-pitch.

Above
Drawing by Paul Davis, 2009

do. If we want an easy life, we just say 'yes' to every invitation to pitch. Yet stop for a minute and think about what this says about us. It says we don't value our skills. It says we don't value the service we offer. It says we are compliant. But if we do the opposite and say 'no thanks' to unpaid pitches, what are the likely consequences? Politely refusing invitations to free-pitch on the grounds that we don't believe our client's best interests are served in this way need not be commercial suicide. I've done it frequently, and it's surprising to discover how often clients I've said 'no' to have come back with offers of work. There's a rough magic in the word 'no'. Clients often react badly at first, but they usually end up respecting the designer who says 'no' to unpaid pitching more than the one who says 'yes'.

Saying 'no' to clients requires self-confidence and, for most designers, it takes time to acquire this. When I started my studio in 1989, I said 'yes' to everyone who asked me to take part in unpaid pitches – even when I knew it was a waste of time. Eventually I learnt that this wasn't right and I found the inner belief to say 'no'. But is there a middle way in all this?

One technique that sometimes works is to ask for a fee to cover costs. Mostly, clients will say 'no', but sometimes they will offer a token payment, so it's always worth asking; it also lays down a marker that say we are not a doormat, and places a value on what we do.

Some designers won't do creative work, but instead offer to produce written submissions that detail their creative and strategic thinking. Their view is that they are creative practitioners and to give away creativity is to give away their primary asset: a bit like a laptop manufacturer saying, free laptops everyone! But is producing a written proposal really any different from giving away design skills? In the new sophisticated media landscape we occupy, strategic thinking is more valuable to clients than creative executions.

My own personal philosophy on unpaid competitive pitching is this. If someone asks me to pitch for work in an area where I have a track record, I say 'no'. I explain that they can look at the work I've already done in this sector, and take a view about my suitability. If, however, I am approached by a potential client in a field where I have no track record, and assuming the job is a good one, I will agree to pitch. I usually regret the decision, but I recognize that the only way I'll ever break into a particular sector is through the trapdoor of pitching.

Further reading:
www.aiga.org/content.cfm/position-spec-work

1 A written offer to contract goods or services at a specified cost or rate; a bid. The *American Heritage® Dictionary of the English Language, Fourth Edition*. Houghton Mifflin Company, 2004.

2 The AIGA makes this statement on its website. 'AIGA believes that doing speculative work seriously compromises the quality of work that clients are entitled to and also violates a tacit, long-standing ethical standard in the communication design profession worldwide. AIGA strongly discourages the practice of requesting that design work be produced and submitted on a speculative basis in order to be considered for acceptance on a project.' www.aiga.org

3 I was working as a consultant for a design group that had been invited to take part in a paid pitch for an interesting project by a leading charity. We were one of four studios invited to pitch. We presented our submissions and waited for the verdict. A few days later I got an email from a friend. He included a web link to a site where the charity had posted all four submissions and invited the public to vote on them. As designers we should be willing to submit to this sort of scrutiny, but the charity didn't tell us they were going to do this, and it came as a shock to see speculative, exploratory work posted on the Internet with an open invitation to viewers to pass judgement on it.

4 A friend who runs a well-established London design group was invited to pitch for some work by one of the UK's main, publicly-funded arts centres. This world-famous institution sent him a brief and asked him to make a creative response. He looked for a pitch fee – and to his surprise found there was one: £30.00. As he said, this would probably pay for the tube fares for him and a couple of his design team to attend the presentation.

Portfolios

The process of impressing employers or clients with our design skills begins with the design of our portfolios. When we show them we are not only judged on the content, but also on the way we have designed them. A badly designed portfolio sends out a message: bad designer.

MY WORK IS POWERFUL, SO VERY POWERFUL

IT CAN MAIM.

Above
Drawing by Paul Davis, 2009

For designers looking for employment, and for studios and individuals trying to impress clients and win assignments, it is essential to have a portfolio of work. There are two important aspects to portfolios. The first is the actual physical receptacle we use to show our work, and the second is the methodology we employ to visually present the work within our portfolios. We need to get both aspects right. We can spend a small fortune on a beautiful custom-made steel flight case, but if the work inside is poorly presented we might as well put it in a supermarket carrier bag.

For an increasing number of designers, the online portfolio (see Online portfolio, page 220) is the most obvious way to display work, and more and more designers are abandoning the old cumbersome portfolio bag with its zips, clips, handles and plastic envelopes. But clients still want to meet designers, they want to talk to them and they want to view their work in their presence, which means that designers, even in this digital era, are obliged to have a physical portfolio as well as an online (or digital) one.

However, I often look at websites and then meet the designers to look at their portfolios, and two things frequently strike me. The first is that many designers don't bother to maintain visual continuity across their printed and online portfolios. This is a fundamental flaw and indicates a designer who can't maintain a stylistic voice. The other thing I notice is that the featured work is the same online as it is in the physical portfolio. For a young designer with not much work under his or her belt, this is unavoidable, but for more established designers it is essential that they do not show the same examples online as in their portfolios. Mix it up – make it different.

If we accept that we still need a physical portfolio, what are the options available to us? The slim, black vinyl zipper bag with spring clips and plastic envelopes containing printouts of work is the most common variety of portfolio case. There's nothing wrong with this traditional case, except that it's what nearly everyone else uses, and as a result it gives a drab uniformity to presentations.[1] It's a bit like turning up at a fancy dress party dressed as Superman and finding ten other people in the same costume. No marks for

If you've designed a billboard, think how much more impressive it would be to photograph the actual billboard in a busy urban setting. Clients understand this. It makes the work real for them. They rarely care about the formal aspects of design, but they care about its effectiveness.

originality. But if we are going to use one, we should at least keep it clean. The American designer Gail Anderson described interviewing someone and seeing a cockroach run out as soon as the portfolio was opened. Can't say that's happened to me, but I've lost count of the number of times I've felt my heart sink as an earnest young designer invited me to leaf through sheets of plastic envelopes, thick with dust and thumbprints.

So what are the alternatives? There are three choices: we can design and manufacture a custom-made case; we can buy a ready-made box or container; or we can go electronic, and do away with a physical portfolio and use a laptop or data projector. A custom-made box is a smart idea if we have the money, and if we can come up with a suitable design that is both eye-catching and functional. An unusual design means our portfolio will stand out and it will provide a talking point with employers or potential clients.

Buying a ready-made container is usually a good (and cheaper) alternative to a bespoke one. I like a simple box with a lift-off lid (the type favoured by photographers) that holds A3 (16½ × 11½ in) run outs, which I protect with clear lightweight acetate sleeves. The box does two things. It allows sheets to be freely handed round (rather than held in the piranha-like grip of ring-binder clips), and it allows the acetate sheets to be cleaned or replaced when they become dirty – or are attacked by hungry cockroaches.

But if we are going to use one, we should at least keep it clean. The American designer Gail Anderson described interviewing someone and seeing a cockroach run out as soon as the portfolio was opened.

Today, portfolios are less and less likely to be physical artefacts. Since many presentations will involve web design, interactive elements and motion graphics, it is essential to be able to make some sort of screen-based presentation. Presentations made on laptops or via data projectors can be highly effective. Somebody recently showed me their work on an Apple iTouch. Novelty value: high. Effectiveness: low. Personally, my favourite way to make a formal presentation is to use a data projector, with printed samples as back-up (see Presentation skills, page 250). These smart little machines are cheap and easy to transport, and when hooked up to a laptop they allow designers to make sophisticated audiovisual presentations. However, it's always advisable to check to see whether a presentation with a projector is possible.

But no matter how our work is transported, the question of how to 'show it' remains paramount. The obvious solution is to present it in flat 2-D. A double-

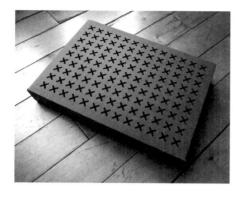

page spread from a book, for instance, will look perfectly acceptable as a digital file placed elegantly on a page. But if size, scale and dimension are important factors, we have to consider photographing items. Packaging nearly always looks best when photographed.

Regardless of whether we photograph our work or simply call up the digital files and place them on a sheet, this has to be done with style and grace. Every page must show our design ability and we must pay attention to factors such as background colours, labelling and visual consistency.

But the most important rule to remember when showing work is to show it in context. What does this mean? Here's an example. My studio was asked by an advertising agency to design a series of images to be used on billboards. We designed the images and handed them over to the agency's production department, who added a logo and made them into giant billboards. They were striking as billboards, but when we placed our images on a page for use in our portfolio they looked flat and uninspiring. So I sent someone out with a camera to shoot a few of the billboards in busy urban locations, and instead of the flat digital files we used these shots. By doing this we gave our work context. Clients understood what we had done. They rarely care about the formal aspects of a design, but they do care about its effectiveness. Of course, it's not always possible to photograph work in situ, but we should always attempt to show context – even if it means mocking it up, in the same way that architects make lifelike models of their buildings to show their 'reality'. Doing this is an enormous benefit.

I don't mind seeing examples of personal work, but I also need to see how a young designer has tackled an identity for a local dentist. How designers design mundane stuff is one of the best measures of their ability.

I'm often asked whether it is necessary to provide detailed descriptions to accompany work in a portfolio. In my view, it is usually enough to state the name of the project, name of the client, the date, and the briefest of descriptions – 20–30 words at most. This raises the question of whether it is a good idea to send out a portfolio unaccompanied. It is not uncommon for clients to ask designers to send in their portfolios for assessment. This means they are not present to explain their work, and therefore the work must function on its own. I always try not to send unaccompanied portfolios, but sometimes there is no choice.

The other question that comes up whenever portfolios are discussed is whether to show actual specimens of work

Opposite
Sturdy portfolio flight-case as used by Intro. Designed by Mat Cook, the bright yellow container is a constant talking point at presentations. www.introwebsite.com

Above
Portfolio case of designer Darren Wall, who works under the studio name Wallzo. His work can be seen here: http://wallzo.com

rather than reproductions. There are certain sorts of design – books, brochures, packaging – that need to be seen, touched and sniffed to be fully appreciated. When making portfolio presentations in person it's a good idea to show physical specimens, but only if they enhance the presentation; they can sometimes be a hindrance and could be better displayed photographically, especially if the presentation is to a large group of people.

What are the most common mistakes designers make with portfolios? Showing too much work is a frequent offence. As a general rule, don't show more than one or two examples of the same sort of work. Personally, I don't mind seeing examples of personal work (see Personal work, page 234), but I also need to see how a young designer has tackled an identity for a local dentist. How designers design mundane stuff is one of the best measures of their ability.

To the list of common failings I'd add not showing work properly (see Presentation skills, page 250), sloppiness, people who talk too much, and people who think there is unlimited time for them to show their work. Graduates should be able to get through their presentation in 15 minutes – if it takes longer something's wrong, or you're a genius. This takes us to the heart of any portfolio presentation, whether by a job hunter or a seasoned professional. The most important factor is the personality of the person making the presentation. I've been interviewing people for about 20 years. In that time I've seen hundreds of portfolios. I don't often remember portfolios, but I remember people.

Few things are more important than a designer's portfolio, and this means portfolios demand constant attention. If we become complacent about them, they will reveal our complacency.

One last thought about portfolios: we should never consider them finished, and we should always be dissatisfied with them. At Intro, the studio I co-founded, we employed someone whose main task was to look after our studio portfolio, which included a print portfolio on paper, a number of showreels, a digital presentation and a website. Few things are more important than a designer's portfolio, and this means portfolios demand constant attention. If we become complacent about them, they will reveal our complacency. A state of constant flux and enquiry is the natural state to be in when contemplating our portfolios.

Further reading: www.youthedesigner.com/2008/06/30/12-steps-to-a-super-graphic-design-portfolio/

1 I was once sitting in the reception area of a large advertising agency. I was kept waiting for 45 minutes (common practice in agencies) and while I sat there 20–30 portfolios were delivered. They made an impressive portfolio mountain – but every one was the same: the standard black zipper case. If one of them had been different it would have stood out like a light on a dark night.

Posters

Is there a future for posters in the era of text alerts and email marketing, and when commercial interests now control public spaces? There is a future for the poster, but it will mean adopting new technologies, and it will mean designers having to commission their own posters.

The International Poster and Graphic Arts Festival in Chaumont, France,[1] is a remarkable event. For a few days each year this little town is invaded by a determined army of design fans and students (poster tubes sticking out of their rucksacks like rifles) who fill up the bars and cafés, and flock to the numerous exhibitions, talks and events. At the heart of the festival is the famous Chaumont poster competition.

But it was while attending the festival that I realized that the poster is an endangered format. And yet, when I first arrived in Chaumont, the opposite seemed true. Here was an event – in fact, a whole town – celebrating the poster, but on closer inspection I saw that the many glorious examples of the art of poster design were mainly done for arts organizations and cultural institutions. Hardly any of the posters in the competition had been made for commercial purposes, or for the conveying of public information – both tasks to which the poster is well suited. Beyond the world of the arts the poster is in terminal decline, or so it seemed.

Why is this? In an interview with Kevin Finn, the designer Milton Glaser noted: '… it would be very hard to justify the poster as a major means of communicating, certainly in industrialized countries at the moment.'[2]

Now that the entire urban environment seems to have been colonized by the owners of outdoor advertising sites, it's simply too expensive to put up a poster unless you are a big-brand owner. And big-brand owners want billboards.

Cost mainly; but not the cost of printing, rather, the cost of displaying posters. Now that the entire urban environment seems to have been colonized by the owners of outdoor advertising sites, it's simply too expensive to put up a poster unless you are a big-brand owner. And big-brand owners want billboards. Billboards occasionally show a bit of wit and style, but for the most part they reduce communication to a single blunt proposition, something that can be absorbed in a millisecond as we speed past in our cars on the way to the local supermarket. Posters are different. They function on a human scale. The best ones deliver a message at a distance, but they often repay up-close inspection.

Graphic designer Mark Blamire runs the poster and design archive website Blanka.[3] Blamire knows a lot about posters, and he studies the role of the poster within commercial graphic design. 'To some degree, the poster is showing early signs of decline,' he notes. 'It has to compete with all of the new ways to promote a product. Designers definitely have fewer posters on their job lists today. I used to spend most of my graphic design life working for the music industry and the best part of the job was [usually] working on the fly-poster for the campaign. Due to fly-poster laws changing and record companies diverting their budgets to other forms of media, the poster has definitely suffered.'

Despite the lack of opportunities for designers to do commercial posterwork, there's a healthy scene for self-initiated posters, plus a growing interest (thanks to sites like Blanka) in collecting vintage graphic-design posters. There are also parts of the world where the poster is alive and well – take the perennially vibrant Seattle music scene. As a recent book by Seattle designers Modern Dog showed, the poster isn't quite dead yet.[4]

Poster design is the art of reduction. Great posters are made by what is taken away, and not what is added.

Robynne Raye, a founder member of Modern Dog, is a shrewd observer of the scene: 'Most of our poster work is in the arts sector, probably 20 to 1. But we've also done posters for Nordstrom, Oakley, K2 Snowboards and a computer-software company. Much of this work is used in-house or for retail display.' She sees the use of posters by Barack Obama in his bid for the White House as giving the poster a fillip. 'For me the biggest obstacle is finding a corporate client with a need for posters,' she notes. 'But unfortunately, when you do clients often have art directors that are heavy-handed. Seldom do they trust the designer. That's why you don't see as much great poster work being done outside the music and art scenes.'

What makes a great poster? For Blamire, the art of good poster design is simply put: 'It needs to be concise, striking and powerful.' Hamish Muir, a founder of the design group 8vo and designer of some of the best posters of the modern era, defines the poster format as 'the closest design comes to painting'.[5]

Poster design is the art of reduction. Great posters are made by what is taken away, and not what is added. Blamire quotes an example of this reductive thinking at work. 'For an exhibition of posters I was staging, I asked the Irish design company Image Now[6] to design a poster. They delivered a poster which included a graphic diagram of every punch that was landed in the famous "rumble in the jungle" fight between George Forman and Muhammad Ali. It is a really beautiful and (excuse the pun) striking idea. The original submission had an explanation on how the fight came about and all of the politics going on behind the scenes in Kinshasa at the time. The explanatory copy changed the poster. It was reminiscent of a page from a magazine and the information was a secondary piece of information that the poster didn't need. When

Opposite
Title: 2nd Amsterdam Film Night
Date: 2004
Client: Amsterdam Film Night
Designer: Experimental Jetset
A2 poster announcing the second edition of Amsterdam film festival, showing the numeral 2 consisting of several black stripes, referring to strips of film.

Tweede Amsterdamse
Filmnacht

Zaterdag
18 December 2004

2E
A'DAMSE
FILM
NACHT

De Balie
Filmhuis Cavia
Filmmuseum Cinerama
Filmmuseum Vondelpark
Bioscoop het Ketelhuis
KIT Tropentheater
Kriterion
Melkweg Cinema
Rialto
De Uitkijk

www.filmnacht.nl

Image Now revised the design with the absolute minimum of copy alongside the graphic diagram of the fight, it became a poster again. It allowed the viewer time to interact and engage with the poster and there was enough information for them to work it out for themselves. This made it infinitely more powerful. A poster doesn't need an explanation; it should explain. It should send a message without being verbose.'

Blamire foresees a new sort of poster: 'People are already creating posters which you can interact with. When you touch a certain part of the poster, it will play a piece of music or give you some secondary information or project a message over the top of the poster. As this area of technology evolves, it could make for an even more interesting experience for the viewer of the poster.' He sees no need for pessimism: 'Designers still love designing posters. It is one of the sexiest formats in their repertoire and, even with the decline in clients commissioning the poster for print, I can't see it dying out completely. Maybe that's because you see more posters in the modern day which are done as self-initiated projects under the designer's own steam.'

Further reading: Cees W. de Jong, Stefanie Burger and Jorre Both, *New Poster* Art. Thames & Hudson, 2008.

1 www.ville-chaumont.fr/festival-affiches/index.html
2 'Dissent Protects Democracy: a conversation between Milton Glaser and K. F.', Open Manifesto {4}: Propaganda, 2007. www.openmanifesto.net
3 The Blanka website features original, vintage and limited-edition posters and prints. It says: 'Our ever-expanding website includes art, design, photography, film and music, brought together by collectors and leading creatives. We collect prints to sell or just to inspire, and we are constantly adding new, historic and unusual work to our permanent visual archive.' www.blanka.co.uk
4 Michael Strassburger and Robynne Raye, *Modern Dog: 20 Years of Poster Art*. Chronicle Books, 2008.
5 Mark Holt and Hamish Muir, *8vo: On the outside*. Lars Müller Publishers, 2005.
6 www.imagenow.ie

Presentation skills

When a designer's ideas are rejected it's usually because they have been presented badly, and not because they are bad ideas. Few skills are more important to the modern designer than the ability to present work. Considering the importance of presentations it's surprising we're not better at doing them.

Since design should be self-explanatory, designers might be forgiven for thinking presentation skills are unimportant. Surely the work should succeed on its own merits without our advocacy? True; except I've never met a client who didn't want an explanation for every aspect of the creative work they've commissioned.

Designers frequently imagine that presenting work is a trick – like walking on a high wire – which only certain people are able to do. It's seen as something alien, a skill not suited to introspective graphic designers. It's certainly true that it can be effective to introduce a level of theatricality and performance into presentations. But it's not necessary. Presentation is a matter of simple logic and common sense, and is one of the most fundamental skills a designer needs to acquire.

The single most important thing to remember when presenting work to clients is that they are terrified of what they are going to be shown. For clients, commissioning design is like buying something without seeing what they are buying. Imagine going into a furniture showroom to buy a sofa and the nice smiley sales person says: 'I can sell you a sofa, but I can't show it to you.' If you were told this you'd walk out. Who ever spent money on something they couldn't see? Yet this is what we ask our clients to do. They commission us, they brief us, they might even tell us what they want, but until we turn up with our proposals they don't know what they are getting. As a result, most presentations begin in an atmosphere of nervous tension. The clients are nervous. The designers are nervous. The atmosphere is inflammable.

So, first rule of presentations is: be reassuring. We need to do everything we can to make our clients feel unthreatened. The best way to do this is to take lots of tiny steps.

Let's imagine you have been asked to design a new logo for a new company. You have been asked to present your ideas to a group of the company's senior people. You are in a small room, and you have one hour.[1] Here are a few simple rules that build reassurance and confidence.

State what you are there to do:
It may seem obvious, but designers often turn up at presentations to be confronted by people they've never met before, who might only have a sketchy idea about the purpose of the presentation. By quickly and precisely restating the aims of the presentation, you can create a sense of purpose and calmness.

Summarize the brief:
Again this sounds obvious; surely the client knows the brief inside out? Perhaps they do. But clients are often worried that designers have failed to understand the brief, or that they have deviated from it. Therefore a careful and accurate summary of the key points can be reassuring. It shows that you have understood the task, and reinforces a sense of shared objectives.

Present any research or important findings:
Have you learnt something about the project over and above the brief? Have you gleaned some information that has helped you to formulate your approach? Have you investigated what the competition is doing? If so, this is the moment to add any vital insights. Do this quickly and succinctly, because by now your audience is developing a hunger to see some work.

Show the work in stages:
Break presentations down into a series of small steps. You should not begin by unveiling the new logo; instead, you should begin with some basic building blocks. You might start by showing a colour palette and explaining your thinking on colour; you might then move to typefaces or letterforms. In both cases it is often advisable to show developmental

HELLO, I'M THE CLIENT

Hello, I'm the designer – nice to meet you. At the moment

thinking. You might explain that you looked at red, but decided it was too reminiscent of 'x', and therefore decided to use blue. Or you might show some letterforms that illustrate the direction you have elected to take. Only when you have presented all the components do you move on to show the complete logo.

Announce what the client is going to see before they see it:

If you are about to show a final version of the logo, you should actually say: 'I am now going to show you the completed version of the logo' – and only then show it. This is one of the most important aspects of a presentation: whatever you show you should say what it is before you show it. If you thrust a piece of work in front of the client it will almost certainly not be what they are expecting, and while you are pointing out its subtleties and dazzling brilliance, they are not listening. They are thinking: what am I looking at? But by simply describing exactly what they are about to see before they see it, you greatly increase your chances of a favourable response.

Once you've shown a piece of work, you should shut up:

This is hard. You want to point out the many good features of your design. But you need to give the client time to absorb what they are seeing. You've lived with the work for days – perhaps weeks, even months – but to the client what you are showing them is shockingly new. If you talk while they are adjusting to what they are seeing, they won't be listening. So you should shut up and wait for questions. If no questions arrive you can assume one of two things: you have either produced a perfect piece of work, or you have produced something that is so off target your audience is lost for words.

These are six simple steps towards making effective presentations. Of course, sometimes we are thwarted in our plans. I've turned up to present to clients who are impatient and demanding. They want to be shown ideas immediately – they don't want preamble or 'bullshit'. But we should gently insist on following our way of doing things. It's easy to be rattled by clients, and when this happens we usually end up with failure. Think of a presentation as being like directing a group of people wearing blindfolds. You are the only one who can see, therefore you have to work extra hard to make sure your charges don't amble off and get lost.

Above
Drawing by Paul Davis, 2009

What else can we do to make our presentations more effective? Well, I'm a big fan of data projectors (see Portfolios, page 243). It's worth investing in one because a major problem with presenting to a large group of people is knowing where to stand and how to display your work. A projector allows you to project an image on to a wall or screen, which means everyone will be facing the same way. My favoured route is to make the initial presentation with a projector, then hand round printed copies of the work for closer inspection.

You should always make eye contact with whomever you are presenting to. This becomes doubly important when presenting to a group of people. There's a natural inclination to address the 'boss' or main decision-maker. Big mistake; you need to involve everyone in your presentation, and you shouldn't forget to include the shy intern sitting in the corner.[2] Their opinion might be canvassed and if you've blanked them throughout the presentation you shouldn't expect a good word from them.

Watch anyone who is good at presentations and you will see that they automatically make their audience relaxed and receptive. They are unthreatening and they take everyone with them on a short and rewarding journey. They may not follow exactly the steps listed above, but they nevertheless create the warm buzz of mutual discovery.

One last point: when we've been unsuccessful in a presentation, we need to find out why. It's never an easy question to ask, but we have to force ourselves to discover what we did wrong. Sometimes the reasons are depressingly mundane – oh, the winning company said they could do the project quicker than you. Sometimes the responses are downright unfair – sorry, we really like your ideas but we decided to stick with the designer we've worked with for the past four years. Sometimes the reasons are hurtful – well, we didn't think you understood the project. Whatever the reason, we have to know.

Clients commission us, but until we show them what we've done, they don't know what they are getting. As a result, most presentations begin in an atmosphere of nervous tension. The clients are nervous. Designers are nervous. The atmosphere is inflammable.

Further reading: *Essays on Design: AGI's Designers of Influence*. Booth-Clibborn, 2000.

1 We know this because we have called up beforehand to check where the presentation will be held, who will be attending and how much time we have. (I've done presentations in crowded cafés; and one businesswoman was so busy she asked me to walk with her to her next meeting presenting on the way – it was a verbal presentation. Needless to say she rejected all my ideas. Just as I should have rejected her invitation to present on the hoof.)

2 I once made a successful presentation to a panel of 14 people. Some time later, when the project was under way, I asked the project leader why the panel had chosen my studio. 'Most of the presentations we saw were liked,' he said, 'but we had two interns on the panel, and they both said your ideas were by far the best, and that swung it for the rest of us.'

Problem solving

Graphic designers are often called problem solvers. Many are happy with this description; it satisfies the enquiring analytical mind designers often have. But does it really describe what designers do? And what if seeing every task as a problem limited our potential for creative thinking?

Is designing a logo for a new company solving a problem? It might be the case that the company has an identity 'problem': no one knows what it does, or who it is, therefore it has to get itself noticed. But is it right to view this as a problem that needs to be solved? Surely it's an opportunity that needs to be taken? Take the iPod – it wasn't a response to a problem, it was a response to an opportunity.

Consider another example. A client asks a designer to make improvements to a website that is failing because it is hard to use. The designer looks at all the issues of content, display and usability, and then makes recommendations that enable the website to function more efficiently. Surely this is problem solving?

I think there's a fundamental difference between these two tasks. In the case of the logo, the designer is given a blank canvas. In the second example, the designer is given a canvas with elements on it and asked to rearrange them. All design boils down to one or the other: designers are either working with a blank canvas or they are working with existing elements. Both the blank-canvas designer and the problem-solving designer require intuition and rationality. But problems are mainly solved by rationality (although intuition can play a part) and creativity is about intuition (although rational thinking can play a part).

But what if regarding every brief as a problem that has to be approached in a logical and rational manner means we are limiting our potential to find radical and unexpected ideas?

The distinction between these two tasks seems worth making since it describes a fundamental difference in the way designers operate. If we see all design as problem solving we run the risk of eliminating one of the most important aspects of creative thinking: the rebel yell of irrational intuition.

Most of the graphic designers I know are happy with the term 'problem solver' – even those who might also be legitimately described as blank-canvas designers. It confers intellectual status, and for many designers it's the most useful term to describe the process of translating a knotty brief into a visual equation.

There's a whole science of problem solving. Books have been written on the subject; courses can be taken on all its aspects. *How to Solve It* was written by the Hungarian-born mathematician George Pólya in 1945. It became a best-seller. 'If you can't solve a problem,' wrote Pólya, 'then there is an easier problem you can't solve: find it.' He also suggested the following four steps for solving a problem:

1. First, you have to understand the problem.
2. After understanding, then make a plan.
3. Carry out the plan.
4. Look back on your work. How could it be better?

For many designers, this is an accurate description of the correct procedure for most graphic design tasks. But what if regarding every brief as a problem that has to be approached in a logical and rational manner means we are limiting our potential to find radical and unexpected ideas? By seeing all design as a problem to be 'solved' we become more like mathematicians and people who do puzzles. To do maths and solve puzzles, we need a logical brain that moves through various stages with stately grace. But to have a creative idea that fizzes with genius, we need a blinding moment of inspiration and we need intuition. Sometimes we need to think like a pinball in a machine played by a drunk; sometimes it's beneficial to ricochet around bumping into ideas we won't find through rational thought processes. Sometimes we need to think the unthinkable – or at least have ideas that are frankly a bit loopy. Yet out of loopiness, out of postulating an unlikely scenario, out of thinking 'what if' rather than 'how come' – we are more likely to arrive at ideas that are fresh, radical and unobtainable through step-by-step rational thought.

Most graphic designers are happy with the term 'problem solver'. It confers intellectual status, and for many it's the most useful term to describe the process of translating a knotty brief into a visual equation.

Pragmatists and business people are suspicious of words like intuition and inspiration. But intuition, inspiration and creative leaps don't come out of nowhere; they come from deep pools of knowledge, experience and observation. To get at them we sometimes need to dive into these pools without any regard for our safety, and that's just not logical, is it? I'd also say we need to adopt the Miles Davis approach to creative thinking. Miles said: 'I'm always thinking about creating. My future starts when I wake up every morning … Every day I find something creative to do with my life.'[1] Sound advice, even if it comes from a fearless creative genius who, time and again, risked his reputation by adopting a radical new approach to his music. If we only turn the creative overdrive on when we have a problem to solve we will become dull designers. It should always be on.

1 Miles Davis, *Miles: The Autobiography*. Simon & Schuster, 1990.

Further reading:
www.copyblogger.com/mental-blocks-creative-thinking

Professional bodies

Graphic designers have various bodies that claim to look after their interests. But we rarely agree on the value of these institutions. Are they elite clubs for the already successful, or useful bodies with educational and professional value? And what should we expect from membership?

The desire to herd together in mutually beneficial groups seems less strong in design than it does in other professions. Yet national design associations exist throughout the industrialized world, in France, Italy, Germany, Australia, Canada and many other countries, offering a mix of professional advice, forums for discussion, and – most commonly – awards schemes. There are also smaller bodies – often no more than clubs – that cater for special interest groups, most commonly typography and illustration. The International Council of Graphic Design Associations (Icograda[1]) attempts to do globally what the various national bodies do at a national and local level.

The national bodies are professional non-profit associations run with the intention of improving the status of creative practitioners. Two well-known examples are D&AD founded 1962, in the United Kingdom, and the AIGA founded 1914, in the United States.

D&AD is unusual in that it caters for both the design and advertising communities. On its website it tells us that it is an 'educational charity that represents the global creative, design and advertising communities. Since 1962, D&AD has set industry standards, educated and inspired the next generation and, more recently, has demonstrated the impact of creativity and innovation on enhancing business performance.' It claims to stand for 'excellence, education and enterprise'. It makes no mention of that other word beginning with E: ethics.

AIGA is less shy about mentioning ethics: 'AIGA, the professional association for design, is the place design professionals turn to first to exchange ideas and information, participate in critical analysis and research and advance education and ethical practice. AIGA sets the national agenda for the role of design in its economic, social, political, cultural and creative contexts.

The other important aspect of professional bodies in fields other than design is that they offer accreditation. What is meant by accreditation? It is a certification process that holders can use to claim professional competency in a given area.

AIGA is the oldest and largest membership association for professionals engaged in the discipline, practice and culture of designing.' It also claims to assist designers in 'five critical functions for a profession: Information, Communication, Inspiration, Validation, and Representation'. AIGA offers useful guidance on ethics on its website, but in keeping with most other bodies it doesn't have an enforceable code of ethical behaviour. It has much good advice, but no rule book.

Opposite
Symbols and logos for various professional design associations: VIDAK (Visual Information Design Association of Korea); AGDA (Australian Graphic Design Association); HKDA (Hong Kong Designers Association); D&AD (Design and Art Direction); JAGDA (Japanese Graphic Designers Association); Grafia (Association of Professional Graphic Designers in Finland); Trama Visual AC, Mexico; SGD (Swiss Graphic Design); GDC (The Society of Graphic Designers of Canada); AIGA, the professional association for design; MU (Society of Hungarian Graphic Designers and Typographers); TGDA (Taiwan Graphic Design Association).

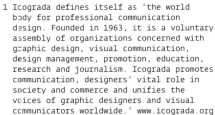

The other important aspect of professional bodies in fields other than design is that they offer accreditation. What is meant by accreditation? It is a certification process that holders can use to claim professional competency in a given area. It's a badge of professional fitness. Beauty technicians have it, and real estate agents need it, as do health care workers – but designers don't. The argument against accreditation for designers is that it isn't possible do anything as crass as 'measure' creativity. The consequence is that design is a huge global industry, but offers no professional accreditation.

The Design Association,[2] based in the UK, announces itself as a 'Chartered Society of Designers[3] initiative', and offers accreditation. It says: 'The Society is unique in accrediting and representing professional designers across the spectrum of design disciplines, including; Exhibition, Fashion, Graphic, Interactive Media, Interior, Product and Textile design. Within these categories are included myriad specialist design disciplines. With members in 34 countries around the world, CSD offers a truly diverse and inclusive base of professional designers, each committed to operating to the highest professional standards in whichever field or country they practise.'

Yet the notion persists that design associations are clubs usually run by elected councils of designers who have reached some eminence, and for whom service represents both recognition of professional status, and their desire to 'put something back'. Most design associations seem to put their efforts into making design attractive to business. This is an important role, but it is not the only one, and the feeling persists that bodies around the world duck the really big issues: ethics, sustainability and accreditation.

Is membership advisable? Usually, because without these bodies designers have nothing, and in the new climate of accountability professional associations that rely on membership fees are likely to be far more willing to listen to members than they might have been in the past. A good example of this was D&AD's willingness to review the way they run their annual awards scheme after the graphic design jurors delivered a damning verdict and awarded hardly any prizes. This caused uproar and debate raged in the design press and on the blogs, but the result was that D&AD agreed to review its procedure for attracting and assessing graphic design. It is doubtful that this would have happened in the past.

Further reading: www.icograda.org

1 Icograda defines itself as 'the world body for professional communication design. Founded in 1963, it is a voluntary assembly of organizations concerned with graphic design, visual communication, design management, promotion, education, research and journalism. Icograda promotes communication, designers' vital role in society and commerce and unifies the voices of graphic designers and visual communicators worldwide.' www.icograda.org
2 It says: 'The Design Association accredits the design of the business and the business of design.' www.design-association.org
3 The Chartered Society of Designers was formed in Great Britain in 1930. It says that it 'is not a trade body or association and membership is only awarded to qualified designers who must also prove their professional capability during an admission assessment. If a designer has MCSD™ or FCSD™ after their name you can be assured of a professional service.'

Protest design

There is a small but rich tradition of designers using their skills to register a protest. The iconography of the modern era is commercial – the Coca-Cola logo or the McDonald's arches. But is there a symbol more recognizable than the peace logo? Who says designers can't have an impact?

Above
Authentic protest badges from 1960s American counter-culture protest movements.

One of the world's most enduring pieces of iconography has nothing to do with commercialism. It was designed in 1958 by Gerald Holtom, a graduate of the Royal College of Art, London. In Britain it is recognized as the logo of the Campaign for Nuclear Disarmament (CND). In the United States, after its widespread adoption by the 1960s protest movements and the hippies, it is known as the peace symbol.

Gerald Holtom was a conscientious objector who had worked on a farm during the Second World War. He has described how the symbol came to be created. 'I was in despair. Deep despair. I drew myself: the representative of an individual in despair, with hands palm outstretched outwards and downwards in the manner of Goya's peasant before the firing squad. I formalized the drawing into a line and put a circle round it.'[1]

After CND and the huge cultural upheavals of the 1960s, oppositional and campaigning groups adopted logos and slogans and used them in exactly the same way that the global corporations did: as powerful rallying points; as instantly recognizable symbols that reduce complex messages to a concise visual gesture – think of the clenched gloved fist of the Black Panthers, or the scribbled logotype of Solidarity, the Polish anti-Communist movement of the 1980s.

Of course, graphic design has been used just as effectively in support of establishment and reactionary forces. We think of Uncle Sam urging United States citizens to enlist in the army, and the British government using the image of Lord Kitchener to tell its citizens to sign up and fight in the First World War – both are graphic images that have entered the bloodstream of iconography. But the real masters of graphic propaganda were the Nazis. The swastika – adapted from an ancient symbol used in religions such as Hinduism – has become for ever associated with them (and shows no sign of losing its potency as a symbol of evil, thanks to its continued use by neo-Nazi groups today).

As designers find themselves increasingly enmeshed in commercial life, it is more and more the case that they feel a need to use their skills for causes and social campaigns that they believe in. Nothing new in this, designers have always done it. We need only think of the agit prop work of Grapus in France and the politically motivated output of Dutch designer Jan van Toorn. Today, using graphic design to register a protest or create an oppositional stance is unusual. On the contemporary

Jonathan Barnbrook is a campaigning graphic designer in the same way that a campaigning journalist tackles issues and perceived inequalities.

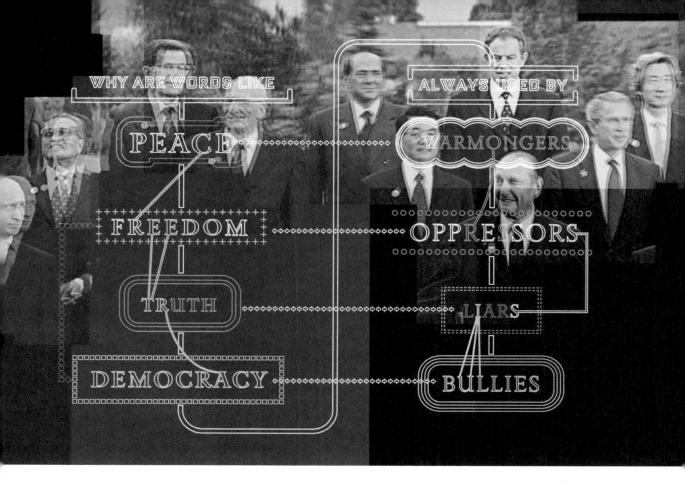

WHY ARE WORDS LIKE

PEACE

FREEDOM

TRUTH

DEMOCRACY

ALWAYS USED BY

WARMONGERS

OPPRESSORS

LIARS

BULLIES

scene, Jonathan Barnbrook is one of a handful of designers who use their skills to make graphic statements that demonstrate opposition to, among other things, wars and corporate encroachment into civil liberties. He is a campaigning graphic designer in the same way that a campaigning journalist tackles issues and perceived inequalities. Barnbrook's work has a rare potency, but its effectiveness is due to his ability to use the slick machine-tooled graphic language of commerce to attack some of modern life's most deserved targets: warmongering governments and ruthless corporations.

Barnbrook is proof that design can make a difference and that designers are not impotent. Some of his work has attracted legal action from the corporations he has caught in his cross hairs. We are quick to boast to our clients about design's ability to drive commercial activity, therefore, those of us who feel a commitment to social change and the elimination of unfairness in society should not be shy about offering our views. The Internet gives radical campaigning designers a platform that didn't previously exist.

Further reading: Milton Glaser, *The Design of Dissent: Socially and Politically Driven Graphics*. Rockport, 2006.

Above
Project: Why Are Words like Peace, Freedom, Truth, Democracy Always Used by Warmongers, Oppressors, Liars, Bullies
Date: 2003
Designer: Jonathan Barnbrook
Image Credit: Antônio Milena/Abr
Barnbrook explores the contradictions inherent in the use of language by those in positions of power. Note his use of sophisticated graphic design and typography to make an oppositional political statement, and how he avoids the raw and blunt modes of graphic expression normally found in agitprop design.

1 Letter to Hugh Brock, editor of *Peace News*. www.docspopuli.org/articles/ PeaceSymbolArticle.html

Q

Questions

Interrogating clients is an essential part of being a designer. If we don't learn to ask questions, we run the risk of never getting to the heart of what good design can be. No question is ever too dumb to ask, and if we are frightened of exposing our ignorance we will never understand anything.

It's surprising how often we shy away from asking the most obvious – OK, let's say it, dumb – questions. I've lost count of the number of times I've sat in briefing meetings and failed to understand everything that I've been told. What did I do about it? For years I kept quiet; I thought if I asked too many questions I would look stupid. But when I finally learnt to ask 'stupid' questions life as a professional designer improved tenfold.

What I'm talking about here is the habit clients have of failing to explain the stuff that to them is grindingly obvious. They are quick to accuse designers of failing to understand their businesses, yet they often make the mistake of not explaining what they understand implicitly. They just assume everyone knows what they know.

I once worked for a man who ran an insurance business. It wasn't even a conventional insurance business: it sold insurance to other insurance companies. The man who ran it was a super-smart guy, who'd left school at sixteen but had got himself to university and then to business school and earned an MBA. He was taking a gamble by hiring my studio – he knew we weren't the usual kind of company that did this sort of work. But he genuinely wanted a novel approach to his communication materials. I was aware of the fact that he was taking a risk and I was nervous about showing any weakness in my understanding of his business. Big mistake.

I went to a couple of briefing sessions and left with gaps in my knowledge. When I returned to present our creative ideas, I received an

For years I kept quiet; I thought if I asked too many questions I would look stupid. But when I finally learnt to ask 'stupid' questions life as a designer improved tenfold.

instant lesson in the need to ask questions until perfect knowledge is achieved. As soon as I showed some work, my client immediately started to ask questions. They were alarmingly basic; some were almost childlike. And they indicated someone who knew nothing about the workings of creative companies. It was a level of questioning that I'd never encountered before. It wasn't aggressive; it was an example of someone with an analytical mind, someone who simply had to understand what he was looking at before he could accept it. It was easy to imagine him doing the same with a contract or a complex business deal.

This degree of interrogation was a revelation to me. Sitting in a grey office with grey carpet tiles, a white board and a water cooler, I had a small epiphany. I realized that in future I had to do what my smart businessman interlocutor was doing. I had to ask questions until there were no gaps in my knowledge, and I had to be fearless about asking questions that made me look dumb.

Further reading: Peter Hall, Sagmeister. *Made You Look*. Thames & Hudson, 2001.

Quotation marks

These little tadpoles cause more trouble than just about any other typographic detail. Double and single quote marks are one of the main causes of typographic crime. But what is right, and how do we avoid making embarrassing mistakes that require the attention of the typo police?

In an interesting post on *Design Observer* entitled 'The Cuckoo Bird and the Keyboard' the designer Matthew Peterson wrote: 'Easily the most maligned key on your computer's keyboard lies just to the left of "return" and represents what appear to be single and double quotation marks. It is a cuckoo's egg in the designer's nest. It doesn't belong. Unless we put a finger on the key's history and purpose, we risk being cuckolded, in the truest sense of the word.'[1]

What we're talking about here is a commonly found confusion between what are known as primes and 'proper quotation marks'. A prime mark on its own stands for inches or minutes. The double prime represents feet or hours. But with mind-numbing frequency, we see primes used wrongly to indicate reported speech and apostrophes. When double primes are used in quotations they are known as 'dumb quotes'.

On the other hand, 'proper quotation marks' look similar to apostrophes. The opening quotes resemble two little sixes (66), while the closing quotes look like two little nines (99). The precise shape of proper quotation marks can vary depending on the typeface being used, and different countries and languages have their own styles and customs.

A prime mark on its own stands for inches or minutes. The double prime represents feet or hours. But with mind-numbing frequency, we see primes used wrongly to indicate reported speech and apostrophes.

When to use double and single quotation marks is determined by house style and national conventions. In Britain the custom is to use single quotes and if the quotation carries a quote within it double marks are used. In American English it is the other way round.

Further reading: www.1000timesno.net/?p=261

1 www.designobserver.com/archives/entry.html?id=21498

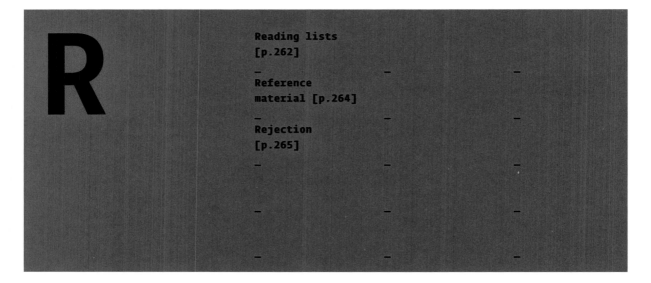

R

Reading lists
[p.262]

Reference
material [p.264]

Rejection
[p.265]

Reading lists

How do we know which design books to read? There are so many to choose from we couldn't read them all – not to mention the blogs and magazines – even if we wanted to. One of the ways we decide is by studying reading lists. And there's no shortage of reading lists to choose from.

Reading about design is as important as the act of designing itself. And it's not only design books that designers need to study; in fact, it's unhealthy for them to only read design books. It's like eating only one type of food; without a varied diet we become sluggish.

In an interview in *Eye* magazine, Michael Bierut describes a typical bibliographic rite of passage for a young designer: 'When I found out it [graphic design] had a name – I was fifteen years old – I went to the Parma Regional Library in Ohio and looked up graphic design in the card catalogue. They had one book: *Graphic Design Manual* by Armin Hofmann … All these pictures of dots and squares hypnotized me. After repeatedly taking this book out of the library I went to a department store in downtown Cleveland and asked if they had it, expecting to get a frown and a puzzled look. Instead the saleswoman said, "Oh, yeah, we just got that in for Christmas." She led me to this pile of books, but it was a book called *Graphic Design* by Milton Glaser, with Bob Dylan on the front. So there were two books – one by Glaser and one by Armin Hofmann, that seemed diametrically opposed.'[1]

Books are like ladders. We climb one, and when we get to the top there's another one waiting to take us higher. Even today, when the computer screen threatens

Above
Project: *50 Reading Lists – Spin/2*
Date: 2007
Designer: Spin
A self-published project by London design group Spin. Printed on newsprint, the publication features lists of recommended reading by 50 leading graphic designers including Ben Bos, Karl Gerstner, Peter Saville, Wolfgang Weingart and the late Alan Fletcher. It is available to buy from www.spin.co.uk

1 Steven Heller, 'The shortcomings of ideology and the role of design criticism', interview with Michael Bierut, *Eye* 24, Spring 1997. www.eyemagazine.com/feature.php?id=24&fid=164

to replace printed text as our main source of information and entertainment, books offer a vehicle for study and learning that will never be surpassed.

There are designers who don't read much, and who find reading difficult, and it is perfectly possible to be a designer without being a reader. He or she is capable of having a well-developed instinct for colour and shape, and the rhythmic arrangement of elements in space. But they might struggle to excel in typography and text-based design, since the fundamental requirement of this aspect of graphic design is the ability to render words readable.

The assertion that 'designers don't read' is a familiar refrain, but it is no longer true. There's a strong emphasis on reading and writing in the education of the modern designer, and as a result writing about design is everywhere. Blogs are hugely popular. Magazines are full of in-depth articles. Books flood out of the publishing houses. The non-reading designer is becoming a rarity.

But we still need help in choosing what to read. Design schools provide students with plenty of information about must-read books, and designers love to produce lists of recommended reading. So, in homage to the new designer-literacy, here is my reading list.

Reyner Banham, *A Critic Writes: Selected Essays by Reyner Banham*. University of California Press, 1999.
Michael Bierut, Steven Heller, Jessica Helfand and Rick Poynor (eds), *Looking Closer 3, Vol. 3: Classic Writings on Graphic Design*. Allworth Press, 1999.
Robert Bringhurst, *The Elements of Typographic Style*. Hartley & Marks, 1992.
Mark Holt and Hamish Muir, *8vo: On the outside*. Lars Müller Publishers, 2005.
Tibor Kalman, *Perverse Optimist*. Princeton Architectural Press, 2000.
Robin Kinross, *Unjustified Texts: Perspectives on Typography*. Hyphen Press, 2008.
Lars Müller, *Josef Müller-Brockmann: Pioneer of Swiss Graphic Design*. Lars Müller Publishers, 4th edition, 2001.
Rick Poynor, *Jan van Toorn: Critical Practice*. 010 Publishers, 2008.
Stefan Sagmeister, *Things I Have Learned in My Life So Far*. Harry N. Abrams, 2008.
Gerald Woods, Philip Thompson and John Williams, *Art Without Boundaries 1950–1970*. Thames & Hudson, 1972.

Further reading: Spin/2.50 Reading Lists. Available from made@spin.co.uk

Reference material

**All designers need reference
material, to inform but also to
inspire. Yet information and
inspiration are not always
found in the same place, which
makes it essential to go beyond
the obvious. Many designers
keep scrapbooks, but in the age
of Google, all we need do is
hit 'search'.**

Give a designer a brief and watch what happens. After
the document has been scrutinized (see Briefs, page 48)
most designers start looking for reference material.
But what is meant by 'reference material'? Reference
material fulfils two functions for designers. The first is
practical. It is anything that helps us respond to a brief
in a more informed way. It helps us in our search for
background information and gives us a deeper understanding
of our subject. The second is inspirational. It stimulates
or excites us into discovering ways of responding to a
brief with freshness and originality.

Let's deal with the practical role of reference
material first. If we are asked to design a logo for a new
company we will look at the sorts of logo commonly found
in its sector to avoid duplicating a design or colour
scheme already in existence, and to find out the graphic
styles that characterize this particular territory. In
other words, we will accumulate and sift through material
that will make us better informed about the subject. This
is a necessary part of the design process.

However, information is not enough. We also need the
steroid injection of inspiration – that creative jolt
we get from discovering something that leads us to an
exciting and fresh idea. And for this we must look beyond
the obvious reference materials. If we only look at other
logos – there are plenty of books on the subject – we will
most likely end up with what is already in existence. Like
curing hiccups with a slap on the back, true inspiration
needs to come from a sudden and unexpected source.
The quest for inspirational reference
materials is, in my view, one of the
best parts of being a designer: leafing
through strange books and bumping up
against unfamiliar worlds is a never-
ending joy.

The Internet has taken a lot of
the legwork out of inspiration hunting.
Google image search is terrific, as is
Flikr and the numberless other sites
that have turned the Internet into a
cosmically proportioned lexicon of

**The only rule
in searching
for inspiration
is not to look
in the obvious
places. That
way we end up
with obvious
solutions. Think
tangential.**

visual reference points that makes the viewer gasp with
amazement. But the sheer volume of material means we
have to hunt smart. If, for example, we are looking for
inspiration for a sports-related task, it might be better
to avoid searching the word 'sports': instead try 'speed',
'stamina', 'velocity'. A picture of a speed camera might
be a more interesting image, with greater metaphorical
bite, than a close-up of straining neck muscles.

So the only rule in searching for inspiration is
not to look in the obvious places. Following that route

means that we end up devising obvious solutions. Think tangentially. Lift those stones that haven't been lifted before – it's amazing what's to be found under them. I'd also say that we have to build up an internal reference system. We have to develop a way of storing images, ideas and visual metaphors so that we can call on them when needed. Notebooks and sketch pads are essential adjuncts for this.

In *Things I Have Learned in My Life So Far* Stefan Sagmeister describes the way most of his ideas come from his memory banks. As a young designer he'd worked in Hong Kong where one of the great sights is bamboo scaffolding. Sagmeister stored this potent image in his head, and when he was asked to return to the city to undertake a project he remembered the scaffolding and used it to create giant self-standing 3-D letterforms.

For me, hunting for references and visual stimuli has to be done constantly. I used to keep scrapbooks, but I quickly reached a point where I needed a separate room just to house them. Now, it's a mental scrapbook (augmented by Google Search). But it's one I never stop adding to.

Further reading: Stefan Sagmeister, *Things I Have Learned in My Life So Far*. Harry N. Abrams, 2008.

Rejection

It would be a strange designer who didn't mind having his or her work rejected. But it's a poor designer who can't cope with rejection. Rejection is as much a part of design as success. And it needn't always be bad: sometimes it makes us do better work and sometimes we deserve it.

I was talking to a designer friend recently. She said: 'I've just finished two big projects and both clients were nightmares.' I thought about the number of times I'd heard designers say this. Are all clients always nightmares? But then my friend said, 'Of course, I shouldn't have taken on these jobs. I wasn't right for either of them.' Suddenly the reason her clients were nightmares became phosphorescently clear: they were nightmares because she had done a bad job. If we are honest with ourselves when our work is rejected, we will probably come to the same conclusion: nightmare clients are nightmares for a reason.

Of course, some clients really are nightmares, and sometimes the rejection of creative work is unfair and unmerited. There are hopeless clients who wouldn't know good design if it bit them on the nose. But usually if our work is rejected it is our own fault: we have either presented our ideas badly (see Presentation skills, page 250) or we have not spent enough time preparing; occasionally it is because we have done a bad job.

Even more important than being able to admit to ourselves that we have failed, we also have to be able to admit to the client that we have failed – and that's not easy.

We can improve the way we present our work, we can set up systems to ensure that we are properly prepared, but if we can't spot when we have done a bad job we will experience the pain of failure with dull regularity. But, even more important than being able to admit to ourselves that we have failed, we also have to be able to admit to the client that we have failed – and that's not easy. Owning up that we have bellyflopped? Surely that is commercial suicide? And certainly, walking into a client's office after working on a project for six months and saying 'I've messed up' probably is a sort of suicide. It's too late then. I'm thinking of those earlier sessions, perhaps by the water cooler showing initial ideas to a creative director or meeting a client in a coffee shop and showing work on a laptop. It's here in these informal, exploratory settings that it is easiest to admit that sometimes, just sometimes, we get it wrong – and that this is one of those occasions.

When we are wrong, we must own up. This is difficult for designers. We imagine that our professional integrity is dependent on always being right. But no one is always right, and the designer who can admit to failure scores higher than one who is in denial.

In more formal settings, when presenting to a big group of people for example, it's less easy to own up to mistakes. But even here, owning up is sometimes the best route. Someone recently asked me what to do when work is rejected or criticized in a public forum (she worked for a large company that required its designers to present to large groups, including people participating via a satellite link). I suggested two options. One is that if we believe in what we've done, we must defend it. To do this we will need a solid rationale for our work. We may still lose the argument but at least we will have the satisfaction of knowing we stuck up for what we believed in; and as long as we do this with good grace and don't sound petty or peevish, people will respect us for defending our work (even if they shoot us down and we lose the argument).

The other option is more dramatic: if we are in the wrong, we must own up to having got it wrong. This is difficult for designers. We imagine that our professional integrity is dependent on always being right. But no one is always right, and the designer who can admit to failure scores higher than the one who defends himself or herself even when they know they are wrong.

Owning up has a remarkable effect, even on the most boorish of clients. They suddenly want to talk about ways of fixing rather than destroying work. All the tension drains away and is replaced by an air of cooperation. To

Above
Drawing by Paul Davis, 2009

1 The writer Clive James observed: 'A wrecked
  project can hurt worse than heartbreak,
  so it's no wonder that some people give up
  altogether, even though their talents would
  have merited another chance. Noel Coward
  was right when he said that the secret of
  success is the capacity to survive failure.
  The failure can hurt so much. But unlike
  heartbreak, which really is a dead loss,
  failure has a function.' Clive James, *North
  Face of Soho*. Picador, 2006.
2 In *Things I Have Learned in My Life So
  Far*, Sagmeister reproduces the letter he
  received from his Japanese client. 'Dear
  Stefan, I have to tell you bad and sad
  news today. The cover that you designed for
  Esquire has been rejected by the advertising
  dept. of *Esquire* magazine Japan last night.
  Reason why it was rejected: "Street piss"
  is a crime in Japan, and it is against the
  moral. It looks that piss targets the car,
  and when reader turns the cover, Nissan
  car appears.'

get a sympathetic hearing it sometimes helps to hold a hand up and say, 'Guilty'.

Of course, rejection comes in various forms. The worst of these is when no reason is given. This often happens in competitive pitches, when three or four studios compete for a project (see Pitching, page 240). The losers get a polite message saying, 'Sorry, you were unsuccessful'. Well, in these situations it is essential to ask why we were rejected. It's a tough phone call to make, but if we are to learn from our failures we need to know the reasons for our rejection – especially if we are confident that we did a good job and answered the brief properly. The reasons can often make for painful listening – and, as I've said, are frequently downright unfair – but if we are to avoid repeating a mistake in the future, we have to know what they are.[1]

Another sort of rejection is even harder to take. Sometimes designers are given an open brief: they are invited to 'do what they want'. Most of us jump at these opportunities, and are surprised when our ideas are rejected. Stefan Sagmeister tells a great story about receiving a 'do whatever you want' brief. A Japanese magazine asked him to design a cover. The cover – although never used – has become famous: it shows Sagmeister and another person peeing. Their projectile urine spells out (with the aid of 'elaborate post-production') the words, 'Everybody thinks they are right'. Although it was clearly a fantasy image, when the Japanese client saw the outcome they rejected it.[2] 'Do what you want' only rarely means do what you want.

Learning to deal with failure is an essential skill for all creative people. Everyone has work rejected. But good ideas are good ideas, and what one client rejects might find acceptance with another, so we should never see failure as being total. However, the only way to deal with rejection is to accept responsibility for it. It's only by doing this that we can turn rejection into success.

Further reading: Clive James, *North Face of Soho*. Picador, 2006.

> **Rejection comes in various forms. The worst of these is when no reason is given. This often happens in competitive pitches, when three or four studios compete for a project. The losers get a polite message saying, 'Sorry, you were unsuccessful'. Well, in these situations it is essential to ask why we were rejected.**

Sacking clients

Why would designers ever want to sack clients? We spend half our lives wooing them, so it seems odd to show them the door. But sometimes it's necessary. The trick is to avoid getting involved with the wrong clients in the first place.

Most designers find it difficult to sack a client. We'd rather suffer than wield the axe. This is for two reasons. The first is the simple economic reality that as soon as we start a project we incur costs we need to recoup. The second is that most designers have developed the service gene, and have a professional commitment to seeing the job through no matter what this involves.

But we should ask ourselves this: how many projects have ended up as creative, financial and moral failures because the designer knew the client was wrong for them, but did nothing about it? If the answer is none, he or she probably never even thought about sacking a client. If, however, the answer is quite often, dumping a client is not something they find unthinkable. Of course, we should only ever consider sacking a client in extreme circumstances. It is our duty as professionals to persevere with even the most miserable clients; it is our ethical obligation to finish what we have started, and to do what we have promised to do.

I've only had to sack a client on two occasions, and in each case I found they were in agreement with my decision. They both accepted that it was a failed relationship and divorce was the best option; in both cases the parting was amicable. But knowing when to open the trapdoor is a valuable skill.

The best way to avoid having to dump a client is to have criteria by which we assess all clients before agreeing to work for them. We must draw up a set of rules covering payment terms, schedules, approval processes and accountability, and it's for this reason that it's advisable for even small studios to have Terms and Conditions. Many professionally minded studios run credit checks on new clients and ask for references. Be sure to follow these up. Good clients have no problem filling out credit-check forms. Dodgy ones are evasive: 'Oh, did you send me the form? Didn't see it. Send it again.'

But there is no better way to spot troublemakers than to develop a 'nose' for them. In other words, we need to develop an instinct for danger and act before we get in too deep to pull out. We must learn to spot the telltale signs of evasiveness and reluctance to agree on the parameters of a project. If a client is slow to hand over a purchase order, or commit to payment terms, they are sending out warning signals. It's sometimes a good idea to talk to someone who has worked with them before and get a 'character' reference.

But some clients reveal their bad habits only when we start to work for them.[1] When this happens we have to be prepared to dump them. So let's assume we've initially failed to spot any monster-like tendencies: what are the reasons that might make us sack a client? We only ever do it when their actions have caused us, or are likely to cause us, to lose money or our integrity. Here are two examples: those admittedly rare clients who pile on extra tasks as soon as a job has started; and the ones who are cavalier about copyright and demand that we hand over artwork so that it can be used in other contexts without additional payment.

One last thought. Dishonest clients are rare, and long before we think about sacking them we should be taking steps to avoid this outcome. When things go wrong, the first thing to do is to ask for a clear-the-air meeting. If this fails, we should wield the axe quickly. But only as a final act of self-preservation, and only when every other avenue has been explored. And only if we are sure that it's not us who are at fault.

Further reading:
www.aiga.org/content.cfm/professional-practices

1 The opposite is more often true. Many clients begin as difficult, untrusting and hostile, but once we have gained their trust they turn into model clients.

Salaries

It's possible to make a good living as a designer. Salaries may not rival those in other creative disciplines such as advertising, but design isn't the financial ghetto it once was. The only problem is, the more money we earn, the more commercial we have to become.

When we start out as designers we don't care how much we earn. All we want to do is work. We want to learn our craft and see our work used, disseminated and published. But there comes a time when the need to earn a decent living becomes important. The usual culprits emerge – marriage, mortgages, children, expensive habits and tastes – driving us to earn more money.

When these prompts arrive, some big decisions have to be made. If we want to earn more money, it's necessary to negotiate salary increases, gain promotion, take on extra work or start up on our own. Let's assume we are working in a small, independent studio. We've been there a couple of years and our salary has crept up, but when we talk to friends in other studios, we discover they are earning more than us (funny isn't it, our friends always seem to be earning more than us). So what do we do?

We need to ask ourselves a tough question: if I announced my resignation tomorrow would my employer beg me to stay, or would my departure be greeted with polite acceptance? Assuming the answer is that our employer wants to keep us, how should we go about getting a pay hike?

The first step is to get a realistic idea of what our remuneration should be. How do we do this? If we work in-house there will probably be salary structures that enable us to see what we should be earning. For designers working in studios, information on salaries can be found by looking at one of a number of surveys that track salaries in the design sector. In the United Kingdom, *Design Week* publishes one every year; other countries have similar reports. The ever-enterprising AIGA even offers United States designers a helpful salary calculator.[1]

Once we have an idea of our 'market value' we need to approach our employer. Having employed lots of designers, I was always pleased when people told me what they wanted. If I was in a position to grant them their wishes, I did so. If, however, I didn't think they merited an increase, or if I wasn't in a position to give pay rises – even to those who deserved it – I appreciated the opportunity to say so. It got the issue out into the open. Employers and employees tend to be secretive about salaries. It's much better to be frank about them.

For most of us, being a designer is about earning enough money to live and doing the sort of work that makes us feel proud.

But what should be done when the answer is a flat no? When that happens we must ask for a reason. If it is that the studio can't afford to pay us more, we might have to consider leaving. But if the reason is that we don't deserve it (too much poor work, for example, being a serial latecomer, or worse), at least it's possible do something about it. We can decide to improve or start planning a new career.

If we are offered a pay increase, how do we know that it is fair? In most cases, the figure will be what the studio can afford and there will be little room for negotiation. However, being familiar with local pay scales will help. It will at least let us know whether to accept the offer or move on. Small design studios usually pay what they can afford, which is less than bigger studios or working in-house in the corporate sector.

There are a few blessed individuals who have everything: a great job and a handsome pay packet. For most of us, being a designer is about earning enough money to live and doing the sort of work that makes us feel proud. It's widely accepted that to earn big salaries designers have to work in areas where design is not greatly valued, such as mass-market branding and consumer-facing businesses. For designers who find this unpalatable, the alternative is to start up a studio. The rewards are there for anyone who can sustain a successful business. It is a hard road to travel and risks lurk at every corner – but since when did that dissuade smart people from trying?

Further reading: www.designweek.co.uk/Articles/134235/ Design+Week+Salary+Survey.html

1 http://designsalaries.org/calculator.asp

Sans serif

Sans serif type is associated with mechanistic precision. Sans type is modern, serif type is traditional. But it's not the lack of serifs that makes sans typefaces special. It's the fact that sans type is usually monoline, which distances it from typography's ancestry in calligraphy.

ABCDEFGHI JKLMNOPQ RSTUVWXY Z012345678 9,.:;""''!?*/& %£$()[]{}@

Berthold Akzidenz Grotesk Bold

In the village where I grew up there was a sign by the roadside. It was hand-lettered and said DEAD SLOW CHILDREN. The parents of one of my school friends had erected it to encourage drivers to slow down. It had been made (designed?) by an architect friend of theirs. It had red and black sans serif lettering on a white background. I remember being struck by its elegant simplicity.

Even then, as a snotty little urchin, I knew this was something interesting. The brutalist poetry and ambiguity of the message had an effect on me, but it was the way the architect had stacked all three words in a justified block, and the impact of the stark sans-serif lettering, that affected me most.

If the sign had been made by a professional signwriter it is doubtful that it would have had this stark Modernist look. It took an architect to make it elemental and urgent. But that's what sans serif typefaces do: they have a direct effect. The Modernists recognized the fusion of pure form and explicit functionalism in their letterforms. Writing in *Pioneers of Modern Typography*, Herbert Spencer noted: 'After 1925, Herbert Bayer, at the Bauhaus, and Jan Tschichold, at the Munich School, both energetically encouraged the use of sans serif types and both designed geometrically-constructed sans-serif alphabets. Sans serif types reflected the notion of "beauty in utility", which had become the pivot of Bauhaus experiments …'

The theory of 'beauty in utility' in sans serif typefaces is still dominant in modern communications. No one uses a serif font for road signage; the word 'police' on a flak jacket is not often rendered in Palace Script. The stark authority of sans serif letterforms has turned the great serif-free

Today, the sans serif typeface no longer spells rebellion. It is as likely to be found on a toothpaste tube as on a brochure for a publicly funded arts project. But it still stands for a certain cool detachment.

ABCDEFGHI JKLMNOPQ RSTUVWXY Z0123456 789,.:;!?*& %£$(){}@

Bell Centennial BT Bold Listing

ABCDEFGHI JKLMNOPQ RSTUVWXY Z012345678 9,.:;""!?*/& %£$()[]{}@

Frutiger 65 Bold

ABCDEFGHI JKLMNOPQ RSTUVWXY Z01234567 89,.:;""!?*/ &%£$()[]{}@

Futura Bold

Previous page and above
Sans-serif fonts can be classified into various categories: Grotesque (Akzidenz Grotesk, Franklin Gothic); Neo-grotesque (Bell Centennial, Arial); Humanist (Frutiger, Gill Sans); Geometric (Futura, Avant Garde).

1 Rick Poynor, 'Rub out the Word', I.D., September 1994. Republished in Design Without Boundaries, Booth-Clibborn, 1998.

fonts of Helvetica, Univers, Franklin and others into the command system of authority. Yet, to the probable dismay of the Bauhaus founders, the sans serif 'look' has become the predominant 'cool' graphic design style statement of the 1990s and the first decade of the twenty-first century.

The sans serif style was widely viewed as old-fashioned and sterile until the arrival in the 1990s of a new generation of designers who were in love with the originators of the Modernist style, but also with contemporary masters such as Wolfgang Weingart, who offered a less strict and more intuitive approach in tune with the emergent computer-based design culture.

I first became aware of the neo-Modernist graphical syntax when Neville Brody used Helvetica in his first major post-*Face* project: the design of *Arena* magazine. Here he moved away from the rich Constructivist-inspired 'look at me' graphics that had made his name to a new sans serf understatedness. Brody told Rick Poynor in 1990, that he did this because his 'ideas were weakened into styles. The very thing I used in order to get the ideas across – a strong personal style – was the thing that defeated reception of the ideas.' Poynor went on to note that Brody's 'switch to stylistically neutral Helvetica for *Arena* headlines was an act of both atonement and self-denial ('I hate Helvetica'), but it did no good. They copied that, too: for the last eight years in Britain a spotlessly white, drip-dry neo-modernism has been the dominant graphic style.'[1]

What Brody did was become the most visible adopter of the sans serif International Style – the version of Neue Grafik (the New Typography) that had been exported from Switzerland, and which had conquered the United States where, from the 1960s onwards, it had become the dominant graphical style of corporate America. Brody was to play fast and loose with Swiss rationalism, but in his wake came a generation of young British designers who were to turn to the Swiss, asymmetric style as a way of rebelling and rejecting British traditionalism and formalism. Foremost among these sans-serif pioneers were 8vo, the iconoclastic British design team.[2]

Today, the sans serif typeface no longer spells rebellion. It is as likely to be found on a toothpaste tube as on a brochure for a publicly funded arts project. But it still stands for a certain cool detachment. Perhaps

The theory of 'beauty in utility' in sans serif typefaces is still dominant in modern communications. The word 'police' is not often rendered in Palace Script on a flak jacket.

2 'The context in which 8vo started in 1984/5 was important as it gave us something to react against and made it easier to define our approach to graphic design. Post-war UK graphics had developed a reputation for being ideas led. Creative solutions were as much literary as visual. In contrast to the rationality of Swiss design, for example, and without the need to communicate across language groups and borders, the subtlety and humour of the English language strengthened the development of the ideas-led approach in the UK.' Mark Holt and Hamish Muir, *8vo: On the Outside*, Lars Müller Publishers, 2005.

more than the absence of serifs, it's the fact that most serif typefaces are monoline – no thick and thin letterforms – that gives the characters their machine-like purity. Of course, many typefaces that appear monoline are in fact 'faked' – in other words, line thickness varies microscopically to give the illusion of uniformity. Not so pure after all?

Further reading: http://typefoundry.blogspot.com/2007/01/ nymph-and-grot-update.html

Semiotics

Semiotics is the study of signs and their meanings. The subject is often cloaked in difficult language and more suited to the university lecture theatre than the working world inhabited by graphic designers. But designers are natural semioticians – signs and their meaning are the designer's stock in trade.

Semiotics was defined by one of its founders, Ferdinand de Saussure, as 'a science which studies the life of signs at the heart of social life'.[1] Saussure was a linguist, and revolutionized the study of language by proposing that words are part of a system of signs. Words, like signs, he postulated have no meaning beyond the meaning we invest in them. For instance, the word for a house varies from language to language. If we read or hear the Japanese word for 'house' it won't give us a mental picture of a house – unless of course we understand Japanese.

If we saw a picture of a house, however, surely there would be no confusion? Not necessarily. If you lived in a tree house in Papua New Guinea, you might fail to recognize a semi-detached house in suburban Britain – or a penthouse in Manhattan. Take the example of a teddy bear. To Western eyes a cuddly bear made out of fabric with buttons for eyes is a symbol of childhood and innocence. But this is not a universally understood interpretation. At the time of writing, the news is full of a distressing story about a British teacher who has been prosecuted in Sudan for allowing her class of six- to seven-year-olds to name a teddy bear Mohammed. She was charged with insulting the Prophet and sent to prison for 15 days.

Studying semiotics and the ways in which meaning is perceived and understood will help designers communicate with a semiotically literate audience.

Officials from the Sudanese Embassy in London pointed out that in Sudan bears are not viewed as cuddly bedtime companions for children and sentimental adults; they are seen as vicious and deadly predators. But to Brits, the teddy bear is an unequivocal piece of signage. If a British graphic designer used the image of one it would be seen as symbolizing innocence and intimacy.

This science of signs, and what they signify, is clearly of the utmost importance to graphic designers. A designer who failed to understand that graphic design is about signs and their meanings would be like an

Above
Project: *Decoding Advertisements. Ideology and Meaning in Advertising* by Judith Williamson, book cover.
Date: First published 1978
Cover Design: Eleanor Rise
Publisher: Marion Boyars Publishers
Writer and critic Judith Williamson's seminal work on signs, symbols and meaning in advertising. She writes in the foreword: 'As a teenager reading Karl Marx and *Honey* magazine, I couldn't reconcile what I knew with what I felt. This is the root of ideology, I believe. I knew I was being "exploited", but it was a fact that I was attracted. Feelings (ideology), lag behind knowledge (science). We move foreword as the revolutionary becomes the obvious.'

ornithologist who failed to grasp that birds had wings and could fly. Yet when I first encountered the subject of semiotics I felt it was stating the obvious – or, rather, that it was describing a way of viewing the world that is instinctive to designers and advertising people.

In her great book *Decoding Advertisements*, Judith Williamson makes an exhaustive study of modern advertising and its use of signs and meanings. She writes: 'A sign is quite simply a thing – whether object, word, or picture – which has a particular meaning to a person or group of people. It is neither the thing nor the meaning alone, but the two together. The sign consists of the Signifier, the material object, and the Signified, which is its meaning. These are only divided for analytical purposes: in practise a sign is always thing-plus-meaning.'

'Thing plus meaning' is a good description of visual communication. Designers create a thing (a poster, logo, etc.), which is invested with meaning. Their task is to ensure that the meaning is the correct meaning. As we've seen with the teddy bear, this is not as simple as it might appear. Meaning is always open to interpretation even in cultures that share a language and a common heritage. Even abstract decoration has a meaning. It might suggest decadence or luxury – but it is never free from meaning.

A designer who failed to understand that graphic design is about signs and their meanings would be like an ornithologist who failed to grasp that birds had wings and could fly.

If we were asked to design the packaging for a toilet-cleaning product, for example, we wouldn't show human excrement floating in a toilet bowl – we'd show sparkling whiteness and imply the squeak of clean porcelain.

Roland Barthes, the French philosopher and semiotician, and a follower of Saussure, noted that signs had two qualities: denotation and connotation. The denotative quality of a sign is the thing itself.[2] An image of a house is an image of a house. No argument. But the connotative quality is the type of house shown and the way it is depicted. For example, a picture of a very grand house – such as a palace – is radically different from a drawing of an igloo or a tree hut, yet they are all houses.

All graphic design is therefore about using the connotative value of signs. But to do this effectively and honestly requires mental sharpness and visual agility. What was a striking image a few years ago is laughable and nakedly hypocritical today. Just think of all those cigarette advertisements showing cool guys wearing golf sweaters, leaning against sports cars and being admired by glamorous women, or cowboys in Montana living a John Ford dream of rugged manliness.

Today, designers have to manage the signs and symbols of visual communication with much greater aplomb — and truthfulness. Studying semiotics and the ways in which meaning is perceived and understood will help them to communicate with a semiotically literate audience, and help to expose falsity and heavy-handed attempts at manipulation.

Further reading: Sean Hall, *This Means This, This Means That*. Laurence King Publishing, 2007.

1 www.britannica.com/EBchecked/topic/525575/
    Ferdinand-de-Saussure
2 www.ubu.com/sound/barthes.html

Studio management

Studio management rarely gets mentioned in books and articles about design. For some, the studio manager is the person responsible for keeping the colour printer stocked with ink and rounding-up the time sheets. For others, a studio manager is the difference between success and failure.

Once a studio reaches a certain size — say around 10 to 15 people — it becomes unmanageable without a dedicated studio manager. Studios can survive without managers but usually in a froth of chaos and wasted effort. Normally it's only the big design companies who can afford their services, yet all studios — even small ones — need to be managed. This means that most designers have to do their own management, just as they have to do their own bookkeeping, IT consultancy, print buying and light-bulb changing.[1] But by investing in a good studio manager, they can increase efficiency and make the working day more enjoyable, not to mention boosting profitability.

None of these tasks can be accomplished effectively without a cooperative and sympathetic attitude; good studio managers are team players, not moody loners.

The key to making the most out of studio management is not to think of it as a burdensome overhead. It is to think of it as a key factor in the way we look after our clients. Viewed like this, studio management (and its sibling, project management) becomes a way of looking after clients more efficiently and thus boosting income. So it pays to employ someone in this role, and it pays to employ someone good.

But what exactly is the role of the studio manager? Put simply, a studio manager deals with all non-design matters, leaving designers free to design. He or she might be required to empty the paper recycling bins and manage software upgrades all in the same day. Studio management used to be about keeping materials like pens and layout pads in stock, and managing printers and other suppliers, as well as dealing with technical questions from clients. Studio managers used to be bossy individuals who chivvied everyone into working harder.

Today, good studio managers require production and project management skills, sophisticated and sympathetic communication skills, and ruthless efficiency backed up by 360-degree vision. Their remit includes any or all of the following: work scheduling; budgeting; profitability reporting; invoicing; maintaining IT capabilities; booking freelancers; managing time sheets; and, most important of all, keeping accurate records (logging every call and email, noting every request). It might also include more practical tasks such as ensuring the colour printer doesn't run out of ink half an hour before a major presentation. But none of these tasks can be accomplished effectively without a cooperative and sympathetic attitude; good studio managers are team players, not moody loners.

No studio manager is worth employing if they can't combine an internal coordination role with an ability to deal with outsiders – clients, suppliers and freelancers all need to be treated with professionalism. In the ideal world, clients talk to designers about design, and to studio managers about non-design matters. But clients always talk to whoever gives them the information they want. So if a studio manager (or project manager) has poor communication skills, clients will avoid talking to them, thus reducing their value. The same applies to suppliers and freelancers. One of the many definitions of a good studio manager is someone who external contacts want to speak to.

Good studio managers require production and project management skills, sophisticated and sympathetic communication skills, and ruthless efficiency backed up by 360-degree vision.

The impression clients receive when they arrive at a studio, and the care and maintenance of a good working environment, are vitally important factors in running a design business. There is a widespread belief that design studios have to be sexy, high-design statements. Not so. Good clients are rarely impressed by showy offices; they have come to see the designers, not where they work. But they don't want to see chaos and scruffiness, and if reception areas are untidy, or if they aren't offered a decent cup of coffee in a clean mug, or if there are only three-day-old newspapers lying on the reception table a studio will struggle to attract good clients. So, we must give the responsibility for the look and upkeep of our studios to a studio manager, and turn our working environments into places people enjoy working in, and places clients enjoy visiting. Simple stuff – but easily neglected by deadline-junkie designers who are working day and night.

And yet, despite the impeccable logic of hiring a good studio manager designers are notoriously reluctant to employ non-designers. It took me a long time to get over my apprehension about employing one, but when I employed my first studio-cum-project manager the results were astonishing: we increased our income, our profitability, and the quality of our working environment, not to mention our work.

But how do we evaluate the success or failure of a studio manager? The person doing the job must be given enough time to introduce systems and procedures. But the first visible sign of success should be that designers are free to do what designers do best: design. Secondly, despite the increase in the salary bill, we should notice our profitability improving. If we don't (and we must allow enough time for this to show itself – say six months) we've got the wrong person, or we're not managing them properly. A good studio manager should pay for himself or herself many times over. And, instead of having to work all night, we might get to go home when other people go home. How bad is that?

I've always thought the secret of a successful studio was to make everyone client-facing. In other words, expose them to clients as often as possible. If studio personnel (designers and non-designers) know that everything they do has an impact on the studio's clients, they tend do their jobs better. This is especially relevant in the case of studio managers and production people, who are usually internal-looking. But the successful managers know that if they can combine good internal organizational skills with good client skills, they have a winning combination. To do this, they need to run studios for the benefit of clients as well as designers. Every decision must be assessed by two criteria: does it improve internal working, and does it also improve the way clients are serviced? If the answer to both parts of this question is 'Yes', it's the right move.

The secret of a successful studio is to make everyone client-facing. In other words, expose them to clients as often as possible. If studio personnel (designers and non-designers) know that everything they do has an impact on the studio's clients, they tend do their jobs better.

Further reading: Tony Brook and Adrian Shaughnessy, *Studio Culture: How to form, run and manage a graphic design studio.* **Unit Editions, 2009.**

1 Even when I employed over 20 people in my studio, I still changed the light bulbs. I was able to ask designers to perform heroics involving all-night working, but I never felt I could ask anyone else to change the light bulbs.

Swiss design

Switzerland is the spiritual home of graphic design. For many designers, the work that came out of this little central European country represents graphic design perfection. For others, Swiss design is a soulless conflation of graphic rigidity and arid expression. It can't be both, so which is it?

Above
Switzerland (Vista Books). An illustrated tourist guide to Switzerland published in 1961, containing images of typical Swiss mountain scenes and Swiss national life. Perhaps surprisingly, the book also contains examples of Swiss graphic design. The spread shown above features a poster for Basle Zoo (Ruodi Barth – 1947), and an advertisement for Schwitter AG (designer uncredited). The text notes: '… the modern poster has been brought, in Switzerland, to a point of perfection.' Hard to imagine any other country bothering to mention the national genius for graphic design in the context of a popular tourist guide.

In the movie *The Third Man*, the anti-hero played by Orson Welles says: 'In Italy, for 30 years under the Borgias, they had warfare, terror, murder, bloodshed – they produced Michelangelo, Leonardo da Vinci and the Renaissance. In Switzerland, they had brotherly love; they had 500 years of democracy and peace, and what did that produce? The cuckoo clock.' It's a much-quoted line (and usually accompanied by the observation that the cuckoo clock was a German invention anyway), yet the notion of Swiss orderliness persists. When we think of Switzerland we think of calmness and order; tranquillity and absence of ostentation. Which is also pretty much what we think of when we consider Swiss graphic design: calm, ordered, tranquil and absence of ostentation – with a bit of geometry thrown in to hold it all together,

Theo Ballmer's grids were often clearly visible in his design work; where subsequent generations sought to make the grid an invisible controlling presence, Ballmer and others let the viewer see how their pages were built.

But there's another word that comes to mind when we think of Switzerland: neutrality. As the only central European nation not to take sides during the Second World War, the suspicion that it is a country with an overdeveloped sense of self-interest, is widespread. This impression is not lessened by the infamous Swiss banking system, with its reputation as a safe repository for hot money, not to mention Nazi plunder from the Second World War.

For many graphic designers, Swiss graphic design is also tainted by the aroma of neutrality. Its traditional grid-based rigidity and mathematically derived sense of structure are seen as, well, too neutral. It's a view shared by most modern clients. With its limited number of fonts and point sizes, with its tightly controlled structure and its predilection for white space, design based on the Swiss model is often dismissed by clients as 'cold' and 'unwelcoming'.

Philip Meggs makes it sound much more appealing in his *History of Graphic Design*. In a chapter entitled 'The International Typographic Style', he describes the main characteristics of Swiss style as including a 'unity of design achieved by asymmetrical organisation of the design elements on a mathematically constructed grid; objective photography and copy that present visual and verbal information in a clear and factual manner, free from the exaggerated claims of propaganda and commercial advertising; and the use of Sans-Serif typography set in a flush-left and ragged-right margin configuration. The initiators of this movement believed Sans-Serif typography

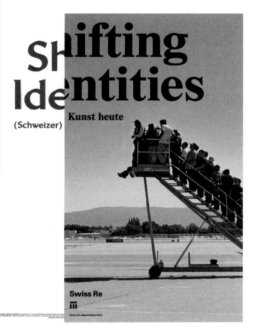

Above
Project: 'Shifting Identities'
Date: 2008
Client: Kunsthaus Zürich
Designers: Elektrosmog
Various communications elements for
Zürich exhibition, 'Shifting Identities'.
Elektrosmog are Valentin Hindermann and
Marco Walser. They exhibit many of the
stylistic and conceptual characteristics of
young Swiss designers. Walser has said: 'I'd
like to be more in the position of an editor
and a publisher in future projects. I just
realize that whenever we get involved in a
project at an early stage, we always deal
with all the tasks editors, publishers or
curators deal with.'

expresses the spirit of a more progressive age and that
mathematical grids are the most legible and harmonious
means for structuring information.'[1]

At the heart of all Swiss design is the grid. Theo
Ballmer was the first Swiss designer to make use of the
system. His grids were often clearly visible in his design
work; where subsequent generations sought to make the grid
an invisible controlling presence, Ballmer and others let
the viewer see how their pages were built.

Important early Swiss designers included Max Bill,
who introduced the concept of art concrete, which stated
that art could be made from mathematically constructed
elements, into Swiss design. Meggs quotes Bill as saying,
'It is possible to develop an art largely on the basis of
mathematical thinking.'

The German-born Anton Stankowski, who worked in
Zürich, pioneered the use of graphic design to express
abstract – or invisible – forces such as energy,
radiation, heat and the transmission of information,
all vital elements in a new technologically equipped
world. Stankowski's 1968 design programme for Berlin
was an early example of how major cities can develop
a coherent graphic identity.

Swiss design was to achieve lasting prominence
with the publication of the journal *Neue Grafik* (New
Graphic Design),[2] edited by Carlo L. Vivarelli, Richard
Paul Lohse, Josef Müller-Brockmann and Hans Neuburg.
The *Neue Grafik* philosophy found many adherents in the
United States, where it became the dominant style for
large companies, and also among the growing band of global
corporations, such as those that comprised the Swiss
pharmaceutical industry, where a genuinely international
style was required. The mathematically constructed clarity
of Swiss design was ideally suited for communications in
the new global village.

Müller-Brockmann emerged as the most influential of
the post-war Swiss designers. I knew countless designers
who had a copy of *Josef Müller-Brockmann: Pioneer of Swiss
Graphic Design*[3] permanently open on their desks, taking
inspiration off the page like sunbathers absorbing the
rays of the sun. Müller-Brockmann, who died in 1996 aged
eighty-two, remains a potent influence;[4] a reminder that
in the hands of a master (and a Swiss master at that)
graphic design can reach levels of poise and grace that
defy its status as merely one of the applied arts.

Among Swiss designers who succeeded the *Neue Grafik*
generation, the typographer and educator Wolfgang Weingart
has the strongest claim to be regarded as a major figure
in the Swiss canon. An influential teacher, Weingart
broke from the dogma of Swiss Modernism and began a
process of typographic experimentation that was to prove

Above
Project: Kunsthaus Glarus poster
Date: 2009
Client: Kunsthaus Glarus
Designers: Elektrosmog
Elektrosmog's work has been described by
Back Cover magazine as a 'smart and nice
synthesis between pop, vernacular culture
and Swiss modernism.' www.esmog.org

1 Philip Meggs, *History of Graphic Design*,
  4th edition. John Wiley & Sons, 2006.
2 Starting in 1965, a total of 18 issues were
  published by Verlag Otto Walter, Olten.
3 Lars Müller (ed.), *Josef Müller-Brockmann:
  Pioneer of Swiss Graphic Design*. Lars Müller
  Publishers, 2001.
4 The British designer Michael C. Place has two
  cats – they are called Müller and Brockmann.
5 Wolfgang Weingart, 'My Typography Instruction
  at the Basle School of Design/Switzerland
  1968 to 1985', originally published in *Design
  Quarterly*, 130, 1985.

revolutionary. Yet he never quite abandoned his roots in Swiss pragmatism. He has written: 'I try to teach students to view typography from all angles: type must not always be set flush left/ragged right, nor in only two type sizes, nor in necessarily right-angle arrangements, nor printed in either black or red. Typography must not be dry, tightly ordered or rigid. Type may be set centre axis, ragged left/ragged right, perhaps sometimes in chaos. But even then, typography should have a hidden structure and visual order.'[5]

Weingart taught the important American designers April Greiman and Dan Friedman, and left his imprint on the New Wave American typography of the 1980s. His influence on a generation of young British designers – most noticeably 8vo – was profound.

Switzerland remains a powerhouse of graphic invention. A new breed of Swiss designers has emerged, among them Cornel Windlin, Norm, Lehni-Trüb, Körner Union and Elektrosmog. Along with others, this group exhibits the intelligence and poise of their predecessors but injected with a new, more fluid sensibility; they have absorbed the messages of post-Modern international eclecticism, and while something of traditional Swiss restraint exists in their work they are far more expressive and undogmatic than their predecessors.

My own view is that Swiss design (which usually means Swiss and German design, since many of the greatest Swiss designers were educated, worked or taught in German design schools) of the 1960s and 1970s, set the standard by which all future graphic design has to be measured: it invariably delivered an unmistakable message, but it did so with style, poise and supreme graphic elegance. Surely there is no higher praise for graphic design?

When designers in my studio were struggling with delivering a message, I often sent them to look at the Swiss masters. It usually worked.

Further reading: Richard Hollis, *Swiss Graphic Design: The Origins and Growth of an International Style 1920– 1965.* Laurence King Publishing, 2006.

Swiss design (which usually means Swiss and German design, since many of the greatest Swiss designers were educated, worked or taught in German design schools) of the 1960s and 1970s, set the standard by which all future graphic design has to be measured: it invariably delivered an unmistakable message, but it did so with style, poise and supreme graphic elegance.

T

Theory

Few subjects cause more friction in graphic design than theory. To its detractors it is a worthless intellectual exercise that has nothing to do with what clients like to call the 'real world'. Yet to others it is a conduit for fresh thinking and a way of expanding the creative and social role of the designer.

We associate theory with the experimental end of graphic design. Yet paradoxically, the most dramatic and long-lasting theorizing of graphic design has not been done by intellectually inclined designers and educators, inflamed by the writings of French post-Modern philosophers. It has been done by the design-as-business-tool wing of graphic design. These 'theorists' saw design as the panacea for the corporate world, and produced a robust theoretical infrastructure for the craft that gave designers a body of arguments with which to promote design with evangelical zeal. It was a different sort of theory from the theoretical thinking and writing that radicalized design in the 1990s. It was business-school theory; it was marketplace theory; it was Thatcher and Reagan theory. But it was theory nonetheless.

The study of theory – asking designers to consider the intellectual ramifications of their craft, and to ponder its historical, social and cultural role in contemporary life – runs counter to the way most designers think.

The benefits to be derived from a business-orientated theory were easy for designers to grasp. It enabled most of them to advance their careers and earn a living in a way previously undreamt of. But this was not cultural theory. It was not theory that forced designers to question their role in the world or examine the ethical implications of what they did for a living. It was not theory that caused designers to interrogate the hidden meaning of the work they produced.

However, a new kind of theory emerged that did engender critical thinking and analysis. The philosophies of radical French thinkers such as Derrida and Barthes, and their theories of deconstruction and authorship, hit certain American universities with a resounding thump. As Ellen Lupton has written: 'Graphic designers in many U.S. art programs were exposed to critical theory through the fields of photography, performance and installation art during the early 1980s. The most widely publicized intersection of post-structuralism and graphic design occurred at the Cranbrook Academy of Art, under the leadership of co-chair Katherine McCoy. Designers at Cranbrook had first confronted literary criticism when they designed a special issue of *Visible Language* on contemporary French literary aesthetics, published in the summer of 1978. Daniel Libeskind, head of Cranbrook's architecture program, provided the graphic designers with a seminar in literary theory, which prepared them to develop their strategy: to systematically disintegrate the series of essays by expanding the spaces between lines and words and pushing the footnotes into the space normally reserved for the main text.'[1]

Theory's entry into the bloodstream of graphic design has meant that designers can no longer be neutral water-carriers. Even those who ignore questions such as ethics and responsibility (and many do) are nevertheless aware of the debate.

In her tightly argued and lucid essay, Lupton explains how Derrida's theories offered graphic designers a new way of viewing their practice. She writes: '"Deconstruction" became a banner for the advance guard in American literary studies in the 1970s and 80s, scandalizing departments of English, French, and comparative literature. Deconstruction rejected the project of modern criticism: to uncover the meaning of a literary work by studying the way its form and content communicate essential humanistic messages. Deconstruction, like critical strategies based on Marxism, feminism, semiotics, and anthropology, focuses not on the themes and imagery of its objects but rather on the linguistic and institutional systems that frame the production of texts.'

Such was the interest in theory that Pentagram designer Michael Bierut was able to say, in a 1998 interview with Steven Heller,[2] that there was an argument brewing between a 'theoretical approach to design versus – I don't want to say an anti-intellectual, more pragmatic approach – a less theoretical approach to graphic design. There's this new mania now for writing about design instead of doing it.'

But not everyone was in favour of this new-found interest in theory at the expense of action. Paul Rand described the 'obsession' with theory as 'instead of being fuel for action as it was at other times, during the

Renaissance, for example, (it) is merely the vehicle for fathomless language, variously described as "extravagantly obscure, modish, opaque verbal shenanigans – masters of impenetrability"'.[3]

He's got a point. A lot of theoretical writing is impenetrable and heavily codified, and this is at odds with the spirit of graphic design, which is about clarity and instant comprehension. The study of theory – asking designers to consider the intellectual ramifications of their craft, and to ponder its historical, social and cultural role in contemporary life – runs counter to the way designers think. The majority of designers function on an intuitive level: they use innate perception skills to grasp complex subjects; they are capable of sophisticated responses to complex briefs, but they do it with 'visual thinking' rather than by systematically intellectualizing the task.

The study of theory – asking designers to consider the intellectual ramifications of their craft, and to ponder its historical, social and cultural role in contemporary life – runs counter to the way most of them think.

And yet, the increasing interest in a theoretical approach to graphic design over the past two decades has caused designers (and perhaps more importantly, educators) to engage in a period of interrogation and scrutiny that has benefited the craft and altered it in untold ways. To see how graphic design has enriched itself by engagement with theory we need only turn to illustration, which in the same period has failed to look at itself through the lens of theory; as a consequence, a huge area of illustration has become a decorative craft reduced to filling gaps in editorial spreads (although the position is changing and illustration is entering a new period of self-scrutiny).

But what do we mean by theory? The word itself often acts as a barrier for designers, who are habitually concerned with doing and making, and the production of real world objects such as books, signage and websites. Louise Sandhaus, who teaches a theory course at CalArts, adopts a pragmatic approach to the definition: 'I think there may still be some traces of confusion over what theory is and means to graphic design specifically. The critical frameworks of gender, race, semiotics, etc., were a very important moment of maturity for the discipline as it began to point a finger at itself and probe its role and participation in the social and political landscape. There were varied outcomes for designers engaging in critical theory, probably emblematized by the influences of deconstructionist thought on the work produced at Cranbrook. To crudely paraphrase critical theorist, Jonathan Culler theory is the challenge that reorients thinking beyond the scope of design itself. This seems like just common sense for design given that it can't be discussed outside of a context since that's what gives the work meaning and relevance in the first place. It's like discussing dancer and dance – they inhabit one another. But my favorite definition of theory comes from a former student who described it as the inquiry that pushes the practice.'

Typography is one of the ways in which we convey added 'meaning' in the modern world. It's no longer enough for type to be type. It has to impart resonance and depth to the messages it is delivering.

In Sandhaus's view the study of theory has had far-reaching effects: 'It was thanks to this vital and imperative conversation,' she notes, 'that we began to see many types of graphic form, including vernacular practices, as part of graphic design. It brought the breakdown of the single, monolithic definition of graphic design.' But she is not starry-eyed about this theoretical on-rush. 'There's still a way to go as I watch the debates among colleagues and the profession still arguing as if there's a single set of values and only one correct understanding of the discipline. And giving nice pats on the head to people of color. Argh.'

But does overemphasis on theory mean that more and more designers will turn away from doing in favour of theorizing? 'I'm not sure that I'd agree with the way the question is put,' notes Sandhaus, 'it suggests that "doing" means doing commercial work. I'd rather the question was about whether smart designers will find great intellectual satisfaction in creating design theory rather than producing work. Otl Aicher in his essay *Design and Philosophy*, points out via Kant that philosophy's outcomes live in the head and on paper, while design's outcomes live in the world – manifesting ideas as lived, tangible things and experiences and at times having great effect and consequence. It's an argument that sees that making things (and I don't mean necessarily objects) is a form of thinking – a really important one since it becomes actual lived experience.'

The fruits of graphic design's encounter with theory can be seen in many places: the rise of serious content in the trade magazines (where once they merely gave editorial puffs to star designers, and indulged only in boosterism for the commercial value of design, they now regularly feature articles on ethical and social issues); the rise of a more effective and deep-running design education for students; and, most importantly, a gradual realization among professional designers that the work they do is not done in an airless vacuum – it has political and cultural repercussions.

Theory's entry into the bloodstream of graphic design has meant that designers can no longer be neutral water-carriers. Even those who ignore questions such as ethics and responsibility (and many do) are nevertheless aware of the debate. And for this we owe a debt to the pioneers of a theoretical discourse within design. As Louise Sandhaus notes: 'With two major new programs now in place – Alice Twemlow's Design Criticism Program at SVA and Teal Triggs's MA program in Design Writing Criticism at London College of Communication along with the PhD programs at NC State and elsewhere, we're finally witnessing a maturing of graphic design as a discipline and in part we can thank the theory revolution for that.'

Further reading: Victor Margolin, *Design Discourse: History, Theory, Criticism*. University of Chicago, 1989.

1 Ellen Lupton, 'Deconstruction and Graphic Design: History Meets Theory', first published in a special issue of *Visible Language* edited by Andrew Blauvelt, 1994. www.typotheque.com/site/article.php?id=99
2 Steven Heller, 'Michael Bierut on Design Criticism', interview with Michael Bierut, in Steven Heller and Elinor Pettit, *Design Dialogues*. Allworth Press, 1998.
3 Paul Rand, 'Confusion and Chaos: The Seduction of Contemporary Graphic Design'. www.paul-rand.com/thoughts_confusionChaos.shtml

Typography

At the heart of typography is a massive paradox: the hallmark of good typography is that it should go unnoticed, yet there has never been more demand for the sort of typography that grabs the reader's attention and excites the retina. Does this mean typography is the new illustration?

When I visit a new country, the first thing I usually notice is the typography on shopfronts, posters and road signs. If I was in the waste disposal business I might pay more attention to the design of rubbish bins and garbage trucks, but I'm a graphic designer so I notice typefaces. I've found that typography is a pretty reliable guide to a nation's character. Typography in Tokyo is feverish and urgent; typography in rural France is languid and traditional; Dutch typography is intellectual and restrained; typography in the United States is strident and omnipresent. Of course, in our globalized world big business (aided by us, the world's graphic designers) is doing its best to turn the planet into a homogenized shopping mall, where everything looks the same no matter whether it's in Tokyo, Moscow or Papua New Guinea.

But typography is stubborn. Like following the bloodline of a racehorse, we can trace the ancestry of type: Helvetica grew out of Akzidenz Grotesk, which grew out of Walbaum and Didot.[1] And despite the typographic law that states it's the message that matters not the messenger, typography is one of a dwindling list of ways in which national quirks and personal idiosyncrasies can be asserted. Its ability to flavour a message with cultural, tribal and national seasonings is, well … magical.

Nor is it only a sense of place and nationality that can be conveyed through typography. So recognizable is its footprint that entire eras can be defined in a few stray letterforms. All we need is a few characters of an Art Deco font and we are propelled back to the 1930s. A single

fact:

"Bobby Kennedy is the most vicious, evil _ _ _ _ _ in American politics today," says lawyer Melvin Belli.

fact: Paul Goodman says, "I don't give a rap who killed Jack Kennedy." Harry Golden:"Senator Kennedy told me, 'The family is satisfied there was this one fellow.' He couldn't even mention Oswald's name!" Dwight Macdonald: "If I had to say yes or no to Oswald's sole guilt, I'd still say yes." Melvin Belli:"The real villain in this piece is that latter-day King Farouk, J. Edgar Hoover." Mark Lane:"I myself don't see any evidence that President Johnson was the assassin." Other comments by Allen Ginsberg, Arthur Miller, Al Capp, Cleveland Amory, John Updike, Theodore Bikel, Marya Mannes, Gordon Allport, and many others.

fact:

Coca-Cola can cause tooth decay, headaches, acne, nephritis, nausea, delirium, heart disease, emotional disturbances, constipation, insomnia, indigestion, diarrhea and mutated offspring.

Above
Fact: magazine covers. The art director responsible for the striking typographic covers was Herb Lubalin (see Avant Garde typeface, page 26). The magazine's editor was Ralph Ginzberg. It describes itself as 'An antidote to the timidity and corruption of the American press.' Issues shown are from 1964 (top); 1966 (middle); 1964 (bottom).

Opposite
Project: poster to promote Kada typeface
Date: 2004
Designer: Joel Nordstrom, RGB6
Described as a 'photographical story and a comparative type specimen for Kada font.' Sold as two-sided poster at www.lineto.ch

scrap of psychedelic lettering can evoke the fervid 1960s. Neville Brody's Industria typeface is as emblematic of the 1980s as rolled-up sleeves on the mint-green linen jacket of a member of the Miami Vice squad. This works throughout history – even back to runes in prehistoric caves. Typography provides a compelling alternative guide to our past cultural life – we just need to know our typographic history and everything is revealed.

But what is typography? Can a hand-painted sign on a fruit stall in a street market be part of the same discipline that produced the pages of *Neue Grafik*? My dictionary defines it as: 'noun 1 the art or process of setting and arranging types and printing from them. 2 The style and appearance of printed matter.'[2] If we accept this definition, typography is typography whether it's found on a fruit stall in Mumbai or in a Swiss typographic journal from the 1960s.

But for me, there's an element missing from the above description: the personal. On the surface, typography appears to be a precise and detailed discipline, much like architecture and engineering. You learn the rules and then you apply them. What could be simpler? Except there's nothing simple about typography. To become an expert, you have to learn the rules, but you also have to, at all times, exercise aesthetic judgement.

Looked at from an historical perspective, today's typographers are doing what they've always done: they're changing and adapting to developments in technology, media and literacy.

The American typographer Beatrice Warde wrote a famous essay, 'The Crystal Goblet, or Printing Should Be Invisible',[3] in which she put forward the notion that typography was like a crystal wine glass – if you noticed the glass you wouldn't notice the perfection of the wine. She argued that if you noticed the typography you wouldn't get the message it was delivering. She memorably called those who deviated from this principle 'stunt typographer(s)'. Warde's view chimes in with that of the arch-traditionalist Oliver Simon[4] who in 1945 opened his *Introduction to Typography*[5] with this: 'The old artists of the classical school were never egotists. Egotism has been and remains responsible for many defects of modern typography.'[6]

Looked at from an historical perspective, today's typographers are doing what they've always done: they're changing and adapting to developments in technology, media and literacy. We have more typefaces and more methods of disseminating type than ever before. And, although Warde and Simon were writing before the rise of electronic media and the countless other contexts in which typography is

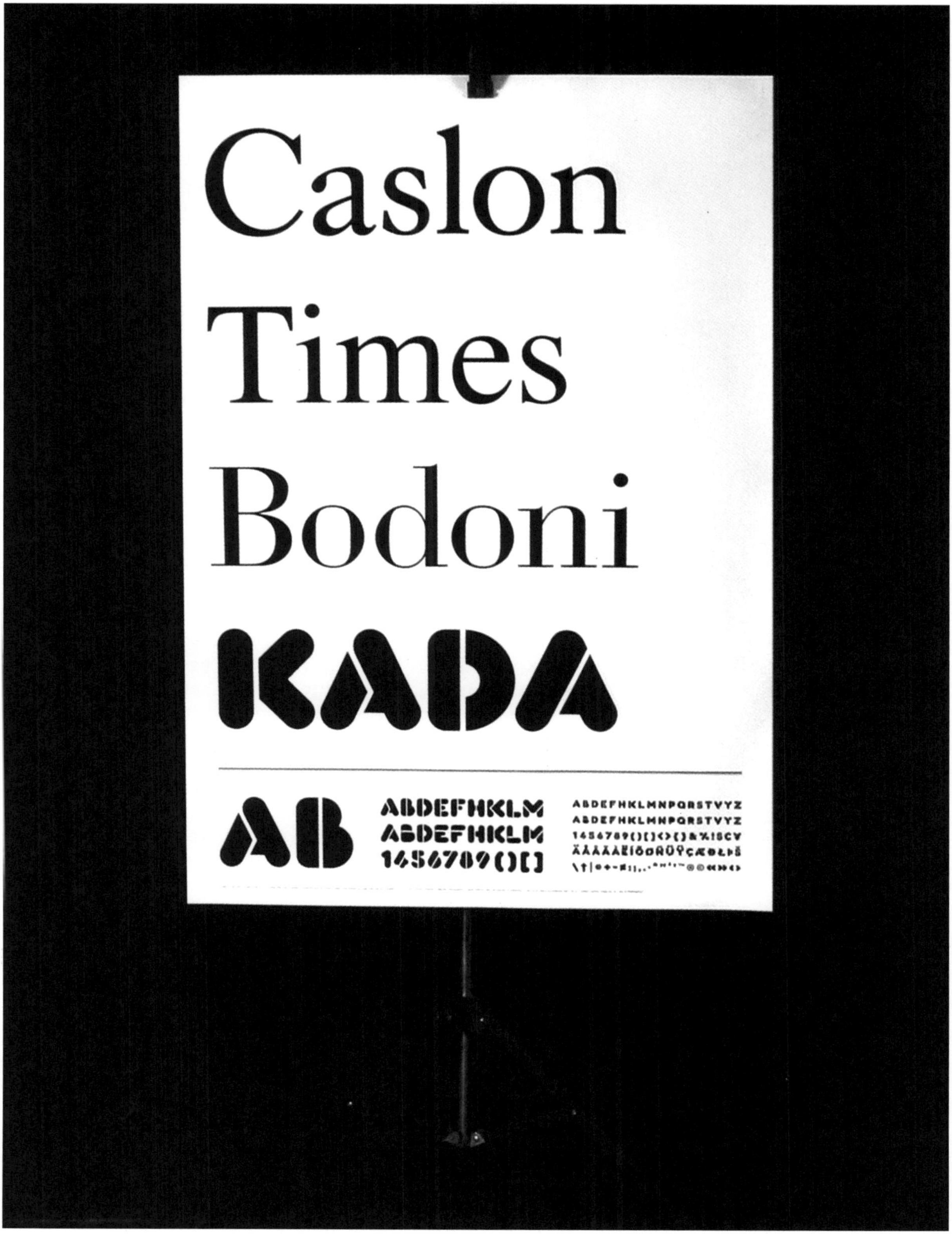
Caslon
Times
Bodoni
KADA
AB

required to function, their views are oddly prescient. In the new electronic domain, and in areas such as user-interface design and information graphics, stunts and egotism are unwelcome.

But we also live in a world where communication is conducted on many levels, and typography – its style, size and colour – is one of the ways in which we convey added 'meaning'. It's no longer enough for type to be type. It has to impart resonance and depth to the messages it is delivering. And it's this requirement that turns on its head the notion that type is an invisible crystal goblet: modern type is required to fulfil the role of both the wine and the goblet. In some cases, the glass is more important than the wine. We see this most clearly in brand names that have no obvious meaning. How we identify these 'brands' is through the typographic rendition of the name; change the type, and the brand 'value' evaporates. This makes type a powerful force in the modern brand economy. It also affords typographers and designers with plentiful opportunities for experimentation and expression.

Not only that, but animated type is now as common as static type. And when this is coupled with the ubiquity of graphics software and powerful blogging tools that allow anyone to make sophisticated type layouts, we see that typography has gone super nova; it is now as common as the spoken word.

Entire eras can be defined in a few stray letterforms. All we need is a few characters of an Art Deco font and we are propelled back to the 1930s.

Typography has come a long way since the discovery of movable type. Successive generations of typographers have learnt to jettison the tools, conventions and methodologies of their predecessors. When I became a designer, photomechanical typesetting freed designers from reliance on professional compositors, and allowed them to create typography that they themselves could place in mechanical artwork. This was liberating, but the arrival of the Apple Mac and Postscript fonts sent phototypesetting to the typo graveyard almost overnight, and turned the designer into a typesetter. Will there be another technological revolution that will render computer-generated type redundant? In a way, it has already happened: the Internet has a new technical and aesthetic typographic grammar that has had to be learnt. Type on the Internet is radically different from type on the printed page, and numberless designers, typographers and type designers are engaged in defining the new on-screen paradigms of online text.

Further reading: Erik Spiekermann and EM Ginger, *Stop Stealing Sheep & Find out how Type Works*. Adobe, 2003.

1 'Akzidenz Grotesk was probably cut by some experienced but anonymous Berthold punchcutters rather than designed by an individual type designer. This means the punchcutters had to have a general idea for the serifless forms, and they could probably only derive these ideas from the then popular classicistic typefaces such as Walbaum or Didot. This can be seen clearly upon superimposing Walbaum and Akzidenz Grotesk characters.' Martin Majoor, 'My Type Design Philosophy'. www.typotheque.com/articles/ my_type_design_philosophy.html
2 www.askoxford.com
3 Beatrice Warde, 'The Crystal Goblet, or Printing Should Be Invisible', 1955. http://gmunch.home.pipeline.com/typo-L/misc/ward.htm
4 Oliver Simon, English typographer (1895–1956).
5 Oliver Simon, *Introduction to Typography*. Faber, 1945.
6 Roger Fawcett-Tang (ed.), *New Typographic Design*, with an introduction and essays by David Jury. Laurence King Publishing, 2007.

U

Univers

Less fashionable than Helvetica, Univers is a near-perfect example of a modern, no-frills, sans-serif typeface. Yet it's a face that retains an aura of humanity and practicality that is missing in the more precise and machine-tooled perfection of its Swiss cousin, Helvetica. And there is no shortage of weights!

I once employed a designer – a very good one – who had a calm, systematic nature that made him perfect for the role of lead designer on large, long-running, highly detailed projects. But there was a problem; his typographic creed only allowed him to use a tiny number of typefaces, Univers being one of them. Occasionally this caused problems, and there were one or two instances when he had to be taken off projects because they required the use of a typeface he wouldn't – or couldn't – use. When we won the largest job we'd ever undertaken – a year-long graduate recruitment assignment for a large German firm – we got lucky. The company's house typeface was Univers.

Designed by the Swiss type-designer Adrian Frutiger, Univers appeared in 1957. Along with Helvetica, it shares a common ancestor in Akzidenz Grotesk. It has a somewhat smaller x-height than the former, and its subtle variation of stroke – clearly visible in the lower case 'm' and the upper case 'R' – make it a less mechanistic alternative to Helvetica. This hint of a calligraphic ancestry means that, unlike Helvetica, Univers can be successfully paired with certain serif typefaces such as the newer cuts of Baskerville. It is also notable for its numbering system and its vast range of weights. Another successful pairing is Frutiger, produced in 1975 and named after its designer, who in 1997 reworked and updated the entire Univers family for linotype. This new version consists of over 60 weights.

I can't pretend that Univers hasn't dated. Even in its most recent 1997 incarnation, it drags us back three or four decades.

Adrian Frutiger was born in 1928 in Switzerland. He began his working life at sixteen, as a printer's apprentice. After attending the Zurich School of Arts and

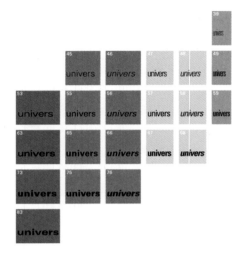

Above
Synoptic table showing the Univers family
of typefaces. Univers 55 sits centrally.
Condensed weights are on the left, expanded
on the right. Odd numbers show roman, even
ones italic.

1 Taken from a discussion between Adrian
Frutiger and Friedrich Friedl at the
presentation of the new Linotype Univers
in 1997 in Frankfurt am Main.

Crafts he moved to Paris and worked at the famous type foundry Deberny & Peignot, where he designed his first typefaces. He went on to produce many of the most enduring typefaces in the modern typographic canon. As well as Frutiger, these include: Méridien (1955); Serifa (1967); OCR-B (1968); Glypha (1979); and Avenir (1988), a geometric sans serif similar to Futura.

Frutiger has said: 'I believe that Univers – without exaggerating – is a classic typeface. But a classic typeface of the 1950s, as Futura is a classic typeface of the 1930s. There have always been classics that correspond to the spirit of the age. And therefore I stand completely behind Univers, but I also stand completely behind Helvetica. Univers was already a bit more nuanced, maybe a little closer to humanist typefaces, and naturally had the advantage that all of the heights were in agreement. But we have to be clear that every epoch creates its classics.'[1]

Despite my affection for Univers, I can't pretend it hasn't dated. Even in its most recent 1997 incarnation it drags us back three or four decades. But its wonderful sense of completeness and its vast range of weights mean it is still usable. Personally, I like the rather odd Linotype Univers Typewriter, a subfamily of fixed-width fonts. I considered using it as the typeface for this book, but it was supplanted at the last minute by the more up-to-date Fedra. But it's a smart typeface with a blunt, no-frills appearance. Just like its venerable parent.

Further reading: Neil Macmillan, *An A–Z of Type Designers*. Laurence King Publishing, 2006.

USA design

Much American graphic design works on the 'shock and awe' principle. It uses maximum firepower to sell the guilt-free joys of consumption. Yet the USA is also home to some of the most imaginative and intellectually rich graphic design the world has seen. How can both strands coexist?

Current graphic design in the United States reflects two distinct strands of American life. One strand represents the America former President George Bush famously appealed to after 9/11 when he said, 'Get shopping', and the other reflects a quieter America – the America of education, culture and sophisticated modernity – perhaps the America of Barack Obama.

Undoubtedly, the steroid-pumped graphic design used to promote second-hand automobiles and burger joints predominates. It can be seen everywhere; it assaults us from all angles. But there's another kind of design; it is the design that the designer, educator and blogger Jason Tselentis describes as 'a highbrow design culture … where up-and-comers worship studios like Pentagram, Cahan &

American commercial design has always had a buy-me-now directness that sets the gold standard for immediacy and lack of equivocation.

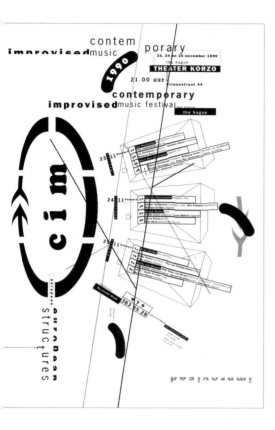

Above
Project: CIM poster
Date: 1990
Client: Ooyevaer Desk, Den Haag
Designer: Allen Hori, Studio Dumbar
Two-colour silk-screened poster utilizing
'improvisation' as both visual theme and
methodology.

Associates, and IDEO. And where the polarity between design and art continues to shrink: many artists are using design tools and aesthetics for gallery work; many designers strive to have gallery showings to escape the boardrooms and client revision requests.'

But to Europeans, American graphic design will always be characterized by an unmistakable mercantile swagger. Throughout the American Century,[1] graphic design has been a tireless foot soldier helping US businesses to sell their products and services. You only have to look at American restaurants and diners to see this at work. I'm always struck by the ostentatious and vigorous way that even small eating places utilize graphic design to ramp up the culinary delights on offer. In the United Kingdom, restaurants and cafés have tended to be discreet, almost apologetic in the way they announce themselves. Of course, this has changed in recent years (McDonald's came to Britain as long ago as 1974) and the country is now much more American in how it advertises the pleasures of eating out. But nothing compares to the way American designers use the full arsenal of graphic effects to promote the orgiastic joy of eating.[2]

Even if we go back to a time before W. A. Dwiggins (the man who in 1922 coined the phrase 'graphic design') we see that American commercial design has always had a buy-me-now directness that sets the gold standard for immediacy and lack of equivocation; it can make European design look undercooked and lacking the fizz of commercial intent.

Yet European and American design are deeply entwined. The story of American graphic design before the Second World War was written largely by Europeans; it was a time when the art director was king, and most of the great art directors were European-born. Mehemed Fehmy Agha and Alexey Brodovitch defined the modern role of the art director as a master manipulator of photography. Their work for leading magazines set in motion a trend that marked the decline of illustrators like Norman Rockwell whose *Saturday Evening Post* covers defined America. Sophisticated and systematic corporate graphics began as early as 1930 with the celebrated work commissioned by the Container Corporation of America (CCA). The company's owner, Walter Paepcke, aimed to give it 'a distinctive personality and identify it with the best in graphic arts'. But it was a generation of Europeans – among

Carson's work for Ray Gun – texts bleeding off the page and, famously, a whole article rendered in dingbats – catered for a new, young post-literate audience who craved the frenetic swagger of MTV and the buzz of the new always-on electronic media landscape.

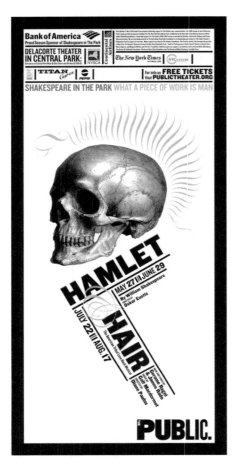

Above
Project: Shakespeare in the Park poster
Date: 2008
Client: The Public Theater
Designers: Paula Scher,
Lisa Kitschenberg/Pentagram
Campaign for the 2008 Shakespeare in the
Park productions of *Hamlet* and *Hair* that
also introduced a refreshed graphic identity
for The Public Theater as an institution.
The campaign appeared all over New York,
in subway and rail stations, on public
transportation and in print.

them, Herbert Matter, Will Burtin, Ladislav Sutnar, Herbert Bayer and Josef Albers – who were to pioneer a new intellectually and aesthetically sophisticated brand of graphic communication. This restrained European sensibility could also be seen in the New Advertising of the 1950s, which veered away from the traditional hard sell towards a more cultured and less frenetic stance (typified by the revolutionary advertisements for Volkswagen, designed by Helmut Krone in the 1960s).

But it wasn't all in the hands of European émigrés. Three American-born designers – Lester Beall, Alvin Lustig and, most celebrated of all, Paul Rand – emerged as Masters of the Graphic Universe. Rand was to become the most celebrated post-war American graphic designer; his work for IBM and Westinghouse in the 1950s and 1960s set a benchmark for designers around the world. A controversial figure, Rand combined elements from modern art with the clean contours of Modernist design. In later life he was to become a trenchant, sometimes reactionary commentator on the design scene.[3]

Accelerating technological change, and developments in mass media, allowed graphic design to proliferate beyond the printed page. Saul Bass moved between animation, print and film, and the typographer Herb Lubalin seized the opportunities provided by photo-mechanical and computerized typesetting to create a dynamic new typographic syntax.

The 1960s saw the rapid advancement of corporate design as practised by Raymond Loewy, Chermayeff & Geismar and Landor Associates. It was also a decade of cultural eruption: a new youth culture emerged, centred on oppositional politics, rock music and psychotropic drugs. San Francisco poster artists turned psychedelic art into an emblem of the age, and into one of the most distinctive and globally recognizable modes of graphic expression.

Few American designers have exerted the influence of PushPin Studios. It was formed in 1954 by Milton Glaser and Seymour Chwast, whose hybrid melding of psychedelicized Victoriana and a sort of funky Modernism turned them into the darlings of professional designers everywhere – especially in 1970s London. Glaser's 1973 book, *Milton Glaser Graphic Design*, was to prove stunningly influential among European graphic designers, this writer included.

Europe was to exert its influence on US graphic design again in the 1980s. Tibor Kalman, a Hungarian, produced work of sly intelligence. He was a vocal supporter of the vernacular (see Vernacular, page 296), and made frequent eloquent pleas for designers to question the nostrums that had grown up around the business of graphic design.

Above
Project: Shakespeare in the Park poster
Date: 2009
Client: The Public Theater
Designers: Paula Scher,
Lisa Kitschenberg/Pentagram
Campaign for the 2009 Shakespeare in the Park
productions of *The Bacchae* and *Twelfth Night*.
Both posters demonstrate Scher assured touch
when designing cultural posters. Note the
deft way the sponsors logos are handled in
both posters.

Equally influential were Dan Friedman and April Greiman. Both travelled to Switzerland to study with Wolfgang Weingart, and both returned to the United States and introduced a new post-Modern sensibility into its graphic thinking. Greiman in particular, with her early adoption of the Apple Mac, introduced a new complexity into the bloodstream of American graphic design. The Apple Mac created a new computer-flavoured graphic vernacular, and designers revelled in the potential to introduce layers of overlapping richness at the click of a mouse. Rudy VanderLans and Zuzana Licko at *Émigré* – the highly influential magazine and font house that they founded – were to prove lastingly influential.

In the 1990s US graphic design was dominated by the controversial figure of David Carson. Carson emerged as art director and designer of *Beach Culture*, a small magazine for surfers, but it was at the more ambitious *Ray Gun* that he was to forge his reputation and celebrity. His work for the magazine – texts bleeding off the page and, famously, a whole article rendered in dingbats – catered for a new, young post-literate audience who craved the frenetic swagger of MTV and the buzz of the new always-on electronic media landscape. This was a generation who skated on the surface glare of the information glut, absorbing only what was needed, rejecting what failed to engage them. Carson even had a brand name for his philosophy: he called it the End of Print. By reducing communication to a seductive graphic babble, Carson created a maverick persona for himself that appealed to a generation of designers who craved rebellion, yet who were locked tightly into the maw of brand culture: if you can't have real rebellion, let's have designer rebellion, they seemed to be saying. Carson was their messiah.

Today, if we were to ask young designers in Tokyo or Jakarta to name the leading American graphic designer most would name Stefan Sagmeister. The Austrian-born Sagmeister has a legitimate claim to be the most famous graphic designer alive today, and is undoubtedly brilliant and a visionary. His two monographs[4] are essential reading for designers of any age, particularly those who have become jaded; his enthusiasm and energy are contagious.

Yet, as with nearly all the eminent designers named above, Sagmeister can hardly be said to represent the

Few American designers have exerted the influence of PushPin Studios. It was formed in 1954 by Milton Glaser and Seymour Chwast, whose hybrid melding of psychedelicized Victoriana and a sort of funky Modernism turned them into the darlings of professional designers everywhere – especially in 1970s London.

great oceanic wave of American graphic design. He belongs to the highbrow tradition that Jason Tselentis alluded to earlier. But it's these 'highbrow' figures who are inspiring designers currently studying design in schools around the United States. Tselentis, who is a professor at Winthrop University in South Carolina, is optimistic about the future of American graphic design: 'Opportunistically, we seem poised for another industrial revolution,' he notes, 'centred on new or renewable energy, and this will present creatives with unique communication challenges ranging from brand development to identity design. And from a communication standpoint, the signals and noise that surround us will only get denser and denser as technology and its messages pervade our lives, so breaking through to audiences will require a very specialized approach that only designers can offer.'

If we were to ask young designers in Tokyo or Jakarta to name the leading American graphic designer most would name Stefan Sagmeister. The Austrian-born Sagmeister has a legitimate claim to be the most famous graphic designer alive today,

Tselentis sees an entrepreneurial spirit in the emerging generation: 'It's similar to the one that pervaded American design culture in the 1980s with type foundries like Émigré or the 8vo workshop, and then in the 1990s along the lines of fictional products like Shawn Wolfe's Removerinstaller & Beatkit or Shepard Fairy's OBEY Giant, and the subversive Adbusters. Even if designers of tomorrow start out with multiple side projects on top of their nine-to-five full-time work, it's through that after-hours experimentation, doodling, freelancing, or research that their questioning spirit challenges the day-to-day. It's also where some of the best work can happen, but it rarely gets seen because of limited budgets or poor publicity. In fact, failing to "get noticed" is a good thing, and a little humility could go a long way for the entire industry because getting attention isn't that important. Even though the fame game tempts designers with the lure of celebrity, they have to recognize that doing good work (or simply doing good) means more than getting noticed or becoming viral.'

Further reading: R. Roger Remington and Barbara J. Hodik, *Nine Pioneers in American Graphic Design*. MIT Press, 1989.

1 The term 'American Century' is attributed to Henry Luce, the publisher of *Time*. He used it to define the historical role of the USA during the twentieth century.
2 http://blog.pentagram.com/new-york/index.php?page=2
3 Paul Rand wrote: 'Most of this "new" style of design is confined to pro bono work, small boutiques, fledgling studios, trendy publishers, misguided educational institutions, anxious graphic arts associations, and a few innocent paper manufacturers, who produce beautiful papers, but then spoil them with "the latest" graphics, and who, undoubtedly, see themselves as the avant-garde — and are comforted by the illusion that this must be progress.' Paul Rand, *Design, Form, and Chaos*. Yale University Press, 1993.
4 Stefan Sagmeister, *Things I Have Learned in My Life So Far*. Harry N. Abrams, 2008. Peter Hall, *Sagmeister: Made You Look*. Booth-Clibborn, 2002.

V

Vector
illustrations
[p.295]

Vernacular
[p.296]

Vector illustrations

Like all new eye-catching graphic innovations, vectorized images were overused almost as soon they appeared. It's inherent in all seductive, easy-to-use, readily available technologies that they are adopted on such a scale, and with such rapidity, that they become suffocating in their ubiquity.

Vector files store information as mathematical formulae. Images, type and artwork can all be vectorized to make them scalable to any size: the quality of resolution is determined by the amount of data in the file.

Vector illustrations became ubiquitous in the late 1990s. Their ability to create an idealized, posey elegance suited the mood of luxury and designer fetishism that was sweeping through the Western world at the time. It was no accident that one of the pioneers of the vectorized image was *Wallpaper* magazine, the style bible for a generation of designers and fashion mavens. Vectorized images that seek to replicate the effect of drawing are highly distinctive, and are commonly made from scanned-in photographs using the trace tool (rather than being drawn with a tablet and pen). Adobe Illustrator is the program most often used to create them.

When done skilfully, the quality of line and purity of colour can make for seductive images that retain their vividness in both print and on-screen usage. One of the early pioneers of vectorized image-making was Fred Deakin of the London design group Airside. Deakin is also a member of the band Lemon Jelly, and together with Airside colleagues he produced a body of work for his band that gave it an unmistakable twenty-first-century high-tech sheen, mixed with a whimsical playfulness. It was the perfect visual accompaniment to the band's music – itself a technologically enabled mix of old and new.

It's hardly surprising that Deakin's inspiration came from British Transport posters from the 1930s, by artist such as Tom Purvis and Frank Newbould – both artists used screen-printing to create areas of rich flat colours, often involving up to ten different hues and strangely similar to modern computer-made vectorized images. 'My early vector designs were specifically produced to be screen-printed,' notes Deakin. 'I outputted each spot colour as a single black area to be exposed on to a screen for printing so I got very close to my vectors. I think I got to 12 individual colour passes on a single A1 poster before I switched to CMYK.'

Using Flash animation, Deakin discovered that online design also thrives on flat, vectorized, spot-colour designs as it kept data size to a minimum. As he notes, 'Embracing the vector turned out to be futuristic as well as backward looking.' But as Deakin was quick to spot, vectorized images became overused when they were widely adopted by designers and illustrators keen to utilize the fashionable seductive technique.

Can vectorized illustration be used convincingly today? In Deakin's opinion, anyone using it has to 'push things forward. There's no doubt that the market has been flooded. But the humble vector isn't the criminal here; it's still a great tool, just like the more traditional pen or pencil. I see new forms emerging every day. My thing at the moment is geometric patterns, and vectors are the perfect way to create them given that they are intrinsically nothing more than mathematical formulae made visual. The geek in me really likes bezier curves!'

Further reading: _Airside by Airside_. DGV, 2009.

Vernacular

As graphic design becomes slicker and ever more calculating in its effect, there is a growing interest in vernacular design – the stuff that hasn't been designed and commissioned by sophisticated designers and their clients. The stuff we take for granted and barely notice. The undesigned.

When, in the late 1990s, Tibor Kalman commissioned a portrait of himself by Mumbai-based Vanguard Studios for the cover of his monograph, _Perverse Optimist_,[1] the portrait was raw and didn't seek to aesthetisize its subject. Kalman was an evangelist for the undersigned, and by commissioning a Mumbai artist rather than a Manhattan one, he was taking a stand against slick anodyne graphic design and illustration that served no purpose beyond commercial messaging.

This was against the grain of the conventional graphic design orthodoxy of the time – and of today. Over the past four or five decades, graphic designers have worked hard to convince the business world – and anyone else who'll listen – of the benefits of design. It's been a long hard slog – a crusade, even. If we went back 50 years we'd find that only a few enlightened corporations had signed up to the cause (IBM under the spell of Paul Rand, for example), but the great mass of companies and institutions were deaf to the argument that good design was good for business.

This just made designers more determined. They could see that design was the magic ingredient – the wonder drug – that would give modern businesses the edge they craved.

Above
Photographs from the book *Chicken: Low Art, High Calorie* by graphic designer Siaron Hughes. Her book celebrates the visual qualities of fast food signage, and the people who create the visuals. As she notes: 'On the surface it may all look the same, but the differences reflect a ubiquitous and humorous vernacular design. It will make you laugh, ponder and hungry for chicken!'

Designers looked at every aspect of modern life – from shop windows to business cards; from pet-food packaging to television idents – and said, 'We can make these things so much better'.

A designer from the 1950s or 1960s would be astonished to see how successful this design crusade has been. Everyone gets the design argument now: politicos get it; charities get it; even cities get it. You can't do anything today without the sheen and lustre of good graphic design.

But there's a price to be paid for this victory. Today, the beautiful machine-tooled, high-sheen graphics that we see everywhere have been so successful that they are creating their own redundancy. Here's an example of what I mean. I was talking to someone who works as a senior designer for a major mobile phone company. He told me that the market for mobile phones has reached saturation point, and now that everyone has one his job is to come up with initiatives that encourage people to use their phones more. In other words, commercial design has been so successful it has created its own superfluousness.

In the world of super-modernity, a bus ticket can't be just a bus ticket. It has to exhibit the branding of the bus company; it might carry an advertisement; and it will use sophisticated computerized typography. It's only a bus ticket, yet we've turned it into a scrap of commercial graphic theatre that utilizes the brainpower of designers, marketing people and IT people. My point is that commercial graphic design has become over-purposed. When a bus ticket can no longer be simply a bus ticket we know the inmates are running the prison.

A consequence of this superfluity is the rise of an alternative graphic design: a design of rebelliousness and a return to style for style's sake. This in turn has led to a new recognition of the power and value of vernacular design – a re-evaluation of the undesigned.

At the time of writing, Wikipedia has an entry on Vernacular Photography, but not on Vernacular Graphic Design. Thanks to the intellectualization of photography, its vernacular aspect has been extensively discussed and theorized. According to Wikipedia, vernacular photography is made by 'amateur or unknown photographers who take everyday life and common things as subjects'. This definition would hold for vernacular graphic design, too. It is design by amateurs and the unknown.

When graphic designers talk about vernacular design they are talking about design that lacks the over-purposed self-consciousness of the great suffocating mass of graphic material we see around us.

So what are we talking about here? Design without designers? Possibly. There is already a boom in online self-publishing that was undreamt of ten years ago; sophisticated blogging tools enable untrained people to make and publish sophisticated multimedia. Domestic PC software allows anyone to produce material that would once have needed a skilled graphic designer. There are numerous books on do-it-yourself design.[2]

This explosion of work by 'amateur or unknown' designers neatly fits the definition given above. But what is produced is far too sophisticated and purposed to be a truly vernacular statement. When graphic designers talk about vernacular design they are talking about design that lacks the over-purposed self-consciousness of the great suffocating mass of graphic material we see around us. It is design, in other words, that is unselfconscious and lacking any sense of ambition or intent beyond its functionality. Or to put it another way – it's authentic. When we stick a bus ticket from an underdeveloped part of the world in our scrapbook, we are doing so because it screams simplicity and purity.

When we stick a bus ticket from an underdeveloped part of the world in our scrapbook, we are doing so because it screams simplicity and purity.

When Steven Heller asked Tibor Kalman how he differentiated between 'garbage' and the vernacular, Kalman replied: 'Vernacular is the result of a lot of time, very bad tools, and no money. In New York it might be a bodega sign in Spanish Harlem or the graphics on the side of an ice delivery truck. A tremendous amount of care is taken with the work, and there's no real concern about beauty and stuff like that. However, because there is no skill, it comes out kind of clunky – but beautiful, in my opinion. Garbage is bad, stupid, but professional graphics: junk mail, the Korvette's signs and Citibank brochures we designed.'[3]

Further reading: Jessica Helfand, *Scrapbooks: An American History*. Yale University Press, 2008.

1 Tibor Kalman, *Tibor Kalman: Perverse Optimist*. Princeton Architectural Press, 1998.
2 Ellen Lupton, *DIY: Design It Yourself* (Design Handbooks). Princeton Architectural Press, 2005.
3 'Tibor Kalman on Social Responsibility', interview in Steven Heller and Elinor Pettit, *Design Dialogues*. Allworth Press, 1998.

W

Wayfinding

For designers who crave a socially useful role, designing effective wayfinding systems that enable others to find their way around a given environment is one of the best uses to which their skills can be applied. But we need more than graphic design skills to make effective wayfinding systems.

The term 'wayfinding' was first used by the urban planner Kevin A. Lynch in *The Image of the City*,[1] published in 1960. He defined wayfinding as 'a consistent use and organization of definite sensory cues from the external environment'. Note that he doesn't use the word 'signs'. Directional signs are part of wayfinding, but to provide a total system of orientation many other elements are needed. These include maps, the extensive deployment of language (often multiple languages), the coordination of architectural elements (street names and numbers), colour coding, pictograms and, increasingly, the use of electronic aids such as audio and interactive elements.

Wayfinding systems are essential in countless situations. Navigating through hospitals, large buildings and complex urban environments without help is unthinkable. Imagine the London underground, the Paris metro or the New York subway without maps and signs. No one could use them.

When we are using an underground railway (where our field of vision is usually limited) we rely on numerous aids to help locate our positions and our destinations: we listen for the roar of trains; we feel the onrush of air telling us one is imminent; we might even find that our sense of smell tells us when we are near an exit; we follow other people who seem to know where they are going.

You'd have thought that devising wayfinding systems for above ground would be far easier. But most great

Satellite navigations systems in cars have transformed the way drivers locate destinations; is it science fiction to imagine that all wayfinding will be done by personal GPS systems – perhaps implanted in our bodies?

cities have been in existence for centuries and have developed haphazardly. Take London with its almost incomprehensible structure – how would you set about creating a system for this urban tangle?

In a sense, all graphic design is wayfinding. But there's something about helping people to move their bodies, that requires knowledge of the way they think.

The London-based design consultancy Applied Information Group (AIG)[2] is doing exactly that. Headed by graphic designer Tim Fendley, it has been charged with creating the graphic infrastructure for a publicly funded initiative called Legible London – 'a new pedestrian wayfinding system to help people travel around the capital'.[3] In an essay, the design writer Jim Davies notes: 'Over 200 million people visit the West End [of London] each year, spending over £4.7 billion. Some 87 per cent of them choose to move around on foot. Towards Christmas, these figures bulge significantly.'[4] That's a lot of people, and any wayfinding system that is going to help them to make sense of London will have to offer more than a few signs and directional arrows.

Tim Fendley defines wayfinding as 'the method we use to understand, navigate and recall the relationship between spaces and how we navigate them. In terms of a profession it is the architects, interior designers, urban designers, graphic designers and, increasingly, information designers, who tackle the problem of guiding people within places. It starts with thinking about how people understand places, leading to the creation of a mix of tools that can provide knowledge and offer help. Signage is just one of these tools, wayfinding is the whole set, a legible programme is the complete package.'

Fendley's interest in wayfinding started with orienteering and mountain hiking as a teenager: 'Also an early career in typography taught me humanist design and to see the spaces between things. Then working as a designer of graphic systems for magazines and corporate identities, which taught me how to tackle complexity and coherence at the same time, and which led to designing animations, videos and interactive environments and thinking of them as physical spaces and stories. This led me to usability design, and designing by watching people use things. I'd also say I was helped by working with product designers who have an excellent developmental approach – they prototype! Finally, I'd add a desire to think beyond the bounds of the brief, because that's what people do when they try to find somewhere.'

In a sense, all graphic design is wayfinding. But there's something about helping people to move their

Opposite and overleaf
Project: Legible London
Date: 2007
Client: Transport for London, Westminster City Council, New West End Company
Photography: Philip Vile
Creative Director: Tim Fendley
Designers: AIG: Applied information Group
Clear and precise directional signs offering a guide to the labyrinthine London streets. The 'heads up' maps provide a simple way of marrying the view ahead with cartographic representation.

bodies (rather than, as is the case with a magazine or a website, just their eyes and minds), that requires knowledge of the way they think. Jim Davies notes: 'Cognitive science and research work in other related areas has shown we develop "place cells" in the brain corresponding to points in the physical environment and gradually build them up into a mental map of places, routes and, eventually, areas. The mental map we build is not strictly geographic, but revolves around the relationships between memorable locations and routes insofar as they are relevant to our needs. This is a function of the hippocampus area of the brain which, it is said, is enlarged in London's black-cab drivers.'

Part of the creation and implementation of any wayfinding system involves real-world testing. As part of their Legible London programme AIG placed a prototype sign with its rich mix of information near their London office, and within a short time it had attracted unprompted interest from people keen to use it and comment on its efficacy. The signs are sophisticated assemblages that require the skills of a wide variety of disciplines. 'We strive to have an environment where knowledge from many sources can be pulled together,' notes Fendley. 'Our people are urban and transport planners, researchers, information designers, graphic designers, digital developers and GUI experts.'

But the elegant Legible London signs may already be redundant. Some mobile phones come fitted with GPS navigation systems, and in the future we may not need anything other than road names and building numbers. Satellite navigation systems in cars have transformed the way drivers locate destinations; is it science fiction to imagine that all wayfinding will be done by personal GPS systems – perhaps implanted in our bodies?

Most great cities have been in existence for centuries and have developed haphazardly. Take London with its almost incomprehensible structure – how would you set about creating a system for this urban tangle?

Further reading: Edo Smitshuijzen, *Signage Design Manual*. Lars Müller Publishers, 2007.

1 Kevin Lynch, *The Image of the City*. The MIT Press, 1960.
2 www.aiglondon.com
3 www.legiblelondon.info
4 Jim Davies, 'Which Way Christmas', introduction to 'Legible London – Yellow Book', produced and published for Transport for London by Applied Information Group, 2007.

Web design

The future of graphic design is in the hands of web designers. Print design has an unmistakable whiff of formaldehyde about it. But if web design is to rival print design's glorious heritage, it has to do it at a time when web design is increasingly falling under the control of non-designers.

With the arrival of the Internet, graphic design has met its greatest challenge since its establishment as a recognized craft in the early part of the twentieth century. At first glance, designing for the World Wide Web appears to have changed the nature of design itself. But has it? Perhaps it has done the opposite. Perhaps it has caused graphic design to revert to its original values. For the traditional graphic designer with a classical view of the craft as a neutral delivery system at the service of content (with the designer as an egoless conveyor of someone else's message), web design represents a return to fundamentals. In web design, fundamentalism is everything: the overriding consideration is the information and how it is accessed. If that means every typographic convention and every graphic design nostrum is chucked out the window – so be it.

For many designers, usability experts assist greatly in the designing of functionality – for others they impede progress and lag behind the web zeitgeist.

Effective web design also means that the designer recognizes that users decide how websites are used, not designers. But hang on! Graphic designers are control freaks. Anyone who wants to poke fun at them need only point to a collective obsession with the sort of graphic detail that is visible only to other graphic designers. The Internet offers a sharp challenge to a designer's control freakery. With the arrival of web pages that can be put together by pretty much anyone and then delivered via the Internet to a global audience, designers have begun to lose the ability to control graphic communication. This control has been further decreased by the fact that most web pages can be altered by the user; that different browsers alter the appearance of web graphics and that variations in monitor quality mean that there is no such thing as a definitive version of a website – even the sizes of fonts can be altered to suit the viewer.

The Internet also offers a facility to clients that was not available to them in traditional media, namely the ability to test the functionality of sites – and if they don't measure up, the ability to change them. In other words, websites are never finished; they are always a work in progress, and this fact alone adds a level of complexity to web design that designers have rarely had to contend with in the past. On a purely practical note, for example, it makes billing for web work difficult since clients never seem to agree when a site is finished. Andy Cameron was a member of the pioneering interactive design collective Antirom.[1] Today he is Creative Director of Interactive Fabrica and Benetton Online.[2] Cameron

neatly expresses the conundrum at the heart of web design: 'The best web design is minimal, preferably invisible. Content is what matters, and web design's only function is to give the visitor access to as much information as possible in the fastest, cleanest way. A rule of thumb is the uglier it looks the better the design – think YouTube and Amazon. When you have a graphically beautiful page, the design is probably rubbish.'

Web design, with its overarching emphasis on functionality is forcing designers to return to the fundamentals of design: the web designer is not concerned with creating passive one-way-only communication; he or she is designing user experiences. This is causing designers to expand their horizons and find new ways of thinking and new skills (the most important of which is coding).

Professor Gerry Derksen is Associate Professor in the Visual Communication Design and Digital Information Design programmes[3] at Winthrop University in South Carolina. For him, web designers must have knowledge of coding: 'I am an advocate for designers who learn how to code websites themselves, but I also know when you need to call in an expert. Understanding, at least in theory, what is technologically possible is necessary because web designers work in a fixed context of the computer and network constraints.'

He also urges designers to keep up to date with technological developments: 'New languages, web standards, browser functionality become more complex as they allow greater interaction and should be on a designer's mind. Understanding that web technology is mainly about efficiency and scale economy should drive a designer to keep up with technology to ensure the best experience a user can have with the information they are communicating.'

For Andy Cameron, knowledge of coding is equally important: 'It's about having a basic experience of, and basic respect for a medium as part of the design process. It's about the direct, visceral relationship between thinking and doing. There have been many creative projects which attempt to put together artists and programmers and they usually fail. Why? Because the artist doesn't get it, the artist doesn't feel the medium. The artist has no way to play with code, to sketch with interactivity, to feel their way into the medium and test its limitations and possibilities. And it's hard to make

In web design, fundamentalism is everything: the overriding consideration is the information and how it is accessed. If that means every typographic convention and every graphic design nostrum is chucked out the window – so be it.

Opposite
Project: Vitsœ website
Date: 2009
Client: Vitsœ
Designer: Airside
Content management system built by
With Associates.
For 50 years Vitsœ has created and evolved
furniture that allows its customers to live
intelligently and responsibly by buying
less, but of better quality. The website
neatly conveys the style and practicality
of Vitsœ products in a disciplined and
entertaining way. www.vitsoe.com

Above
Project: Monocle website
Date: 2009
Client: Monocle
Designer: Richard Spencer Powell
Creative Director: Ken Leung
Art Director: Dan Hill.
Too many magazine websites are pallid
offspring of the printed parent. The
Monocle website is different. It is full
of multimedia content, and offers a rich
mix of features that enhance the printed
publication. www.monocle.com

an intervention within a medium without being able to play with it. It seems strange to talk about interactive art or design as if it's a plastic medium like sculpture or painting, but in a way it is – it's handcrafted. If you do have to hire a coding expert, best thing to do is to consider him/her as creative lead and take his/her ideas, tastes and opinions seriously. Chances are they understand interaction design better than you do.'

Yet even when the designer has mastered coding technique and theory, there is still the thorny problem of usability. Usability experts have invaded the Internet. Their views carry weight and some – like Jakob Nielsen[4] – have acquired considerable influence. For many designers, usability experts assist greatly in the designing of functionality – for others they impede progress and lag behind the web zeitgeist.

Usability theory is employed in the construction and management of many websites. Yet for many web designers, usability thinking is not part of their everyday practice. 'This is due, in part,' according to Gerry Derksen, 'to the fact that designers are using prepackaged tools, ecommerce, blogs, wikis, etc., and they assume the tools have been tested or one tool functions the same as the next. Adding custom features or designs that "skin" these tools can affect the usability. What may have worked before no longer possesses the same design considerations when it was first implemented. As new tools are developed or as tools become easier to customize, designers are well positioned to take on the responsibility for implementing usability theory. Traditional "user centred" approaches make designers naturally suited for working with end users. In addition usability encourages an iterative process that improves designs, correcting assumptions we make about the user, adding to the skill set of the designer.'

Andy Cameron adopts a more skeptical approach to usability theory. In his view, usability thinking often fails to keep up with changes in technology and user expectations: 'What's interesting about people like Nielsen is how puritanical they seem – how religious the whole tone of the discussion can get. Nielsen is famously against pictures on the Internet. Now, this might have made sense in 1995 when the best connection you could get was a modem. But it doesn't really make sense now. YouTube has 100 million download/views per day and we are still

Anyone who has lived through the past two decades, will have seen technological change on a scale never before witnessed by the human race. No one feels the hot backdraught of this more keenly than the web designer.

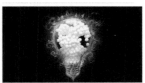

being told that graphics are bad for the web! My eleven-year old kid thinks the Internet is a kind of TV – a video delivery mechanism. So much for usability. It's a funny kind of theory that doesn't take changing circumstances – bandwidth, graphic power, cultural development, etc – into account and treats usability as if it is something eternal, something fixed outside of history. Just like a religious belief.'

What is the ideal mental make-up for the web designer? For Andy Cameron its blindingly obvious: the web designer is someone who 'doesn't think the web is made up of pages. Someone who doesn't wish they were really doing a book or a magazine. I know there are designers who miss the choices they can make with typefaces in print, who resent that the web offers much fewer choices. I never felt the lack of 5,000 typefaces myself. Does the world really need more than 15 to 20 typefaces?'

In Cameron's view, the web designer is inhabiting a new terrain. But he still envisages a role for traditional graphic skills. 'Principles of information design, typography, legibility etc., still apply,' he notes. 'But they apply in different ways within different contexts. I think graphic designers have a great deal to offer in web design, as long as they adapt to the limitations and opportunities in what is a new medium.'

Gerry Derksen also sees a role for traditional design and typographic skills: 'In the broadest sense web designers still control readability, legibility, and other functions of typography. Because there are constraints in the number of standard fonts that are available on both Mac and PC machines, designers are limited to styles for longer portions of texts. Since the advent of Cascading Style Sheets (CSS code) we have had more control over the spacing and styling of type, but this and other design concerns should be seen as fluid. The user can still change the size of font in the browser, for example, if they are visually impaired. This will change the layout of the page but makes it accessible to a larger audience. Text that is displayed within images or video, for example, is free to be anything imaginable and reflect more of the typical typographic concerns. A larger issue for the web designer is how people read text off a computer screen (the physical) and how they put information together from a non-linear source (the intellectual). I guess it is an expansion of type skills and at the same time giving up some of the control.'

Despite envisaging a role for traditional graphic design skills within web design, Derksen also sees a need for a wider palette of skills: 'Web designers need to be visual thinkers in the third and fourth dimensions. Web designers also need to be planners/organizers of information represented visually — of what is now "information design". If designers assume these areas of expertise we will elevate the web to new experiences and to a variety of platforms.'

That innocuous sounding phrase 'variety of platforms' seems to haunt current web design practice. Even when the web designer becomes a skilled thinker in multi-dimensional space, perhaps the biggest issue to be faced is the accelerating pace of technological change. Anyone who has lived through the past two decades, will have seen technological change on a scale never before witnessed by the human race. No one feels the hot backdraught of this more keenly than the web designer. Mastery of web-page design is only the beginning. As Gerry Derksen points out: 'We already see web information being displayed on a variety of formats such as phones, PDA's, and in cars. I suspect more varieties of devices are coming, but will be specific to a task or context in which they are used. Information delivered over the web may look more like what we have seen at kiosks or ATM machines, but portable. More importantly it will be the visual representation and manipulation of data seen on these devices that will define designers of digital media. Our programme at

> **Web design is not only the future of graphic design, it is the reality of graphic design.**

Winthrop is called "Interactive Media Design" for this very reason. I am sure other human electronic interaction devices will be added to our culture that need new designs for interactivity and content.'

In 2008, I acted as host for a day-long event investigating interactivity. The event was organized by my friend Malcolm Garrett[5] and featured a variety of experts in interactivity (including Andy Cameron) giving short presentations of their work. What struck me was the degree of intellectual vigour on show. There was a palpable sense of barriers being jumped and new landscapes being colonized; a sense of a new, more expansive definition for the role of the designer. It would be hard to match this display of mental fireworks in the traditional graphic design world. And it's this sense of redefining the parameters of design that gives me optimism about the notion that I began this entry with — namely that web design is not only the future of graphic design, it is the reality of graphic design.

Further reading: www.fivesimplesteps.co.uk

Opposite
Project: Maxim Zhestkov website
Date: 2009
Designer: Maxim Zhestkov
Spartan website of motion designer Maxim Zhestkov. Based in Ulyanovsk, Russia, Zhestkov claims to be obsessed with 'contemporary art, illustration, design, sculptures and cg graphics'.
www.zhestkov.com

1 The Antirom collective was formed in London in 1994 as a protest against 'ill-conceived point-and-click 3D interfaces' grafted on to re-purposed old content — video, text, images, audio — and repackaged as multimedia. www.antirom.com
2 www.fabrica.it and www.benetton.com
3 www.winthrop.edu/informationdesign/infd.pdf
4 www.useit.com
5 www.dynamolondon.org

Writing about design

Graphic designers are supposed to deal in imagery. Yet today, fuelled by the rise in the number of high-quality design books, better writing in the magazines, and the blogging revolution, there is a widespread interest in design writing and critical thinking. But will this result in us becoming better designers?

Designers often say they can't write. Yet many use language with skill and style, both in their work and in their everyday speech. Many designers have a ready facility for sharp phrases and economical expression, and most are better with words than they realize. So where has this slander that designers can't write come from? Like the old adage that designers don't read, it sounds plain wrong.

Unfortunately, the assertion that designers and the written word don't mix comes mainly from designers. They believe that they need to do everything visually, and there's a fear that they are betraying their design skills if they exhibit language skills. Yet look at all the smart designers who have clout and status. What distinguishes them? They all have language skills and aren't afraid to show them.

It's not as if designers don't have plenty of contact with language. Most of them 'handle' language daily as the raw material of their design work. All design students have to write a dissertation as part of their degree course. And there is a long tradition of designers writing about design with clarity and the vivid insight that comes from being a thinking practitioner: William Morris, Paul Rand, Milton Glaser, Ken Garland, Jessica Helfand and Michael Bierut are all examples from this small but influential group.

Yet something is stirring in the undergrowth: designers writing about design and designers reading about design is now normal. It's no longer something that happens only in design schools and academia. This surge of interest in the written word can be partly explained by the huge rise in the number of design books published over the past two decades (publishers will tell you that book buyers no longer want pages of eye candy; they demand commentary, analysis and criticism). But perhaps a bigger impetus has come from the plethora of design blogs that have filled cyberspace in recent years (see Blogs, page 33). Blogging has contributed to a huge upsurge of interest in design writing – both doing it and reading it. The visitor figures for these blogs are phenomenal, far more than any print magazine could hope to achieve.[1]

This upswing of interest has prompted the arrival of a number of graduate courses devoted to design criticism. The United States-based, British-born writer Alice Twemlow is chair of MFA (Master of Fine Arts) in design criticism at SVA (School of Visual Arts) in New York. The online prospectus describes the course as an 'innovative two-year program that trains students to research, analyze,

> **Look at all the smart designers who have clout and status. What distinguishes them? They all have language skills and aren't afraid to show them.**

Above
Project: *Open Manifesto 1*
Date: 2004
Client: Self-initiated
Designer/Editor: Kevin Finn
Cover and spreads from *Open Manifesto*,
a series of books (four volumes to date)
by designer and editor Kevin Finn. Based in
Australia, Finn describes *Open Manifesto* as
an 'egalitarian publication' which 'includes
opinions from students, academics and
practitioners, as well as various thinkers
from different fields. Rather than showcase
samples of work, the focus is on sharing
viewpoints and ideas.' www.openmanifesto.net

and evaluate design and its social and environmental
implications.'[2] Twemlow is quick to emphasize that her
programme is not just about design writing. She says:
'We are interpreting criticism very broadly to include
many kinds of media and our diverse choice of faculty
reflects this approach. For example, in addition to
learning how to write critically about design in
conventional formats such as articles, essays and posts,
students will also learn how to make radio documentaries,
exhibitions, conferences, syllabi,
blogs, magazines and websites. In this
way we expect graduating students to
pursue careers in publishing, curating,
design management and event production,
as well as in design journalism
and criticism.'

Twemlow's aim in establishing an
MFA in design criticism is 'to provide
students with all the intellectual
equipment they need to make thoughtful
and historically informed analyses
of the designed objects, images and
experiences that surround them. By
training 12 graduate students a year,
we hope to improve the standards of
design criticism and writing generally
and, by exploiting mainstream channels rather than merely
the design trade press, we hope to make sure design
criticism reaches readerships, viewers and listeners well
beyond the design community.'

It is to be hoped that graduates from Twemlow's
course – and the others that have opened – will enrich
the design scene and beef up the intellectual muscle it
currently lacks. But how does design criticism – and the
act of reading it – make designers better designers?
Twemlow thinks that 'being able to write enables designers
to own a much larger share of any project they are
involved in'.

This is undoubtedly a major incentive for designers
to become more proficient in linguistic matters. But
Twemlow sees even more benefits: 'Where criticism gets
really interesting, in my opinion, and where it deserves
its title rather than "design journalism", for example,
is when, in addition to evaluation and explication, it's
also using a designed object as a lens through which to
make much larger and perhaps politically or theoretically-
fuelled observations about society. To me, the design
critic has a vital role to play not only within the design
community, but well beyond it too, as a kind of social
conscience and public provocateur. When discussing the
implications of an Olympic logo, a Nike shoe, the latest

**To get respect
from opinion-
formers we need
critical writing
about design
that shows
self-awareness
and cultural-
awareness. For
this we need
writers who can
rise above the
professional
concerns of
design.**

Facebook functionality, or a new park bench that prevents homeless people from sleeping on it, design critics speak to designers, but they also address manufacturers, consumers, governments and society at large.'

But it's not all rosy in the garden. There are still a substantial number of designers who view critical writing as anti-design. The only sort of design writing this group wants is public relations puff and cosy, mutual backscratching profiles. These are the same people who demand that design is respected and revered by clients and decision-makers. Yet while design writing panders to this demand (and until recently this is what it did almost exclusively) design will remain a minor encrustation on the flank of the media world. Ironically, the way to get respect from opinion-formers is through critical writing about contemporary design that shows self-awareness and wider cultural awareness. For this we need writers who can rise above the professional concerns of design (important as these are) and writers who can translate the often non-verbal reasoning that designers apply to their best work. And who better to do this than graphic designers?

Further reading: www.aiga.org/content.cfm/content.cfm/ writing-awards

1 *Design Observer* (I'm a contributing writer) has just celebrated its fifth birthday, and has had 40 million visitors.
2 http://designcriticism.sva.edu/

Writing proposals

In design's competitive arena, few projects are awarded to designers without a written proposal. If we can't make our proposals fizz with clear and lucid arguments, we will miss out on opportunities. Is there a correct way to write a proposal?

Opposite
Project: proposal cover
Date: 2003
Client: NHS
Design: Intro
Cover for 64pp proposal document to the British National Health Service in response to an open invitation to tender. The document cover was printed litho, and the text pages were printed digitally. Four copies were made and submitted as part of the official tendering process. The bid was successful.

I've written and edited seven books – this will be my eighth – and I regularly write articles for blogs and magazines. I did English at school but rarely got good grades; not because I didn't try, but because I was reading William Burroughs and Jean Genet when I should have been reading Thomas Hardy and Ernest Hemingway. I didn't learn to write, but I learnt to read. And reading taught me what little I know about writing. Yet I hardly wrote a word until I started to write proposals for projects that my studio was pitching for.

I soon discovered that if we were going to win jobs I would have to learn to write compelling and readable proposals, and over time I acquired a small ability to write terse and clear prose. I also discovered that unless it was terse and clear, it didn't get read. And if it didn't get read, we didn't win work.

Clients will often demand that designers submit written proposals for even the smallest jobs. Personally, I like doing them regardless of the project. They often bring to the surface issues that are submerged, and allow for these and other thorny questions to be tackled early. Furthermore, certain sorts of client are more comfortable reviewing a written proposal than with viewing creative work (though there are others who can barely be troubled to read the opening paragraph of a proposal).

NHS

NHS Graduate Schemes tender
a response from
Intro 27/01/03

But written proposals are also a way of avoiding doing speculative creative work that gives away our most valuable asset: creativity (see Pitching, page 241). Although many designers argue correctly that even to produce them is to give our prime assets away.

If you are going to write a proposal it has to be readable and compelling. Typically, it will be a response to a brief from a client, and should include everything that is requested: creative, technical, strategic, scheduling and costing information. This list will grow in relation to the complexity of the job. Web proposals, for instance, often require highly detailed and far-ranging responses. Here are my ten golden rules for writing proposals:

1 Always make the document attractive, legible and easy to use regardless of whether it is printed or delivered electronically. Many design studios create a house style for written proposals. I prefer to design the document in the style and spirit of the proposal to give a pointer towards the visual style I'm proposing.

2 Always make the client's logo the first thing they see, and always make it bigger than yours.[1]

3 Provide a contents list. Most clients like to go straight to the page marked 'Costs', so make it easy for them to find it.

4 Begin with a summary of your intentions – and keep this short and to the point. By telling the reader what your intentions are, you can often lead them to the conclusion you'd like them to reach.

5 Restate the brief. Why? Surely the client knows the brief? Yes, but it may be read and assessed by others who are unfamiliar with the project.

6 Write in short sharp sentences. It is always possible to say something in a more concise way. Always.

7 Write in plain English – avoid jargon. Even if your client uses it, this doesn't mean you have to.

8 If your proposal is a specific response to a written brief from a client, always respond in the same order as the brief.

9 Make sure your contact details are clearly visible. I was once asked to review some proposals on behalf of a client, and the writers of two out of six of them had neglected to supply contact details on their documents. All these proposals were submitted as PDFs, and although the emails to which they had been attached had contact details it was the PDFs, and not the emails, that were printed out and circulated).

10 Always finish with a conclusion. This must be short (no more than 100 words) and should be an at-a-glance overview of the proposal. It allows those who can't be bothered to read the entire document to have it all in one hit – and, besides, many readers turn to the last page as a matter of course. It is always advisable to add a copyright line to any proposal. And a cheerful 'thank you' rarely goes amiss – a proposal is a communication between human beings; normal rules apply.

Further reading:
www.creativepublic.com/write_winning_proposal.php

1 A management consultant once told me that she had been told by more than one of her clients – mostly big corporations – that they resented the way reports and documents were always plastered with the consultants' logos. By reversing this, and having the client's logo centre stage, designers can create a sense of the transfer of ownership in a proposal. It's not the designer's document; it's the client's.

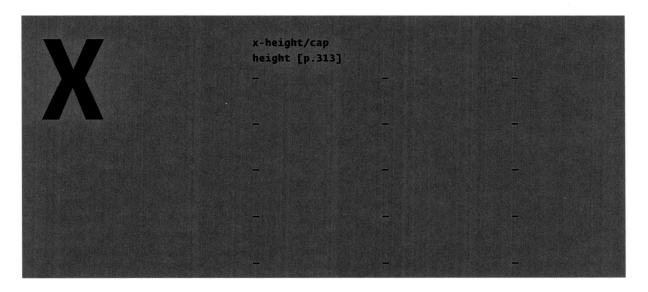

x-height/cap height [p.313]

x-height/cap height

The relationship between x-height and cap height in a font is one of the most important factors in determining legibility, readability and a typeface's visual appearance. As with everything else, this relationship is subject to fads and fashions: big x-height means modern, small x-height means old-fashioned.

Technically, the x-height of a letter is the height of a lower-case letter from the baseline to the mean line, in any given alphabet. Of course, it has to be a lower-case letter without an ascender or descender – an 'x' for example. Lower-case letters with descenders (g, q, p, y) extend beneath the baseline, and letters with ascenders (b, d, l, k) extend above the x-height.

The cap height of a letter is the extent to which an upper-case letter[1] sits above the baseline. It normally refers to letters with a flat top such as M or T, rather than letters with curved tops such as O and S, which may not sit exactly on the cap height line for optical reasons.

In most typefaces, the ascender height of lower-case letters is slightly higher than the cap height. The ratio of the x-height to the cap height is one of the key ways in which the appearance of a typeface is determined. Typefaces with proportionally large x-heights are generally compact and highly legible. They make good text fonts. Typefaces with small x-heights (in relation to cap heights) tend to be more showy and elegant. They are suitable mainly for display purposes.

Further reading: http://typeindex.org/tutorial_anatomy.php

1 Capitals were known as upper-case letters because in the days of metal typefaces they were found in the 'upper cases' of the furniture typesetters used to store letters.

Young designers
[p.314]

Young designers

It's not only the number of design students that has increased – the standard of their work has also risen. Graduates are far superior to those of even a decade ago. But are expectations too high? Have the schools produced a superstrain of designers who will inevitably be disappointed with their working lives?

Something extraordinary is happening around the world. More and more people are studying design. The figures are astonishing enough for a double take.[1] But there is something else that is even more amazing: the standard of undergraduate and graduate work is mind-bogglingly high.

Ten years – maybe even five years – ago I couldn't have said that. But today's students are producing work that puts many professionals to shame. The main reason for this is the teaching; it has improved beyond recognition. A new generation of tutors, many of them radicalized by the theoretical discourse that has swept through design over recent years, is offering students an enlightened curriculum that reflects the breadth of possibilities in design – and doesn't just concentrate on what the mundane world of work requires. Another significant factor is the growth in the number of books, magazines and blogs, not to mention lectures and exhibitions, that have combined to ferment a design culture that barely existed a decade ago.

There are those who say the market is flooded: we are often told that far too many designers are being produced. It's not a view I share. I think there are opportunities in abundance for graduates and, besides, anyone with a good design education is fit for many roles in life, not just that of a graphic designer. A mastery of publishing tools and web programming alone will guarantee countless opportunities. Plus, the intellectual qualities gained through a comprehensive design education mean that graduates are well positioned to work in many areas. But I do have another concern: how to prevent all this creative excellence going sour. As graphic design becomes increasingly over-purposed, and increasingly deployed to micromanage business problems, opportunities to use design in expressive, adventurous and meaningful ways becomes increasingly rare.

This is not to say that every designer wants to do expressive, adventurous and meaningful work; there are many who relish the intellectual tussle of problem solving, and who want to specialize in user-centred applications. But the problem with being the recipient of an enlightened education is that the graduate wants enlightened clients and employers; and when this is not possible, it leads to disillusionment and disenchantment.

For many graduates, doing the kind of work they want to do means starting up on their own, or it means a long hard search for the right sort of job. It also means seizing every opportunity that comes along. Here are my five golden rules for starting out:

1. Get your presentation material in perfect order and never assume you are finished. Be prepared to update it constantly and to rethink it every time you have to present it to someone.

2. When you get a job or an internship, approach it on the assumption that there is no such as thing as a bad task in design – only a bad attitude towards it.

3. Design is increasingly a team activity; if you can't work in a team, you are going to struggle. Interpersonal skills are more important than design skills – in fact, design skills are interpersonal skills, when you think about it.

4. Learn as many technical skills as possible, but remember: it's the brain that makes design, not software (although software allows us to do the things our brain imagines).

5. Never lose sight of your vision of the sort of work you want to do.

1 In the United States, The National Association of Schools of Art and Design accredits about 250 post-secondary institutions with programmes in art and design. www.bls.gov/oco/ocos090.htm

Further reading: Adrian Shaughnessy, *How to Be a Graphic Designer, Without Losing Your Soul*. Laurence King Publishing, 2005.

Zeitgeist

The Zeitgeist – the spirit of the age – is in design, just as it's in pop music and movies. When we lose touch with the zeitgeist it is usually because we have lost interest in the modern world. This is not the same as saying we have to be slaves to the zeitgeist, but we have to be able to recognize it.

Designers are usually thought to be in touch with the zeitgeist. It's certainly true that many designers have an intrinsic grasp of nowness. It's a sort of cultural antennae that designers possess as part of the mental equipment needed to do the job; like an accountant having a grasp of mathematics, designers tend to have two hands around the neck of the zeitgeist.

And when you think about it, how can we help our clients to communicate with people if we don't know how people think and what they are thinking about? You could answer that no one knows what anyone else is thinking about. But there are dominant emotional and behavioural currents that run through society, and designers often have the knack of being able to read these cultural waves.

Design has its own zeitgeist. We might define it as the dominant spirit within design – it can be stylistic, it can be conceptual, it can be both. Most designers instinctively absorb it and reflect it in their work. I've always been struck by how trends, fashions and conventions become embedded in design and how other trends, fashions and conventions get ejected. It's an invisible process. There's no one orchestrating it; no one policing it; it just seems to happen. Each generation has its own, and like a baton in a relay race, it gets handed on to the next generation. Yet each time the baton is transferred, it changes. But what happens when designers don't feel in touch with their times? Is it possible to be a designer without a sense of the zeitgeist? It's a mysterious thing the zeitgeist. It is possible not to feel its presence, but if a designer has no grasp of it they are either behind it, or ahead of it. It can be argued that both positions are viable: to be behind the zeitgeist is to be free from its influence and to be unhindered by its constraints; to be ahead of it is to be a trailblazer and free to innovate. In truth, the only real offence we can commit against the zeitgeist is to be unaware of it. We don't have to immerse ourselves in it, but we have to be able to spot it.

Further reading: Rick Poynor, *Designing Pornotopia*. Princeton Architectural Press, 2006.

Zzzzz

A row of 'z's is a brilliant piece of graphic shorthand, instantly recognizable to anyone who has ever picked up a comic or watched an animated cartoon. But what is a row of 'z's doing in a book about graphic design? Graphic designers never sleep – they are far too busy to bother.

A small graphic design studio at night. Congealing remnants of a takeaway meal. Messy piles of books – some open, some closed. Sheaves of papers. A teetering tower of CDs. An iPod with non-standard headphones. A book called *Flash for Beginners*, its pages festooned with Post-it notes. On the walls are pinned sheets of paper, each containing endless iterations of the same few graphic marks; twice every minute, a silent fan makes them flutter like Tibetan prayer flags. Next to them are shelves filled with books and box files; the box files have decoratively lettered descriptions of their contents: Software; Rent; Reference; Fonts; Leasing Agreements; Teaching – 2nd Year coursework. On the floor, a pair of trainers. Not new, but exuding an unmistakable whiff of fashionability. We see computer kit. Some of it is old and wedged under desks. We see cables snaking across the floor in flagrant disregard of health and safety regulations. We see poster tubes, a cutting mat, a bicycle.

There are three workstations. Two of the workstations are empty. One is occupied. A clock shows 3.45 a.m. The window is open. Lights twinkle in the distance. It's the fourth or fifth floor of a warehouse-type building.

The figure we can see is Joe. His parents are both graphic designers and revere Josef Müller-Brockmann. Joe is working late. He is designing a website. Some text he was waiting for didn't arrive until 6.00 p.m. and the pictures an hour later. In other professions, the client would be told the deadline had been missed. But this is graphic design, and Joe is working through the night to make up the lost time. It's not that he didn't think of telling his client to take a hike; it's just that he was looking forward to doing this job. He's done most of the site and was agonizing over the homepage when it occurred to him that half an hour of sleep might revitalize him.

If this was a frame from a comic novel – Joe is a fan of Chris Ware – we might glimpse a stream of 'z's hovering above Joe's head. In Akzidenz Grotesk, of course.

Further reading: Chip Kidd, *The Learners: A Novel*. Scribner, 2008.

Index

Thanks / Colophon

Many individuals helped with the making of this book: Michael Bierut with his sharp-brained Foreword; Paul Davis with his acid-laced drawings; Tony Brook, Mason Wells and Jason Tselentis read the text and made helpful comments; Mark Blamire for numerous image suggestions; the editors who have regularly commissioned me to write for their publications – Lynda Relph-Knight (*Design Week*), Patrick Burgoyne (*Creative Review*), Étienne Hervy (*étapes*) and John L Walters (*Eye*); Jessica Helfand, William Drenttel and Michael Bierut (*Design Observer*); the many people who gave me quotes and allowed me to plunder their knowledge – all the good bits in this book are down to them. Warm thanks are also due to the dozens of people who enthusiastically and generously contributed images.

Maximum gratitude to Laurence King for his patience and unfailing support throughout the making of this book. Special thanks to my editor Donald Dinwiddie for cheerful forbearance and helpful advice. Thanks also to Jo Lightfoot, Felicity Awdry and the Laurence King Publishing team.

Big dollop of respect to Dan Simmons, Ian McLaughlin and Tom Browning for InDesign skills, hot music tips and biscuits.

Finally, heartfelt thanks to Lynda, Ed, Alice, Moll, Roy, Fred and Flora, and especially to Josh, who slept through the making of so much of this book.

Design and art direction: Adrian Shaughnessy
Additional design and artwork: Tom Browning (Tea Design)
Photography: Jessica McLaughlin

Typeface: Fedra Mono Standard Bold, Bold Italic, Book and Book Italic.

Images: Every effort has been made to trace and contact the copyright holders of the images reproduced in this book. However, the publishers would be pleased, if informed, to correct any errors or omissions in subsequent editions of this publication.

Published in 2009 by
Laurence King Publishing Ltd
361–373 City Road
London EC1V 1LR
United Kingdom

T: 020 7841 6900
F: 020 7841 6910
E: enquiries@laurenceking.com
W: www.laurenceking.com

© 2009 Adrian Shaughnessy

All rights reserved. No part of this publication may be reproduced or transmitted in any form or by any means, electronic or mechanical, including photocopy, recording or any informational storage and retrieval system, without prior permission from the publisher.

A catalogue for this book is available from the British Library.

ISBN: 978 1 85669 591 6

Printed in China

LAURENCE KING